Further praise for *A Court Divided*

"*A Court Divided* is everything a book about the Supreme Court ought to be: clear, engaging, laced with gossip and mercifully uncluttered by footnotes, endnotes or string citations. It is, in short, a brisk ride through 30 years of high-court jurisprudence with a slightly mussed constitutional law professor in an open Jeep. Tushnet . . . makes the perfect tour guide through this sometimes dusty terrain. . . . *A Court Divided* is a brave book."

—Dahlia Lithwick, *Washington Post*

"A jewel of a book. This important and powerful work is the first advanced look at the views and psychologies of the individual justices on the Rehnquist Court. Because of Professor Tushnet, we can now make better judgments about our justices and the enormous effect of their decisions on the lives of each of us."

—Martin Garbus, Davis & Gilbert LLP

"The book blends juicy morsels with an academic analysis of the political split on the Supreme Court. . . . Tushnet, the Court scholar, is comprehensive and thorough. He addresses a slew of constitutional issues. . . . At times, his thinking becomes even greater by providing non-obvious insights that upon reflection become indisputable."

—Robert L. Rogers, *Legal Times*

"[Tushnet] has captured some of the flavor and romance of what the Supreme Court does and what it has come to represent. . . . Compelling."   —Thane Rosenbaum, *San Francisco Chronicle*

"Illuminating, energetic, fun, clear-headed, and nugget-filled. Tushnet has produced the best book yet on the Rehnquist Court."

—Cass Sunstein, University of Chicago Law School

D0168762

"In *A Court Divided*, one of the nation's most insightful legal scholars provides an exceptionally astute and timely analysis of a Supreme Court that is more powerful than ever."   —Edward Lazarus,
author of *Closed Chambers: The Rise, Fall, and Future of the Modern Supreme Court*

"An incisive consideration of the Supremes, offering erudite yet accessible clues to legal thinking on the most important level."
—*Kirkus Reviews*

"A balanced, insightful assessment of the dynamics of today's Supreme Court. . . . In this calm, unbiased study, Tushnet explains clearly how and why the Supreme Court reflects the nation's uneasy political consensus."   —*Publishers Weekly*

A
COURT
DIVIDED

ALSO BY MARK TUSHNET

*The NAACP's Legal Strategy
Against Segregated Education 1925–1950*

*Making Civil Rights Law: Thurgood Marshall
and the Supreme Court 1936–1961*

Taking the Constitution Away from the Courts

The New Constitutional Order

*Slave Law in the American South:
State v. Mann in History and Literature*

A
COURT
DIVIDED

*The Rehnquist Court and
the Future of Constitutional Law*

MARK TUSHNET

W. W. NORTON & COMPANY
New York · London

Copyright © 2006, 2005 by Mark Tushnet

All rights reserved
Printed in the United States of America
First published as a Norton paperback 2006

For information about permission to reproduce selections from this book, write to
Permissions, W. W. Norton & Company, Inc., 500 Fifth Avenue, New York, NY 10110

Manufacturing by Courier Westford
Book design by Charlotte Staub
Production manager: Anna Oler

Library of Congress Cataloging-in-Publication Data

Tushnet, Mark V., 1945–
A Court divided : the Rehnquist court and the future of constitutional law / Mark
Tushnet.— 1st ed.
p. cm.
Includes index.
ISBN 0-393-05868-9 (hardcover)
1. United States. Supreme Court. 2. Political questions and judicial power—United States.
3. Constitutional law—United States. 4. Rehnquist, William H., 1924– I. Title.
KF8742.T87 2005
347.73'26—dc22

2004013786

ISBN 0-393-32757-4 pbk.

W. W. Norton & Company, Inc., 500 Fifth Avenue, New York, N.Y. 10110
www.wwnorton.com

W. W. Norton & Company Ltd., Castle House, 75/76 Wells Street, London W1T 3QT

2 3 4 5 6 7 8 9 0

To the memory of
JUDGE GEORGE EDWARDS,
*who taught me that it's a privilege
to have the opportunity to serve
the American People*

CONTENTS

INTRODUCTION

The story of the Rehnquist Court is the story of a court divided not simply between liberals and conservatives but, more important, between two types of Republican. Justices speaking for the modern Republican Party, transformed by Barry Goldwater and Ronald Reagan, rejected the principles that animated our government from the New Deal through the Great Society. Sandra Day O'Connor and David Souter drew on more traditional Republican Party themes to temper and resist a transformation of constitutional law. The Court's liberals mostly sat on the sidelines, happy to pick up the victories they could gain when the Court's Republicans divided.

The justices are neither villains nor heroes in some story about whether the United States is about to descend into tyranny or ascend into utopia. They are, rather, ordinary lawyers who have strong views about what the Constitution means, shaped by their personal experiences and their thoughtful consideration of arguments about what the Constitution means. Some of them have quirks, just as the rest of us do. But it would be a serious mistake to reduce their disagreements over the Constitution and its future to those quirks or to personal spats. To understand the Rehnquist Court, we have to look at the history that gave rise to the arguments about the Constitution's meaning and see how competing visions play out in specific legal settings. It's not enough to do a scorecard of "conservative" or "liberal" victories, although that's part of the story. The hardest, but the most important, part of the story of the Rehnquist Court is figuring out *what* conservatism about the Constitution is.

The Court's divisions meant that conservatives prevailed—more or less—on issues associated with the Republican Party's efforts to scale down the size of government, while losing rather consistently on the social issues—abortion, gay rights, and affirmative action—that animated an important part of the party's base. Economic conservatives got some help from the Rehnquist Court even though they didn't need much assistance. In contrast, social issues conservatives might have benefited from the Rehnquist Court's help but didn't get nearly enough. The old-fashioned Republicans were reasonably sympathetic to the liberal side on these issues, while the Court's movement conservatives were dead set against that side but lost.

The reason the Court's economic conservatives won and its cultural conservatives lost is simple. In the arena of politics, economic conservatives were winning and cultural conservatives were losing. The economic conservatives dominated Congress and the presidency, making help from the Supreme Court less important to their cause, though they received some. The cultural traditionalists, on the other hand, needed major assistance but received little, as they were forced repeatedly to retreat. So the patterns discernible in the Rehnquist Court's decisions reproduced the patterns occurring in American politics generally.

That fact raises an obvious question: Why should anyone care about what the Supreme Court does if it is merely a reflection of the broader political and cultural worlds? The answer is that the Court can push some issues higher up on the public agenda (gay marriage after the gay rights decision in 2003) and some issues farther down (affirmative action after the Michigan affirmative action cases in the same year). It can eliminate laws that have fallen out of favor in the general culture (the 2003 gay rights decision barred sodomy prosecutions that few regarded as sensible anyway) but persist in some isolated areas or protect those laws in ways that allow the general culture to push forward elsewhere. Sometimes—not often, but sometimes—a gap can open up between the Court and the culture, making the Court's decisions particularly important and stressful. And then there's always the entirely unexpected: *Bush v. Gore* resolving the 2000 election.

One reason for my writing this book is my frustration with most of what constitutional scholars have written for readers who aren't specialists in constitutional law. Perhaps prodded by the journalists who call them for comments on breaking news, most scholars end up doing little more than cheering or booing the Court's decisions. I think that the general public ought to know about what the Supreme Court does, but I don't think that cheerleading for one or the other side really advances public understanding.

The civics book view of the Court—that conservative and liberal justices divide over whether it should be restrained or activist and that they use original intent or contemporary values in interpretation—is a fairy tale. Nothing like it goes on in the Rehnquist Court. *Everyone* is a judicial activist. The Rehnquist Court has invalidated laws whose constitutionality was clear under long-established doctrine, using novel analyses that it has sometimes acknowledged cannot be tied closely to the Constitution's text or original understandings. In addition, the Rehnquist Court has asserted, more strongly than the Warren Court, a primary role in enforcing the legal boundaries Congress has to respect, so much so that two respected scholars have written an important article with the accurate title "Dissing Congress."

So the Rehnquist Court is a political court. For scholars, tying the Supreme Court to party politics is not all that new. The standard view of the Warren Court, for example, is that it worked in conjunction with the Democratic Party to implement a New Deal/Great Society vision of the Constitution. The Rehnquist Court resembles the Warren Court in implementing a constitutional vision associated with the nation's dominant political party. What makes its story more complicated (and interesting) is that the Republican Party has remained a coalition of economic and cultural conservatives. The Republicans on the Court who would use the Constitution to advance the economic and cultural agendas of the modern Republican Party have been able to lay the groundwork for later advances. But their actual accomplishments have been meager because they have been thwarted, not by activist liberals or by Democrats but by Republicans uneasy about the Republican cultural agenda.

Labeling decisions as "conservative" or "liberal," or even "right" or "wrong," simply preaches to the choir. Perhaps more important, it doesn't advance understanding the true impact of the divided Rehnquist Court. The Court might become united in the future, depending on who replaces which of the justices sitting in 2004 and thus on the processes of judicial nomination and confirmation that emerge after the 2004 elections. It might become a united moderately liberal or a united strongly conservative Court. Or the divisions among Republicans on the Rehnquist Court might be reproduced in whatever happens next. William Rehnquist and Clarence Thomas have laid the groundwork for a revolution that would truly reconstruct constitutional law; that revolution has not yet occurred because of O'Connor and Souter. The real impact of the Rehnquist Court lies in the decisions of the *next* Supreme Court.

CHAPTER ONE

William Rehnquist's Court

As Richard Nixon was trying to decide whom to nominate to the Supreme Court in 1971, William Rehnquist joked to a journalist that he had no chance "at all" of being nominated, because "I'm not from the South, I'm not a woman, and I'm not mediocre." He was, though, "the most conservative lawyer" Barry Goldwater had ever met, and that turned out to be enough.

By 1971 the Republican Party had become committed to a version of conservative constitutional law shaped in reaction to Earl Warren's Supreme Court and particularly to the Warren Court's activism on civil rights. Its constitutional theorists relied on criticisms of judicial activism that had been developed in the generation before Warren became chief justice, as a reaction to the *conservative* activism that New Deal Democrats repudiated. Rehnquist's nomination was part of the party's strategy for transforming constitutional law.

Rehnquist came to the Supreme Court fully shaped intellectually, with the Republican conservative constitutional agenda firmly in mind, including its antipathy to the Court's civil rights interventions. At each point that civil rights entered Rehnquist's work, he responded with an indifference resting on his judgment that advocates of civil rights were exaggerating the importance and underestimating the costs that advancing civil rights would impose on other values he thought important. He explained his concerns by keeping in mind the constitutional theories of Robert Jackson, the Supreme

Court justice for whom he had clerked. Along with other judges and scholars, Jackson developed a criticism of judicial activism from the liberal side that Rehnquist was to turn against liberals on the Supreme Court.

℘

Born in 1924, William Rehnquist grew up in a middle-class, heavily Republican suburb of Milwaukee, Wisconsin. He used the GI Bill benefits he earned for serving in the Army Air Corps in World War II to attend Stanford University. After graduating as a member of Phi Beta Kappa, Rehnquist got a master's degree in political science from Stanford, then a second one from Harvard in 1950. He also enrolled in Stanford Law School, where he was graduated on an accelerated schedule first in his class in December 1951. He went to Washington to work as a law clerk to Supreme Court Justice Robert H. Jackson the next February. The experience of working for Jackson confirmed Rehnquist's conservative instincts and brought him into contact with the civil rights issues that threaded through his career before his Supreme Court appointment. So, to understand Rehnquist, it helps to understand Jackson.

Jackson had been a central player in the constitutional battles over Franklin Roosevelt's New Deal. By 1952, when Rehnquist went to Washington, Jackson was seen as one of the Court's conservatives—not in terms of his policy preferences, which remained firmly liberal, but in terms of his views about the Supreme Court's role in government. Rehnquist's conservatism about policy was refracted through the lens of his experience as Jackson's law clerk, while Jackson's perspective was shaped by his understanding of the constitutional history he had lived.

By the early 1930s liberal lawyers like Jackson had firm—and unfavorable—views of the Supreme Court and judicial review. As they saw it, the Court had persistently obstructed their legislative agenda. The liberal lawyers took *Lochner v. New York* (1905), a typical Progressive-era case pitting the interests of labor against those of employers, to exemplify all that was wrong with the Court. A long campaign by workers and sympathetic newspapers had drawn public attention to what advocates of limiting working hours called appalling conditions in bakeries. In 1895 New York's legislature had responded by passing a law saying that bakeries couldn't make their workers stay on the job for more than ten hours a day, six days a week. Joseph Lochner owned a small bakery in Utica, New York, and was charged with hiring Aman Schmitter to work more than sixty hours a week. Lochner challenged the law as a violation of the doctrine known as substantive due process.

A sharply divided Supreme Court agreed that the Fourteenth Amendment's due process clause protected the right of bakers to enter into voluntary contracts on whatever terms they wanted. Limiting that right, the Court said, was an arbitrary interference with every worker's right to make decisions about his working life. Legal progressives derided the Court's doctrine as unfounded in the Constitution's text and considered it the majority justices' way of expressing their preference for an ideological laissez-faire economics.

The New Deal brought the conflict between a conservative Court and a liberal president to a head. The Court held some important New Deal programs unconstitutional, and its doctrines posed real threats to others. After his landslide reelection in 1936 Roosevelt took on the Court. He proposed (disingenuously) that in order to help the justices with their work, the president should have the power to appoint a new justice for every one over the age of seventy. What became known as the Court-packing plan failed in the short run, but Roosevelt soon had the opportunity to change constitutional law by filling Supreme Court vacancies caused by retirements.

Having taken over the Court, the liberals had to figure out what to do. As memorably put by political scientist Martin Shapiro two generations later, the New Deal justices now occupied the fortress previously held by their enemies and had to decide whether to dismantle it or to turn its weapons against the enemies, now on the outside. Jackson inclined to the first position. As he saw it, nearly every important question of public policy should be resolved through politics. Interest groups would fight it out, and the Court would not stand in the way of whatever they managed to accomplish.

Eventually Jackson's position put him at odds with some of his liberal colleagues on the Supreme Court. His position made sense when it was applied to the economic issues that were at the heart of the New Deal's fight with the Court. There was a problem, though, with his placid attitude toward politics. Interest-group politics would work only when every group had a chance to lobby the legislature. Everyone in the 1930s knew that some people didn't have that chance. In particular, African Americans in the South were denied the right to vote, either by law or by terrorism. How could anyone think that laws resulting from a *distorted* interest-group process were fair?

The Court itself pointed the way to a theory that could justify restraint in economic matters, where the political process worked reasonably well from the New Dealers' point of view, and judicial activism on human rights matters. The decision involved an economic regulation—Congress had banned shipment of filled milk, an inexpensive but nutritious substitute for whole milk, across state lines—and the Court easily upheld the regulation against a challenge brought by Carolene Products, a producer of filled milk.

The opinion was written by Justice Harlan Fiske Stone, a liberal Republican. Stone used the Carolene Products case as a vehicle for what Justice Lewis F. Powell later called "the most celebrated footnote in constitutional law." Footnote 4 was attached to a statement in the text saying that the Court wouldn't examine closely to see if economic regulations really did a good job of protecting the public health or safety. The footnote had three paragraphs. The first was an unexceptional statement that the Court might engage in close examination of statutes that seemed "to be within a specific prohibition of the Constitution." The next two paragraphs contained the meat of the footnote. The second paragraph referred to "legislation which restricts those political processes which can ordinarily be expected to bring about repeal of undesirable legislation" and said that perhaps such laws would be examined more closely. This meant statutes disfranchising voters and perhaps laws restricting speech. The final paragraph looked to the situation of African Americans, again suggesting that close examination would be given "statutes directed at particular religions, or national or racial minorities." It added that "prejudice against discrete and insular minorities" might be a "special consideration, which tends seriously to curtail the operation of those political processes ordinarily to be relied upon to protect minorities."

Footnote 4 provided the weapons New Deal justices could turn against their enemies. They could develop an aggressive stance on laws limiting expression because such laws impaired the political process. They could be equally aggressive against denials of the right to vote and against southern segregation. The only question was whether Jackson's view or Stone's would prevail.

For the next two decades, including the Term Rehnquist worked for Jackson, the Court remained divided. The division was exacerbated by deep personal conflicts. Felix Frankfurter, a former law professor who thought of himself as a sophisticated constitutional theorist, basically couldn't develop a decent theory to help him decide what to do, but he knew he despised William O. Douglas, the quintessential activist. So Frankfurter inclined in Jackson's direction and Douglas toward the Footnote 4 position. Jackson believed that Hugo Black had connived to steal the chief justiceship away from him. Roosevelt had promised to make Jackson chief justice after Stone's death, but unfortunately for Jackson, Roosevelt died before Stone did, and Jackson believed—almost certainly erroneously—that Black had poisoned his reputation with Harry Truman, who instead appointed an old crony, the former secretary of the treasury and court of appeals judge Fred Vinson. Because Black leaned toward Footnote 4 jurisprudence, Jackson inclined against it. That inclination was entirely consistent with the political conservatism of his young law clerk in 1953, although Jackson was more ambivalent about judicial restraint than Rehnquist was.

Two important civil rights cases that came to the Court during Rehnquist's clerkship brought out his conservatism and placed him at odds with his boss. The first involved a peculiar system of primary elections in Fort Bend County, Texas. The Jaybird Association was nominally a private organization open only to whites, but it dominated the Democratic Party in the county, and the Democratic Party was in effect the only one there was. The Jaybirds ran a preprimary in which candidates sought the association's endorsement. The winner of the preprimary always won the Democratic nomination and then the election. Starting in the 1940s, the Supreme Court had struck down primaries in which only whites were allowed to vote, and what happened in Fort Bend County looked a lot like a white primary. Fitting it into the right doctrinal category was tricky, though, because of the association's "private" character. Eventually, after a lot of pushing and hauling, the Supreme Court held the Jaybird primary unconstitutional.

Jackson wasn't sure what to do, but Rehnquist was. In his first memo to Jackson on the case, Rehnquist observed that several clerks "began screaming as soon as they saw this that 'Now we can show those damn southerners, etc.' " Rehnquist told Jackson that he took "a dim view of this pathological search for discrimination." As the Court struggled with the case, Jackson suggested to his clerks that he might want to dissent from a proposed opinion striking down the Jaybird primary. Rehnquist's response adopted Jackson's writing style. "Surely the justices of this Court do not sit here to ruthlessly frustrate results which they consider undesirable, regardless of the Constitution." The key idea, in Rehnquist's words, was that it "is about time the Court faced the fact that the white people on [*sic*] the South don't like the colored people." Further, Rehnquist wrote, asserting that he was representing Jackson's ideas—as he was, as a general matter—the Constitution "most assuredly did not appoint the Court as a sociological watchdog to rear up every time private discrimination raises its admittedly ugly head." Adverting to liberal positions during the New Deal, Rehnquist said that liberals "should be the first to realize . . . that it does not do to push blindly through towards one constitutional goal without paying attention to other equally desirable values that are being trampled on in the process." In the end Jackson didn't go along with Rehnquist and simply joined one of the opinions stopping the Jaybird primary.

Rehnquist tried again to push Jackson in a conservative direction in *Brown v. Board of Education*, the NAACP's challenge to segregated education in the South. *Brown*, which was joined with four other segregation cases, was clearly the most important case the Court considered while Rehnquist was a law clerk, and he wrote another memorandum to Jackson detailing *someone*'s position on the issue. When the memorandum became public late in Rehnquist's 1971 confirmation process, the question was *whose* position it reflected: Jackson's or Rehnquist's. The answer seems clear: Rehnquist took the opportunity provided by Jackson's ambivalence about judicial activism to put down on paper his own views about the Constitution and civil rights.

Jackson asked his two law clerks to prepare memoranda on the segregation cases. Rehnquist's coclerk, Donald Cronson, headed his "A Few Expressed Prejudices on the Segregation Cases." Cronson said that *Plessy v. Ferguson*, the 1896 decision upholding segregation, "was wrong" but that it had become embedded in the law and in the southern way of life. For Cronson, "where a whole way of life has grown up around such a prior error, then I say we are stuck with it."

Rehnquist's memo was titled "A Random Thought on the Segregation Cases." It began with a quick overview of Supreme Court history, written from the perspective of someone who had learned about judicial restraint through the New Deal experience. History taught, Rehnquist said, that "it was no part of the judicial function to thwart public opinion except in extreme cases." The memo then turned to the segregation cases. Having earlier written that judicial review had to rest on "standards . . . other than the personal predilections of the Justices," Rehnquist said that the NAACP's position did not. Rather, the Court was "being asked to read its own sociological views into the Constitution." The NAACP's position was "palpably at variance with precedent and probably with legislative h[is]tory." It was trying "to convince the Court of the moral wrongness" of segregation. But, Rehnquist continued, whatever an individual justice thought about segregation as a matter of policy, it was not "one of those extreme cases" justifying judicial intervention. For Rehnquist, "if this Court, because its members are individually 'liberal' and dislike segregation, now chooses to strike it down, it differs from the [pre-New Deal] court only in the kinds of litigants it favors and the kinds of special claims it protects."

Rehnquist returned to history, broadly seen. "To the argument made by Thurgood not John Marshall that a majority may not deprive a minority of its constitutional right, the answer must be made that while this is sound in theory, in the long run it is the majority who will determine what the constitutional rights of the majority are." The Court's earlier attempts to protect minorities had failed. "One by one the cases establishing such rights have been sloughed off, and crept silently to rest. If the present Court is unable to profit by this example, it must be prepared to see its work fade in time, too, as embodying only the sentiments of a transient majority of nine men." Rehnquist's memo concluded: "I realize that it is an unpopular and unhumanitarian position, for which I have been excoriated by 'liberal' colleagues but I think *Plessy v. Ferguson* was right and should be re-affirmed."

His memo surfaced in 1971, as the Senate was debating Rehnquist's nomination to the Supreme Court. His critics, including Senator Birch Bayh of Indiana, said that it raised questions about Rehnquist's "commitment to equal justice." Rehnquist's first reaction, reported to John Dean by Attorney General John Mitchell, was puzzlement; according to Mitchell, Rehnquist "doesn't have the foggiest memory of ever writing it." He quickly drafted a letter "reconstruct[ing] the circumstances after some nineteen years." As he recalled, Rehnquist said, Jackson had asked for the memo "as a rough draft of a statement of *his* views," and it was "not designed to be a statement of *my* views on these cases." Indeed, Rehnquist wrote, "the bald, simplistic conclusion that '*Plessy v. Ferguson* was right and should be re-affirmed' is not an accurate statement of my own views at the time." Jackson's longtime secretary told the *Washington Post* that in asserting that Jackson believed that *Plessy* was right, Rehnquist "had smeared the reputation of a great justice."

So which was it? Did the memo state Jackson's views or Rehnquist's? Most people who have studied the matter believe that it expresses what Rehnquist, not Jackson, thought. They point to the canned history of the Supreme Court at the memo's beginning, claiming that Jackson would have had no reason to lecture his colleagues or himself about the Court's history. They point to the repeated use of the first person in the memo and the scare quotes around the word *liberal*. Rehnquist later acknowledged that he couldn't remember Jackson's saying that he had been "excoriated by 'liberal' colleagues" for upholding *Plessy*, and that Rehnquist himself had defended *Plessy*—at least for debating purposes—around the lunch table with other law clerks. That makes the sentence understandable.

Writing in 2001, when his political views had changed, John Dean said that his first reaction to Rehnquist's response was that he "had lied." Partisan Democrats reached the same conclusion. There's a better way to understand what Rehnquist did and said. Dean suggested that Rehnquist "felt he had to reconstruct history to get himself off the hook." But memory is always a reconstruction of history. Rehnquist always said that his recollections of the events were fuzzy on many details, and indeed, the more specific his assertions were, the less credible they were. So, in 1971—and again in 1986, when the issue resurfaced during the hearings on his elevation to chief justice—Rehnquist tried to paint a picture of the events that made sense to him as he understood his circumstances in 1971 and 1986. The picture he painted may well have been inaccurate, but it overstates things to say that he lied, implying that he put forth an account that he *knew* to be inaccurate. I'm sure that Rehnquist thought that he described the events surrounding the memo accurately, even though he didn't and even though his distortions were all in a direction favorable to him.

Rehnquist's confrontation with the two civil rights cases as a law clerk show a pattern that persisted throughout his career before he became a judge. He used the experience of the New Deal as a vehicle for explaining his strong opposition to judicial activism on civil rights. He took vigorous exception to political liberals who thought that the Constitution provided the remedy for all that ailed the United States, describing himself as the stern nonhumanitarian committed to the true interpretation of the Constitution no matter what the political implications, although the political implications of the interpretations he favored didn't bother Rehnquist at all.

♦

The experience of the Warren Court reshaped the way legal conservatives like Rehnquist thought about constitutional law, confirming for them, at least for a while, the wisdom of Jackson's attack on judicial supremacy. Footnote 4 remained an important theme in the Warren Court's approach to constitutional law. But with the conflict that had divided the New Deal's justices behind them, the Great Society justices added a substantive vision of liberalism to the Footnote 4 jurisprudence.

The Warren Court's most enduring contribution to a substantive vision of constitutional law was undoubtedly *Griswold v. Connecticut*. Justice Douglas wrote the Court's decision striking down a Connecticut statute that made it a criminal offense to *use* contraceptives. (The statute was never enforced against actual users, though; instead, it deterred drugstores and doctors from distributing contraceptives by making them "aiders and abetters" of the offense of using contraceptives.) On the level of constitutional theory the decision reminded critics, including Rehnquist, of the Lochner era, because despite Douglas's valiant efforts, few observers believed that the decision could be justified by invoking the Constitution's text.

The Warren Court's commitment to substantive liberalism was undoubtedly its most important characteristic as seen from the late years of the Rehnquist Court. The Warren Court's decisions dealing with the criminal justice system were far more important in the short run. Driven by the observation that African Americans and other minorities were the primary victims of abusive police practices, the Court set about attempting to reform and professionalize the nation's police agencies. It restricted their ability to conduct searches without getting a judge's permission first, and of course it insisted that police officers give the famous Miranda warnings.

The Warren Court's efforts were a political disaster for it. The Court conducted its campaign to reform the police just as crime rates began a dramatic rise. The increase in crime was due to a combination of demographic changes and broader social trends, such as a decline in the ability of parents to supervise their children. Richard Nixon understood, however, that he could gain political points by a law and order campaign attributing crime and social disorder to the Supreme Court. Nixon's election, and his Supreme Court appointments, were supposed to change the Court's direction.

✐

After finishing his clerkship in mid-1953, Rehnquist decided to pursue his legal career in Arizona. He practiced law in Phoenix and quickly became involved in Republican Party politics. Barry Goldwater had won an upset victory over the incumbent Democratic senator in 1952, and Rehnquist quickly moved into Goldwater's political circle.

Rehnquist used his experience as a law clerk to make his first appearance in national politics. In December 1957, while conservatives around the country were mounting attacks on the Warren Court's decisions dealing with attempts to suppress the Communist Party, and southerners were resisting the Court's desegregation decisions, Rehnquist published an article in the newsweekly *U.S. News & World Report*, which at the time had a distinctly conservative editorial cast. Echoing his criticism of the "liberal" law clerks in his memo on the white primary case, Rehnquist charged that the Supreme Court had come under the control of liberal law clerks, who, the article suggested, manipulated the justices into taking positions that the justices themselves wouldn't have. The law clerks, and through them the justices, showed "extreme solicitude for claims of Communists and other criminal defendants, [and for] expansion of federal power at the expense of state power."

Rehnquist was an important player in Goldwater's long-term effort to transform the Republican Party. Again, the pattern in Rehnquist's career is clear. He was ambitious for himself and for the ideas he thought correct. Among those ideas, the one that crops up over and over is the view that advocates of civil rights were going too far, trampling on other important constitutional values in their misguided effort to cleanse the United States of racism. Rehnquist himself was not a racist, if that means someone who harbored hatred or disdain for African Americans. He was, however, simply indifferent to the situation of African Americans, and he placed the claims of the civil rights movement in a framework of constitutional theory shaped by his experience as Jackson's law clerk.

Rehnquist coordinated poll-watching activities in Arizona, but his main contribution to the Goldwater effort was as a legal adviser and speechwriter on civil rights issues. He testified against a proposal that the Phoenix City Council adopt an ordinance banning discrimination in restaurants and shops because, he said, "I am opposed to all civil rights laws" as intrusions on "the historic right of the owner." He also opposed plans addressing de facto school segregation in Phoenix, writing to the local newspaper that "many . . . would feel that we are no more dedicated to an 'integrated' society than we are to a 'segregated' society," apparently meaning that American society was simply divided between people who thought it should be segregated and those who thought it should be integrated.

Although Goldwater had supported the Phoenix civil rights ordinance, by the time he was running for president in 1964 his political position had shifted. Goldwater was the leading figure in the Republican Party's southern strategy, aiming to shift votes in the South from the Democrats to the Republicans by appealing to whites opposed to the civil rights movement. Goldwater now found Rehnquist's views congenial, and he knew that Rehnquist had the legal talent to translate them into constitutional arguments.

Rehnquist joined with political scientist Harry Jaffa to draft a major speech Goldwater delivered to the American Political Science Association's meeting in Chicago. After drawing on Jaffa for the proposition that Lyndon Johnson's apparent successes in Congress reflected "a totalitarian philosophy that the end justifies the means," Goldwater turned to Rehnquist's constitutional analysis, challenging the Warren Court for exercising "raw and naked power."

Six weeks later Goldwater gave a major speech on civil rights, "Civil Rights and the Common Good," again written by Jaffa and Rehnquist. Using what one historian calls "Bill Rehnquist's mantra," Goldwater said that the nation's aim "is neither to establish a segregated society nor to establish an integrated society. It is to preserve a *free* society." The speech opposed school busing because it was "wrong to take school children out of their normal neighborhood schools for the sake of achieving 'racial balance,' or some other hypothetical goal of perfect equality imagined by the theorists of the so-called 'Great Society.' " Such a goal was "wrong—morally wrong—because . . . it reintroduces through the back door the very principle of allocation by race that makes compulsory segregation morally wrong and offensive to freedom." True freedom, Goldwater continued, was "a double freedom," applying both to those who wanted to associate with others—proponents of civil rights—and to those who wanted to keep away from others—proponents of segregation. "We must never forget that the freedom to associate means the same thing as the freedom not to associate," he said. The speech concluded: "From many races, nations, and creeds we have made, as we shall ever more perfectly make, under God, one people."

Goldwater lost the presidential race in 1964, of course, but he succeeded in changing the Republican Party. Richard Nixon adopted the southern strategy—for electoral purposes at least, although his administration's policies overall were substantially less conservative than Goldwater's would have been. Nixon continued to treat the Republican Party as a coalition between traditional northeastern Republicans, internationalist in foreign affairs, oriented to the interests of large industry and moderately pro–civil rights in domestic matters, and the new southern and western conservative Republicans, heirs to a more isolationist element in the party and strongly in favor of small business and against civil rights.

Nixon rewarded Goldwater's troops—and the new Republican con-servatives—when he won the next election by giving them control over the Department of Justice, while giving northeastern Republicans control of other departments, including State. On the recommenda-tion of Richard Kleindienst, one of Goldwater's closest advisers, Nixon nominated Rehnquist to head the Office of Legal Counsel in the Department of Justice. To legal insiders, the appointment is some-thing of a plum. The Office of Legal Counsel, sometimes described as providing the lawyers for the attorney general, has a much lower pro-file than other parts of the Department of Justice, such as the Civil Rights Division. Lawyers in the know regard it as one of the most elite elements of the nation's legal staff. The person at its head rarely makes his way into the newspapers, but the opinions prepared in the office have a major impact on the shape of every administration's legal and constitutional policy. Still, Rehnquist's appointment was basically patronage for one of Goldwater's smartest supporters. He was not being groomed for the Supreme Court.

∞

Every politically active lawyer fantasizes about becoming a Supreme Court justice, but few get there. Random events define the path to the Court, and Rehnquist benefited more than most from that ran-domness. Until a few weeks before Rehnquist was nominated, his name was basically off Nixon's radar screen. But as other names dropped off the list of potential nominees, Rehnquist's name rose, and in the end he was the last one left.

Richard Nixon knew what he wanted to do with the Supreme Court. He had campaigned against the Warren Court on law and order issues, and his first priority was to name justices who would side with the "peace forces" against the criminals. Moreover, under-standing that Goldwater's nomination in 1964 had marked a turn-ing point in Republican Party history, he wanted to use Supreme Court nominations to strengthen the party in the South and, to a lesser extent, in the West. Finally, he wanted to change the Court by appointing young justices who would be able to shape constitu-tional law after he left office.

His first nomination went down easily. In 1969 he chose Warren Burger, then serving on the federal court of appeals in Washington,

D.C., to succeed Earl Warren. (There's no rule, or even tradition, that only a sitting justice can become chief justice. Earl Warren was governor of California when he was named chief justice; indeed, only two of the men named chief justice in the twentieth century were promoted from associate to chief justice.) As a circuit court judge Burger had spoken out vigorously against the criminal procedure decisions written by the liberals on his court. Probably the best that can be said for Burger as chief justice is that he looked as if he had been cast for the part by a Hollywood director. His ineptness at administering the Court's work raised suspicions among its liberals that he had to be pursuing some sort of deep Machiavellian strategy, although almost always they were observing simple incompetence. Many justices were frustrated at the chief's inability to manage their discussions of the cases; Burger would open the discussion with a long-winded description of the case, which none of them needed, following up with his own views, too often rambling at length on issues that were entirely peripheral to the case and leaving little time for the other justices to explain their positions.

Nixon's second nomination process was a disaster. He and Attorney General Mitchell presented Associate Justice Abe Fortas with information about Fortas's relationship with a financier convicted of securities fraud. They also leaked the information to the press to generate pressure on Congress to open an impeachment inquiry. Fortas resigned in 1969 to prevent his impeachment. Having satisfied the law and order constituency with Burger's appointment, Nixon wanted to use this appointment to bolster the Republican Party in the South. He chose Clement Haynsworth, a respected court of appeals judge from South Carolina. Prodded by labor unions and African Americans, Senate Democrats seized upon the fact that Haynsworth had participated in deciding cases that had had some minor impact on his own investments. In one, for example, he had ruled in favor of a corporation in a bitter labor dispute even though he had been vice-president of a firm that supplied vending machines to the parent company of the plant's owner. The Democrats escalated these trivialities into major breaches of judicial ethics, and Haynsworth's nomination was defeated by a vote of 55 to 45.

Infuriated at the Senate, Nixon decided to stick it to the Democrats by nominating another southerner, this one clearly less qualified than Haynsworth. G. Harrold Carswell barely had any credentials for the job, although he had been confirmed a few months before to serve on a federal court of appeals. When Carswell's talent became an issue in the confirmation process, Senator Roman Hruska of Nebraska came to his defense in a statement (tinged with anti-Semitism) that became famous—and damaged Carswell's chances even further: "Even if he is mediocre there are a lot of mediocre judges and people and lawyers. They are entitled to a little representation, aren't they, and a little chance? We can't have all Brandeises, Cardozos, and Frankfurters, and stuff like that there." Carswell's chances were doomed when it turned out that he had been a staunch segregationist in 1948 and even more recently had helped Tallahassee maintain segregation by converting the public golf course of the state capital into a private, racially discriminatory club. After his nomination was defeated by a vote of 51 to 45, Nixon chose Minnesotan Harry Blackmun for the seat.

Nixon continued to see Supreme Court appointments as an element in his party's southern strategy. Announcing Blackmun's nomination, Nixon said that he had "reluctantly concluded that—with the Senate as presently constituted—I cannot successfully nominate to the Supreme Court any federal appellate judge from the South who believes as I do in the strict construction of the Constitution." His next chance to pursue the strategy came in 1971, when two giants of the Warren Court, Hugo Black and John Marshall Harlan, retired because of the illnesses from which they died within weeks. Rehnquist became one of the nominees, but only because politics had knocked candidates Nixon preferred off the list.

Black was from Alabama, and again Nixon looked for a southerner. He settled on Virginia Representative Richard Poff, who withdrew because he feared a Senate fight would reveal to his young son that the boy had been adopted, a fact that came out anyway, but too late for Poff to come back into consideration. Vindictively recalling the Haynsworth-Carswell episode, Nixon said that he wanted "to get someone worse than Poff and really stick it to the opposition now," but then he calmed down. He eventually selected Lewis F. Powell, Jr., a prominent Richmond lawyer who had been second to Haynsworth earlier but who was then thought to be too old—sixty-one in 1969— to serve long enough to transform the Court.

The real action was for Harlan's seat. It was a process of nomination by trial balloon. Nixon told Mitchell that he wanted to nominate a conservative woman judge. The pool of conservative women judges was small; the great expansion of the number of women in law schools was just beginning, and only a few women—and even fewer conservative women—were serving on higher courts anywhere in the country.

After developing a list of thirteen women candidates (of whom only six were judges, and only five were Republicans, suggesting that the advisers weren't all that serious about the list), Nixon's advisers ended up with another, more serious list of six potential nominees, four women and two men. The list was headed by Herschel Friday, an Arkansas corporate lawyer whom Attorney General Mitchell was friendly with and who was Warren Burger's leading suggestion, and Mildred Lillie, a judge on California's intermediate court of appeals. Hruska's language came back to haunt the administration when *Time* magazine described all six as "mediocre" and "obscure." The American Bar Association asked the administration to look for "some people with stature." Its Committee on the Federal Judiciary evaluated the potential nominees and called Lillie "unqualified," while it was merely "not opposed" to Friday. Nixon, who didn't like having to deal "with all those kikes" on the ABA committee, got fed up.

Taking the selection process away from their aides, Nixon and Mitchell decided to propose Senator Howard Baker of Tennessee, whose Senate membership would make confirmation easy. But when Mitchell met Baker to ask, Baker wanted time to decide, citing concerns about salary. As John Dean put it, Baker "dithered," asking for still more time. Nixon decided that time was up, and Baker lost his chance.

Dean says that he threw Rehnquist's name into the pot. Rehnquist had been involved in vetting some of the potential nominees himself, but Nixon had no idea who he was. Nixon first ran across Rehnquist when Rehnquist led a 1971 meeting on declassifying secret documents. Nixon convened the meeting, then left. He had noticed the person running the meeting, who had bushy sideburns and was wearing a pink shirt and a "psychedelic necktie." Nixon asked Dean, "John, who the hell is that clown?" Dean told him Rehnquist's name, and Nixon asked Dean to spell it and asked,

"Is he Jewish? He looks it. . . . That's a hell of a costume he's wearing, just like a clown." The impression stuck with Nixon; three weeks later he was still referring to "that group of clowns we had around here. Renchburg and that group."

Dean recalled a conversation with Richard Moore, special counsel at the White House, in which Dean praised Rehnquist for his conservatism and sophistication. According to Dean, he said, "Rehnquist is no racist. But he is far to the right of Dick Poff in his thinking on civil rights." At first Nixon was unenthusiastic about the idea of nominating Rehnquist. He agreed with Mitchell that it would be "a great appointment," partly because it would "salt away a guy that would be on the Court for thirty years" and be "a rock solid conservative." But he thought he wouldn't get anything politically by nominating Rehnquist. "Maybe he can get a sex change," Nixon joked.

Enamored of Rehnquist's general conservatism, Dean and Moore continued to lobby for him, and eventually, as Mitchell got frustrated over Senator Baker's unwillingness to commit, the attorney general overcame his earlier concern that there was no political advantage to be gained by naming Rehnquist. Describing him as "an arch conservative," Mitchell briefed Nixon on Rehnquist's background. The next day Nixon still seemed unenthusiastic about Rehnquist, commenting to Moore, "How the hell could you just put a guy who's an assistant attorney general on the Court?" His interest perked up when Moore mentioned Rehnquist's clerkship with Robert Jackson, and after a few more minutes of discussion, Nixon called Mitchell to say that he might "reevaluate" the nomination. Politics again came up, as Mitchell reminded Nixon that he wouldn't get "political mileage" from a Rehnquist nomination. Nixon had persuaded himself that he could get enough mileage simply by "appointing a highly qualified man." He joked with Mitchell about getting Rehnquist baptized so that they could claim to be appointing a Catholic. By the end of the conversation Nixon was pretty much committed to naming Rehnquist when, as he expected, Senator Baker turned the appointment down.

Unfortunately for Nixon's plans, Baker had decided to accept the nomination, and the president then had to figure out how to withdraw the offer. He had Mitchell call Baker and say that the Republicans couldn't afford to lose his seat in the Senate. With that

out of the way, Nixon prepared his speech. The leaks and trial bal-
loons had worked to rule out a number of candidates, but Rehnquist
had never surfaced as a serious contender. It was, as Nixon said, "like
China," an initiative held secret until he himself revealed it. Nixon's
speech dwelt at length on the criteria he had used in choosing Powell
and Rehnquist and praised Rehnquist as "among the very best
lawyers in the nation," who "has been outstanding in every intellectual endeavor he has undertaken."

Rehnquist's confirmation hearings began on November 3, 1971.
They were more contentious than the administration had expected.
Democratic Senator Birch Bayh of Indiana asked Rehnquist about
his poll-watching activities. Rehnquist replied that he had
"absolutely nothing to do with any sort of poll watching" in 1968
(true enough, his poll-watching activities had taken place in 1964)
and that he had never worked as a challenger at the polls in any other
election. Although Democrats assembled a few affidavits claiming
that Rehnquist had hassled potential African American voters in
1964, he categorically denied the charges. After the hearings had
ended, *Newsweek* published the text of Rehnquist's memo to Jackson
in the Brown case. As Dean put it, "Democrats jumped on it," with
Senator Bayh taking the lead. He tried to delay a confirmation vote
by moving to reopen the hearings, but the motion lost.

Apart from the question of the accuracy of Rehnquist's recollections, what can we make of the substance of his positions on civil
rights? It's telling that at least as John Dean recalled the conversation in which he proposed that Rehnquist be added to the list of
people to be considered for the Court, Dean thought he had to *say*
that Rehnquist was not a racist. In 1986 the Federal Bureau of
Investigation, checking his background in connection with his promotion to chief justice, discovered that the deeds on houses he
owned in Phoenix and in Vermont contained restrictive covenants
inserted some time before he bought the houses. The covenants purported to bar sale of the houses to members of disfavored races or
religions. The deed for the Vermont house, for example, said that it
could not be sold to "anyone of the Hebrew race." A 1948 Supreme
Court decision—widely criticized by conservatives—had held that it
was unconstitutional to enforce restrictive covenants, and those in
Rehnquist's deeds were legally meaningless. Fastidious buyers, how-

ever, often insisted on the removal of the provisions. Rehnquist first said that he didn't know that the deeds contained restrictive covenants and then, after finding a letter in his file on the Vermont house stating the covenant's terms, said that he must have read the letter but didn't remember doing so. There's a pretty obvious pattern here, as with the poll-watching charges and the Brown memo. Questions of civil rights and racial justice were simply a matter of complete indifference to Rehnquist. It's not that he was actively hostile to civil rights claims; it's just that he didn't care about them one way or the other—except when, as they often did, they ran up against interests, like those of small businesses, that he did care about.

Neither the poll-watching charges nor the Brown memo made a large difference. In the end the Senate confirmed Rehnquist's nomination, 68 to 26. That day Nixon had a private conversation with Rehnquist. Nixon gave him "one last bit of advice, because you're going to be independent, naturally." He said, "Don't let the fact that you're under heat change any of your views. . . . So just be as mean and rough as they said you were." Rehnquist replied politely, "Thanks, Mr. President."

☙

Nixon's nominations did change the Supreme Court, but not as much as Goldwater conservatives hoped. Mostly the Court drifted along the course set by the Warren Court, moving more slowly but never abandoning the commitment to substantive liberalism. Its abortion decisions in 1973, written by Nixon appointee Blackmun and joined by Nixon appointees Burger and Powell, extended the idea of privacy developed in the Griswold case into a far more controversial area. As the title of one overview of the early years of the Burger Court put it, that Court was "the counterrevolution that wasn't." Instead, it was characterized by a "rootless activism." It never adhered to a consistent theory of judicial restraint, but its decisions striking down statutes fitted no obvious pattern of liberalism or conservatism.

The Burger Court's drift reflected the state of politics generally. Liberals were beleaguered, but they still controlled Congress, and their voices were heard on the Supreme Court, through Justices William Brennan and Thurgood Marshall. Even more important, the Republican Party was in transition from one in which Nelson Rockefeller and those who thought like him played some significant role to a party dominated by true conservatives like Goldwater and Rehnquist. Lewis Powell, one of Nixon's appointees, was a patrician southerner, nominally a Democrat, but more comfortable with so-called country club Republicans than with the more ideological new conservatives in the party. Burger was a midwestern, moderately conservative Republican, firm on law and order issues but, again, more in tune with more liberal Republicans on other issues, particularly on separation of church and state. Combine this sort of conservatism with the continuing role liberals played on the Burger Court, and the counterrevolution was bound to fail.

⁄⁄

Warren Burger retired as chief justice in 1986 to head a national commission to celebrate the Constitution's bicentennial. The Reagan administration had no problem figuring out who to appoint in his place. Rehnquist was an "intellectual giant" to the conservative lawyers in the Department of Justice and at the White House. William Bradford Reynolds and Charles Cooper, two leaders of the administration's conservative lawyers, headed the selection team and had no doubts. Rehnquist was, according to Reynolds, "quite clearly the justice who most represented" the Reagan administration's constitutional vision. Of course, promoting Rehnquist from within also gave the administration a chance to name a new justice, Antonin Scalia, sharing that vision as well.

Rehnquist's confirmation hearings were only a bit less contentious than they had been the first time even though Republicans controlled the Senate and the outcome was never in serious doubt. Democrats, again led by Edward Kennedy, revived the charges of racism, particularly emphasizing the poll-watching issue, this time with some new evidence. Rehnquist denied the charges again, although in a somewhat qualified way. Sixty-five senators voted to confirm Rehnquist's promotion to chief justice, but the thirty-three votes against him were—at that point—the largest number of negative votes on a successful nomination. (Clarence Thomas was to break the record a few years later, winning confirmation by a vote of 52 to 48.)

For his colleagues on the Court, Rehnquist was a relief from Burger's pomposity and bumbling administration of their work. The other justices knew that Rehnquist was an affable ideologue, and his experience under Burger made him insist on expediting the Court's work. For Thurgood Marshall, Rehnquist was "a great chief justice"; for William Brennan, he was "the most all-around successful" chief justice with whom Brennan served (including Warren). He ran the Court's discussions so efficiently that sometimes a justice—most often, John Paul Stevens—would grumble that they never really discussed the cases but simply staked out positions. Rehnquist pushed his colleagues to get their opinions out promptly and did so himself. He insisted that his law clerks get draft opinions to him within ten days of getting their assignments. The short time frame meant that Rehnquist opinions were models of brevity, sometimes suffering for it. A typical Rehnquist opinion stated the facts in one or two paragraphs, described the relevant precedents, offered a paragraph or two explaining why the precedents supported or compelled the outcome, and then simply stopped. His opinions got cases decided but sometimes left unclear why they came out as they did or, more important, what the implications were for other cases.

Rehnquist presided over a dramatic reduction in the Court's workload, which surely made it easy for his colleagues to like him. The Court heard just about half the number of cases it had heard in the 1960s and 1970s. It had heard oral arguments for two hours in the morning and one or two in the afternoon, three days a week; with their docket cut, the justices now sat for oral arguments only in the mornings and sometimes only two days a week. The justices appointed to the Court in the 1980s and 1990s seemed to have strict standards for determining which cases to hear. The Warren and Burger courts occasionally heard cases simply to rectify what seemed to the justices were injustices. The Rehnquist Court did not, except in a handful of death penalty cases.

How the Court decided which cases to take up—which cert petitions to grant, in the Court's jargon—also changed. A cert pool of law clerks from nearly all the chambers prepared memoranda describing the cases—according to a peculiarly bureaucratic format to fit a computer template—that were sent to all the justices. They recommended whether the case was worth hearing, but the cert pool process slightly skewed the recommendations toward denying review because a law clerk who recommended denying review would be only mildly embarrassed if the justices decided to hear the case anyway, but one who recommended granting review on a case they took and then found boring or not worth their time imposed real costs on everyone who had had to slog through the briefs and oral argument.

∾

When Rehnquist became chief justice, the Court could be divided up along these lines:

The Conservatives

- BYRON WHITE, appointed by John F. Kennedy in 1962. White was a New Frontiersman in his views. Like Robert Jackson, he believed that the Supreme Court should generally stay away from contentious social issues, leaving them to be resolved by Congress. Among those issues were the law and order questions that came to characterize the Warren Court. Like Jackson, White relaxed his skepticism on the issue of race discrimination. He saw the national government as a vehicle for social and economic progress and the states as obstacles.

- LEWIS F. POWELL, nominated in 1972 at the same time as Rehnquist. Powell's instincts, nurtured sometimes by his law clerks, were conservative, but he could also be moved when particularly appealing human stories brought home to him the reality of constitutional law in everyday life. He was a consistent supporter of abortion rights, for example, largely because his daughters explained why abortion mattered to women and because he had seen how the illegality of abortion had ruined the life of an employee of his law firm.

- SANDRA DAY O'CONNOR, whose 1981 nomination fulfilled Ronald Reagan's campaign pledge to name a woman to the Supreme Court.

- ANTONIN SCALIA, one of the thinkers most admired by conservative legal activists, second only to Robert Bork in their eyes. The Justice Department officials who vetted the nomination described his opinions as "brilliant" and "ground-breaking" and said that he was "especially creative and successful" in developing "a set of coherent principles about what courts should not do." A White House official said, "What a political symbol. Nino would be the first Italian-Catholic on the Court. . . . He's warm and friendly. Everybody likes him. He's a brilliant conservative. What more could you want?" Scalia got the nomination rather than Bork because Reagan wanted to get political points for naming an Italian American to the Supreme Court, because he was younger than Bork and because conservative legal activists thought that Bork's turn would come soon.

The Liberals

• WILLIAM J. BRENNAN, named by Dwight Eisenhower in 1956 because Brennan was a Catholic Democrat whose appointment during an election year might boost Eisenhower's reelection chances. Within a few years Brennan had become the intellectual leader and tactical coordinator of the Warren Court's liberals, to the point where many scholars think it's more accurate to refer to the Brennan Court than to the Warren or Burger Court. Each year Brennan asked his law clerks to name the most important rule in constitutional law. Brennan gave them the answer after they stumbled around, naming one great case after another. "This," he said, holding up one hand with his fingers spread, "is the most important rule in constitutional law." Brennan knew that it took five votes to do anything, and, he may have thought, with five votes you can do anything.

• THURGOOD MARSHALL, a giant in U.S. legal history. It became a cliché that he would have been in the history books even if he had never served on the Supreme Court, because he had led a twenty-year battle in the courts against segregation, culminating in *Brown v. Board of Education*, the defining decision for the Warren Court and perhaps for the Supreme Court in the twentieth century. Lyndon Johnson knew that he would go down in history as the president who nominated the first African American to serve on the Supreme Court, and he knew that the only possible candidate was Thurgood Marshall. Yet the job as justice never quite suited Marshall. He was an outgoing man who felt isolated from social contacts on the Court, and he never devoted a great deal of attention to its work. Within the Court, however, some of his colleagues found him engaging and—particularly on issues of race and criminal justice—a person whose views carried great moral authority, more because of who he was and what he had done than because of the depth of the constitutional analysis he offered.

· HARRY BLACKMUN, named by Nixon in 1971. Blackmun was at first quite diffident about his views on the Constitution, but his experience, especially the experience writing the abortion decisions and living with their aftermath, transformed him. Someone took a potshot at his apartment window, and he regularly received, and read, an enormous volume of hate mail on the abortion decisions. His Court experience affected him in other ways. Burger dealt with Blackmun in a way that Blackmun perceived as condescending; Brennan became his friend. Blackmun at first voted to uphold the death penalty's constitutionality although he thought it bad social policy, but just before he left the Court, he reflected on the impact of his experience in death penalty cases and wrote that twenty years of dealing with those cases convinced him that he could no longer participate in operating what he called "the machinery of death."

· JOHN PAUL STEVENS, an antitrust lawyer in Chicago who had been named to the court of appeals by Richard Nixon and promoted to the Supreme Court by Gerald Ford on the recommendation of Attorney General Edward Levi, himself from Chicago.

Conservatives luxuriated in the thought that Rehnquist and Scalia would lead the Court sharply to the right. What did the legal conservatives want to do once they took charge? In February 1988 the Department of Justice published a booklet, nominally to "help government litigators think clearly about issues of constitutional and statutory interpretation that arise in the course of their litigation," actually a road map for the course constitutional conservatives hoped to take. The document was prepared by the department's Office of Legal Policy, the justice's internal think tank, as well as the clearinghouse for judicial nominations. Its head was Stephen

Markman, a conservative legal activist who when a congressional staffer had made many appearances at Federalist Society events. (He was appointed to the increasingly conservative Michigan Supreme Court by Republican Governor John Engler in 1999.)

As Attorney General Edwin Meese noted in the booklet's preface, the publication was "more than just an aid to government attorneys." It was also a statement of the conservative legal vision. Of course the "guidelines" denied that they were "conservative" or "liberal." Quoting Meese, the booklet said that it sought to provide "a jurisprudence faithful to our Constitution." The Office of Legal Policy offered guidelines on six topics, some with several subdivisions. In each, the booklet described the principles that government lawyers should follow and identified cases that were faithful or unfaithful to those principles.

Unsurprisingly, the first section dealt with constitutional interpretation and insisted that government lawyers base their arguments "solely on the ordinary usage" of the Constitution's words "at the time the provision at issue was ratified." The poster children for decisions inconsistent with this approach were the abortion decisions and *Miranda v. Arizona*, famous for its requirement that police officers inform those they arrested of their rights to remain silent and to have a lawyer.

Another section dealt with "the limited power granted to the federal government." Here the pamphlet mostly recited restrictive language from Supreme Court decisions that actually upheld congressional legislation and suggested that in many cases the dissents had the better argument. It criticized the Court for "stretch[ing]" constitutional principles in one of the major cases from the New Deal, in which the Court upheld a restriction on the amount of wheat a farmer could produce even for consumption on his own farm, because the impact of *all* the home consumption on the interstate market for wheat was substantial. That result, the booklet said, was "untenable" because the matter regulated wasn't commerce *among* the states. The booklet also criticized a decision upholding a federal prosecution for loan sharking, which was in all its essentials a local crime. The booklet urged government lawyers to "use . . . quotations" from Supreme Court cases recognizing the possibility of judicial protection for state sovereignty.

Turning to individual liberties, the booklet insisted that "If the government violates one of these expressly guaranteed liberties, attorneys should refuse to defend the violation." But, it continued, "expanding an express constitutional right beyond its legitimate scope is as improper as creating additional constitutional rights out of whole cloth." (It listed the Second Amendment among the expressly guaranteed rights but didn't devote any more attention to it.)

This is not terribly helpful in the abstract, but examples fleshed out the meaning. The Court had read the First Amendment too narrowly in upholding a requirement that broadcasters give time for a reply to those who were attacked on the air; it had read the Sixth Amendment's guarantee of a right to counsel too broadly in barring the use at trial of a statement elicited from a defendant by a jailhouse informant after the defendant had been indicted. The booklet was particularly critical of Supreme Court decisions that "create fundamental rights not specified in the Constitution." It approved the then-recent decision upholding a state's power to make homosexual sodomy a criminal offense and again criticized *Griswold* and the abortion cases.

The Department of Justice booklet expressed the hopes of the legal conservatives in charge of the executive branch's activities. To realize those hopes, they had to get the Supreme Court to agree. The appointments of Rehnquist, Scalia, and the other supposed conservatives were the mechanism to achieve success. But in the end only some parts of the agenda were carried out.

ℂℂ

The English philosopher Jeremy Bentham said that law was made by "Judge and Company"—by judges and the lawyers who appeared before them. Conservative lawyers learned from their liberal counterparts how to use Supreme Court litigation to advance their political agendas by carefully selecting sympathetic plaintiffs, nurturing lower court litigation until the time was ripe to present an important issue to the Supreme Court, and dividing the work once cases got to the Court.

The conservative lawyers were innovators as well as imitators. Liberal public interest litigators were basically individualists who pursued their own agendas and coordinated cases only when absolutely necessary. The conservatives developed networks of personal connections that promoted coordination. They created the Federalist Society as an organization where they could come together, discuss their common interests, and provide a way for young conservative lawyers to meet—and get jobs from—more senior lawyers. These innovations meant that conservative positions were presented to the Rehnquist Court more coherently than liberal positions ever had been.

The idea of constructing strategic litigation campaigns to reshape the law one case at a time is at least a century old. At the turn of the twentieth century business interests supported a series of cases aimed at weakening labor unions. Businesses also mounted coordinated challenges to aspects of Franklin Roosevelt's early New Deal programs.

The idea that social movements could benefit from strategic litigation really took hold after *Brown v. Board of Education*. Liberal lawyers told a story about *Brown*, treating it as a case that was the end point of a strategy that had been carefully thought through and then implemented step by step over a twenty-year period. That story was inaccurate, but it is the story that liberal public interest litigators—and later, conservative ones—told. During the 1960s liberal organizations like the American Civil Liberties Union put together strategic litigation campaigns on women's rights (headed initially by Ruth Bader Ginsburg) and prisoners' rights. Legal aid offices, supported by the national Legal Services Corporation, pursued what its proponents called impact litigation, designed to challenge state welfare policies as inconsistent with the federal income support statutes and as unconstitutional.

Conservatives noticed this activity and decided to emulate it. Lewis F. Powell wrote a memorandum to the U.S. Chamber of Commerce shortly before he was nominated to the Supreme Court, criticizing the influence consumer and environmental groups were having on policy making. Powell proposed that the chamber help create a counterweight, a public interest litigating group oriented to business interests. The Chamber of Commerce was interested and started to look for such a group to support. The chamber found it in California.

As governor of California, Ronald Reagan pushed for welfare

reforms. Liberal public interest groups challenged the reforms in court. Two Reagan advisers—Ronald Zumbrun, who lobbied for the reforms in the legislature, and Raymond Momboisse, who defended them in court—concluded that the state's litigators needed help. They consulted other conservative legal activists, including Edwin Meese, Reagan's chief adviser on law enforcement issues, and raised enough money from the Chamber of Commerce and others to open the Pacific Legal Foundation in 1973. The foundation, the first conservative public interest litigating group, started with Zumbrun and Momboisse as the legal staff in Sacramento, then expanded to hire more lawyers and to open an office in Washington, D.C. By the end of the 1990s the PLF had five offices and a budget with over $4 million from grants from conservative foundations like the Lilly Endowment and the Olin and Scaife family foundations. Its total budget in 2001 was over $8.6 million. PLF lawyers have been involved in cases raising a number of issues dear to conservatives' hearts.

Reagan administration veterans founded two other conservative public interest litigating organizations in 1991. Roger and Nancie Marzulla both had worked with Meese in Reagan's Justice Department. They created the Defenders of Property Rights in 1991 and supported more than one hundred legal cases involving challenges to government regulation. Chip Mellor, a second-level political appointee in Reagan's Department of Energy, and Clint Bolick, who had been one of Clarence Thomas's assistants at the Equal Employment Opportunity Commission, set up the Institute for Justice as a libertarian law firm. In 2001 its budget was over $2 million.

The money for these projects came from conservative foundations. William Simon, Richard Nixon's treasury secretary, headed the John M. Olin Foundation through the 1990s. Under his direction the foundation provided substantial financial support to a wide range of conservative organizations, including over $2 million to the PLF from 1985 to 2001 and $1.3 million to the Institute for Justice in the same period. Richard Mellon Scaife headed two foundations that supported the property rights lawyers. The Carthage Foundation was the single largest supporter of the Defenders of Property Rights in the 1990s, although it had ended its support by 2001. The Sarah Scaife Foundation gave the PLF $200,000 in 2001, continuing its traditional support for that group; the Defenders of Property Rights and the Institute for Justice each got $100,000 from it in 2001. This is a decent amount of money, particularly if you can rely on the foundations to keep the checks coming, but it won't support a really large organization.

The conservative public interest litigators faced continuing chal-lenges. Basically they had too much to do. They wanted to use consti-tutional law to downsize the government, but big government did so many things that the litigators had too many targets. They couldn't possibly take up every case that presented what they saw as an injus-tice. Their budgets, though substantial, were not inexhaustible, and their legal staffs were relatively small. In 2003 the Institute for Justice had eight staff lawyers who could be involved in litigation along with Mellor and Bolick; the PLF listed four lawyers in its main office in Sacramento dealing with property rights and environmental law, with a few other lawyers scattered around the country in branch offices.

Responding to these resource problems, the conservative litiga-tors took another lesson from the liberals. They developed proce-dures to screen out cases so that they would support only the most sympathetic clients. In 2003, if you went to "Meet Our Clients" on the Institute for Justice's Web site, you'd find the headline WIDOW WINS, PRIVATE PROPERTY PROTECTED, with a picture of Vera Coking flashing a V for Victory sign in front of Atlantic City's Trump Plaza Hotel—and her house, which the city had tried to condemn so that it could sell the property to the hotel for use as a parking lot for lim-ousines. (Or at least that's what the Web site says; usually when you look into the stories, there's a little more ambiguity about what the government was really trying to do and how sympathetic the clients really ought to be.)

Even these screening procedures aren't enough to construct a viable litigation strategy. Representing a lot of plaintiffs who didn't like government regulation isn't always helpful. A lot of the cases, particularly the strongest ones, will wash out. The regulators will give the developer a variance or change their regulation. The clients may want to pull out of the case at that point, even though doing so would deprive the litigators of a case that would contribute to their step-by-step strategy. The litigators might actually win some of the cases—again, often the ones presenting their claims in the most sympathetic light—at trial or in the first appeal, before the Supreme Court could get a chance to hear the case. The losing side might not want to appeal. The Institute for Justice, for example, got the New Jersey courts to stop the condemnation proceeding of Mrs. Coking's house, and Atlantic City decided not to take the case to the U.S. Supreme Court. Building a case from the beginning gives the lawyers the greatest control over the legal theories they want to develop, but it also reduces their chances of getting the case to the Supreme Court.

Clearly, bringing lawsuits and pursuing them from start to finish weren't the most cost-effective ways to develop the law in a conservative direction. So the conservative litigators looked around for cases that someone else—a landowner, a business, a real estate developer—had already started and found ways to piggyback on those cases. In addition, in yet another imitation of liberal public interest litigators, the conservative lawyers in each field—property rights, religion, family values—formed an informal network among scattered groups that could watch out for interesting and possibly important cases. According to one count, for example, about a dozen separate groups were involved in challenging government regulations as "takings" of private property.

Once the lawyers identified a promising case, the best outcome was that they could take over the case after the Supreme Court had decided to hear it so that they could present the arguments that had the greatest chance of moving the law in the direction they wanted. That happened in several ways. Experienced and well-heeled clients sometimes conducted so-called beauty contests, in which lawyers with substantial Supreme Court practices paraded before the client and its lawyers, attempting to show why this particular lawyer was really the best to present the case to the Court. Sometimes lawyers contacted the attorney who had been representing the client and made the case that he or she should relinquish the oral argument. They "volunteered" their expertise, pointing out that they had argued many more cases in the Supreme Court than the local lawyer.

If you can't take over a case, there's another possibility: presenting your position to the Supreme Court in an amicus curiae brief. An amicus brief is a written argument presented to the Supreme Court by an amicus curiae—literally, a friend of the court. Filing amicus briefs is easy. The Court's rules require that the amicus, including organizations like the PLF and the Institute for Justice, describe why it is interested in the case the Court has decided to hear. In one property rights case, the Institute for Justice filed an amicus brief, saying that it could help the Court because of its mission "to strengthen the ability of individuals to control and transfer property and to demonstrate that property rights are inextricably connected with other civil rights." That was enough to satisfy the Court's rules.

The rules also require either that the parties agree to allow the amicus brief to be filed or that the Supreme Court grant a motion for permission to file. Consent to filing is almost always given. It's courteous. Most of the time the amicus brief isn't going to do any more damage to your side than the opponent's brief does. Sometimes parties think that refusing to give consent will signal to the justices that they shouldn't take the other side's position seriously. It doesn't. Sometimes parties think that the more amicus briefs there are on the other side, the weaker their position will look. It won't. Experienced Supreme Court litigators knew this and gave consent routinely. Frank Lorson, the Court's chief deputy clerk during the 1980s and 1990s and a revered figure among Supreme Court practitioners, always told inexperienced practitioners that they should give consent because the Court was going to grant permission to file anyway and all that refusal accomplished was to make more work for the justices, which they might remember.

The Court's rules also require that the amicus declare if the lawyer for the actual party helped write the brief and who made a monetary contribution toward the brief's preparation. As a specialized Supreme Court practice matured, this requirement became pretty much a sham. In any important case the party's lawyers did the best they could to coordinate amicus filings. The Supreme Court's rules limit the number of pages in a brief. A party has fifty pages for an opening brief and twenty pages to reply to the other side. Sometimes that wasn't enough to get out all of a party's arguments. With any luck, an amicus would make the other arguments in the thirty pages the Court's rules give it. The most sophisticated Supreme Court advocates increased the odds by coordinating amicus filings, so that one amicus made one point and another, instead of repeating that point, made another. Again, with a bit of luck, the justices would pay attention. In the affirmative action case the Court decided in 2003, for example, some justices referred to the amicus brief from a group of retired military officers, drafted by Carter Phillips, one of the advocates the justices respected most. One justice asked the solicitor general about "the position taken in Mr. Phillips' brief." This is the gold medal for an amicus, rarely awarded.

The amicus practice can also bring well-known academics into the process of strategic litigation. The academics can devote their time to writing briefs rather than actually conducting trials or even making oral arguments. The conservative property rights litigators landed a notable catch in the University of Chicago law professor Richard Epstein. Epstein's 1985 book *Takings* made the case for a sweeping interpretation of the takings clause, so sweeping that it would essentially eliminate most of what modern governments do in regulating businesses, including, as Epstein wrote, "zoning, rent control, workers' compensation laws, . . . [and] progressive taxation." To Epstein, any interference with a property right, no matter how small, required compensation. His position in *Takings* was extreme. One respected student of both property law and the Constitution wrote that the book "belongs with the output of the constitutional lunatic fringe."

Epstein acted as a lawyer, not an academic, in writing his briefs for the Institute for Justice, and the positions he asked the Court to take weren't at all extreme. Instead, they were a lawyer's building blocks, positions that once adopted would allow the property rights lawyers to push ahead on their larger agenda. What the Institute of Justice got out of Epstein were very good briefs, some publicity, and—important—the value of his good name as a widely known legal academic who was happy to associate himself with the institute.

All in all, the amicus strategy is cheap and easy, perfect for ideologically oriented litigators. They used it effectively, but so did their opponents.

⚬∕∕⚬

Within the liberal public interest community, conflicts of interest—and ambition—were notorious. Lawyers with large egos who had devoted their lives to "their" causes resisted taking advice from people who they thought had other interests. The conservative public interest lawyers worked out some ways of reducing these conflicts.

The first was simple: the network of personal connections. One academic study identified five issue areas in which conservative constitutional lawyers operated: abortion, Christian religion, family values, libertarianism, and business orientation. Their most interesting discovery was five lawyers they called mediators. These lawyers bridged the gaps among the other issue-oriented groups, serving as advisers sometimes to one, sometimes to another. The mediators were Theodore Olson, who became solicitor general in George W. Bush's administration, Michael McConnell, appointed by Bush to a federal court of appeals, and William Bennett, Charles Cooper, and Edwin Meese, all of whom had held high positions in the Reagan administration. Working out of the conservative Heritage Foundation, Meese convened regular sessions at which lawyers representing the various issue areas met to discuss their common interests and to iron out their differences. The foundation held biannual legal strategy forums, bringing lawyers from around the country to Washington to "talk about joint efforts and cooperation" as well as monthly meetings of conservative lawyers in the Washington area to "keep them informed about each others' [sic] activities." As the conservative challenge to affirmative action developed, the Heritage Foundation joined with the Center for Equal Opportunity, a conservative think tank that focused on affirmative action and bilingual education policies, to hold monthly meetings of what they called the Civil Rights Working Group to inform participants about what the various conservative groups were doing. These meetings didn't always suppress disagreement, which was sometimes quite pronounced between social issue conservatives and libertarians on issues like gay rights, but they did create a forum for establishing the kinds of personal connections that reduce conflict.

The second innovation was, in the long run, even more important. Conservative lawyers created the Federalist Society to provide a forum within which they could meet, network, and develop the ideas that gave shape to conservative constitutional thought.

Stephen Calabresi, Lee Liberman, and David McIntosh got to know one another in the late 1970s as undergraduate members of the Yale Political Union, a debating society. Liberman later explained that she had a conservative "epiphany" when she discovered "Yale's intolerance . . . toward outside speakers whose theories offended some segment of the student body." Her colleagues shared her views. They were concerned not just about outside speakers but about an atmosphere that they believed discouraged conservative students from expressing their views.

All three went to law school: Calabresi to Yale, Liberman and McIntosh to the University of Chicago. They got the idea of re-creating a "debating group" in law school that would "attract bright conservatives who would challenge the Burger court and Warren court legacies." The three founders of what they called the Federalist Society were soon joined by Peter Keisler, Calabresi's roommate, and Spencer Abraham, a Harvard Law School graduate (later senator from Michigan and, after his defeat for reelection, George W. Bush's secretary of energy). The society took its name from the famous series of newspaper columns written by James Madison, Alexander Hamilton, and John Jay in 1787–88 to persuade Americans to adopt the Constitution and adopted a silhouette of Madison as its logo, displayed prominently on ties its members proudly wore.

The Federalist Society got support from conservative foundations. Seed money for its first convention came from the Institute for Educational Affairs, headed by conservatives William Simon and Irving Kristol, editor of *Commentary* magazine. Eugene Meyer, the son of an important editor at William Buckley's conservative magazine the *National Review*, became the society's executive director in 1984, a position he held through 2003. The Federalist Society also had an outlet for presentations from its meetings, the *Harvard Journal of Law and Public Policy*, which Abraham had helped found in 1978 as a vehicle for conservative ideas in law school. By 1986 Calabresi was able to boast that "more than half of the 153 Reagan-appointed Justice Department employees and all 12 assistant attorneys general are members or have spoken at Federalist Society events." As he put it, "we do not run the Justice Department," but "we definitely have had an influence in bringing in conservatives who would otherwise not go into Government."

The Federalist Society provided a chance for conservatives to present their positions on legal questions. Probably more important, it provided law students with a chance to meet prominent conservative judges and, during the 1980s, administration officials. Some conservative judges regarded Federalist Society members as particularly attractive candidates for jobs as law clerks, and law clerk positions were an important credential for getting good permanent jobs. In 1996 the Federalist Society expanded its job-networking activities by creating practice groups, where lawyers in private practice could get together to discuss legal strategies that would help their clients. The opponents of affirmative action, for example, were prominent members of the Civil Rights Practice Group.

Liberman went on to clerk for Scalia; Calabresi first for the conservative judges Ralph Winter and Robert Bork and then, after an interval at the Reagan Justice Department, for Scalia. Their career paths were typical of high-flying Federalist Society members. Other members got good clerkships, good jobs in the government, and good jobs in private practice—enough, at least, to make the Federalist Society attractive to ambitious conservative law students. They knew that their membership was an asset in applying for some jobs, a drawback for others, and some accordingly developed two résumés, one showing their membership and the other not.

From a handful of law students in the early 1980s with a budget of fifty thousand dollars, the Federalist Society had grown to an organization with more than twenty-five thousand members and a budget of over three million dollars by 2000, provided by substantial grants from such conservative foundations as the Olin Foundation and the Lynde and Harry Bradley Foundation. After 2001 the Federalist Society provided many of the lawyers who staffed the Bush administration's highest legal positions. As James Piereson, the executive director of the Olin Foundation, put it, "It is satisfying to see all these Federalist Society members in the White House." They were not just in the White House. According to one report in April 2001, over one-quarter of the candidates for federal judgeships "had been recommended directly by the Federalist Society's Washington headquarters." Liberals described the Federalist Society as a "cabal," and liberal interest groups used the society's connections to administration figures to show how the right wing had come to dominate the Bush administration and threatened to take over the courts. Conservatives responded by charging the liberals with playing "guilt-by-association" games. Both sides were right. Federalist Society connections were a good indication of what the new officials—and prospective judges—thought, yet each potential nominee had an individual take on what exactly it meant to be a conservative.

Conservative lawyers had built "a monstrous infrastructure" through the Federalist Society and their more informal networks. Whether they would be able to put that infrastructure to good use remained an open question.

∽

Conservatives would need more justices before they could take firm control of constitutional law. They thought that Ronald Reagan's election, which consolidated Goldwater's transformation of the Republican Party, gave them their chance. It did, but their victories were compromised by continuing divisions within the party. It turned out that it wasn't enough to nominate Republicans as justices. The *kind* of Republican who was named to the Supreme Court mattered too. Rehnquist was the first of the Republican nominees to the Court who were committed to a strongly conservative vision of constitutional law. He was to be joined by two others with equally strong commitments to that vision, Antonin Scalia and Clarence Thomas. However, that left the most conservative justices short of a majority. In the end Rehnquist moved the Court to the right, but not nearly as far as he would have liked because other Republican justices, particularly Sandra Day O'Connor and David Souter, were Republicans of a different stripe.

CHAPTER TWO

Two Kinds of Republican

Rehnquist represented the modern Republican Party transformed by Goldwater and Reagan. Justices Sandra Day O'Connor and David Souter—one appointed by Reagan, the other by Reagan's successor—nonetheless represented an older Republican tradition. Divisions on the Supreme Court mirrored divisions within the Republican Party and gave the Rehnquist Court its distinctive combination of activism in invalidating laws the modern party's social conservatives liked and invalidating laws that its economic conservatives disliked.

⁂

Lawyers arguing their cases before the Supreme Court dreaded hearing a couple of words from Sandra Day O'Connor. When she said, "My goodness" or "for goodness' sakes," you could be pretty sure that she was signaling how she was going to vote. David Boies, representing Vice President Al Gore, could have sat down in the middle of his argument in *Bush v. Gore* when O'Connor asked, "Well, why isn't the standard the one that voters are instructed to follow, for goodness sakes? I mean, it couldn't be clearer. I mean, why don't we go to that standard?" Because O'Connor's was often the only vote advocates thought might be "in play"—the only justice whose views weren't entirely predictable—hearing "My goodness" meant that the advocate probably had lost her vote and so the case.

Sandra Day was born in 1930 in El Paso, Texas, and was raised by her parents on their huge ranch on the Arizona–New Mexico border. Like most farms and ranches in the pre–New Deal United States, the Lazy B, with its 198,000 acres and two thousand head of cattle, didn't have electricity or running water until O'Connor was seven years old. Her memoir of her childhood is filled with stories about how isolated she was, learning to mend fences and drive a truck by the time her sister and brother were born in the late 1930s. O'Connor was clearly a bright child, whose mother read to her not only from standard childhood books but from national newspapers and magazines. Her father was emotionally restrained and sometimes difficult; O'Connor idolized him.

Starting when she was five, O'Connor spent the school year in El Paso with her grandmother, so she could attend a private school for girls, although when she was thirteen, O'Connor got so homesick that she stayed in Arizona for a year, attending school there. She finished school at a public high school in El Paso, then attended Stanford University, where she majored in economics, intending to learn enough about business to be able to run a ranch. She shifted gears, though, when one of her professors, a lawyer, inspired her to go to law school so she could go into some form of public service.

Finishing in two rather than three years, O'Connor ended up third in her class (two places behind William Rehnquist) at Stanford Law School. She met John O'Connor there, and they got married when she graduated while he still had a year to finish in law school. The only offer O'Connor got from a law firm was to work as a legal secretary, and she decided instead to spend the year in the county attorney's office. After John graduated and went into military service in Germany, O'Connor worked as a civilian lawyer for the army.

The O'Connors decided that prospects for careers in Arizona were good, and they settled near Phoenix in 1957. John started working for a large law firm, while O'Connor and a colleague started a practice in a minimall, doing what small law firms do for individual clients, drafting wills, handling insurance claims, and the like. After her first child was born, in 1958, O'Connor scaled back her legal practice and turned to the volunteer work expected of educated suburban Republican women in the late 1950s. She advised the Salvation Army, worked as an administrative assistant at the Arizona State Hospital for the mentally ill, volunteered at a school attended largely by African Americans and Hispanics, and was active in the local Fellowship of Christians and Jews.

She also took up public service. She sat on the local zoning board, wrote questions for the bar exam, and started working as a Republican Party precinct officer, becoming her district's chair in 1962. As O'Connor later said, she wanted a family *and* she wanted to work. So, in 1965, when her youngest son was three years old, O'Connor went back to full-time legal work in the state attorney general's office. Four years later the state's Republican governor appointed her to a seat in the state senate that had become vacant when the incumbent moved to Washington to take a position in the Nixon administration. She was elected twice on her own and in 1972 became majority leader in the state senate, where she shepherded legislation through a body with sixteen Republicans and fourteen Democrats, fashioning bipartisan compromises to get the job done. Regarded as a moderate conservative in Barry Goldwater's Arizona, O'Connor backed Reagan's challenge to Ford in 1976 and was one of the local party's rising stars.

She left the state senate in 1974 to run for trial court judge, and her reputation in the party led people to encourage her to run against Democrat Bruce Babbitt for governor in 1978. She declined, and Babbitt, perhaps to forestall a threat, promoted her to the intermediate state court of appeals in 1979. O'Connor came to the attention of Warren Burger when she attended a conference with him in England. He had become resigned to the fact that a woman would soon join the Court. When Potter Stewart retired in 1981, Reagan had the chance to fulfill his campaign pledge to nominate a woman to the Supreme Court. O'Connor had given a talk at the William and Mary Law School strongly defending state legislatures and judges against claims that Congress had to deal with social problems that state legislatures and judges had fumbled. Seeing O'Connor as holding views compatible with his own, Burger suggested her name to William French Smith, Reagan's attorney general, who put her on the list of potential nominees and then lobbied hard for her nomination. With Smith's support O'Connor was the easy choice.

Pro-life advocates started to worry about her record when they learned from leaks to the press about the possibility that Reagan would nominate O'Connor. She had been a member of the state senate's Judiciary Committee in 1970, when it passed a bill—before *Roe v. Wade*—to repeal Arizona's abortion law, but in 1981 no one could find a record of how she had voted. There were snippets of information about her position on abortion, but nothing solid. During her interview with Reagan, which his assistant Michael Deaver said "all but clinched her nomination," O'Connor said that she was "personally opposed to abortion," which doesn't quite say what her views as a judge would be. Responding to pressure from pro-life groups, Smith directed his assistant Kenneth Starr to follow up with O'Connor. Starr's report reflects how careful O'Connor was to navigate between the sides of the controversy. According to Starr, O'Connor said "that she had never been a leader or outspoken advocate on behalf of either pro-life or abortion rights organizations." She "knows well" the local right-to-life leader, Starr wrote, "and has never had any disputes or controversies with her." In the end the controversy fizzled out, and O'Connor was confirmed by a vote of 99 to 0.

O'Connor understood that she had been appointed because she was a woman, not because of her stellar academic credentials and reputation among those who knew her, though she had those assets too; you have to go back some decades to find a Supreme Court nominee with as slender a record as O'Connor's prior to her nomination (perhaps Charles Whittaker, appointed in 1957, but even Whittaker had been a federal judge for three years before he was nominated). She got floods of letters, which in her first years she strove to answer personally, and was at least for a while uncomfortable with all the attention she got in the press. Soon, though, she and John settled in to Washington, becoming fixtures on the party circuit. At one party in 1985 she received some particularly unwelcome attention when a drunken John Riggins, a star on the Washington Redskins football team, said loudly enough for many in the room to hear, "Lighten up, Sandy. You're too tight."

Her background led O'Connor to believe in the importance of people taking responsibility for their own lives. In her memoir of her childhood she recounted a long anecdote whose point was her father's lesson to her: "No excuses accepted." She wrote that her life on the ranch probably made her "more generous, open, and independent." There certainly is a tradition of farmers and ranchers' believing that they have made it the hard way and that so can others, without recognizing the importance of the government in having made their successes possible, but O'Connor's description of her ranch life shows how much it was improved by New Deal programs.

Perhaps more important, O'Connor took control of her own career. As the law professor Walter Dellinger put it, O'Connor was not "passively plucked, but [was] rather a woman who reached out and grabbed history for herself." At each stage in her life, she pushed to the outer limits of what people thought women could do and then broke through those limits, essentially by force of will. Blocked from a job in private practice, O'Connor turned to the government for a job. Uncomfortable with the role assigned to suburban wives in the 1950s, she resumed her career as a lawyer while her children were still young. Confident in her ability, she believed she could have beaten Babbitt in an election, but *she* chose a different path.

Inside the Court, O'Connor was somewhat formal and remote, and in her first years some of her colleagues wrote notes to each other gently mocking her stiffness. Her law clerks dealt with her in a fairly formal way, engaging in more like a staff briefing for a legislator than a discussion. She leavened the long hours she demanded from them with brunches and excursions—described as "mandatory" by some, taking a bit of the fun out of it—to museums and for white water rafting. Some clerks found her too demanding, though, and, in terms that sound quite sexist, called her "a witch" whose moods could swing from cordiality to snappishness without warning. Having attended an exercise class in Arizona every day before she went to work, O'Connor started an aerobics class for the women who worked at the Supreme Court, which morphed into a somewhat less stressful yoga class as she aged.

O'Connor had one characteristic that mattered a lot: She was decisive. Her office has a throw pillow with the inscription "Maybe in error, but never in doubt," and her approach to decision making was to figure out what she thought she should do (or what she thought the law required her to do), do it, and move on. As she told a group of cancer survivors in 1996, "I make my decision, and I don't look back. I do not look back and say, 'Oh, what if I had done the other thing,' or 'Oh, I should have done something else.' "

Her position on the Rehnquist Court made O'Connor, in the eyes of some observers, the most powerful justice and—to those who think the Supreme Court matters a lot—the most powerful woman in the United States. Academics used some statistical techniques to measure the power of individual justices. O'Connor did indeed come in first according to some measures, while Anthony Kennedy was more powerful according to others. There was no question, however, about O'Connor's importance because her vote seemed often up for grabs. Susan Estrich and Kathleen Sullivan, two prominent legal scholars, published an article about how they developed arguments in one abortion case. Their subtitle was "Writing for an Audience of One," O'Connor.

Her vote was up for grabs not because she was uncertain about what to do in any particular case but because her way of approaching cases made it hard for anyone other than her to know what she might think about specific cases. O'Connor tried to take everything into account, balancing every possible consideration against every other one, in a way that was often tied quite specifically to the facts of the case at hand. In political scientist Nancy Maveety's words, O'Connor's opinions "frequently justify exceptions within rules, arrive at limited, context-specific solutions, or articulate balancing tests for specific fact situations." Her approach was "loose, flexible, [and] malleable."

This approach had some important virtues. It displayed for all to see the things that mattered to O'Connor's resolution of the case. It allowed everyone involved in the case to believe that she had understood, and taken into account, the things that mattered to them. On a closely divided Court, it allowed the justices to resolve problems step by step when they couldn't agree on a broader holding. Even when someone might think that O'Connor had not given enough weight to some consideration, at least her opinions gave the critic something to point to that demonstrated where she had gone wrong.

Her approach also had some important defects. Change the facts a bit, and the outcome might change because the modified facts might, in her eyes, mean that something suddenly had taken on new importance. A reader could know *what* mattered to O'Connor, but often not why it mattered so much—or so little.

Probably most important, O'Connor's approach gave legislators, litigants, and lower courts very little guidance about problems just a bit different from the ones resolved by specific cases. Thinking about adopting some new regulation of abortion? An affirmative action program? You wouldn't know whether your plan was constitutional or unconstitutional until you asked Sandra Day O'Connor. The joke was that people could save a lot of time and effort in making laws and filing lawsuits if only O'Connor would answer her phone and let them know what she thought beforehand. The constitutional law the Supreme Court develops has to thread its way carefully between making overly broad statements that control too many problems beyond the one presented in a specific case and making overly narrow decisions that resolve particular controversies without making anything that can fairly be described as law. O'Connor's approach to constitutional adjudication came too close to the latter method.

A few years after O'Connor's appointment, the law professor Suzanna Sherry suggested that O'Connor's opinions reflected a distinctively feminine approach to constitutional law. Sherry drew on the work of the prominent psychologist Carol Gilligan, which many people took to show that boys like rules, girls like balancing and accommodation of competing interests. O'Connor was amused and a bit offended by Sherry's argument. After summarizing Sherry's argument, the justice wrote, "I would guess that my colleagues on the Court would be as surprised as I am by these conclusions," although one of the conclusions seems indisputable: that O'Connor uses "a contextual approach and tend[s] to reject so-called bright lines rules." O'Connor thought that a feminism emphasizing the differences between men and women—even one that purported to identify virtues women had that men lacked—threatened to bring back the days when women were placed on pedestals because they were too good for the messy world below.

O'Connor was fond of quoting Jeanne Coyne of the Minnesota Supreme Court: "[A] wise old man and a wise old woman reach the same conclusion." Of course the real work here is done by the word *wise*, and it could be that fewer old men than old women are wise. But in the jargon of legal academics, O'Connor was a sameness feminist, who thought that men and women were the same (or, more precisely, that the distribution of attributes between men and women was similar enough to make the differences unimportant), rather than a difference feminist, who thought that men and women differed in interesting ways that were important to shaping public policy—and approaches to constitutional law.

O'Connor was of course the best witness to her own mental processes, and if she said she didn't resolve constitutional questions as a woman would, but only as a wise person would, she must be right. Still, some things almost certainly came on her radar screen because she was a woman. The abortion cases show that she was particularly concerned about domestic violence. The Court was reasonably united in creating a federal right against sexual harassment at work and at school, but O'Connor broke with her more conservative colleagues to impose liability on a school board that failed to respond to complaints about the harassment of one student by other students.

Obvious criticisms of O'Connor's positions illustrate the problems facing a centrist on a divided Court. Pro-lifers might have noted that she ranked violence against women over violence against the unborn, but not over "violence" to states' rights; O'Connor voted with the conservative majority to overturn the federal Violence Against Women Act in 2000, thereby barring women from suing their attackers in federal court. On the other side, liberals could note that O'Connor was not as sensitive to issues of race discrimination as she was to issues involving women.

O'Connor will always be the first woman Supreme Court justice, and connecting her gender to her jurisprudence will preoccupy students of her work. She was more right than they, though, in thinking that her gender played only a part in constructing her approach to law, a part that was more important on some issues than on others, but that was overall less important than the focus on her firstness would suggest.

❧

Observers disagree about whether David Souter is a man of the eighteenth century set down in the twenty-first or merely a man of the nineteenth century. Compromising, his colleagues in the New Hampshire attorney general's office celebrated his 1976 promotion to attorney general with a cake saying, "Forward into the 19th century." The judgment that he is somehow out of step with the world seems to be almost universally shared. He is an ascetic in a world concerned with material things. He doesn't mow his lawn (or hire someone to mow it), his house in New Hampshire needs painting, and he drives a car seemingly too old to get from one end of town to the other, much less from New Hampshire to Washington and back. He is an intensely private person, who dislikes even the rare occasions when someone recognizes him as a Supreme Court justice.

There's a good deal of truth to all this, but Souter has also carefully cultivated his own image. Everyone who knew him knew that he was a sophisticated, well-read, and urbane man, hardly a hayseed from New Hampshire. He loved New Hampshire and preferred Boston to Paris, but he read English history and French novels.

David Souter was born in Massachusetts and moved when he was eleven to a small town in New Hampshire, where his father worked as a banker and his mother as a store clerk. At school he was a classic nerd, carrying a battered briefcase with his schoolwork in it. Harvard College was the natural next stop for a talented New England boy, and Souter did well enough there to get a Rhodes scholarship to spend a year at Oxford University in England. On his return he enrolled in Harvard Law School. He did not become consumed with his law school work and spent so much time as a proctor at a Harvard dormitory, counseling the college's young men, that his grades weren't good enough to get him a place on the law review. After graduation he returned to New Hampshire, where he worked for two years at a small law firm in Concord.

Souter decided to change jobs and joined the staff of the state attorney general in 1968. Two years later Warren Rudman became attorney general and, impressed with Souter's intellect and talent, made Souter his principal deputy. Eventually the two men became close friends. Rudman urged the very conservative governor Meldrim Thompson to name Souter attorney general when Rudman left to run successfully for a seat in the U.S. Senate in 1976. Thompson, a political opponent of Rudman's in the state's Republican Party, saw the appointment as a way to calm the waters. As attorney general Souter had to defend some of Thompson's more extreme positions, and to keep the office out of the Republicans' internal combat, he also used the argument that the attorney general was a professional lawyer.

Souter wanted to become a state supreme court justice and

turned down a couple of offers from Thompson for a seat on the state's trial court. In 1978 Thompson tried again, and again Souter declined. Thompson then offered the job to Thomas Rath, Souter's deputy and a close friend. That night Souter talked with Rudman about the appointment and concluded that the only way he would get to the state supreme court would be by becoming a trial judge. The next morning Souter called Rath and asked if Rath would "step aside and become attorney general." Rath agreed, and Souter became a trial judge in 1978. His judgment about what was needed to get on the state supreme court was confirmed when John Sununu, Thompson's successor as governor, finally appointed him in 1983. Souter found work as a judge so easy that he took on the additional task of chairing a local hospital's board of directors. (Souter had been on the board in 1973, when it approved a resolution allowing doctors to perform abortions. There was no record of the board vote or even of Souter's attendance at the meeting, though.)

Rudman's sponsorship continued. He put Souter on the radar screen when the Reagan White House was trying to recover from the Bork nomination, but the Californians in charge decided on Anthony Kennedy. In 1990 Souter agreed to let Rudman secure his nomination to the federal court of appeals in Boston, thinking that he could live in New Hampshire and work in Boston. Souter was sworn in as a federal judge on May 25, 1990. William Brennan announced his retirement from the Supreme Court on July 20, and Rudman persuaded Sununu, at the time President George H. W. Bush's chief of staff, to put Souter on the list of finalists.

The original list included Kenneth Starr, serving as solicitor general, and Laurence Silberman, a conservative court of appeals judge from Washington. The White House quickly eliminated them, leaving Souter and Edith Jones, a federal judge from Bush's Texas, for interviews. Jones's interview with Bush was a Texas "lovefest," but the president found Souter "most impressive." Rudman later observed that Souter and Bush "came from similar backgrounds: Yankee, white Anglo-Saxon Protestant families that believed in the old values of hard work, integrity and public service." Bush's note to himself was: "I like his manner—scholarly, serious approach—right age—temperament = A OK." Bush divided his advisers to argue for Jones and Souter, asking Sununu and Vice President Dan Quayle to present the case for Jones, and Attorney General Dick Thornburgh and White House counsel C. Boyden Gray for Souter. Jones fitted the Republicans' continuing interest in strengthening their position in the South and was known to be quite conservative. That was her major drawback too. Her nomination would be "a strong 'in your face' political appointment," Bush was told. The president was not anxious for a tough nomination fight during an election year, and Souter was a perfect stealth nominee, whose views on controversial questions were so unknown that he couldn't be attacked for them.

Conservatives were a bit nervous about Souter but accepted Sununu's assurance of his reliability. Liberals were nervous too, and pretty much for the same reason: Anyone who could satisfy John Sununu couldn't be good news for liberals. Mostly, though, people tried to find out who David Souter was. The fact that he was a fifty-year-old bachelor who lived with his mother in the house where he had grown up led to speculation that he was gay. Reporters located several women he had dated in his twenties, and the standard line became that he was married to the law. Still, the inquiry bothered Souter, who wondered about the relevance of "getting quotations from old girlfriends and so on of 20 years ago." Neither reporters nor liberal interest groups came up with anything that damaged Souter, and his nomination went through by a vote of 90 to 9.

Souter settled in to work in Washington, keeping his usual long hours and continuing to eat his peculiar lunch of yogurt and an apple—seeds and all, reporters noted. His office became as cluttered with books as his house, which he described as looking "like someone was moving a bookstore and then stopped." He tried to use his summers to catch up on his reading, with such projects as rereading Marcel Proust and reading a multivolume history of Great Britain. He genuinely disliked living in Washington, leaving town as soon as possible when the Court's term ended to drive home to New Hampshire; his law clerks joked that if he became chief justice, his first act would be to move the Supreme Court there.

Souter is a witty man in private. He does good imitations of other public figures, although his thick New England accent limits the range of people he can effectively parody to other New Englanders (and sometimes puzzles lawyers arguing cases before the Court). He occasionally sent thank-you notes written in Latin, and one of his law clerks discovered a bar of soap on her desk the day after she had used a four-letter word in the office. At his confirmation hearings Souter responded to a senator's comment that his staff had spent "an arduous August" looking into Souter's work, "If they were reading my opinions, they did." When one of his law clerks was working a case involving a Massachusetts law barring the state from buying goods made in Myanmar, formerly known as Burma, day after day the clerk received short three- or four-word notes from Souter containing, as the baffled (and of course young) clerk later learned, the sequence of Burma Shave signs that used to be posted on the nation's roads.

I met Souter for the first time at a reception a few weeks after he had chosen my daughter to be one of his law clerks—on the basis of her spectacular academic record, not any family ties—and told him that hiring her confirmed that he was a person of wisdom and good judgment. To which he immediately replied, "And if your daughter is discreet, you'll continue to think that."

Souter played down his wit in his opinions, although it's not true, as some commentators suggested, that "there are no sound bites in a typical Souter opinion." Addressing a Scalia dissent, Souter quoted Justice Benjamin Cardozo's comment that dissenters are "gladiators making a last stand against the lions" and then observed that Scalia's "dissent is certainly the work of a gladiator, but he thrusts at lions of his own imagining." Souter's opinion in a school prayer case reviewed the history of the establishment clause and included a footnote on Thomas Jefferson's views. The footnote observed that Jefferson's practice as president sometimes deviated from his statements of principle and concluded elegantly, "Homer nodded."

What happened to David Souter on the Supreme Court? Conservatives certainly felt betrayed. One, who worked in the Bush White House, said, "The guy lied; he just snowed everybody to get his appointment." The conservative economist Thomas Sowell invented the term *Greenhouse Effect*, referring to the *New York Times'* Supreme Court correspondent Linda Greenhouse. The Greenhouse Effect worked its magic by leading conservative justices to become liberal so that they would be praised by Greenhouse for having "grown" . . . away from their conservatism. That's particularly unlikely in light of Souter's evident indifference to the Washington scene. Perhaps conservatives discovered that the problem with a stealth nominee is that even the nominee's supporters may not know which way the plane is flying.

The real story is simpler. Souter simply hadn't dealt with the issues he faced when he got to the Supreme Court. As New Hampshire's attorney general and then as a state supreme court judge he handled routine criminal cases, zoning cases, car accident cases—but nothing major about the U.S. Constitution. As far as anyone could discover, the only national issue Souter had ever addressed was affirmative action, which he criticized as "affirmative discrimination" in a speech he gave in 1976. At his confirmation hearings Souter finessed the speech, saying that he wasn't sure that the newspapers quoted him correctly, but that he thought that actions "simply for the sake of reflecting a racial distribution" were wrong and that the nation probably had "a need for affirmative action."

It wasn't that Souter had views about controversial issues but hadn't expressed them but that he actually hadn't formed views on them. As he told a law clerk, "I never had to think about these things until I came to Washington. I never thought about them. I had no settled views." That was precisely what made him an attractive stealth candidate for the Bush White House.

Still, even Antonin Scalia had to start thinking about constitutional law at some point, and the fact that Souter had to learn constitutional law doesn't explain why he drew relatively liberal rather than relatively conservative conclusions from his study. A close friend from Souter's days in England recalled that he had been deeply influenced by an aunt who worked as a medical social worker and was "politically and socially conservative" but "fulfilled liberal causes." As attorney general Souter had to deal with the rabidly conservative governor Thompson, defending his client's positions but never really accepting them. At his confirmation hearings Souter uttered some conventional platitudes about the greatness of William Brennan, whom he was replacing. It turned out that Brennan and Souter became good friends, having coffee together nearly every morning Brennan was in his chambers after his retirement. But Souter's predispositions were almost certainly more important than any of this. He was a Republican, but a northeastern Republican, representative of the party before its transformation by Goldwater and Reagan.

Souter hadn't concealed his inclinations from anyone who paid attention at his confirmation hearings. He told the senators that the justice he admired most was John Marshall Harlan, appointed to the Supreme Court by Dwight Eisenhower in 1955. Like Souter, Harlan had come from the northeastern wing of the Republican Party. Harlan was a conservative who understood the importance of tradition and stability, and he had a powerful sense that government, while obviously a good thing in general, had a tendency to be too intrusive on people's privacy. His concern about overreaching governments led him to write a powerful opinion concurring in the Court's decision to overturn Connecticut's law against using contraceptives. Describing the concept of substantive due process, Harlan wrote that "its content cannot be determined by reference to any code." Rather, "it represented the balance which our Nation, built upon postulates of respect for the liberty of the individual, has struck between that liberty and the demands of organized society." Giving content to that idea was "a rational process," in which the courts paid attention to tradition, "a living thing." Souter's version of this, at his confirmation hearings, was: "Principles don't change but our perceptions of the world around us and the need for those principles do."

The Justice Department booklet that set out the conservative legal agenda was cavalier about the law built up before it was written. Decisions were right or wrong, depending entirely on whether they conformed to the conservatives' interpretation of the original understandings about the Constitution. Wrong decisions should simply be discarded. Souter was a different kind of conservative. Tradition mattered, and among the traditions that mattered were the Supreme Court's decisions. The constitutional law Souter inherited had been shaped by the Warren Court and modified only around the edges by the Burger Court. *Roe* had been on the books for twenty years when the Pennsylvania abortion case arrived at the Supreme Court in 1992; Justice Powell's opinion in *Bakke* had guided universities for twenty-five years when the Michigan affirmative action cases arrived in 2003. These were facts of life—traditions, in a sense that mattered to Souter—and he believed that he had a duty to preserve the law he had been given.

◯◯

Journalists, some political scientists, and some of the rest of us think that how the justices get along with one another has to matter in Supreme Court decision making. Surely, they think, it has to matter to O'Connor that Scalia writes that her position is "irrational" and to Kennedy that Scalia finds a Kennedy opinion "really more than one should have to bear"—two phrases Scalia used in his opinions in abortion rights cases.

Some observers suggest that this personalized rhetoric pushes O'Connor or Kennedy away from Scalia. The very conservative court of appeals judge Alex Kozinski, who clerked for Burger in 1976 (and for Anthony Kennedy when he was an appeals court judge), invoked this idea in 1991, writing that Scalia's dissents were "verbal hand grenades," which "throw shrapnel at anyone near the blast without attention to who they are—or how they might vote in the next case." Yet the justices have positions on what the Constitution means. The effect of personal relations among the justices has to be swamped by the effect of those positions, except occasionally and mostly on the margin.

The fact that Scalia and Ginsburg are friendly, for example, seems to have had no effect whatever on their positions in important constitutional cases—except, perhaps, that Scalia didn't go after Ginsburg when he disagreed with her with nearly as much personalized rhetoric as he did when O'Connor or Kennedy departed from his vision of a true conservative jurisprudence. Even that might have resulted less from friendship than from a sense that O'Connor or Kennedy had strayed off the reservation, while Ginsburg was never on it.

The justices routinely deny that they are anything but friendly at work. In an interview with George Stephanopoulos in 2003, for example, O'Connor said, "When you work in a small group of that size, you have to get along, and so you're not going to let some harsh language, some dissenting opinion affect a personal relationship." Breyer agreed, saying that when he read "rather sharp words about something I've written, perhaps it's sort of a question of rhetoric, more than it is of actual human feeling." He continued, "So if I'm really put out by something, I can always go to the person who wrote it and say, 'Look, I think you've gone somewhat too far here.' But it isn't, it doesn't hang on as a personal matter, because we get on quite well, personally." Notably, though, neither one used the name of the one person to whom they could have been referring. The fact that they talked only in general terms about a problem, if it is one, associated almost entirely with Scalia casts some doubt on the degree to which their denials captured the entire story.

One indication that personal relations might matter a bit sometimes is that the justices on the Rehnquist Court really don't interact with one another much on a personal basis, at least with respect to their work. The justices are a small group of people that are almost like a family, but like a family that never really talks about things that matter. Thomas regularly described the Court as congenial, by which he meant that the justices never raised their voices to one another. His explanation was simple: "You live your professional life with eight other people and not like them and see how difficult that is." Fair enough, but Thomas's description doesn't sound like one of a group that works together toward some common goal.

Lewis Powell was disappointed in the 1980s to discover that the Court operated like nine separate law offices, with each justice processing the paper that flowed into and out of the chambers rather than discuss questions with another justice. The discipline Rehnquist imposed on getting the Court's work done only reinforced that way of doing business. Justice Thomas reported that "internally we rarely see each other." He added, "You don't walk to your colleague's office and try to decide something informally."

The justices have to get together at their conferences, the meetings to decide which cases to take up and to "discuss" and vote on cases that have been argued. Getting a discussion going in the conference is a difficult task for anyone. The justices need to get through a lot of material at each conference and can't possibly have a full-fledged discussion of every case. Moreover, discussions of even a handful of cases can become tiresome. Felix Frankfurter annoyed his colleagues by treating them to minilectures on constitutional law and history; some responded by turning away from the table or simply noting their positions rather than respond to Frankfurter. Rehnquist's push for efficiency was partly a reaction to Burger's long-windedness. At the conference he leads, efficiency means that each justice states his or her position, without trying to engage anyone else in a real discussion.

As O'Connor told Stephanopoulos, "The real discussion takes place in the writing of opinion drafts." A justice who had trouble with a draft would, she said, "write a letter that shared with all the other justices perhaps and then they can all weigh in and say, yeah, I agree, that needs clarifying or, no, I don't agree." Even there, however, real engagement was unusual. People get attached to the words they—or their law clerks—have written. The justices occasionally modified their opinions to get a vote or two. They didn't have much bargaining leverage on the language of dissents, though. It's hard to imagine Souter going to Scalia as opinions circulate and saying something like: "You know, it seems to me that your tone is inappropriate." At most someone on Scalia's side might be in a position to raise questions about his personalized rhetoric. Mostly, though, the justices on his side when he let loose shared his outrage and were willing to let him put things however he wanted. Occasionally, Scalia himself would tone down his rhetoric, eliminating from later drafts the more egregious phrases he used in earlier ones. But, of course, his colleagues, having seen the early drafts, knew what Scalia, unrestrained, really thought.

In Scalia's early years on the Court, his colleagues were sometimes taken aback at his tone but then came to say, in effect, "Don't take it personally; that's just how Nino writes." By and large, they didn't take it personally. Still, the point about acid is that it can gradually eat away at things, and that too seems to have happened. Personal relations may have contributed to the outcome of Scalia's campaign against the use of legislative history in statutory interpretation. The Justice Department booklet on guidelines for conservative jurisprudence emphasized the primary role of a statute's words in guiding interpretation. The general principles allowed government attorneys to rely on legislative history "to give meaning to the words employed," but the section ended with a quotation from Scalia, when he was a circuit court judge, cautioning against the use of that history.

Scalia carried that approach to the Supreme Court, and for a while it seemed as if he would succeed in eliminating references to legislative history from Court opinions. The campaign then stalled and ultimately failed. One reason was that the argument against using legislative history always had an air of unreality about it. It was convenient to deploy the argument when, as it often did, it limited the reach of the regulatory statutes Congress adopted. But anyone

familiar with the legislative process knew that refusing to look at legislative history to find out what a statute's words meant was pretty
artificial. Anthony Kennedy, with his background as a lobbyist, and
Sandra Day O'Connor, a former legislator, might have brought a
reality check to Scalia's campaign. But they had worked with state
legislatures and might have been reluctant to take him on in connection with Congress.

Breyer was another, far stronger adversary for Scalia on this issue.
Like Scalia, Breyer had specialized in administrative law as a law professor, but Breyer was a more accomplished academic in the field. In
addition, he had worked *in Congress* as chief counsel to the Senate
Judiciary Committee. He knew how Congress worked from the
inside. Scalia's challenge to the use of legislative history was based
on theory and, perhaps, on his experience in the executive branch. It
couldn't withstand the response Breyer mounted inside the Court.

By the mid-1990s Scalia's campaign against the use of legislative
history had come down to this: He had to write opinions saying that
he concurred in all but Section X of the Court's opinion or that he
concurred in the Court's opinion except for its footnote Y, when
Section X and footnote Y relied on legislative history. What's notable
here is that often Kennedy or O'Connor wrote the majority opinions. They were willing to accommodate Scalia by separating out the
discussion of legislative history so that he could concur separately,
but they weren't willing to accommodate him any further. Some of
their unwillingness surely resulted from the way Scalia treated them
in his more pointed opinions on other matters.

Something like a change affected by personal relations does seem
to have happened in the abortion cases with O'Connor. She came to
think that Scalia was "not a very polite man," and she valued the
social graces. Her stance hardened, probably in part because she
found his tone so distasteful. Even here, however, there was a lot
more at work. Scalia was right to see that O'Connor thought of herself as a stateswoman. O'Connor believed that overruling *Roe* would
be a bad thing: bad for women, bad for the country, and perhaps bad
for the Republican Party.

Personal relations have some effects on Supreme Court decisions,
but they are small and operate only around the edges of the important issues. Move in a bit from the edges toward the core, and views

about the Constitution, the Court's role, politics, and society are all that matter.

∽

Remarkably, the Rehnquist Court went from 1994 to 2004 with no changes in membership. You have to go back to the years from 1811 to 1823 to find a longer period with no changes in personnel on the Court (and then there were only seven justices anyway).

The Court's stability mattered for a couple of reasons. The Supreme Court is a small institution, nine people working together on projects that require most of them to come to some agreement. The justices rarely know one another before they become colleagues. They have to get comfortable with one another's personality quirks and figure out what really matters to each justice. On a stable Court they know one another reasonably well.

Also, justices say that it takes about four or five years to get used to the Court's work. No justice, ever, has been exposed to the full range of issues the Court considers. Some may have known something about constitutional law before they arrived at the Court, others something about criminal procedure, still others something about administrative law, but almost no one knows anything about federal tax or pension law before becoming a justice. It takes time simply to get one's sea legs. A stable Court is one where the work can get done reasonably efficiently.

In a 2002 analysis of the Rehnquist Court, the law professor Thomas Merrill suggested that there were actually two Rehnquist Courts, one running from Rehnquist's promotion to chief justice in 1986 to 1994, and the other from 1994 to 2002 (and now 2004), the period when the Court's membership didn't change.

Merrill observed that the first Rehnquist Court dealt with the social issues, particularly abortion and religion, that mattered to one segment of the Republican coalition and that those issues "receded from the scene" during the second Rehnquist Court, to be replaced by issues of federalism. According to Merrill's count, the first Court decided twice as many social issues cases as the second, while the second Court decided twice as many federalism cases as the first. The Court heard five abortion cases from 1986 to 1992; it heard only one from 1993 to 2004. It heard four affirmative action cases from 1986 to 1992; it heard one in 1995 and then revisited the issue definitively in 2003. And according to Merrill, the Rehnquist Court was far more innovative on federalism than on the social issues.

Why did the second Rehnquist Court differ from the first? Merrill thought that the changes flowed from a complex combination of personal and ideological factors. He pointed out that observers characterized both Rehnquist Courts as having five conservatives and four liberals but said that that simple labeling obscured too much. During the first Court the conservatives were Rehnquist, O'Connor, Scalia, Powell and his replacement, Kennedy, and Byron White, and the liberals were Brennan and his replacement, Souter, Marshall, Blackmun and his replacement, Ginsburg, and Breyer, whose appointment when White retired restored a balance briefly upset when Clarence Thomas replaced Marshall. But, Merrill said, calling White a conservative was accurate for some purposes but inaccurate for others. White was "an old fashioned New Deal liberal," a strong supporter of the constitutionality of expansive exercises of national power, which fitted together with a suspicion of judicial activism reminiscent of the New Deal battles. A "conservative" Court with White on it could not engage in a federalism revolution, and it did not. His departure provided the opportunity for changing the rules on national power.

What about the social issues? For Merrill, the key actor was Scalia, who arrived at the Court in 1986 with "an extraordinarily ambitious agenda," mapped out a few years later in the Department of Justice pamphlet. Some items on the agenda were more important to him than others, of course. Scalia cared a lot about the social issues but was only mildly interested in the conservative federalism agenda. In a 1982 Federalist Society speech Scalia urged conservatives to think strategically about federalism. Sometimes, he said, national power was a good thing, when it reined in states that adopted economic regulations that interfered with "market freedom."

It turned out, though, that even the first Rehnquist Court couldn't muster majorities for major changes on the social issues agenda, most notably, again, abortion. In Merrill's eyes, when Scalia lost the battle over the social issues, he turned his attention to the federalism agenda, where he had more consistent allies in O'Connor and Kennedy, perhaps, Merrill suggested, to bide his time until new

Republican appointees could take on the social issues once again.

Merrill supplemented these arguments with attention to what was happening generally in politics. From 1986 to 1992 Democrats controlled Congress, and Republicans the presidency. Merrill suggested that the first Rehnquist Court had to worry about going too far and provoking some sort of response from Congress. Indeed, when the Court issued a series of opinions restricting the scope of federal civil rights laws in 1989, Congress did respond with a Civil Rights Restoration Act, vetoed at first by George H. W. Bush but then signed by him after its supporters had made some cosmetic changes and after he had suffered political damage on the issue of civil rights in the bruising fight over Clarence Thomas's nomination to the Supreme Court.

The date the second Rehnquist Court began, 1994, was a turning point in the American political system. Newt Gingrich led conservative Republicans, with their Contract with America, to take over the House of Representatives for the first time since the 1950s, and the Senate came under Republican control as well. Bill Clinton's State of the Union address in 1996 showed how much had changed when he acknowledged that "the age of big government is over." The federalism agenda then became consistent with what politicians were saying, and the conservatives had nothing to fear in pursuing it. In contrast, the social issues remained politically volatile. As a matter of sheer power, probably a conservative majority could have gotten away with pretty much anything it wanted to do on the social issues, because liberals couldn't possibly have managed to get enough votes to amend the Constitution. If the conservatives overruled *Roe v. Wade*, for example, there was no way that pro-choice forces would have gotten the required two-thirds votes in the House and Senate even to submit to the states a constitutional amendment protecting the right to choose.

But, of course, there *wasn't* a conservative majority on the Court to overrule *Roe v. Wade* or to pursue forcefully the social issues agenda. Merrill suggested that O'Connor and Kennedy "blinked" when they were confronted with the congressional reaction to their civil rights decisions and with the role the abortion issue played in Thomas's confirmation hearings. This overlooks the fact that O'Connor and Kennedy were conservatives, but of a different stripe from Scalia and Thomas. Scalia and Thomas came from and expressed the values held by the most conservative elements in the Republican Party coalition. By the end of the Rehnquist era those elements had succeeded in almost entirely eliminating opposition from moderate Republicans . . . in Congress. Membership on the Supreme Court changes more slowly, though, and O'Connor and Kennedy were perhaps the last representatives of an older, country club Republicanism, keenly interested in keeping the size of the national government down and limiting government regulation of businesses, but not all that interested in the social issues that animated the core constituencies of the modern Republican Party.

There were indeed two Rehnquist Courts, and Merrill's analysis came close to the mark. A better way to see the two Rehnquist Courts, though, is in stark political terms: The Rehnquist Court was a Republican Supreme Court, with one wing concerned primarily with the size of government (the traditional Republican concern), and the other with the newer issues animating the modern Republican Party. Rehnquist spanned both wings, but the divisions between O'Connor and Kennedy as traditional Republicans and Scalia and Thomas as modern ones meant that the Rehnquist Court would be able to advance further on the economic and federalism agenda than on the social issues agenda. The Court's movement conservatives gradually learned that they couldn't win on the social issues, accounting for the differences between the two Rehnquist Courts.

CHAPTER THREE

Clarence Thomas's Constitution

Clarence Thomas's bitter confirmation hearings in 1991 left a permanent scar. In 2003 the dean of the law school at the University of Georgia abruptly decided to resign, in part because of the controversy among his faculty and students about his decision to invite Thomas to speak to that year's graduating class. Legal scholars, predominantly liberals, have found it impossible to take his work on the Supreme Court seriously. At most (and at worst), they mistakenly treat him as simply a clone of Antonin Scalia.

In 1995 I published an essay about a book dealing with Thomas's confirmation. After presenting what I still think was a relatively sympathetic account of what I thought had happened between Thomas and Anita Hill, I concluded that he had almost certainly lied in denying that anything at all had happened. Under normal circumstances the discovery that a Supreme Court justice had lied about something important in the course of his nomination hearings would lead to an impeachment, but because that outcome was politically impossible, I wrote that legal scholars and ordinary citizens ought to take the position that Supreme Court decisions rendered by five to four majorities when Thomas was in the majority should not be regarded as law at all. I wasn't entirely serious about that proposal (and said so at the time); the proposal was part of a larger scholarly project I had, about thinking through the ways in which ordinary citizens can participate in making constitutional law.

I no longer think that Thomas probably lied. Just as I think that what happened between Thomas and Hill was more complicated than nearly every account suggests, so I think that Thomas's reaction to the charges against him was more complicated—more like an honestly stated reconstruction of the events, motivated by a combination of outrage and puzzlement about the source of the charges, than assertions of facts he knew to be false.

No discussion of Thomas's performance on the Court can avoid dealing with the confirmation hearings. But Thomas has now been on the Supreme Court for more than a decade, and as he said after his confirmation, he is going to be there many more years. What he has done on the Court is certainly more interesting and distinctive than what Scalia has done and, I think, has a greater chance of making an enduring contribution to constitutional law. Basically, *anyone* whom Ronald Reagan selected for the Supreme Court who had strong ties to the Federalist Society would have done just about what Scalia did. The Department of Justice booklet described in Chapter One set out the program, and Scalia pretty much followed it, as would anyone else Reagan picked.

Clarence Thomas is different. There was no close competition for the seat he got, but the others who were at least considered—Judges Laurence Silberman and Edith Jones—were more or less standard Federalist Society conservatives. *They* might have been Scalia's clones. Not Thomas.

$\mathcal{O}\!\!\mathcal{D}$

"Every Clarence Thomas profile I've ever read begins with a discussion of [his] grandfather." Thomas kept a portrait of his grandfather Myers Anderson in his Supreme Court office and mentioned Anderson in nearly every speech he gave. Anderson, whom Thomas described as "the strongest man in the world," taught him the importance of self-confidence in the face of disparagement and the virtues of self-reliance in a world where other people didn't always have your best interests at heart. Thomas rebelled against Anderson's teachings in his college years but came back to them in law school. Anderson taught him, as he put it in 1987, "You don't have any control over" what the government does, but "What you do have control over is yourself. . . . You've got to learn how to take care of yourself, learn how to raise your kids, how to go to school and prepare for a job and take risks like everybody else."

Born in 1948, Thomas spent his first years in Pin Point, Georgia, a small town outside Savannah. His father left a year later, just after Thomas's brother was born. Thomas later described Pin Point as "a small community of blacks, most of whom are my relatives." His immediate family may have been somewhat unstable, but his extended family watched over Thomas while his mother worked at the local shellfish-packing plant. He spent most of his time with a great-aunt, Maggie Devoe, who taught him to read from books her family got from two white families for whom her husband worked. Other members of the extended family did their best to make sure that he ate decent food, attended church, and otherwise stayed in line.

When Thomas was six, he moved with his mother and brother to a small room in a run-down part of Savannah, while his sister, Emma, one year older, stayed in Pin Point. In Savannah, their living conditions changed. They lived in a one-room flat without electricity, and according to Thomas, his mother often left him and his brother to fend for themselves. His mother remarried in 1955, and her new husband didn't want the children from the first marriage around. His mother sent him to live with her father, a self-employed construction worker and handyman.

For the first time Thomas lived in a place with indoor plumbing. Anderson ran the house with a strict hand. Barely able to read himself, Anderson insisted that Thomas go to school, and he paid tuition of thirty dollars a year for Thomas to attend a Catholic school for African American children, where Thomas found another mentor, Sister Mary Virgilius, who, he said, "was not one of these people who would placate you and worry about your self-esteem." Thomas was a decent student, receiving B+ grades. He absorbed Anderson's passion for education, going off to the segregated library for blacks in the evenings after he had finished doing the chores his grandfather set for him. In 1964 Anderson sent Thomas to St. John Vianney Minor Seminary in the tenth grade, where the boy was one of the first two African American students. The other black student dropped out a year later, and Thomas ended up as the school's pioneer in integration. He did well in class, although his self-consciousness about his accent led him to refrain from speaking unless he was called

on. He had an A average over his three years at the seminary, even as
he participated in the school's athletic and drama programs. He
believed he had a vocation for the priesthood.

Thomas was never entirely comfortable with his place at school or
in Savannah. Segregation pervaded the city, and Thomas had his
share of racial insults at school. He didn't even find the black community to be a welcoming home. He remembered bitterly that he
was called "ABC—America's Blackest Child." Other students at the
seminary made fun of Thomas's blackness. Later he told a reporter
that it wasn't so bad that some students yelled, "Smile, Clarence, so
we can see you," after the lights went out; what hurt was that no one
said, "Shut up." Thomas tried to shape himself to fit in, eliminating
the dialect and slang from his speech, working hard to get grades
that his grandfather used to show his fellow NAACP members that
"black people were as good as white people." But as reporter Juan
Williams put it, "acceptance did not come," and Thomas concluded,
"There is nothing you can do to get past black skin. I don't care how
educated you are, how good you are at what you do—you'll never
have the same contacts or opportunities, you'll never be seen as
equal to whites."

In 1967, pursuing his religious vocation, Thomas began studies
for the priesthood at another seminary, in Missouri. His classmates
were impressed with his intellectual, athletic skills, and maturity,
and his booming laugh became his hallmark. But he lost his vocation while at the seminary. Some of his acquaintances thought that
he had been gradually drifting away from the idea of becoming a
priest. Thomas told a more dramatic story. He pinned down the
moment he lost his vocation to the evening, eight months after he
had started at the seminary, when Martin Luther King, Jr., was assas-
sinated. Thomas said that the triggering event occurred when he
overheard another seminarian, someone who Thomas believed
shared his religious commitments, say, "Good, I hope the son of a
bitch dies." Thomas left the seminary and in the fall of 1968 enrolled
at Holy Cross College in Worcester, Massachusetts.

Thomas continued to be a bit awkward socially, both with his
male classmates, who sometimes found him arrogant and brusque,
and with women. He rarely took part in campus social activities. In
1969, Thomas met Kathy Ambush, a young woman from Worcester

who was attending a small local Catholic college. Kathy, the daughter of an African American man and a Japanese American woman, was active in her campus's politics. Thomas was smitten with her, dated her for a year, then proposed. They were married in June 1971, the day after Thomas graduated from Holy Cross.

By his own account, Thomas was something of a rebel in college. He was the secretary-treasurer of the school's Black Student Union in his sophomore year. He admired the Black Muslims because of their self-help orientation and was, he later said, "very partial to Malcolm X" for the same reason. He rejected Anderson's integrationism and worked in a free breakfast program consciously modeled on one set up by the Black Panthers while opposing the college's creation of a separate dormitory corridor for its African American students. He had come to college, he said, to learn how to live with white people, not to live apart from them; when the college did create the corridor, Thomas took a room on it—with a white roommate. He also spoke against a proposal that black students withdraw from Holy Cross to protest the college's treatment of some political protesters. But as with the black corridor, Thomas reluctantly went along when the students prepared to move out. He stayed with his sweetheart's family for a couple of days until the dispute was resolved and the students returned to the campus. He then wrote a rambling column for the campus newspaper defending the walkout in terms that sound just like other radical publications of the period; it referred to the college's "blatant manifestation of attitudes that were previously concealed in articulate justifications and rationalizations" and spoke of "the social shackles of racism" and of "the inhuman tradition of permitting and apathetically foisting upon the black man a role that lies some place between animal and human."

In college Thomas discovered the writings of the black radical Richard Wright, which "captured a lot of the feelings" of anger and frustration he had. In 2001, Thomas told a student audience that he wished he could "go back to college. One of my great regrets is that I knew so much when I was in college and was so angry and was such a Mr. Know-It-All that I missed many opportunities to learn." As he had been in high school, Thomas was quiet in his college classes, getting better than average but not spectacularly good grades.

Thomas was admitted to Yale Law School, almost certainly as part of the school's affirmative action program. He came to resent the fact that as he saw it, the faculty and his classmates believed that the school's minority students weren't "qualified to be there." He later said, "You had to prove yourself every day because the presumption was you were dumb and didn't deserve to be there on merit." Yet he didn't stand out among the school's students; he sat in the back of the classrooms, spoke only when called on, took core business courses rather than courses in constitutional law or civil rights law.

Thomas got a summer job at a small Savannah law firm, which offered to hire him when he graduated. He turned down the offer, perhaps because his wife wasn't interested in moving to the Deep South, but then discovered that no other law firm in Savannah or Atlanta was prepared to offer him a job. Decades later he continued to refer to his disappointment: "No one can ever know the trials and tribulations, the loneliness, the swirl of emotions" he felt when his "dream of going back to Savannah evaporat[ed]."

He took a job as an assistant attorney general in Jefferson City, Missouri, working under the state's Republican attorney general, John Danforth, who was to push Thomas's career forward. According to Thomas, Danforth told him, "There's plenty of room at the top," to which Thomas later responded, "Easy for him to say. He was white. I was black." Thomas arrived in Missouri with Kathy and their newborn son, Jamal. At the attorney general's office he first worked on criminal appeals, then shifted to tax issues. After two years Thomas left the attorney general's office to take a job with the Monsanto Corporation in St. Louis.

While in Missouri Thomas read the conservative black economist Thomas Sowell's book *Race and Economics*, which, he said, "was like pouring half a glass of water on the desert." Sowell's work emphasized economic improvement of impoverished communities by local entrepreneurs, an idea that, Thomas declared, "moved" him "back to an approach that was consistent with my own predisposition and my own background." Sowell's approach resonated with the sense Thomas had that self-reliance was crucial for America's blacks, and Thomas began to fit the views he had intuitively held about self-reliance into a broader conservative framework.

In 1979 he moved to Washington as an aide to then Senator Danforth, specializing in energy and environmental issues. The move put a further strain on Thomas's marriage. His wife had returned to school to obtain a college degree, even while she had primary responsibility for raising Jamal, and she appeared to resent the path that Thomas's ambition was taking. The couple separated briefly in January 1981, as Thomas was about to join the Reagan administration, and then permanently in August of that year.

In December 1980, shortly before Reagan's inauguration, Thomas attended a meeting of black conservatives, where, in a statement that came up repeatedly when he was nominated for the Supreme Court, he used his sister's experience to explain why he opposed welfare payments: "She gets mad when the mailman is late with her welfare check. That's how dependent she is." The meeting was something of a job fair for positions in the new administration, and Thomas was interested in finding one—but not, he said, a job dealing with civil rights. His career would "be irreparably ruined" because "the monkey would be on my back to prove that I didn't have the job because I'm black." Still, in May 1981, when he was thirty-three years old, he took a job as the assistant secretary for civil rights in the Department of Education even though he was, by his own account, "insulted" by the offer.

He pursued the administration's conservative civil rights policies. He reduced the pressure on southern states to integrate their colleges, fearing that doing so would damage the historically black colleges set up to maintain segregation. Within a year Thomas moved on, to become chair of the Equal Employment Opportunity Commission. He shifted the commission's focus from large-scale class actions, where proof of discrimination often rested on complex statistical arguments attempting to demonstrate that the defendants didn't hire "enough" minority employees in light of the pool of eligible minorities. Thomas believed that such cases often did not involve companies that were discriminating in the only sense he thought legally relevant: acting with a purpose of harming minorities. Moreover, even if the companies had discriminated, class action remedies didn't really benefit the victims of discrimination, who needed jobs and back pay, not changes in the employer's practices.

Thomas called class action remedies "playing the group game" and rejected it. Instead, he directed the EEOC's resources to its large backlog of complaints by individuals that they had been discriminated against and wanted jobs and back pay, and he made good progress in getting the backlog cleaned up. His critics observed that he did so by dramatically increasing the number of cases that were dismissed with a finding that there had been no discrimination and decreasing the number that were settled. His defenders pointed to examples of frivolous or unsupported claims that had caused the commission's caseload to blossom without, however, showing that there really was a lot of discrimination going on.

Thomas had critics even within the administration. They believed that he wasn't taking a strong enough public stand. They wanted him to be the face of the administration's civil rights policies, precisely the kind of role he hated having foisted on him.

More important in the long run, Thomas decided to continue his education by putting together a sort of internal think tank, substituting academic political theorists for the usual cadre of speechwriters. He sat in on an informal seminar in political theory. The participants discussed Ayn Rand's objectivism, a strongly individualist defense of capitalism that attracts many young people, who usually outgrow their enthusiasm. The academics in the seminar tried, with only modest success, to show Thomas that Rand was hostile to the religion that played such a large role in his life. The seminar devoted more time to discussing the ideas of the somewhat eccentric political theorist Leo Strauss as transmitted through his disciple Ken Masugi. Strauss's thinking is impossible to summarize, except to note that it stressed the importance of the virtues exhibited in classical Greece and Rome. Its most ingenious component was the idea that philosophers actually concealed what they meant from ordinary people, who couldn't accept the truth, and revealed what they meant only to an elite band of insiders who had the fortitude to accept the truth and then advise politicians on how to implement it without arousing rebellion in the masses. Thomas used the seminar to "think through what protects individual liberty most" and started thinking seriously about states' rights in that connection.

When Thomas was sworn in for his second term as head of the EEOC, William Bradford Reynolds, who had himself been denied Senate confirmation and then been appointed to a position that did not require one, toasted him as "the epitome of the right kind of affirmative action working the right way." Thomas winced. It was a demonstration that he could not escape the burdens that he believed affirmative action placed on all successful blacks.

The burden remained on his shoulders when he was nominated for the Supreme Court. Shortly after he arrived in Washington, Thomas told a reporter, "I want to be on the Supreme Court." Getting there meant mounting a campaign, which he did through his speeches to conservative groups establishing himself as a serious thinker. Given the criteria Republicans had established for Supreme Court nominations, it also meant becoming a judge on a federal court of appeals. Thomas had developed a wide circle of friends and supporters in the Reagan administration, and many of them carried over into the administration of George Bush. They suggested an appointment to the circuit court in Washington. Thomas hesitated, in part because he feared being isolated as a judge. In the end he agreed to accept the nomination because he saw it as a "stepping stone to the Supreme Court."

The nomination was announced in early July 1989. Liberal interest groups that accepted his role on the EEOC as inevitable now went into action against giving him a lifetime appointment to the federal courts, which they, like Thomas himself, saw as a precursor to a Supreme Court nomination. Six months later the Senate Judiciary Committee held its hearings on the nomination, preceded, for Thomas, by a visit to a church, where, he said, he prayed "as Jesus prayed in the Garden of Gethsemane." Despite his concerns, the one-day hearing was routine, and the Senate easily confirmed him to the circuit court, where, at forty-two, he was the youngest judge.

Only a year later Thurgood Marshall retired from the Supreme Court, and Thomas was the obvious candidate to replace him. He flew to the Bush summer home in Kennebunkport, Maine, for the official announcement. It went smoothly at the start. President Bush read a short statement describing Thomas's life as "a model for all Americans" and concluding that Thomas had "earned the right to sit on this nation's highest court." Thomas responded with a statement invoking his grandparents, his mother, and the nuns who had taught him. Then things began to fall apart. A reporter asked Bush to reconcile the fact that he had vetoed a civil rights bill because according to the president, it was a quota bill with "a nomination that could easily be seen as quota-based." Bush fumbled for an answer. He said that he had looked "for the best man" but then continued with words that gave Bush's and Thomas's opponents ammunition: "The fact that he is black and a minority had nothing to do with this in the sense that he is the best qualified at this time." This was so patently untrue that it forced Thomas's supporters to scramble for an explanation as the nomination went forward to the Senate.

✌

The president's aides knew that the Thomas nomination would be as controversial as Robert Bork's had been. This time they were prepared—they thought. They created a war room, prepped Thomas extensively for the hearings, and, most important, reached out to African American interest groups. The latter strategy was particularly helpful in preventing the liberal interest groups from forming a united front of opposition to Thomas. The mock hearings—rehearsals of questions Department of Justice officials thought he would get—were less satisfactory. Washington insiders counseled Thomas to keep as low a profile in his answers as he possibly could, offering generalities and distancing himself from his more controversial speeches. Their best advice was to use the Pin Point strategy, aimed at keeping the focus on Thomas's life history and away from his ideas. The strategy's weaknesses became apparent only as the hearings developed. It forced Thomas to refrain from talking about what he thought, reinforcing the perception among his opponents that he had no ideas of his own but was simply a shill for hard right constitutional ideas, and it opened the way to a detailed examination of his personal life, which made Anita Hill's allegations about his behavior toward her far more relevant to the confirmation process.

The hearings had two stages. In the first the senators tried to get Thomas to talk about his ideas about the Constitution. They used his speeches praising natural law to justify saying that his jurisprudence would allow him to enact as constitutional law whatever his personal preferences were. Thomas dodged all the questions, sometimes saying that his speeches simply presented ideas he found interesting although they weren't ones he endorsed, sometimes saying that he didn't remember exactly why he had mentioned the issues that were being used against him. His interest in natural law, he said, "was purely in the context of political theory," not constitutional adjudication. He was just about as evasive whenever he was pressed to explain his views.

And then Anita Hill came forward.

Books have been written—and retracted—about the episode, and the views people have about it are almost certainly as fixed as the views they have about what happened in Florida after the 2000 presidential election. I don't think Hill was fantasizing or inventing events that never happened. I also think that Thomas either was describing the events as he remembered them in 1991 (even though his description was that the events never happened and so was flatly inconsistent with Hill's description) or was trapped by the circumstances into misdescribing the events, a completely understandable—and not disqualifying—response.

The episode really has two parts: What happened in the early 1980s, and what happened when Thomas testified about what happened?

In 1981 Thomas's marriage to Kathy Ambush had deteriorated to the point of collapse, although the formalities of a divorce weren't completed. Thomas began dating after the couple separated, but he wasn't entirely comfortable with trying to strike up a new romance while he remained married. Also, he had built his self-image around the fact that he had repeatedly succeeded in overcoming obstacles that would have defeated other men. The ending of his marriage—the separation concluded with a divorce in 1984—was his only failure so far. And of course Thomas had been out of the dating game since early in college, when he met Kathy.

Thomas was a bit clumsy in approaching women for dates. Almost all the women in the dating pool were young professionals, many from the African American middle class about which Thomas was so ambivalent. He remained resentful under the surface about the fact, as he believed it to be, that many African American women wouldn't consider romance with a man as dark as he. He tried a number of ways of approaching women to see if they would be interested. Some of his methods of exploring the possibility of dating were ordinary, like asking if he could help a woman move into her new apartment or if she would help him move into his. Another involved raising issues about sex in a joking way, a technique that wasn't rare when Thomas was a college undergraduate, to see if the woman's response suggested that she might be interested in exploring the possibility of developing a closer relationship. That technique was outdated by the 1980s and, probably more important, wasn't well suited for the young professional women Thomas was approaching.

Some women he approached in *this* way were mildly amused at what they regarded as Thomas's ineptness but not offended. Anita Hill was different. She was really offended. Like many men testing the dating waters, Thomas didn't take a single turndown as definitive. But after trying a couple of times to see if Hill would be interested in dating him, Thomas moved on.

In 1986 Thomas met Virginia Lamp at a panel discussion of affirmative action, sponsored by the Anti-Defamation League in New York. Lamp, a white woman from Nebraska who was then twenty-nine, was a lobbyist for the Chamber of Commerce and was politically active in the Republican Party. After getting sucked into a cultlike organization, Ginni, as she was known, also became active in the anticult Cult Awareness Network. Shortly after meeting Lamp at the conference, Thomas called to ask her to lunch. The two quickly fell in love, and they were married a year later.

Then, a decade after Thomas had reentered the dating market as his first marriage was deteriorating, the events with Hill resurfaced. He may or may not have recalled his efforts to date her in detail. The one thing he knew, though, was that whatever had happened wasn't anything like the way it was being presented in the media. No fair-minded person could interpret what had happened as a gross episode of serious sexual harassment (indeed, even Hill herself didn't describe it that way, although some senators—some Thomas's supporters, some his opponents—did). The right stance to take was the one taken by some of the women Thomas had approached—no more than moderate amusement, perhaps a bit disdainful, at his ineptness, but certainly not shock and horror over sexual harassment.

What was Thomas to do? Knowing that he hadn't done what people seemed to think he had done, he denied that anything at all had happened. Several years had passed between the events and the nomination hearings. He had remarried, and his efforts to date women before he met Virginia weren't that important to him. Perhaps his memory blurred all his dating efforts into one large group. He may not have specifically remembered approaching Hill, and he certainly didn't remember approaching her—or anyone—in the way people were saying he did. Indeed, perhaps he had constructed his recollections of how he had gone about dating in light of his *later* success and didn't remember being clumsy about dating at all. In any case, his flat denial that anything had occurred was accurate as a representation of what he remembered in 1991.

Or—this is the interpretation I prefer—Thomas was trapped by the simplifications of the media story of his successes. The Pin Point strategy was designed to present him as a real human being with an interesting and potent story. His clumsiness in attempting to date Hill actually made him a more real—and complex, and not terrible—human being. But there was no way he and his supporters could possibly tell a story about human complexity without ending his candidacy.

The truth about Thomas's interactions with Hill should not have been discrediting. In the media and political world of 1991, though, it would have been. So, it never got out, either because Thomas reconstructed his memory in a way that obscured the truth or because he and his supporters shaped his testimony in response to the media and political world.

∽

Thomas salvaged his nomination with an emotional statement attacking his attackers as people conducting a "high-tech lynching." When the dust settled, the Senate confirmed his nomination by a vote of 52 to 48. The confirmation battle left marks that haven't been eradicated. Seven years later Thomas reported to a group of black conservatives, "I've been called names, I've been accused of things that didn't happen. Fine, but I'm still here." In the same year, referring to criticisms of his work on the Court, he told another conservative group, "I, for one, have been singled out for particularly bilious and venomous assaults." He referred not only to what had happened at the hearings but to his isolation from the African American community since then. As he put it to a reporter in 1984, "I don't fit in with whites, and I don't fit in with blacks." Thomas retained that sense of alienation as a Supreme Court justice.

He rarely got invitations to speak at black organizations whose members were part of the black middle class. He never concealed his disdain for those who were said to speak for that class. As head of the EEOC he told a reporter, "Quotas are for the black middle class. But look at what's happening to the masses. Those are my people. They are just where they were before any of these policies." The leaders he criticized were "out of touch with reality," a reality he appreciated because he "came from among the people" he was "most concerned about." Having leveled these criticisms at the black leadership class, Thomas shouldn't have been surprised at their reaction. Still, as he told one group, "It pains me . . . more deeply than you can imagine, to be perceived by so many members of my race as doing them harm." He told the National Bar Association of African-American lawyers, "Isn't it time to move on? Isn't it time to realize that being angry with me solves no problems?" He dismissed the "psycho-silliness" that attributed his positions to "forgetting my roots or self-hatred." Yet his comments on these criticisms had a bitter and angry tone that showed that Thomas, like his critics, had not completely come to terms with the fact that the divisions between them were as deep in 2004 as they had been when he was nominated.

The disdain in the legal academy and some of the press for Thomas infected interpretations of his role on the Court. A standard trope is to note that Thomas almost never interjects a question during oral argument. The implicit suggestion is that he is too slow to keep up with the rapid-fire questions and answers forced on advocates by his colleagues. A more sympathetic account referred to his experience as a child, mocked in school because of "his Gullah dialect," which led him to develop "a habit of listening." Alternative interpretations—that he figures that someone else is likely to ask whatever he's interested in, that he has no need to satisfy his own ego by demonstrating that he's smarter than the lawyer being questioned, that he knows his own mind well enough to think that he's unlikely to be informed by the lawyer's answer—aren't seriously entertained.

Nor could Thomas shake the perception that he was simply a puppet in Scalia's hands. He attributed the perception to racism. After all, he said, "what else could possibly be the explanation when I fail to follow the jurisprudential, ideological, and intellectual—if not anti-intellectual—prescription assigned to blacks? Since thinking beyond this prescription is presumptively beyond my abilities, obviously someone must be putting these strange ideas into my mind and my opinions."

He found himself on the Court's margins. Some of the reasons were personal. Taking his grandfather as a model, at age fifty Thomas started raising his great-nephew Mark (his sister's grandson) after the boy's father went to prison on drug charges. His own son had grown up, and Thomas was reinvigorated by his renewed parental duties. The time he devoted to raising Mark took him away from the Court building, with Thomas often leaving the office by 3:00 P.M. so he could take the boy to afterschool activities.

Thomas used his expertise with computers to work from home as much as he could. He continued to be uncomfortable at the Court. Once he went out of his way to tell a law clerk, a spiky-haired, wild-dressing young woman who stood out among the law clerks, how much he appreciated having her around the Court that year because her presence meant that he was not the only one whom people behind the scenes saw as unusual. He attended church regularly, but as he had said when he was at the EEOC, "God is all right. It's the people I don't like." He and his wife went to a charismatic Episcopalian church in their Virginia neighborhood until he rejoined the Catholic Church of his youth. He called journalist Debra Dickerson to praise a column she wrote about blacks in the George W. Bush administration and, according to Dickerson, kept her on the telephone so long that she thought, "He's a lonely guy."

He seemed to fit in only in two settings. Each summer he, Ginni, and Mark got into a custom-built motor coach—"a condo on wheels," Thomas called it—and traveled around the country, going to campgrounds and RV parks, where he was essentially anonymous and where he could talk with ordinary people about his and their interests in football and NASCAR racing. He also constructed a social circle of admirers. That circle, though, was tightly sealed against intrusions and irritations, in part by Ginni's protectiveness.

◌

Thomas got fewer opinion assignments in important constitutional cases than he might have. The chief justice—or the senior associate justice in the majority, if the chief justice is in the minority—decides who gets to write a majority opinion. (Thomas was so rarely at odds with Rehnquist in important constitutional cases that for all practical purposes, we're concerned here with Rehnquist's assignment practices.) Most political scientists think that chief justices assign opinions on strategic grounds: If one justice in the majority is not entirely sure that she's on the right side, giving the opinion to her is a way of cementing her vote.

Thomas was rarely unsure about the positions he took, so strategy never counseled in favor of giving him an important opinion. Indeed, his very certainty sometimes recommended against doing so. Thomas tended to write strong opinions, drawing sharp lines and rarely acknowledging that different circumstances might produce different outcomes. O'Connor and Kennedy sometimes preferred a more nuanced doctrine than Thomas's opinions articulated. Also, Thomas was more reluctant than other justices to accommodate such concerns. As a result, Thomas "lost a Court" more often than other justices given opinion assignments. That is, instead of garnering the five votes that seemed to be available when the opinions were assigned, his opinions might get only four votes.

There's more, however, to Thomas's low rate of important majority opinions in constitutional cases than the risk that he would lose a Court. Rehnquist had a strong policy of ensuring that every justice wrote a roughly equal number of majority opinions. When the liberals won important cases, Stevens, who got the power to assign opinions, was quite strategic about opinion assignments. Instead of hogging them for himself, Stevens would distribute the important opinions to O'Connor or Kennedy or to Ginsburg or Breyer, knowing that they would write opinions that would hold wavering votes. The cases the conservatives lost reduced the number of constitutional opinions available for Rehnquist to distribute to Thomas, and Stevens's practice boosted the numbers of opinions assigned to the moderates.

To equalize the number of majority opinions each justice wrote, Rehnquist had to give Thomas important and difficult regulatory cases. On these he shone. Breyer, who sat next to him at the Court for over a decade, said that Thomas was a smart lawyer. He based this judgment on Thomas's work on these regulatory cases, in which Breyer had specialized as an academic. Kennedy noted that Thomas had a "photographic memory of the record," a real asset in complex regulatory cases.

Other justices regarded these cases as dogs, cases they had to decide and opinions they had to write just so that they could deal with the constitutional cases they cared more about. Thomas, however, said that these cases were his favorites. Asked in 2000 to name his favorite case, he quickly identified one decided four years before, in which the legal question was whether an injured railroad worker could sue his employer under the federal Safety Appliance Act. The act says that injured workers can sue when they are hurt when working on railroad cars that do not have automatic couplers that are capable of connecting cars without having a worker go between the cars. The case Thomas liked involved a worker who was injured when he went between the cars to adjust a misaligned coupling. His opinion said that the worker couldn't sue because the fact that the coupling was misaligned didn't make it incapable of automatic operation. Thomas called the opinion "a fun little" one, "almost inconsequential," that allowed him to go "back into the history of trains."

The injured worker responded that the case wasn't inconsequential to him: "That's a hell of a thing for him to say." A writer on railroad lawsuits commented that Thomas was "proud of an opinion that makes the railroad workplace less safe." That says nothing about whether he was right about the law, though, and the decision was unanimous.

Thomas's opinions were ordinarily restrained in tone. He said in 1999 that he tried to keep his opinions "dry" and "precise, not cute." He continued, "Cute opinions can lead us astray. Glib terms, glib approaches." He didn't think that an opinion assignment was "an opportunity to engage in lively prose." Sometimes, though, he succumbed to temptation. He described the idea of diversity in affirmative action programs as a "faddish slogan of the cognoscenti" and referred to "know-it-all elites" in the 2003 affirmative action opinion, which may be entirely understandable, but it detracted from the force of his stately quotations from Frederick Douglass. Thomas's ability to make a permanent contribution to constitutional law may depend on his ability to resist the temptation to take up Scalia's writing style.

Skeptics about Thomas hinted that the opinions published under his name were not really his. Legal writer Jeff Rosen suggested that Thomas's opinion in an important case involving the scope of Congress's power to regulate interstate commerce was "lifted, almost word for word in some places," from an article by the University of Chicago law professor Richard Epstein, "which Thomas mysteriously fails to cite."

If not plagiarism, then the law clerks. Whatever Thomas wrote, the suggestion was, came from his Federalist Society law clerks. Finding out how a justice works with his or her law clerks is notoriously difficult, because not to put too fine a point on it, the clerks misrepresent what happens inside the chambers of the justices for whom they work, while they don't know what happens inside the other chambers. Appearing on a television program about the Court's law clerks, Laura Ingraham, one of Thomas's early law clerks before she became a conservative political commentator, said that she drafted opinions for him that he took home, tore apart, and rewrote to the point where she couldn't recognize her own contribution. That almost certainly was not true. A justice ought to fire a law clerk who produced work as unusable as Ingraham said hers was. Rather, Ingraham was doing what all law clerks do: mistakenly trying to protect her justice's reputation by underplaying her role and exaggerating his in the drafting process.

Rehnquist gave a better description of how a good law clerk works with a justice. The law clerk drafted an opinion, Rehnquist said, and then (after the other law clerks had reviewed it) he edited the drafts, sometimes quite lightly. That is how the process *should* work. The drafts should need no more than light editing if the judge has chosen competent law clerks who do good work. The justice gives direction by indicating particular points he or she wants emphasized and may sketch out a general approach. The law clerks, though, do the writing, with some additions from the justice. The fact that Thomas's opinions were products of a collaborative process in which law clerks played a large role does nothing to undermine Breyer's judgment that Thomas's opinions in the regulatory cases show that he is a smart lawyer.

One can't dismiss the possibility, raised by Thomas himself, that racism has affected the way some white academics treat him. The *National Review* once published a cover depicting Thurgood Marshall sleeping on the Supreme Court bench, and I believe that some white liberals have a similar view of Thomas, of a dim bulb who doesn't deserve the position he's attained. African American legal academics also dismiss Thomas, but of course there racism doesn't come into play (though the class divisions within the black community to which Thomas is so sensitive might). Rather, they see him as deeply wrong, as, indeed, do many whites.

Elites in the legal academy disparaged Thomas, and he disparaged them in return. His vehicle was a jurisprudence that the liberal legal academy did not take seriously.

✐

The Constitution Clarence Thomas interpreted was the one adopted in 1789. You might not think that's a controversial statement, but most constitutional scholars think that the amendments added after the Civil War changed our constitutional structure in important ways (and some scholars think that developments in the twentieth century, particularly the New Deal, did so as well). Thomas's Constitution, though, was the framers' Constitution.

Thomas interpreted that Constitution using a rigorously originalist method, but with a twist. He believed that the key to our ability to understand how the framers understood the document they adopted was to read the Constitution against what he described as its background in natural law. That background in turn could best be seen in the opening words of the Declaration of Independence, particularly the Declaration's assertion of the "self-evident" truth that "all Men are created equal" and are "endowed by their Creator with certain unalienable Rights." For Thomas, natural law had a decidedly libertarian spin. Yet his natural law approach to the Constitution sometimes came into conflict with his originalist approach and, even more, with a more or less standard conservative view that legislatures rather than courts were the institutions the framers designed to determine what natural law required.

The interactions among the originalist, natural law, and conservative components of Thomas's jurisprudence have laid him open to the charge of hypocrisy, which his critics have been happy to bring against him. In fact, the problem was not that he was a hypocrite but that his jurisprudence really doesn't hang together all that well. He has many more years, though, to work out the problems.

Begin with originalism, the theory that the Constitution's terms should be interpreted today to express the meaning they were generally understood to have when they were adopted. Rehnquist gave a lecture at the University of Texas in 1976, criticizing "The Notion of a Living Constitution," which he and other conservative jurists saw as the only alternative to originalism. The problem with that notion, conservatives argued, was that it left judges unconstrained. Thomas offered the same argument when challenged at his public appearances. He reported his response to someone who called his approach to constitutional interpretation cramped as: "Well, you and I probably don't agree about much about the world, so I'll tell you from now on I'll do whatever I want to do, when I want to do it, at whim and fancy, for the next forty plus years. Will that satisfy you?" For Thomas, originalism imposed discipline and restraint on his whims and fancies.

Scalia once described himself as a fainthearted originalist. He was fainthearted because he couldn't follow through on a rigorous originalism that led to conclusions dramatically at odds with the cases the Supreme Court had decided over its long history. Conservative originalists tended to focus on the Constitution's *structural* provisions—dealing with the powers of the national government and the state governments and with the power of the president against Congress—rather than on its *rights* provisions. Part of the reason was that the understandings of rights as of 1789 were indeed cramped. After all, the United States in 1789 was a nation in which slavery prevailed, and even apart from slavery the understandings of free speech and freedom of religion were much less expansive than we have become accustomed to.

Thomas distinguished himself from other originalists by his very lack of faintheartedness, his willingness to apply originalism in areas where it led to conclusions that were not merely unpopular among liberals—no problem for conservatives, of course—but dramatically at odds with far more widespread attitudes today.

The best example is a prisoners' rights case that produced one of Thomas's most widely noted opinions, because it was decided in 1992 and was taken as the first indication of the way he would deal with the rights not only of prisoners but of the larger group of people who didn't have a lot of political power.

Keith Hudson, an inmate at the Angola State Prison in Louisiana, sued three prison guards who beat him while they were moving him from one cell to another to break up an argument. One punched Hudson all over his body, while another held him and hit him from behind. The third guard did nothing to stop the beating and indeed, according to Hudson, told the others "not to have too much fun." As a result of the beating, Hudson's face, mouth, and lips were bruised, his teeth were loosened, and his dental plate was cracked.

The Supreme Court has interpreted the Eighth Amendment's prohibition of cruel and unusual punishment to mean that state prison guards can't unnecessarily inflict pain as part of the ordinary incarceration of criminals. There's no question but that under Eighth Amendment law as it stood in 1992, guards who severely beat a prisoner violated the amendment. The question in Hudson's case was a bit different. The judge who heard the case found that Hudson's injuries were "minor," and the appeals court concluded that the Eighth Amendment wasn't violated unless the prisoner suffered "significant injury." The question for the Supreme Court was whether the Eighth Amendment was violated when a prisoner, who was concededly beaten, wasn't severely injured. O'Connor wrote for a seven-justice majority that it was. Even minor injuries could produce the kind of pain that the Eighth Amendment prohibited, she said.

Thomas, joined only by Scalia, dissented. He disagreed with the very premises of the Court's decisions dealing with prisoners' rights under the Eighth Amendment. To Thomas, the Eighth Amendment had nothing to do with what happened after a criminal was put in prison. It applied "only to torturous punishments meted out by statutes or sentencing judges, and not generally to any hardship that might befall a prisoner during incarceration." He concluded his opinion by observing that the Court's decision expanding the Eighth Amendment "beyond all bounds of history and precedent" was "yet another manifestation of the pervasive view that the Federal Constitution must address all ills in our society." The Eighth Amendment wasn't "a National Code of Prison Regulation." That didn't mean that prisoners could be beaten or tortured by their guards, though. People like Hudson might well have an ordinary tort (injury) claim against the guards, and the guards themselves might be prosecuted for assaulting Hudson. It was just that the *Constitution* didn't protect Hudson.

One of the more dramatic moments in Thomas's confirmation hearings—before they exploded over the Hill allegations—occurred when he answered a question about why he wanted to serve on the Supreme Court: "You know, on my current court, I have occasion to look out the window that faces C Street, and there are converted buses that bring in the criminal defendants to our criminal justice system, busload after busload. And you look out, and you say to yourself, and I say to myself almost every day, But for the grace of God there go I. So you feel you have the same fate, or could have, as those individuals. So I can walk in their shoes, and I can bring something different to the Court." This was taken as an expression of Thomas's ability to empathize with the plight of criminal defendants—and, by extension, with the plight of prisoners.

Thomas's critics seized on his dissent in the Hudson case. The *Washington Post* called it "mind-boggling," and the *New York Times* said that Thomas was "the youngest, cruelest justice," whose opinion belied the hope some had had that "he would bring to the Court the understanding born of hardship." The harshest criticism came in a column by William Raspberry, an African American who won the Pulitzer Prize for commentary two years later. Raspberry called the opinion "bizarre." Referring to the "grace of God" statement, Raspberry said that Thomas had "encouraged" the view that his conservatism was "a sort of harsh pragmatism" coming from someone who had "known deprivation and unfairness and racism at first-hand." The Hudson opinion, though, "confounded only those who tried to cut you some slack." Raspberry's column ended, "Of course I don't expect that you will always do what strikes the rest of us as 'the right thing.' But why go out of your way to do the wrong?"

Thomas's defenders, such as George Will, reiterated his point that as Will put it, the Constitution was not a "cure-all," but they did not deal with the critics' observations about the tension they saw between Thomas's opinion in the Hudson case and his "grace of God" statement.

It's sometimes a mistake to take testimony at a nomination hearing too seriously. Nominees will say what they think will get them through the process, whether or not it expresses what they really think. Yet Thomas was probably making the "grace of God" statement in earnest. Liberals trying to reconcile themselves to the fact that he probably would be confirmed, and moderates trying to get comfortable with the nomination, may well have heard the statement in a way that he did not intend.

For liberals and moderates, "But for the grace of God there go I" is a statement about the speaker's empathy for people caught up in circumstances in which the speaker could just as easily have found himself. For Thomas, however, the statement may have been deeply theological. Thomas said that the grace of God had been visited upon him and made him different from—no longer the same as—the defendants he saw from his office window. There may have been no discernible reason for the fact that God's grace had fallen on him rather than them, but the fact that it had done so separated him from the criminal defendants, rather than connected him to them. The "grace of God" statement, then, really shouldn't have given hope to skeptics about Thomas. His originalism in prisoners' rights cases might lead to results that the critics find troubling, but the results weren't at odds with what he said about himself.

∽

Thomas's natural law jurisprudence might have tempered his originalism, at least from his critics' point of view. The "natural law thing," as Senator Joseph Biden called it, became a focal point of the first round of hearings on Thomas's nomination. Thomas had given speeches in which he asserted that natural law should inform constitutional interpretation. A scholar sympathetic to him observed that "Thomas attempted, successfully, to distance himself" from those speeches but also that "it is difficult to take seriously" those attempts.

His problem was twofold. He absorbed an interesting way of thinking about the Constitution from the Straussians around him at the EEOC, but he himself was not a deep political thinker and so found it difficult to spell out—at least in the context of a confirmation hearing—precisely what he meant by his invocation of natural law. In addition, his critics had a strong—and quite mistaken—idea what the content of his natural law had to be, which he wasn't able effectively to counter. Rather than do so, he retreated. But once on the Supreme Court, he again occasionally relied on his natural law approach to constitutional interpretation.

Thomas's speeches could not have been clearer about what he meant in invoking natural law. He said that the Constitution's framers held natural law views and that the Constitution they adopted used terms that should be interpreted in light of those views. Getting specific content out of those propositions is of course quite difficult. Thomas repeatedly said that enforcing civil rights laws to protect individuals against discrimination was a good example of where his natural law views led him, but he did not note that there was real controversy about his view that affirmative action constituted discrimination.

He linked his position on abortion to natural law as well, citing a speech by Lewis Lehrman as a "splendid example of applying natural law." Lehrman argued that fetuses were "persons" endowed with an unalienable right to life. As Thomas's critics observed, Lehrman's position would seem to require that states outlaw abortion to avoid violating the unborn child's rights under the Fourteenth Amendment. At his confirmation hearings Thomas ineffectually attempted to minimize the implications of his natural law views for the abortion issue. He said that his praise for Lehrman's speech was the kind of passing remark a speaker makes to thank those who invited him just before launching into prepared remarks. Of course Thomas's position in the Court's abortion decisions did turn out to be compatible with his natural law views. And on the assumption that fetuses are indeed persons, it would not be inconsistent with his libertarianism.

Thomas's critics poured much more content into "natural law" than he himself did. They identified the connection between his natural law views and his likely positions on economic regulation and abortion. Laurence Tribe wrote an op-ed piece that added another item to the list. Natural law, said Tribe, had been invoked in the nineteenth century as a justification for keeping women in their "natural" roles as wives and mothers. The observation about history was correct, but Tribe had no evidence that Thomas held *that* version of natural law.

Indeed, Thomas used the Declaration of Independence in a way that undermined Tribe's account of what Thomas thought about natural law. The Constitution should be interpreted in light of the Declaration of Independence and its commitment to the proposition that all men are created equal and have inalienable rights. For

Thomas, this meant that the Constitution placed individuals at its heart and required that every person be treated equally under law.

In a 1999 speech Thomas relied on Harry Jaffa, the political scientist who had collaborated with Rehnquist during Barry Goldwater's 1964 presidential campaign. Jaffa in turn had drawn on Abraham Lincoln. The framers, Thomas said, compromised on the question of slavery because creating "a union that, at its root, was devoted to the principle of human equality" was the best alternative available to them that would make it possible to abolish slavery in the future. Political prudence counsels in favor of compromise on some questions as long as you can give "effect to the principles of the Constitution as far as possible." Each generation must judge its own practices against "the laws of Nature and Nature's God."

As Thomas correctly understood Jaffa to argue, those judgments should put the compromises to one side once the need for them disappeared. With slavery's end, the nation could embrace the Constitution's full commitment to equality. The framers cast the Constitution's most important provisions in general terms. The compromises were consistent with those terms, but with the compromises set aside, judges could interpret the general terms to reflect the Declaration's commitment to individualism.

Thomas was once again short on specifics, ending his tribute to Jaffa by saying that he "and everyone else who has the privilege of serving our nation" had to "know the difference between a prudent compromise that advances the cause of liberty and a capitulation on principle that snuffs it out." But even without specifics, Thomas's position did not commit him to the nineteenth-century version of natural law that Tribe invoked.

His distinction between prudent compromises and capitulations on principle may help make sense of one of the most obvious tensions his jurisprudence produced. Thomas's natural law was not identical to other versions of natural law and in particular not to some traditional Catholic versions of natural law that treat same-sex relationships as contrary to natural law. Indeed, Thomas's version, with its emphasis on the inalienable right of every person to liberty, understood in terms expansive enough to encompass ordinary economic activity, pushed him toward the libertarian position in the gay rights case of 2003, where the Court majority struck down

Texas's law prohibiting homosexual sodomy. Yet Thomas dissented, because he believed that the decision to make sodomy illegal or not was basically one for legislatures to make. Unlike Scalia, whose opinion made it clear that he agreed with the ban on homosexual sodomy, Thomas wrote that he would "vote to repeal" Texas's law were he sitting in the Texas legislature.

The law professor Scott Gerber suggests that positions like this reflect a division within Thomas, between what Gerber calls liberal originalism, which tells judges to interpret the Constitution in light of the Declaration of Independence, and conservative or Borkean originalism, which tells them to regard the compromises embedded in the Constitution as expressing the framers' underlying principles. Thomas's position in the sodomy case shows the tension between liberal and conservative originalism. There's surely something to Gerber's position. Thomas himself said during his confirmation hearings that he wasn't a systematic political theorist, and some parts of his jurisprudence undoubtedly were unreflectively picked up from the mainstream of conservative constitutional theory even though they were in tension with other parts of his jurisprudence. The distinction he invoked between his role as a judge and the positions he might take as a legislator may be one of those elements. It was, after all, a commonplace of conservative constitutional thought.

A consistent jurisprudence that acknowledges the importance of compromises on questions of principle might also allow Thomas to make such a distinction. The Constitution's terms protect inalienable rights—in the abstract. But implementing the Constitution requires us to design institutions like courts and legislatures. In doing so we might have to compromise. Saying that courts enforce only *some* inalienable rights, leaving others for legislatures, might be the kind of compromise needed—even today—to ensure that we can have a functioning government that, better than any alternative, protects inalienable rights as best as we can. Thomas never spelled out this account, and he may not have thought it, but at least it diminishes the tension between his libertarian individualism and his position in the sodomy case.

Thomas is the only Supreme Court justice whose opinions quoted both Frederick Douglass and W. E. B. Du Bois. Du Bois was a radical throughout his life, a Marxist historian who joined the Communist Party shortly before his death in 1963. But despite Du Bois's left-wing affiliations, and despite the much closer affinities between Thomas's thinking and that of Booker T. Washington, Thomas used Du Bois and Douglass in support of his natural law, individualist interpretation of the Constitution. Doing so introduced themes of black nationalism into his opinions that were not entirely compatible with his individualism. Education cases gave Thomas the vehicle to develop his ideas about individualism, the Constitution, and (implicitly) black nationalism.

He first discussed education for black Americans in his concurring opinion in a case dealing with the desegregation of Mississippi's universities. The Court insisted that Mississippi do more than it had done to ensure that its universities were desegregated. Opening with a quotation from Du Bois, Thomas was relieved that the Court's decision "portends neither the destruction of historically black colleges nor the severing of those institutions from their distinctive histories and traditions." He saw nothing particularly wrong in the fact that institutions with distinctive traditions and programs "might disproportionately appeal to one race or another." He ended his opinion by noting the irony that would occur "if the institutions that sustained blacks during segregation were themselves destroyed in an effort to combat its vestiges."

For Thomas, racial "imbalance" was not in itself anything of constitutional concern. Imbalances resulting from deliberate state policies designed to separate the races were impermissible, but some imbalances resulting from maintaining institutions with distinctive histories were acceptable. This distinction worked as long as he kept the focus on historically black colleges and universities. Still, the historically white main campus of the University of Mississippi had its own traditions and history, and Thomas agreed that the state could not rebut challenges to the policies that sustained the campus's white character by referring to those traditions. Rather, he insisted that the traditions and histories *of historically black institutions* provided educational justifications for racial imbalances at those institutions. He did not spell out what those justifications were, but there are some obvious ones, including instilling pride in the accomplishments of African Americans, as shown through Thomas's quotation from a scholar who described these institutions as "a symbol of the highest attainments of black culture."

Thomas showed his disdain for constitutional rules predicated on the mere existence of racial imbalance in what is probably his most widely quoted statement on education for African Americans: "It never ceases to amaze me that the courts are so willing to assume that anything that is predominantly black must be inferior." The case in which he wrote that sentence involved the long-standing effort to desegregate the Kansas City schools. In the incarnation Thomas was addressing, the district court had ordered the school district to adopt innovative educational programs, which the judge hoped would overcome the educational deficits the judge thought were associated with racial imbalance (in predominantly black schools). Thomas derided these attempts to "experiment with the education of the [city's] black youth."

He reasoned that "if separation itself is a harm, and if integration therefore is the only way that blacks can receive a proper education, then there must be something inferior about blacks. Under this theory, segregation injures blacks because blacks, when left on their own, cannot achieve." Referring to his discussion of historically black colleges in the Mississippi case, Thomas suggested that black middle and high schools "can function as the center and symbol of black communities, and provide examples of independent black leadership, success, and achievement." He concluded, "We must forever put aside the notion that simply because a school district today is black, it must be educationally inferior."

Predominantly black schools could be educationally sound, but they need not be. Whether they are depends on the educational policies, and financing schemes, implemented in them. In his opinion concurring in the Court's decision upholding Ohio's program for school vouchers for Cleveland's children, Thomas acknowledged that many inner-city schools, with predominantly black student bodies, were educationally deficient. Opening by quoting Douglass's observation that "education . . . means emancipation" and closing by quoting Douglass again, Thomas emphasized that "failing urban public schools disproportionately affect minority children most in need of educational opportunity." He charged opponents of school vouchers with ignoring "the core purposes of the Fourteenth Amendment." The opponents held to a "romanticized ideal of universal public education," but "poor urban families just want the best education for their children." And that desire conformed to the purposes expressed through the Fourteenth Amendment. With those purposes in mind, Thomas argued, public policies should "provide the greatest educational opportunities" for minority children. Vouchers held out the promise that quality education would become available to minority children, and for Thomas, no "formalistic" objections should deny that promise.

He relied on his natural law jurisprudence to oppose affirmative action, which he called racial paternalism. Such paternalism was "at war with the principle of inherent equality that underlies and infuses our Constitution," and here he cited the Declaration of Independence. Applying the Declaration's principles, Thomas concluded: "Government cannot make us equal; it can only recognize, respect, and protect us as equal before the law." Racial paternalism, he said, had "unintended consequences" that could be "as poisonous and pernicious as any other form of discrimination." Affirmative action "teaches many" that "minorities cannot compete with them without their patronizing indulgence."

Thomas described the harms affirmative action caused in more detail in 2003, when the Court upheld an affirmative action program at the University of Michigan's law school. When most African Americans at an institution are admitted through affirmative action, "all are tarred as undeserving," Thomas wrote. He continued, "When blacks take positions in the highest places of government, industry, or academia, it is an open question today whether their skin color played a part in their advancement," and the "question itself is the stigma," because if the answer is yes, it suggests that the person is "'otherwise unqualified,'" and if the answer is no, the very asking of the question singles out "blacks who would succeed without discrimination." Affirmative action programs, he concluded, "will help fulfill the bigot's prophecy about black underperformance."

Thomas's opinions on education and African Americans contain several themes. They are infused with scorn for policies supported by elites that assuage their consciences by seeming to address those prob-

lems without doing so and that allow them to maintain essentially
undisturbed the institutions with which they are familiar and from
which they benefit. His opinion in the Michigan case noted that affirmative action programs were a cheap and easy way for elite institutions to pretend that they were addressing serious problems. If schools
had to eliminate affirmative action programs, he wrote, "legacy preferences . . . might quickly become less popular—a possibility not lost, I
am certain, on the elites . . . supporting" affirmative action. The argument by proponents of affirmative action that it promoted educational diversity treated African American students as instruments for
improving the quality of white students' education, a form of experi-
mentation with black students that Thomas rejected.

His opinions are also concerned with ensuring that individual
African Americans have the opportunity to succeed without being
stigmatized by the existence of public policies that rest on the
assumption that all African Americans need "help" to succeed.
Finally, the opinions stress the value of black institutions, including
the contributions they made in the past, and could continue to
make, in resolving the real problems of African American education.

These opinions make a powerful case for some public policies and
against others. Yet they are not without their internal tensions. The
black nationalist strand in Thomas's thinking can be seen in the
importance he places on policies that really would benefit African
Americans and the indifference the opinions display to whether the
policies benefit whites, even nonelite whites. It can be seen as well in
his approving references to historically black colleges and universities. Nationalism, though, is precisely the kind of group identity that
Justice Thomas's individualism rejects.

⚬

Writing in 1987 before Thomas was appointed to the Court,
Washington Post reporter Juan Williams described him as "something
of a black nationalist." Thomas himself rejected the label. He
affirmed his admiration of the Black Muslims during his college
years "primarily because of their belief in self-help."

Thomas reconciled black nationalism with individualism by
treating nationalism as a choice individuals can make if they want
to. He did so when as head of the EEOC he endorsed black capital-

ism. African Americans can, as individuals and capitalists, choose to give special value to black institutions without committing themselves to the proposition that such institutions have intrinsic value beyond the value each African American chooses to give them.

In Thomas's own life, he has demonstrated a striking fluidity of identity. Raised as a Catholic and attending Catholic elementary schools and a Catholic college, he shifted his religious affiliations, from Catholicism to standard Episcopalianism to charismatic Episcopalianism and back to Catholicism. He flirted with black power ideas as an undergraduate before settling down comfortably as a campus liberal. His first marriage was to an African American, his second to a white. This re-creation of one's self is easily achievable within an individualist framework, much harder within one that gives intrinsic value to any particular aspect of one's self such as race.

Yet treating black nationalism as a choice that should be available to African Americans as individuals does not fully resolve the tension in Thomas's opinions and life. It seems notable that when given the personal choice, Thomas did not seem to place any special value on African American institutions. He attended a mostly white college and a majority white law school, although of course he could have attended historically black institutions. He may have been concerned about how a man as dark as he would be treated at such elite black institutions as Morehouse College in Atlanta, but Georgia had a number of other historically black colleges, including Savannah State College, where he could have received an equally good education.

There is no deep inconsistency between these decisions and the observation that for those who choose them, African American institutions have value and therefore should be within the range of choices available to African Americans. There is some tension nonetheless. Thomas's position might be somewhat uncharitably characterized as asserting that African American institutions were valuable for those who wanted them but not particularly valuable for him personally. Yet the rhetoric of his opinions seems quite different, with Thomas asserting in his own voice the value of historically black colleges and universities.

Beyond this, there is a deeper problem with treating black nationalism as a choice that should be available to individuals. After all, often African Americans simply do not *choose* to participate in predominantly black institutions. The most dramatic examples are the inner-city schools Thomas discussed. True enough, the majority black schools in Kansas City were not by that fact alone inferior schools. But it is equally true that the schools were not majority black because the African American parents in Kansas City wanted them to be. Perhaps the black nationalists among them did, placing positive value on their racial composition. But more likely, the parents of the African American children in Kansas City's schools were mostly indifferent to whether the schools were predominantly black or not. As Thomas said in the voucher case, what they wanted were good schools for their children.

Black nationalism cannot be defended as a choice when the institutions involved are not black by choice. Rather, in such circumstances it must be understood as a way for people to make the best of a bad situation. Thomas adopted Richard Wright's term *defensive solidarity* for this reaction and said that he understood it but "resolutely decline[d] to follow it."

Instead, Thomas praised predominantly black institutions as valuable in themselves. Perhaps the rhetoric was a strategic response to what he saw as the prevailing view that majority black schools are necessarily inferior. That view could demoralize their students. Perhaps he asserted the intrinsic value of mostly black institutions to avoid that demoralization, even though he actually believed that they are valuable only when—as is not the case in inner-city schools— their racial composition results from individual choices.

The dissonances in his views emerged in the tones with which he disparaged liberal elites, particularly in his opinion in the Michigan affirmative action case. The key to understanding Thomas's black nationalism is his observation that when "blacks take positions in *the highest places of government*, industry, or academia, it is an open question today whether their skin color played a part in their advancement." The conventional wisdom is that Thomas was indeed chosen for the Supreme Court in part because of his race. His opinion in the Michigan case said that when that happens, "the person may be deemed 'otherwise unqualified.' " That is, he was concerned that some people would regard *him* as unqualified for his position. And not without reason. The political science professor Mark Graber expressed another aspect of the conventional wisdom, writing that

Thomas "had a relatively undistinguished career by Supreme Court standards" before his appointment. Probably because of the legacy of Thomas's bitter confirmation process, it is hard to locate serious academic commentary on his Supreme Court opinions that is even passingly dispassionate or written by someone without an obvious ax to grind.

Thomas's disparagement of liberal elites, then, is only what they deserve for their disparagement of him. Thomas wrote of liberal positions on desegregation as "a jurisprudence based upon a theory of black inferiority." That theory treats blacks as such as inferior. One natural response to that theory is to treat blackness as such as valuable. That is why Thomas couldn't completely relinquish some elements of black nationalism despite his deep commitment to individualism.

℘

Thomas's willingness to handle complex cases involving statutory interpretation and economic regulation limited what he had to say about major constitutional questions in the Rehnquist years. What he did say was quite interesting, if not entirely worked out. Watching his jurisprudence develop over the next decades is likely to be at least as interesting.

CHAPTER FOUR

Ruth Bader Ginsburg's Equal Protection Clause

Most important Supreme Court cases start when someone thinks that the government has violated her constitutional rights. Not the case holding unconstitutional the policy of the Virginia Military Institute (VMI) barring the admission of women. That case began not when VMI denied admission to a woman who wanted to attend but when a lawyer in the Department of Justice read a news story. It ended by transforming the constitutional law of gender discrimination and vindicating the litigation strategy of Ruth Bader Ginsburg, the opinion's author.

❧

Ruth Bader grew up in Brooklyn, the daughter of a first-generation Jewish immigrant from Russia, who worked in the garment industry, and a second-generation immigrant whose family had come from Central Europe. Like many in that generation, her parents encouraged her academic aspirations, saving money to pay for her college education. Ginsburg's mother, Celia, died the night before her daughter's high school graduation, and Ginsburg carried the memory of her mother's hopes with her throughout her career, wearing some of her mother's jewelry at each important event in her life. At Cornell University, Ginsburg met her future husband, Martin, who was bowled over by her intellect, sense of humor, and wide-ranging interests. They got married when they graduated, and moved to Fort Sill, Oklahoma, where Marty was trained as an army artillery officer.

Ginsburg worked as a typist and claims processor in the local Social Security office, having been denied a better job for which she was qualified because she was pregnant with their first child.

After Marty's military service ended, the couple enrolled in Harvard Law School, where Ginsburg was one of nine women in a class of over five hundred students. Her high grades got her on the law review. When Marty was graduated in 1958, he got a job with a New York law firm, the beginning of a spectacularly successful career as a tax lawyer. The family moved to New York, where Ginsburg enrolled as a transfer student at Columbia Law School. She was on the law review there as well and ended up tied for first in her graduating class. Ordinarily that would have been a route to a good job or a distinguished clerkship, perhaps with a Supreme Court justice, but Ginsburg did not get job offers from any of New York's large law firms, nor was she offered any of the most prestigious clerkships. One of her Columbia professors helped persuade a federal trial court judge to hire her as a law clerk. The next year another professor recommended her for a clerkship with his old friend Felix Frankfurter. However, Justice Frankfurter said he wasn't ready to take a woman law clerk.

The legal academy in the early 1960s was slightly more welcoming to women than were judges and the corporate bar, but not by much. Instead of getting a teaching job at one of New York's law schools, Ginsburg signed on to a project on comparative law operated out of Columbia and spent a couple of years investigating the law of civil procedure in Sweden, for which she learned Swedish (knowledge that she coupled with her love of opera to become a fan of the Swedish tenor Jussi Björling). That project helped her land a job at Rutgers Law School in Newark, where she started teaching civil procedure in 1963. She also began working as a cooperating attorney with the New Jersey affiliate of the American Civil Liberties Union, mostly on sex discrimination cases. Students at the law school asked Ginsburg to teach a course on sex discrimination law. Discovering that there were few teaching materials available, Ginsburg joined with the Berkeley law professor Herma Hill Kay and the Buffalo law professor Kenneth Davidson to create the first casebook on sex discrimination law, published in 1974.

By that time Ginsburg had moved back across the river to New

York, taking a position at Columbia Law School in 1972. The ACLU created its Women's Rights Project in the same year and asked Ginsburg to head it. She negotiated a deal with Columbia that allowed her to run the project while holding her position and teaching half time in her first year at the law school.

Ginsburg's goal for the Women's Rights Project was to change constitutional law. She did.

℘

Ginsburg wanted to get the courts to strike down statutes that discriminated against women. Discrimination means unequal treatment, so the vehicle she used was the Fourteenth Amendment's equal protection clause. The equal protection world was divided into two parts when Ginsburg began her work, the land of suspect classification and the land of rational basis. In suspect classification land the Constitution let legislatures adopt laws that treated groups differently only if a legislature was trying to promote a "compelling state interest" and even then only if the fit between the state interest and the identity of the group singled out for different treatment was extremely good.

In the land of rational basis legislatures could treat groups differently if they had some, often quite modest reason to think that doing so would advance some general public purpose. A classic case involved an Oklahoma statute giving eye doctors better treatment than opticians. The statute said that people with glasses could get new ones only if they had recent prescriptions from eye doctors. Opticians couldn't take old lenses and put them in new frames or make duplicate lenses for a spare set of glasses. The Court upheld the statute, saying that the legislature might have thought that limiting what opticians could do was a reasonable way of encouraging people to get their eyes checked when they wanted new glasses. Pretty clearly, though, the real reason for the statute was that eye doctors had more political clout in the Oklahoma legislature than opticians did.

Obviously it made a lot of difference whether you got into suspect classification land or rational basis land. With suspect classification legislatures could rarely get away with treating one group differently from another, while with rational basis they could almost always do whatever they wanted. A litigator challenging discrimination had to steer the Court toward suspect classification land.

Ginsburg's problem was that the road to suspect classification land seemed narrow. The Court's suspect classification cases involved race, with a handful of suggestions that discrimination on the basis of national origin and religion would also be in that land. Ginsburg had to show that gender discrimination was enough like race discrimination—and different enough from discrimination against opticians—to justify placing gender discrimination in suspect classification land.

The problem she faced was that in the 1960s and 1970s many judges and scholars thought that race discrimination and gender discrimination were different. The history of race relations revealed discrimination of the most vicious sort—segregated schools, terrorism directed at African Americans, and much more—for which there were only a few analogies in the history of gender relations (or so many thought). Most public educational institutions admitted students without regard to their sex. Obviously there were no ghettos separating men and women. Women had the right to vote, and no one interfered with that right, unlike the situation facing African Americans in the South until the Voting Rights Act of 1965. And perhaps most important in the mind-set of the judges Ginsburg had to persuade, most men really did think that treating women differently was good for women. Most judges believed that women were protected by laws giving them benefits men didn't have and shielding them from the worst aspects of the world in which men had to live.

Ginsburg developed a two-prong strategy. The ultimate goal was to get sex discrimination cases into suspect classification land by demonstrating that gender discrimination really was a lot like race discrimination: There was a troublesome history of gender discrimination; your gender was, like race, a characteristic that you were pretty much stuck with whether you liked it or not; and all those laws that judges might think helped women actually kept them in a lower social status by perpetuating stereotypes about what men and women could do. The fallback position was that gender discriminations couldn't survive even in rational basis land because there really were no good reasons for treating men and women differently.

Ginsburg developed this strategy in six cases she argued before the Supreme Court, three others for which she wrote the principal briefs, and another fifteen in which she filed briefs as amicus curiae. Her first major case started as an ordinary domestic relations dispute in Idaho. Sally and Cecil Reed adopted a son, Richard. When the Reeds separated, the courts gave Sally custody while allowing Cecil increased visitation rights as Richard grew up. Richard Reed was a troubled adolescent and committed suicide, using his father's gun. Sally blamed Cecil for their son's death and wanted to get appointed as the administrator of Richard's small estate, worth less than a thousand dollars. Her problem was that the Idaho statute dealing with estates divided potential administrators into classes and said that within each class any man would be preferred over any woman. Under the statute, Richard's estate would be administered by his "father or mother," meaning that Cecil was the administrator.

Marvin Karpatkin, who volunteered his time to the American Civil Liberties Union to help the organization decide which cases to take, noticed the Idaho Supreme Court decision upholding the state's preference for men over women and thought it would be a good case to take to the Supreme Court. The ACLU contacted Allen Derr, Sally Reed's lawyer in Idaho, and offered its help in an appeal to the Supreme Court. Derr agreed and turned over the brief-writing job to the ACLU. Ginsburg asked to write the brief along with Melvin Wulf, the ACLU's chief inside lawyer.

The brief Ginsburg and Wulf wrote followed the two-track strategy. Saying that gender discrimination should be treated as involving a suspect classification, the brief argued that gender discrimination was like race discrimination. It examined the nation's history to establish that women had been and still were "subject to pervasive discrimination." It argued, in addition, that automatically giving men preference over women in administering estates simply was not rational. As between Sally and Cecil Reed, and as between any father and mother, there was no reason to think that Cecil would be better at administering the estate than Sally.

The Supreme Court ruled unanimously in Sally Reed's favor. Chief Justice Burger's short opinion put the case in rational basis land but found the preference for men an "arbitrary" means of reducing the workload of the Idaho courts. The opinion was as short on analysis as it was in length. Its flaw—or, from Ginsburg's perspective, its advantage—was that there were obvious reasons why a legis-lature might think that in general, men would be better administra-tors than women. The Court could certainly have concluded that legislatures could reasonably think that as a general matter, men were more likely to have experience in the business world than women, and so they could reasonably have thought as well that men would do better jobs at administering estates across the entire range of cases in which the issue of choosing between a man and a woman as administrator arose. Of course there might be individual cases where the woman would do a better job than the man, but in the land of rational basis legislatures are entitled to make decisions in the large rather than in the small.

Ginsburg knew that the Reed case's use of the rational basis approach couldn't survive critical analysis. She could, however, turn the criticisms to her advantage. She wanted the Court to say that leg-islatures could not rely on stereotypes about men and women. But the rational basis defense of the statute, invoking the supposed fact that men were more likely to be familiar with the business world than women, relied on precisely that kind of stereotype. For Ginsburg, the Reed opinion *said* that the case was in rational basis land, but its holding, which implied that legislatures could not rely on stereotypes to justify gender discrimination, showed that the Court had implicitly applied the kind of approach appropriate only in suspect classification land.

Ginsburg supplemented her two-track doctrinal strategy with what she called a psychological one. She thought that the justices, all men, would appreciate the problem of gender discrimination better if she could show how stereotypes about women and men actually hurt men as well as women: "By showing them the disadvantage to males of being pigeonholed, I think that got their eye and made them more receptive to the arguments we were making about hold-ing women down than they would have been if they hadn't seen it."

The first case Ginsburg herself argued in the Supreme Court fit-ted her strategy perfectly. Sharron Frontiero was a lieutenant in the air force. Under federal law, married members of the armed forces got additional benefits for their dependent spouses: They could live on base in married quarters or get supplements to their pay for off-base housing, and the dependent spouses could use base medical facilities. There was one catch, though. Wives of men in the armed forces were automatically designated as dependents, but husbands of women in the armed forces had to show that they were in fact dependent on their wives' income for more than half their support in order to qualify for the dependent benefits. Frontiero went to the Southern Poverty Law Center, a public interest group, to complain, and it began a lawsuit on her behalf. The center contacted Ginsburg at the ACLU's Women's Rights Project, and she took on the job of writing the Supreme Court brief, dividing the time for oral argument with a lawyer from the center.

The government defended the statute by saying that after all, most wives of male service members were in fact dependent on them and many husbands of female service members were not. Making the wives show that they were dependent would impose an unnecessary expense on them and the armed forces, but treating the husbands automatically as dependents would cost the government a lot of money. The presumption that husbands were not dependents made sense, was rational enough to survive in rational basis land, which is where the Reed case said it should be located.

Ginsburg relied on *Reed* to show that saving the costs of determining who was and who wasn't a dependent was not enough to justify gender discrimination. Second, and more important for her long-run strategy, she said that the government's system effectively paid men more than women, to the disadvantage of families, which of course had men as well as women in them.

The Court agreed with Ginsburg, although this time it was harder to get there. Burger called the case "a tempest in a teapot," and emphasized that there were "differences between men and women" that the government could take into account. Because Burger initially voted against Frontiero, although in the end he changed his mind, William Brennan had the power to assign the opinion, and he took the case for himself.

Brennan's opinion was all Ginsburg could have hoped for. Relying on the history of discrimination against women and the fact that "sex, like race and national origin, is an immutable characteristic," he wrote that gender discrimination had to survive the test of strict scrutiny. But even though the Court found the statute unconstitutional, Brennan couldn't get five justices to go along with his broad opinion. Partly he overreached. He lost Burger's vote by writing that the Reed case "implicitly" adopted strict scrutiny. He lost Lewis Powell's vote by pointing to the enactment of the 1964 Civil Rights Act and its ban on sex discrimination in employment and to the then-pending Equal Rights Amendment to show that "Congress itself has concluded that classifications based upon sex are inherently invidious." To Powell, the fact that Congress had acted counted *against* putting gender in suspect classification land, not in favor of doing so. Only Rehnquist dissented.

Ginsburg built up a small portfolio of Supreme Court decisions. Overall the court was moving in her direction, although her reform efforts suffered some setbacks. The Court said that it was still working in rational basis land, but as the cases accumulated, that claim became increasingly difficult to sustain as a doctrinal matter.

The turning point came in a case well outside the core concerns of the women's movement. Oklahoma's liquor regulation statutes allowed young women between the ages of eighteen and twenty to purchase near beer but prohibited young men in the same age-group from doing so. A bar owner and a young man sued, claiming that the statutes discriminated against men. Oklahoma said that its rules were designed to reduce drunk driving and provided arrest statistics showing that 2 percent of young men in the relevant age group were arrested for drunk driving, whereas only 0.18 percent of young women were. Brennan wrote the Court's opinion finding the statutes unconstitutional and offered a new formulation that came to dominate gender discrimination cases. Laws discriminating on the basis of gender, he said, had to "serve important governmental objectives and must be substantially related to achievement of those objectives."

Applying this test, Brennan found Oklahoma's case wanting. There was too loose a fit between being a young *man* and drunk driving if only 2 percent of the young men who drive were indeed arrested for drunk driving. His point was that restricting only the young men didn't do much to reduce drunk driving.

The words *important* and *substantially related* signaled a real change in the Court's standard. Equally important, a footnote in the opinion bought in to Ginsburg's theory that gender discrimination was unconstitutional because it rested on stereotypes about men and women. The footnote cast aspersions on Oklahoma's arrest statistics because the same "social stereotypes" that were reflected in the statutes were also reflected in police practices. Brennan observed that " 'reckless' young men who drink and drive are transformed into arrest statistics, whereas their female counterparts are chivalrously escorted home."

❧

In the near beer case Brennan wrote that laws resting on " 'archaic and overbroad' generalizations" were outside rational basis land. That did not mean, though, that such laws were in suspect classification land. Where were they? John Paul Stevens had one answer; Thurgood Marshall another. Eventually people came to agree that the Court's majority had a third.

Stevens came to the Court from Chicago. He finished first in his law school class at Northwestern University and served as a law clerk to Justice Wiley Rutledge. Then he went back to Chicago, where he became a leading antitrust lawyer. In 1975 Richard Nixon appointed him to the federal court of appeals in Chicago. When Gerald Ford needed an uncontroversial nominee in the wake of Watergate and Nixon's resignation, his attorney general, Edward Levi, who had taught at the University of Chicago's law school, recommended Stevens.

Stevens had the idiosyncrasy of always wearing a bow tie. As he aged and as technology improved, he basically started commuting from Florida, where he did most of his work, to his job in Washington, where he listened to oral arguments and participated in the discussions among the justices after each argument session.

His idiosyncrasies weren't just personal. He often looked at the Constitution from a different angle. He wrote a strikingly large number of separate opinions, explaining why he didn't agree with the way the other justices analyzed cases. Lawyers thought him unpredictable, at least around the edges. They could not tell what arguments would appeal to him, although after a few years on the Court they could make a fairly good prediction about which side he would end up on. Stevens's doctrinal idiosyncrasies reduced the influence he had on his more conventionally minded colleagues, but they sometimes served him well.

Equal protection law was one area where Stevens saw the analytic problems more clearly than others. He began his opinion in the near beer case with the precisely accurate observation "There is only one Equal Protection Clause." By that he meant that it was wrong for the Court to divide the world between the lands of rational basis and suspect classification. According to Stevens, little was gained by forcing cases into a mold to see whether they involved a suspect classification, whether the government had a "compelling" interest in what it did, whether there was a good fit or a rational basis for the classification. Instead, he suggested, it would be better to explain the reasons for the actual results in specific cases. So, in the near beer case, Stevens said that the gender classification was "not as obnoxious as some the Court has condemned, nor as inoffensive as some the Court has accepted." It was "objectionable," though, because it was "a mere remnant" of an older tradition of widespread discrimination against young men. Using the gender classification was "not totally irrational," but it was "unacceptable" because it was unfair to restrain "100% of the males in the class allegedly because about 2% of them have probably violated" drunk driving laws; "it does not seem to me that an insult to all of the young men of the State can be justified by visiting the sins of the 2% on the 98%."

Stevens's "one Equal Protection Clause" approach made a lot of sense, but it was formless. Explaining reasons for particular decisions couldn't generate doctrines that reached beyond the particular cases. Marshall developed an alternative approach that imposed more structure on equal protection analysis without losing Stevens's insight that the Court's behavior was more complex than its two domains doctrine suggested. Marshall, and eventually others, described *tiers* of equal protection analysis. The lowest tier was the land of rational basis review, and the highest was that of suspect classifications and strict scrutiny. That terminology immediately suggested the possibility that there might be other tiers, indeed so many of them that it would be better to describe what Marshall called a sliding scale for equal protection analysis. According to this sliding scale approach, "the degree of care with which the Court will scrutinize particular classifications" varies depending on "the constitutional and societal importance of the interest adversely affected and the recognized invidiousness of the basis upon which the particular classification is drawn." The "one Equal Protection Clause" approach converged with Marshall's in Stevens's observation that the government might have to carry a heavier burden of justification in some sex discrimination cases than in others, and his suggestion that it might be easier to justify laws based on physical differences between the sexes than those based on more social differences (like young men's propensity to drink too much).

The Court as a whole treated the near beer case as creating a compromise between the two domains approach to equal protection analysis and the sliding scale and similar approaches. As the jargon had it, gender discrimination was subject to intermediate scrutiny, more intensive than that given in rational basis land but less intensive than that given in suspect classification land. From Ginsburg's point of view, intermediate scrutiny was better than nothing, but she still held out hope for more.

∽

The constitutional problem at VMI began in the 1980s, as Ginsburg's constitutional doctrines took hold. VMI itself went back before the Civil War, having been founded to train young men as soldiers and civic leaders and, perhaps even more important, to change rowdy young men into respectable college graduates. Over the years its alumni, who included General (and Secretary of State) George Marshall, became important figures in Virginia's political and social elite. Their financial contributions gave VMI a large endowment that supplemented the state's expenditures on the school. And their political clout meant that the state's political leaders deferred to VMI's alumni on questions that the alumni cared about.

VMI developed a distinctive educational method in the early twentieth century. Described as the adversative method, a term that may have been invented during the VMI litigation, the VMI system was essentially a multiyear period of physical and psychological hazing. Even at the institute the rituals of hazing were intermittently controversial, but the adversative method became the central feature in its defense of its single-sex education. Using a term dating from before the Civil War, VMI referred to its new students as rats for the first seven months at the school. Having had their heads shaved, the rats confronted upper-class students in their first experience of physical hazing. The upper-class students shouted at the rats assembled in the school's courtyard, yelling at them to improve their posture and the like. For the next seven months the freshmen were at the mercy of upper-class students. They must recite portions of the VMI student handbook on demand and do push-ups if they erred. VMI students lived in barracks; one witness in the VMI trial said that calling the barracks "spartan does them excessive credit."

The adversative method wasn't about what happened in the classroom except to the extent that students under physical stress from hazing might have trouble concentrating on classwork. The best defense that VMI could mount of the adversative method is that it eliminated all distinctions among students (treating them all quite badly), that the physical and psychological stress would "break down the 18-year-old male, inducing utter disorientation and uncertainty, and then slowly build him up again, to make him proud of himself and his unsuspected capacity for survival." Basically the idea seems to have been that if you could survive the hazing, you could survive any challenge life threw at you.

Under pressure from the federal government VMI admitted its first African American students in 1968. Racial integration was difficult for the school; gender integration seemed impossible. The college did a self-study in 1985 in which it considered if it should begin to admit women cadets. The planners knew that running a gender-segregated school might be found unconstitutional, and they were also worried about VMI's ability to attract students. Not many young men found the adversative system congenial, and the attractions of a military career—never a requirement for VMI graduates, but obviously an important part of the institution's image—diminished. Increasing the pool of potential applicants was one way to improve the school's quality. The self-study committee examined what had happened when the federal military academies began to admit women and learned that the academies had adjusted fairly easily to gender integration, merely tinkering with some aspects of their physical training programs. In the end, though, the committee recommended against admitting women to VMI, saying that doing so "would alter the mission of VMI."

The *Washington Post* ran a story about VMI's decision to continue as a single-sex institution at the end of May 1986. Judith Keith, a lawyer in the Department of Justice's Civil Rights Division, where she had worked since 1983 on cases mostly involving race discrimination in education, read the *Post* article about VMI and wanted to get the government to challenge its policy, but she couldn't do anything until a young woman complained about being excluded from the school. In 1989 a young woman did complain to the Justice Department about VMI's policy. Keith used the complaint as the basis for a letter asking if the school did indeed exclude women, a prelude to filing suit against VMI.

The Justice Department letter catalyzed the state government. The governor, Gerald L. Baliles, was, for Virginia, a fairly liberal Democrat, and by 1989 Virginia Democrats needed the votes of suburban women if they were to win statewide elections. Baliles asked the VMI board to change the school's policy, but it refused. VMI deployed its political muscle. The state's attorney general, Mary Sue Terry, who would have to defend VMI's policy against the federal government, planned to run for governor in 1993, and her campaign treasurer was a VMI alumnus. The likely Republican candidate for governor weighed in on VMI's side. As historian Philippa Strum says, the "VMI controversy had become a political hot potato."

That the case was a political hot potato in Virginia didn't matter much to the Department of Justice across the Potomac. In early 1990 the department sent another letter to VMI and the state's new governor, Douglas Wilder, saying that VMI's policy was unconstitutional. VMI took the initiative by filing its own lawsuit, seeking a declaration that its policy did not violate the Constitution. By doing so the school was able to get the trial set in a more conservative part of Virginia, and indeed, it won the luck of the draw by having the federal judge Jackson Kiser, a Reagan appointee, hear the case. Kiser was sympathetic to VMI's claims from the very start and never changed his mind.

VMI's lawyers wanted Judge Kiser to ask, Was there a good reason for Virginia to provide a single-sex education for young men at VMI? He could answer yes by finding that single-sex education at VMI was good for young men. The Justice Department's lawyers wanted him to ask, Was there a good reason for Virginia to deny women access to the VMI program? They thought the answer no followed from the undisputed facts that there were some young women who wanted to experience the adversative method and could do as well as young men in VMI's program and that Virginia didn't offer young women anything comparable to the VMI program anywhere else. Throughout the trial Judge Kiser asked the questions VMI's lawyers wanted to focus on, not the Justice Department's questions.

The government's lawyers were in a bind. They needed to show what the adversative method really was, and then they had to show that young women could perform as well as young men at VMI. But the only witnesses who could describe the adversative method were from VMI itself, and they were sure to paint it in ways that would make it seem as if women simply couldn't learn under the adversative method. Indeed, the government's witnesses testified that VMI would have to change a lot if women were admitted. One witness said that the adversative method was particularly well suited to teaching rebellious young men how to learn, while "Girls do it right the first time."

The government's witnesses said that some changes would be required but that the changes wouldn't impair the basics of VMI's operations. In particular, the school could still use the adversative method with women. Acknowledging that VMI would have to change, though, weakened the government's case by giving the institution's lawyers the chance to argue that changing VMI would impair the benefits its structure provided to young men—that is, that there were indeed good reasons for limiting admission to VMI to men.

VMI's witnesses pounded home the point about change. Admit women, and the school would have to provide them with privacy. That would eliminate the completely equal treatment of all rats. David Riesman, the famous Harvard sociologist and scholar of higher education, was VMI's star witness. Riesman was eighty-two years old, and his doctors told him he couldn't travel to Virginia to testify, so he appeared in a videotaped deposition. His testimony reflected his idealized image of the good college of the 1950s and 1960s; his mind-set came through in his disparaging comment that across the street from his home in Cambridge there was a Harvard dormitory from which he could hear "Rock Around the Clock" (the classic rock song first recorded in 1955, forty-five years earlier). Riesman thought that VMI's structure was particularly valuable because it was "the strongest assault that I'm familiar with in this country at the college level on the rating, dating, mating, youth culture."

Riesman also echoed earlier testimony referring to the scholarship of Carol Gilligan, who stressed that men and women typically have different ways of thinking about problems and different ways of knowing and learning. Coeducation wasn't the best way for every young man—or young woman—to learn. In particular, Riesman said, young women lose self-confidence early on and need to learn in environments that rebuild their self-confidence, whereas young men are typically overconfident and need to learn in an environment that breaks down their confidence, as VMI did.

The outcome in Judge Kiser's courtroom was never really in doubt. The government lost and appealed. The arguments before the court of appeals were a replay of the arguments before Judge Kiser. The outcome was different—and somewhat unexpected. The court of appeals reversed Kiser's conclusion that Virginia could simply continue to operate VMI. Instead, it said, Virginia could admit women to VMI or it could create a separate, parallel program only for women somewhere else.

The court of appeals asked the question the government had wanted asked: What reason was there to deny young women access to the benefits of VMI's program? The court gave the answer the government wanted—there was no good reason for doing so—but went on to say that Virginia could provide those benefits without opening VMI to women. It simply had to provide another program that would give young women what young men got from VMI. In some ways the court of appeals' solution evoked the days of separate but equal education for whites and blacks. Virginia might be able to operate a separate institution for young men, but only if it operated an equal one for young women. As Judge Kiser said when the case got back to him, the idea of separate but equal had been discredited by racial segregation, but institutions that were separate but *substantially* equal, or pretty much alike, might well be possible. That was what the court of appeals offered Virginia.

VMI took up the invitation. Its leaders approached the president of a nearby women's college, Mary Baldwin College, with a proposal to create a special program there that would provide leadership training for women to parallel the leadership training VMI offered to men. Traditionally a haven for modestly talented young women from Virginia's better families, Mary Baldwin was a college in some financial distress because the women who used to attend it had started to go to coeducational institutions. VMI's offer, which ended up providing Mary Baldwin over seven million dollars, was more than attractive.

The Mary Baldwin program was named the Virginia Women's Institute for Leadership (VWIL). The trick was to create a program that was enough like VMI's to satisfy the requirement that Virginia give young women opportunities substantially equal to those it gave young men. The VWIL program did have a military training component, but it had nothing like the adversative method. Even in the military component the young women at VWIL wouldn't wear uniforms or carry weapons for training. And VWIL didn't try to create something like the barracks at VMI.

Drawing on the theories about men's and women's learning that VMI offered in its own defense, the VWIL program was centered on the idea that women could be trained to become civic leaders by participating in "cooperative confidence building" rather than the adversative method that VMI had said was more suitable for men than women. Some of the confidence-building techniques involved physical training, like obstacle courses, and were said to be the equivalent of the VMI rat line. The rat line was designed to break the VMI students' confidence, but the women were supposed to gain confidence in getting through the obstacle course by cooperating with one another.

The VWIL program seemed like a perfectly fine way of training young women to be civic leaders. The legal question, though, was different. It didn't matter whether VWIL was a good leadership training program. What mattered was if it was enough like VMI's program to satisfy the requirement of substantial equality.

The case went back to Judge Kiser. This time VMI's expert witness was Elizabeth Fox-Genovese, a historian with impeccable feminist credentials. Fox-Genovese had played an important part in creating the Independent Women's Forum, which brought together politically conservative women who regarded themselves as feminists trying to navigate a pathway between what they saw as a radical sameness feminism that denied all differences between men and

women and a profligate difference feminism that elevated the differences there were into a distasteful identity politics. Locating that
pathway was not an easy task, because Fox-Genovese and her allies
had to acknowledge and even celebrate women's differences from
men without abandoning the claim that women and men should be
treated equally in law. Fox-Genovese endorsed the VWIL program's
confidence-building approach to developing women's leadership
skills and testified that she didn't think there would be many women
who would want or benefit from VMI's adversarial method.

The government's lawyers noted that VMI had some things that
VWIL didn't: some engineering courses, better athletic facilities, a
better-trained faculty. But the real issue was simpler. It didn't matter,
constitutionally, that most young women wouldn't want VMI's
adversarial method (neither did most young men, of course).
Whatever the merits of the VWIL program on its own, some women
wanted training by the adversarial method. Men could get that
training; women couldn't. There was, in the government's eyes, no
equality here.

Judge Kiser disagreed. All Virginia had to do was create a program
that would do for women what VMI did for men: create civic leaders.
The VWIL program did that. Of course it was different from the VMI
program, but the differences were justified on sound educational
grounds.

This time the court of appeals affirmed Kiser, finding that the
VWIL program satisfied the Constitution's demands. One judge dissented and asked that his colleagues be polled on whether the entire
court of appeals should rehear the case. Six judges wanted to hear
the case; four voted against rehearing. Three judges took themselves
out of the case, presumably because of their connections to VMI. In
one of the oddities of court procedure, the minority of four prevailed
over the majority of six, because the court's rules required that
rehearings would occur only if a majority of the entire court—seven
judges—voted for rehearing. The government then appealed to the
Supreme Court.

℀

By the time the VMI case reached the Supreme Court, Ginsburg was
there waiting for it. Her work on women's rights with the ACLU

made her a national figure, the "Thurgood Marshall of gender equality law." Like Marshall, she got a federal appeals court appointment as a result of her law reform advocacy. In 1980 Jimmy Carter appointed her to the federal court of appeals in Washington, where she served for a dozen years before Bill Clinton promoted her to the Supreme Court.

Ginsburg got a reputation as a cautious and careful judge on the circuit court. In a widely noted law review article that, like many short contributions by appeals court judges, mostly summarized the Supreme Court's decisions, Ginsburg criticized *Roe v. Wade* for going too far too fast and for treating the problem as one of privacy and autonomy rather than of sex discrimination. Endorsing observations made by other law professors, Ginsburg suggested that the decision interrupted a legislative trend toward liberalizing abortion laws and that the Court would have done better to place "the woman alone, rather than the woman tied to her physician, at the center of its attention." The issue implicated "a woman's autonomous charge of her full life's course." Ginsburg concluded that *Roe* "would have been more acceptable" if "it had not gone beyond a ruling on the extreme statute before the Court." (That overlooks the fact that while the Texas statute in *Roe* may indeed have been extreme, the Court also had before it a modern, though still restrictive, abortion statute from Georgia.) "The political process was moving in the early 1970s," she wrote, and "majoritarian institutions were listening and acting." The "heavy-handed judicial intervention" in *Roe* "was difficult to justify."

Ginsburg was Bill Clinton's first nominee to the Court, but she wasn't his first choice. He was looking for a nominee with "a fine mind, good judgment, wide experience in the law and in the problems of real people, and somebody with a big heart." He wanted to put a politician on the Court and asked Mario Cuomo, who delayed so long that Clinton gave up, and Richard Riley, his secretary of education and former governor of South Carolina, who turned the appointment down. Just before concluding that he'd have to go with a judge, Clinton considered asking George Mitchell, the Senate's majority leader, to take the seat, but ended up thinking that he needed Mitchell more in the Senate. Then Clinton considered Bruce Babbitt, his secretary of the interior and another former governor.

Babbitt's nomination faced opposition from westerners who didn't like what he had done at the Interior Department and, perhaps surprisingly, from environmentalists who did like his work and were afraid of losing a friend in the cabinet.

Ginsburg's name had been floating around for a while, although the most prominent women's rights groups weren't enthusiastic about her candidacy because she had recently criticized the theory the Supreme Court used in deciding *Roe v. Wade*. Ginsburg's husband, Martin, ginned up a letter-writing campaign from women's attorneys and legal academics to promote her candidacy. Meanwhile, Stephen Breyer remained high on the list, but Breyer's meetings with White House officials and with Clinton didn't go well. Clinton said that Breyer "didn't have a big heart" and his interests in the law were "too narrow." Ginsburg's interview, in contrast, went swimmingly. She is not generally a warm and open person, but she bowled Clinton over when they met. His aides said that he "fell in love" with her and her story of overcoming discrimination. Clinton teared up when Ginsburg ended her statement at the press conference announcing her nomination by mentioning her mother, "the strongest and bravest person I have ever known, who was taken from me much too soon. I pray that I may be all that she would have been had she lived in an age when women could aspire and achieve and daughters are cherished as much as sons." He also snapped at a reporter who questioned the three-month process leading to her selection: "How you could ask a question like that, after the statement she just made, is beyond me."

With Democrats firmly in control of the Senate, Ginsburg's nomination sailed through on a vote of 97 to 3. As a justice Ginsburg was a careful and meticulous liberal, fierce on issues of gender equality. Some of her law clerks found her somewhat remote and opaque, and sometimes she communicated her displeasure with their work with an icy stare. But if some law clerks were not part of a cheery family during their year with her, they became part of her extended family after they left. She pushed potential employers to hire them and kept up with their marriages and the births of their children.

The Court's two women justices differed on many issues but agreed that gender discrimination was generally unconstitutional. Both O'Connor and Ginsburg were sameness feminists. O'Connor wrote the Court's 1982 opinion that held, over four dissents, that Mississippi couldn't bar a man from attending the nursing school at the aptly named Mississippi University for Women. The state's rule, O'Connor wrote, "tends to perpetuate the stereotyped view of nursing as an exclusively women's job." She knew that just as the men hiring lawyers when she graduated from law school thought that law was a man's job, so Mississippi thought that nursing was a woman's job. Both assumptions, to a sameness feminist, were equally wrong.

Even Supreme Court justices couldn't stay away from discussing sameness and difference feminism, though. Cases involving exclusion of women from juries presented the problem to the justices. A 1994 case gave O'Connor a chance to express how a sameness feminist might be ambivalent about her own commitments. Alabama sued J. E. B. seeking to establish that he was the father of T. B.'s child. (As in many family law proceedings, the parties were identified only with their initials to preserve confidentiality.) When jury selection began, the state used its right to remove jurors from the panel to exclude male jurors, and J. E. B. used *his* right to exclude female jurors. As it turned out, every juror was a woman. J. E. B. objected to the state's use of gender as a reason for excluding jurors.

The Supreme Court agreed that doing so violated the Constitution. Blackmun wrote the opinion, which O'Connor and Ginsburg joined. By 1994 the Court understood that the issue of gender discrimination almost always involved the use of stereotypes that helped perpetuate older practices rather than the kind of almost conscious intent to impose disadvantages that characterized race discrimination. Alabama said that it wanted to eliminate men from the jury because men were more likely than women to be sympathetic to J. E. B. as the alleged father of a nonmarital child. But, Blackmun replied, the state's position rested on "the very stereotype" the Constitution "condemns." Ginsburg simply joined Blackmun's opinion.

O'Connor agreed with the result and with Blackmun's reasoning but wrote a concurring opinion to express her "very mixed feelings" about the case. She explained why the Court's "important blow against gender discrimination" was not "costless." "We know that like race, gender matters," she said. Social scientists had produced "a plethora of studies" showing that women and men voted differently in rape cases. She continued, "[O]ne need not be a sexist to share the intuition that in certain cases a person's gender and resulting life experience will be relevant to his or her view of the case." She agreed that gender should make no difference "as a matter of law," but that didn't mean that gender made no difference "as a matter of fact." Women gained by treating gender like race, but society, she suggested, might lose something important. Despite O'Connor's commitment to a sameness feminism, she was unable to deny the pull of some versions of difference feminism.

⁄

The VMI case posed doctrinal questions—what was the real standard of review in cases of gender discrimination—in a context where the choice between sameness and difference feminism might matter.

The outcome in the VMI case was never in doubt. Rehnquist thought at first that he might join Scalia in dissent, so Stevens had the right to designate the justice who would write the opinion. The only real candidate was Ginsburg. In a closer case Stevens might have worried that the kind of strong opinion she would surely write might scare off enough votes to change the result, but with a margin of six to two that was quite unlikely (Justice Thomas couldn't sit on the case because his son was attending VMI), particularly because Ginsburg knew how to draft opinions that would hold rather than lose votes.

Ginsburg gave her law clerk Lisa Beattie a memo sketching out what the draft opinion should look like, and as Beattie developed the draft, she had the other three law clerks in the chambers look it over and suggest revisions. Ginsburg reconstructed the opinion after getting the final draft and then tinkered with it as other justices offered suggestions. Beattie had been careful to include quotations from Kennedy's opinion in the J. E. B. case and from earlier O'Connor opinions, a sort of "opinion patronage" that often helps cement a vote.

Ginsburg's first sentence called VMI "an incomparable military college" that provided "unique educational opportunities." Race segregation in education lasted while the Court thought that separate schools could be equal. Gender-segregated education certainly couldn't be justified unless the separate schools—VMI and the Virginia Women's Institute for Leadership—were equal. Ginsburg's first sentence, though, said that VMI was unique. That ended the case.

The next two paragraphs briefly described VMI's mission and the adversative method. Ginsburg then observed that "[n]either the goal of producing citizen-soldiers nor VMI's implementing methodology is inherently unsuitable to women." But, she said, Virginia "has elected to preserve exclusively for men the advantages and opportunities a VMI education affords." That ended the case a second time.

The opinion continued with a more extensive description of the adversative method, followed by one of VWIL. Ginsburg's constitutional analysis began by referring to the "pathmarking" decisions in the nursing school and jury exclusion cases, which required an "exceedingly persuasive justification" for gender-based discrimination. The nation's history and the Court's decisions since the *Reed* case showed why "skeptical scrutiny" was appropriate. But not "strict scrutiny" in the technical sense, because the Court had "come to appreciate" that " 'inherent differences' between men and women" were "cause for celebration." They were not, however, cause for "denigration of the members of either sex or for artificial constraints on an individual's opportunity."

The question, then, was whether Virginia had an "exceedingly persuasive justification" for denying women access to VMI's unique program. Ginsburg's opinion acknowledged that single-sex education "affords pedagogical benefits to at least some students" and that Virginia was entitled to maintain "diverse" public institutions. Virginia said that the adversative method wasn't suitable for women and that admitting women would therefore require it to change its program so radically that it would be "destroy[ed]." Here Ginsburg equivocated. She agreed that admitting women would require VMI to change some aspects of the adversative method, "primarily in arranging housing assignments and physical training programs." But, she continued, it was clear that "some women" could do everything the (slightly modified) adversative method required. And as long as some women could, it didn't matter that most women couldn't, and wouldn't want to. (Neither would most men, Ginsburg observed.) She noted that predictions of doom had accompanied many earlier extensions of equality to women, pointedly quoting from decisions and reports purporting to explain why women could never practice law.

This part of Ginsburg's opinion ended by emphasizing that

Virginia's goal of training leaders imbued with deep American values was "great enough to accommodate women, who today count as citizens in our American democracy equal in stature to men." Virginia didn't "substantially advance" that goal by excluding women from VMI, "in total disregard of their individual merit."

Ginsburg then turned to the Women's Institute for Leadership. Her treatment was brisk. VWIL's purposes might be the same as VMI's, but its methods were not. Virginia said that the different methods were appropriate because arrogant men needed to be broken down before they could become good leaders, while self-effacing women needed to be built up. Ginsburg replied, "[G]eneralizations about 'the way women are,' estimates of what is appropriate for *most women*, no longer justify denying opportunity to women whose talent and capacity place them outside the average description." There *were* women who would benefit from the adversative method, and Virginia didn't give them the chance to experience it. She supplemented this central analytic point with more mundane considerations: VMI had a huge endowment, Mary Baldwin College a small one; VMI's faculty had substantially better qualifications than Mary Baldwin's did; and probably most important, no new institution could possibly replicate the extensive old boy network of VMI graduates.

Ginsburg said that she had worked out "an ending that I loved," but she wouldn't say what it was because she "changed it because Justice Kennedy didn't like it." Her substitute was indeed something of a letdown. She referred to the Columbia University historian Richard Morris's description of constitutional history as "the story of the extension of constitutional rights to people once ignored or excluded." There was "no reason to believe" that extending women's rights by requiring their admission to VMI would "destroy the Institute rather than enhance its capacity to serve the 'more perfect Union.' " The striving for effect by quoting the Constitution's preamble is a bit too apparent.

VMI debated whether to open its doors to women or go private. The latter course was financially out of reach even for VMI and its alumni, and the school's board decided, by one vote, to admit women. The school revised its brochures and modified some of its rooms to accommodate the new arrivals. It didn't change its physical requirements; men and women would have to do the same number of sit-ups and run a mile and a half in the same time. It sent out a massive mailing to the 31,000 young women who had applied to the ROTC, inviting them to apply to VMI. In 1997, 30 women and 430 men registered as rats. About one-quarter of the women, and one-sixth of the men, dropped out in the first year.

In 1995 the VWIL admitted forty-two students, twenty-two of whom graduated. Over the next few years it admitted roughly the same number of students each year. Gender integration seemed to have worked at VMI; educating women for leadership seemed to have worked at VWIL.

☙

While on the appeals court, Ginsburg became friendly with Antonin Scalia, who joined her there in 1982. The Scalias and the Ginsburgs entertained each other at home and regularly spent New Year's Eve together. The friendship of the ebullient Scalia and the reserved Ginsburg struck some as odd. Partly the friendship was mediated by Marty Ginsburg and Maureen Scalia. Partly it was nurtured by Marty Ginsburg's gourmet cooking. And partly it grew out of the fact that whatever their political disagreements, both Ginsburg and Scalia were children of ethnic and intellectually ambitious New York. Probably the thing that drew Ginsburg and Scalia together, however, was that among their colleagues, they were the judges most devoted to their families (apart from Justice Thomas's special relationship to his adopted son, Mark). Ginsburg and Scalia agreed that family mattered more than almost anything else in building a life worth living. Others would of course express the same sentiment, but few of their colleagues were as committed to their families as Ginsburg and Scalia.

Scalia went after Rehnquist, who concurred in finding VMI's exclusion of women unconstitutional, with his usual vehemence. Notably, though, Scalia was—for him—rather restrained in discussing Ginsburg's opinion. He did call the Court "most illiberal" for "inscribing one after another of the current preferences of the society (and in some cases only the counter majoritarian preferences of the society's law-trained elites) into our Basic Law." Most of Scalia's opinion, however, consisted of a description of the way on which Ginsburg's opinion departed from settled law. Of course it did, and the most Scalia could do was sound a bit regretful about the change. Friendship could make *some* difference.

So did Ginsburg's ability to fire back when provoked. Her opinions were typically precise and understated, with only an occasional rhetorical flourish. Her opinions went through the precedents with painstaking care, employing something of a verbal tic in describing the "pathmarking" decisions that led to the conclusions she reached. She said that her writing style had been influenced by her courses at Cornell with Vladimir Nabokov, who emphasized the importance of painting "word pictures," and political scientist Robert Cushman, who told her to write more simply. The result was opinions that were clear enough, if hardly models of elegant writing. As one law professor put it, Ginsburg valued "clarity above elegance."

Ginsburg's years as an advocate made her a good counterpuncher. Dissenting from a decision upholding drug testing of high school students who wanted to participate in extracurricular activities, she referred to the majority's vision of "nightmarish images of out-of-control flatware, livestock run amok, and colliding tubas." And responding directly to a procedural rule Scalia proposed that she thought incredibly awkward, Ginsburg wrote, "The sphinx-like, damage-determining law he would apply to this controversy has a state forepart, but a federal hindquarter. The beast may not be brutish, but there is little judgment in its creation." The metaphor here is itself somewhat awkward, and certainly not the kind of thing the news media are likely to pick up. But it carries a sting that Scalia would appreciate. He may have restrained himself in dealing with Ginsburg in part to avoid additional wounds.

◎

The *Washington Post* had a banner headline announcing the VMI decision: SUPREME COURT INVALIDATES EXCLUSION OF WOMEN BY VMI. Marty Ginsburg had the front page framed and proudly hung it outside the door of his office at Georgetown Law Center until it faded.

The opinion, though, was unlikely to fade away. Ginsburg's opinion moved the bar up. From "rational basis" review in the *Reed* case to "intermediate scrutiny" in the near beer case to "skeptical scrutiny" in the VMI case, the Court had traveled a long way, never once acknowledging that any particular decision was actually changing the constitutional standard. True, the VMI case and the skeptical scrutiny doctrine dealt with an increasingly rare situation, a government policy that expressly treated men and women differently. Ginsburg's opinion reflected changing social values about the role of women. The Rehnquist Court, divided on so many social issues, was entirely unified around women's issues appealing to suburban women.

CHAPTER FIVE

Antonin Scalia's First Amendment

The Rehnquist Court years were relatively calm ones for political protest. Civil rights and antiwar demonstrations had provided cases that filled the Warren Court's First Amendment docket, but nothing similar generated cases during the Rehnquist years. Every year the Court decided a few First Amendment cases, although in 1998 the *Harvard Law Review* couldn't find a single First Amendment case worth including in its annual overview of "leading cases" from the Supreme Court. A smattering of cases dealing with the rights of high school students, cases dealing with the power of government to regulate speech that used new technologies like cable television and the Internet, and a few cases involving the only real protest movement of the 1990s, demonstrations at the premises of abortion providers—those represented a good fraction of the Rehnquist Court's First Amendment caseload. And like the pudding Winston Churchill tasted, the cases lacked a theme. Scalia thought that the Court had created a special First Amendment law unsympathetic to abortion protesters, but actually the decisions in those cases were no different from the Court's other decisions.

Scalia treated the abortion protest cases as an example of the Court's improper intervention in the culture wars. Other Rehnquist Court free speech decisions were interventions in the culture wars too. Notably, Scalia enthusiastically participated in the Court's unsuccessful attempt to limit campus hate speech codes.

Leftists sometimes described the challenge for radicals as "the long march through the institutions." That is, leftist political thinkers observed that sometimes political protest and open mobilization weren't the best tactics for moving forward. They argued that activists in politically quiescent times should direct their attention to institutions that in the 1990s were given the trendy name civil society. Conservatives also engaged in a march through the institutions. They created think tanks to make their ideas more prominent and respectable, they sponsored organizations like the Federalist Society to coordinate legal challenges, and they took on universities, which they thought had become dominated by their political opponents.

The vehicle for the challenge to the universities was a decadelong attack on what conservatives called political correctness. They brought their battle into the courts by challenging campus hate speech codes at public universities. Hate speech codes impose penalties on students for what they say, and the First Amendment places some limits on what public universities can do about what people say. Conservatives were thus able to deploy the First Amendment against hate speech codes. Often the conservatives manufactured outrages by exaggerating the facts of the cases they brought to public attention, particularly by insisting that their version of contested facts was unassailable. But sometimes the conservatives were on to something. University administrators are bureaucrats. The low-level administrator faced with a student upset about some other student's comments sometimes saw the problem as something to be managed, not as something implicating free expression. Administrators sometimes overreached, threatening "offending" students with punishment when the sensible course would have been to calm the waters through counseling both parties. Sometimes bureaucratic superiors also felt a need to defend their subordinates, at least in public and until the political heat became too great. These natural responses by bureaucrats gave conservatives a reasonably rich plate of cases they could use to mount their challenge to what they saw as liberal domination of the universities.

Lower courts struck down every campus hate speech code they encountered. The Supreme Court never considered a case directly coming from the conservative attack on political correctness. Instead, the Rehnquist Court used a cross burning case to discourage the proliferation of campus hate speech codes. Its approach was a sort of free speech absolutism historically associated with liberals. The Rehnquist Court turned absolutism to different uses, although liberal causes still sometimes benefited from its absolutism. On balance, though, the Rehnquist Court's First Amendment protected the status quo, rather than open space for dissent that might challenge it.

∾

Legislatures wouldn't bother to enact statutes directed at speech if no one thought that words could be harmful. The problem is that words *can* hurt you and even break your bones. Put a false statement about someone's private life into circulation, and you can make it hard for that person to keep his or her job. Falsely shout, "Fire!" in a crowded theater, and you can cause a panic in which people will be injured.

Ordinarily legislatures figure out what's the best way to deal with harms: They can ban some drugs because they are too harmful, or they can make those drugs available only with a doctor's prescription. Nobody except the most extreme libertarians think that the Constitution limits the choices legislatures can make on these matters. What's so different about the harms words cause? Mainly that history shows that legislatures far too often exaggerate the damage words cause and underestimate the contributions words make to a good society (and do a better job with harms caused in other ways). That's the reason for the First Amendment.

Saying that there have to be some limits on what legislatures can do doesn't get very far, though. The real trick is to figure out *what* the limits are. Start with the idea that words can indeed cause harm. All three of the important terms—*words*, *cause*, and *harm*—have to be unpacked. There are a lot of different kinds of words: political speeches, commercial advertising, epithets shouted in an angry fight, and of course much more. There are a lot of different ways words can cause harm. They can persuade people to break the law, they can make people's blood boil, leading them to hit the person who said them, they can condition the environment in which people think about the world, and of course much more. There are a lot of different harms words can cause. They can lead to lawbreaking, they can harm reputations, they can induce people to think badly of an entire group, and of course much more.

First Amendment law is about limiting legislatures' choices in restricting different kinds of words because of the different ways in which those words cause different kinds of harms. Courts have two basic choices: one size fits all or mix and match. Two generations ago Hugo Black was the most vigorous proponent of the one size fits all strategy. Black said that he was a literalist about the First Amendment. The Constitution says, "Congress shall make no law . . . abridging the freedom of speech," and Black said that "no law" means "no law." Political speech, commercial advertising, hate speech, pornography— the First Amendment stops legislatures from regulating any of that, no matter what damage the words cause. The mix and match strategy says that courts have to be sensitive to all the distinctions among types of speech, types of cause, and types of harm. They have to balance carefully the possibility that legislatures have accurately measured the damage a particular kind of speech causes against the benefits that speech provides to society, all the time being aware of the possibility that the courts' rules will set precedents that guide later legislatures as they address different forms of speech and harm.

The one size fits all strategy, conventionally called free speech absolutism by First Amendment scholars, has the enormous advantage of simplicity. Give an absolutist a law abridging speech, and she can tell you right away that it's unconstitutional. The strategy has the enormous disadvantage of simplicity too: One size may fit all, but it will fit only a few people well. Absolutism sometimes provides more protection to words than it should when in fact the legislature hasn't exaggerated the harm the words cause or undervalued the words' contribution to society.

By the late 1960s the Supreme Court had arrived at a reasonably stable resolution of most of the basics of First Amendment law. Journalists writing about the First Amendment summarized the law with a couple of catchphrases: *clear and present danger* and *time, place, and manner* regulations. Those catchphrases are in the neighborhood of contemporary First Amendment law, but they come from an earlier era and don't accurately describe where the Rehnquist Court began.

Clear and present danger refers to regulations that aim directly at speech. It says that government can't regulate speech—at least political speech—unless the speech creates a clear and present danger of harm. The core idea was that history demonstrated that we had the most to fear from legislatures' attempts to abridge speech that was explicitly political. Criticism of existing government policies undoubtedly increases the risk that somebody will break the law. Criticize the war against terrorism as unjust, and somebody's going to decide to obstruct justice by interfering with investigations of terrorism. Legislatures and prosecutors, we've learned, routinely think that speeches criticizing government policy are more likely to produce lawbreaking than they really are.

In 1969 the Supreme Court crystallized centuries of history in a rule restricting the ability of government to prosecute people for political speech. The justices used a case involving Clarence Brandenburg, an obscure leader of a minor Ku Klux Klan group in Ohio, who made a speech before twelve hooded Klan members in which he said, "We're not a revengent organization, but if our President, our Congress, our Supreme Court, continues to suppress the white, Caucasian race, it's possible that there might have to be some revengeance taken." Ohio prosecuted Brandenburg for advocating violence—presumably, the "revengeance" he threatened.

The justices were acutely aware of the surrounding political context: not a fear that governments were going to try to suppress the Klan because they really worried about threats it posed but a fear that the national government might try to suppress protests against the Vietnam War. Abe Fortas, a close adviser to Lyndon Johnson on the conduct of the war, wrote the Court's opinion, but because Nixon and John Mitchell forced Fortas to resign before the opinion was released, his name doesn't appear on it.

The rule in the Brandenburg case was that the government couldn't prosecute someone for political speech unless the speech was "directed to inciting or producing imminent lawless action and is likely to incite or produce such action." During his nomination hearings Robert Bork referred to this as the Brandenburg clear and present danger test, but it's substantially more restrictive than the way *clear and present danger* had come to be understood in the courts.

Such a restrictive rule seemed clearly—or, to some, less clearly—too restrictive for some kinds of speech and some kinds of harm. A guy in a bar fight may not intend to provoke his opponent into punching him in the nose—imminent lawless conduct—but surely, many judges thought, a police officer could step in before the first punch was thrown. Misleading advertisements may be intended to cause people to buy products that don't work, but there's nothing imminent about the purchases.

The Court's initial solution was to define some words to be inside the scope of the First Amendment and to leave other words outside the First Amendment. The classic formulation came in a 1942 case. The case, like many of the important free speech cases of the period, involved a Jehovah's Witness, this one named Walter Chaplinsky. Chaplinsky was passing out pamphlets on the streets of Rochester, New Hampshire. Some people objected to his activities, and a crowd gathered. A police officer told the crowd that Chaplinsky wasn't doing anything illegal, but the crowd got restless. Eventually someone started to rough Chaplinsky up. The police intervened, mostly to protect Chaplinsky by leading him away. Chaplinsky got angry and said to the police officer something like "You are a God damned racketeer" and "a damned Fascist, and the whole government of Rochester are Fascists or agents of Fascists." New Hampshire prosecuted Chaplinsky for violating a statute making it a crime to use offensive language directed at a person in public. The Supreme Court upheld Chaplinsky's conviction. It said that there were "certain well-defined and narrowly limited classes of speech, the prevention and punishment of which have never been thought to raise any Constitutional problem." Those classes included obscenity, libel, and "fighting words."

Chaplinsky's case said that the First Amendment placed some words—political speech, mainly—inside its protective sphere and other words, those in the narrowly defined classes, outside it. Such a law does avoid the problem of giving too much protection to words that really do cause harms that legislatures *don't* exaggerate and that, as the Court said in the Chaplinsky case, really did not contribute much to "any exposition of ideas." It's not entirely satisfactory, though, as Chaplinsky's words themselves indicate. Calling a police officer a "Fascist" looks a lot like a purely political comment, particularly when the officer is dragging you away instead of arresting the people who have attacked you.

Absolutism for speech inside the First Amendment can work only if there's a pretty clear distinction between speech and nonspeech. Black drew the line between speech and action. For Black, the government could do whatever it wanted when action was involved but was absolutely barred from doing anything when speech alone was involved. Everyone knew that this wasn't really helpful, and the civil rights demonstrations and the antiwar movement of the 1960s made it obvious. Civil rights protesters picketing a store that discriminated were engaged in action *and* speech. Antiwar protesters who burned their draft cards were too.

The Court responded to these difficulties by expanding the First Amendment's coverage to include expressive conduct. Then, though, the problem of harmful conduct that did indeed express something arose even more powerfully. Moving away from one size fits all or absolutism, to mix and match, or, as First Amendment scholars call it, balancing, is one way to deal with the problem. A political assassination is expressive conduct, but the contribution it makes to political discussion has to be balanced against the harm it does, and there's no doubt that the balance comes out in favor of allowing the government to treat a political assassination as murder.

A second way to deal with the problem is more complicated. Each example of expressive conduct falls within some larger category, defined solely by the conduct alone. Political assassination falls within the category of murder. In a case upholding a prosecution for burning a draft card, the Court said that legislatures could go after expressive conduct as part of an effort to regulate the larger category of conduct alone. What mattered was whether the government was trying to regulate the larger category for reasons that didn't have anything to do with the fact that sometimes people engaged in the conduct for expressive purposes. The First Amendment limited the government's power to regulate expressive conduct only if the regulation actually had a fairly large impact on the ability of people to convey their message, even in the face of the fact that the government's reason for regulating was unrelated to speech.

In the draft card–burning case, the Court said, pretty unpersuasively, that the government banned burning draft cards because it was trying to make sure that everyone registered for the draft possessed a card that told him whom to contact about changing his address and the like. The government's interest, Chief Justice Warren said, was "preventing harm to the smooth and efficient functioning" of the draft system, not suppressing speech, even though sometimes people burned their draft cards as a means of dissent. The tag line for this approach is that the government can regulate an activity when the reason for regulation is unrelated to the suppression of expression, unless too much expression is in fact suppressed when the regulation is enforced.

Finally, in First Amendment jargon, the draft card–burning law was content-neutral. Draft card burners violated the law if they burned their draft cards to oppose the Vietnam War, to oppose the president, to support more vigorous prosecution of the war, whatever. Content-neutral laws are what used to be called time, place, and manner regulations, before people realized that what was important about them wasn't that they dealt with when, where, or how people spoke but instead that these regulations were entirely general, neutral as to the content of what people wanted to say or do. Content-neutral regulations are constitutional unless they restrict too much expression because usually the government has pretty good reasons for adopting a content-neutral regulation; the social benefit of having the regulation is large enough to justify the reduction in the amount of speech it causes.

Sometimes, however, the government adopts a viewpoint-based regulation. Suppose a city has an auditorium it rents out. There's little doubt that the city can say, "We'll rent the auditorium for musical performances but not for political rallies." (This is called, somewhat confusingly, a subject matter–based regulation.) It probably can say, "We'll rent it out for family-oriented productions but not for productions that would get an R rating if they were movies." But what it can't do is say, "We'll rent it out to the mayor's supporters but not to the mayor's opponents." Sometimes it's quite tricky to figure out whether a restriction is a permissible subject matter–based regulation or an impermissible viewpoint-based one, but the idea behind the distinction is clear enough. Content-neutral regulations reduce the amount of speech, but everyone suffers equally, no matter what he or she wants to say. Subject matter–based regulations reduce some kinds of speech relative to others, but if we define *subject matter* carefully, no single side in some matter of public importance gets better treatment than any other. Viewpoint-based regulations, however, seriously skew the public debate toward the side the government favors. They are *really* bad, within the First Amendment universe.

☙

Scalia relied on the ban on viewpoint-based regulation to go after political correctness. The vehicle was a case involving Russell and Laura Jones, an African American couple, who moved with their five children into a house in the Dayton's Bluff neighborhood of St. Paul, Minnesota, in early 1990. Dayton's Bluff was an old neighborhood in transition, with whites leaving and minorities replacing them. The Jones family began experiencing harassment within a few weeks of moving in, when someone slashed the tires on their car. On the morning of June 21, 1990, Jones woke up to see in his front yard a small burning cross, made out of the legs of a wooden chair. Within a few days the police arrested Arthur M. Miller III, who lived across the street from the Joneses, and Robert Anthony Viktora, a seventeen-year-old who was identified only by his initials throughout the litigation because he was a juvenile. Viktora, a high school dropout with tattoos on both arms, was "often sullen in disposition," according to his lawyer. He denied that he was a skinhead but did tell reporters that he had "visited" a number of white power groups over the past few years.

The city charged Viktora and Miller with violating its bias crime ordinance, which had been on the books for nearly a decade, having been adopted after a series of "episodes of vandalism" directed at Asians, Jews, African Americans, and others. The ordinance made it a misdemeanor to put on any public or private property a burning cross, swastika, or any other symbol that "arouses anger, alarm or resentment in others on the basis of race, color, creed, religion, or gender." Apparently it had never been invoked prior to Viktora's case. Miller pleaded guilty and was sentenced to thirty days in jail. Edward J. Cleary, the public defender assigned to Viktora, moved to dismiss his prosecution on the ground that the ordinance violated the First Amendment. The trial judge agreed. The city attorney decided to appeal to the state supreme court, bypassing the intermediate court of appeals.

The state supreme court quickly decided against Viktora. It said that the city's ordinance could "have been more carefully drafted" but interpreted the ordinance to deal only with "those expressions of hatred and resorts to bias motivated personal abuse that the first amendment does not protect." Depending on the facts revealed at the trial that hadn't yet taken place, Viktora's cross burning might be outside the First Amendment, like Chaplinsky's fighting words. To treat a cross burning *as* fighting words, the prosecution would have to show that burning a cross is likely to evoke an immediate, visceral response in the target, who will strike back and start, or continue, a fight. It's not clear that cross burning actually does that; the point of burning a cross is to intimidate and instill fear, and if it works, the target won't strike back. The prosecution hadn't put on its case at all, of course, and maybe it could have been able to convince a jury that Viktora's actions were indeed fighting words. The state supreme court's opinion wasn't all that clear, though, and it may have been meant to place cross burning in a new category outside the First Amendment.

Cleary announced that he was going to appeal to the U.S. Supreme Court. As he developed his position, he discovered to his dismay that traditional civil liberties groups weren't enthusiastic about defending a cross burner. The American Civil Liberties Union did file an amicus brief on Viktora's behalf, although Cleary didn't think the brief went far enough in defending his First Amendment claim. He believed, correctly, that the ACLU was divided over hate speech regulation, with its traditional civil libertarians seeing the problem in First Amendment terms and its equality-leaning members seeing it as a problem that required balancing First Amendment and equality concerns. Two conservative organizations also weighed in on Viktora's side, but the groups Cleary thought of as the "big three"—the Anti-Defamation League of B'nai B'rith, the NAACP, and People for the American Way—filed amicus briefs supporting the prosecution (as did a number of state attorneys general and a conservative law enforcement–oriented group, the Criminal Justice Legal Foundation). A Minnesota lawyer who had clerked for Scalia advised Cleary on how to draft a brief that "pushed the right buttons" for Scalia. Pushing the right buttons meant, among other things, citing the conservative Dinesh D'Souza's book against political correctness.

Justice White tried to uphold the ordinance by modifying the "fighting words" doctrine, but he couldn't hold Warren Burger's vote, and Scalia, originally in the minority, got to write the majority opinion. Scalia reversed the state supreme court, for a five-justice majority. He started by saying that some earlier discussions of "fighting words" had been a bit sloppy in saying that they were out-side the scope of the First Amendment. What the fighting words cases meant was that there were some categories of speech the government could prohibit on the basis of their content, without requiring that it satisfy the tough imminence requirements of the Brandenburg case. But, Scalia continued, this didn't mean that these categories of speech were "entirely invisible to the Constitution." His examples were persuasive: The government "may proscribe libel," but not just libel "critical of the government"; it may ban obscenity, but not just "those legally obscene works that contain criticism of the city government." St. Paul's hate speech ordinance was content-based because it prohibited only fighting words about race, gender, and religion but not fighting words about politics, unions, or gays. "The First Amendment does not permit St. Paul to impose special prohibitions on those speakers who express views on disfavored subjects."

But, Scalia continued, the ordinance was even worse because it was viewpoint-based as well. The ordinance, he wrote banned "odious racial epithets," no matter who said them. Yet fighting words that didn't invoke race directly could be used by people "arguing in favor of" racial "tolerance and equality" but couldn't be used "by that speaker's opponents." With his usual flair for unrealistic hypotheticals, Scalia wrote, "One could hold up a sign saying . . . that all 'anti-Catholic bigots' are misbegotten; but not that all 'papists' are, for that would insult and provoke violence 'on the basis of religion.'" He ended this part of his analysis with a flourish: The city "has no such authority to license one side of a debate to fight freestyle, while requiring the other to follow Marquis of Queensbury rules."

Scalia still had some doctrinal problems. His position tended toward saying that given some "unprotected" category of speech, governments can't discriminate within that category. That has weird consequences. Everyone agrees that the government can punish someone for using words to make "true threats" to another person. Does that mean that the federal government can't have a special statute making it a crime to threaten the president? Obscenity is unprotected speech, but it can't possibly be the case that the government has to choose between outlawing all obscenity or none; the Constitution has to allow the government to outlaw only the worst types of obscenity if that's all it wants to do. Scalia addressed this problem by saying that discrimination within an unprotected category was all right if the reason for the discrimination was the very reason for creating the category in the first place: We allow bans on threats because they cause real harms simply by being uttered, and threats against the president create worse harms than threats against me.

But, Scalia said, the government couldn't ban only obscenity that criticized the government, and not any other obscenity, because the reason that banning obscenity is consistent with the Constitution—something about morality and sheer offensiveness—doesn't have anything to do with criticism of the government. St. Paul's ordinance didn't fit this exception, though. Fighting words are outside the First Amendment because "their content embodies a particularly intolerable (and socially unnecessary) mode of expressing whatever idea the speaker wishes to convey." But the city hadn't "singled out an especially offensive mode of expression." It hadn't prohibited only fighting words "that communicate ideas in a threatening (as opposed to a merely obnoxious) manner." Instead, it had prohibited fighting words "of whatever manner" that sent "messages of racial, gender, or religious intolerance."

Scalia's approach to the hate speech problem was rule-based or categorical. Content-based regulations were presumptively unconstitutional, but some content-based regulations were permissible, in narrow categories like fighting words. Within those categories, additional discrimination based on content wasn't allowed, unless the reason for the discrimination was the reason for creating the category in the first place. The structure of the analysis is "rule, with an exception, with an exception to the exception." Nonlawyers might find the structure confusing and overly elaborate. Some of the distinctions Scalia drew make a lot of sense when you think through the problem of creating sensible First Amendment doctrine, but they don't have an immediate intuitive appeal.

The four other justices took a different approach to the problem. They agreed the St. Paul ordinance was unconstitutional because the state supreme court had interpreted it to cover words that caused "only hurt feelings, offense, or resentment," far more than was allowed by the fighting words doctrine. They disagreed with Scalia's analysis, though. Taking that analysis on its own terms,

White thought that the final exception "swallows" the rule. The reason fighting words were outside the scope of the First Amendment—they provoked immediate responses, including fear and violence—did indeed apply with special force to fighting words targeted at groups that had been subjected to a long history of discrimination. White and his colleagues looked at the "rule-exception-another exception" structure and said that what was really going on was a balancing of a number of competing considerations. They thought that the Court ought to acknowledge openly that it was engaged in balancing and then talk about why the balance came out against the ordinance, instead of concealing the balancing behind an elaborate screen of words.

The Court's decision in Viktora's case meant that he didn't face a trial for burning the cross. He continued to get into trouble, though. A few months after Cleary had won his case in the Supreme Court, Viktora was arrested for fighting a police officer after the officer reacted to a shout of "White power" from one of Viktora's friends.

The Court revisited the hate speech question a year later and then again in 2003. The 1993 decision involved a sentencing enhancement statute of a sort that had become fairly common. Todd Mitchell, a young African American, saw the movie *Mississippi Burning*, about the 1963 murders of three civil rights workers (one African American, two white). After talking about the movie with some friends, Mitchell noticed a young white boy across the street and, pointing to him, said, "You all want to fuck somebody up? There goes a white boy; go get him." The group crossed the street and severely assaulted the victim. Mitchell was convicted of aggravated battery, which ordinarily carries a maximum sentence of two years. The state had a sentencing enhancement statute that pushed the maximum sentence up to seven years if a jury found that the defendant had intentionally selected the victim because of his race. Mitchell got a four-year sentence. The Supreme Court unanimously held that the sentence enhancement was constitutional.

The assault of course wasn't expressive conduct protected by the First Amendment. The real question, though, was whether Mitchell got an extra two years because of his thoughts, for his choice of a victim because of race. Rehnquist's opinion said that the enhancement resulted from an ordinary use of motivation in sentencing, similar to the role motivation played in sexual harassment cases. Academic critics puzzled over the distinction between Mitchell's case and Viktora's. Choosing a victim because of his race seems to communicate just about as much as burning a cross does, and the fact that an assault is outside the scope of the First Amendment doesn't mean much because the Court in Viktora's case assumed that cross burning was outside the scope of the First Amendment too. Academic criticism doesn't count for much, though. The point of the Viktora decision was to address campus hate speech codes, not to deal with "ordinary" hate crime legislation.

Cross burning itself came back to the Supreme Court in 2003. The Court dealt with a couple of cases from Virginia, one involving a cross burning at a Ku Klux Klan rally and the other with a crime like Viktora's, teenagers burning a cross at a neighbor's house. The cases were procedurally messy, but in the end the Court agreed that states can ban cross burning when it's done with an intent to intimidate its targets and suggested that Klan leaders who burn crosses at a rally might not have that kind of intent. A majority said that cross burning was "symbolic expression," but that it was all right for Virginia to discriminate against the particular messages sent by cross burning when it was done with an intent to intimidate. The real offense, it seems, is intimidating your neighbors, and "burning a cross is a particularly virulent form of intimidation" that history showed was "a signal of impending violence."

Justice Thomas rarely spoke up during oral arguments. In the Virginia cross burning cases, he interrupted the lawyer representing the United States, which was supporting the prosecution, to ask, "Aren't you understating the—the effects of—of the burning cross?" He then referred to "almost one hundred years of lynching and activity in the South" in "a reign of terror" in which the burning cross was a "symbol of terror." He ended his intervention with "There was no other purpose to the cross. There was no communication of a particular message. It was intended to cause fear and to terrorize a population." As the argument proceeded, Thomas's colleagues repeatedly cited his emphasis on the role the burning cross played in the history of white terrorism in the South.

When the cases were decided, Thomas objected to the suggestion that cross burners could ever invoke the First Amendment. He described a long history in which a cross was a weapon of the Klan, "a terrorist organization." Whatever might be said about burning crosses in the abstract, he said, "In our culture, cross burning has almost invariably meant lawlessness and understandably instills in its victims well-grounded fear of physical violence." Still, that would seem to say that cross burning might indeed be a means of communicating something. But, Thomas concluded, the history of cross burning showed that it was "only conduct, not expression." He described "violent and terroristic conduct" as "the Siamese twin of cross burning." Yet the unhappy doctrinal history of efforts to distinguish between expression and conduct suggests a difficulty with the metaphor: Mystery writers have sometimes posed the question, How can you punish one Siamese twin for something the other one did? The same question, suitably adjusted, could be asked of Thomas.

Blackmun criticized the majority in Viktora's case for succumbing to "the temptation to decide the issue over 'politically correct' speech and 'cultural diversity.'" Charles Fried, a conservative, agreed, saying that "Scalia was putting his finger on" universities where "certain kinds of speech are banned because they upset people who belong to certain categories," even though the opinion didn't refer to campus hate speech codes or political correctness. Initially the R.A.V. decision seemed to put a heavy damper on the development of hate speech codes. College administrators met with their lawyers to redraft existing codes.

In the longer run the adoption of campus hate speech codes continued apace. According to one study, "the number of speech policies clearly rose following the court decisions." In 2003 the war against political correctness continued, with the Foundation for Individual Rights in Education, a legal action group with a conservative-leaning board sprinkled with some liberals, announcing "an all-out assault on speech codes at public universities nationwide." In the same year the federal Department of Education, again under conservative control, sent a letter to universities cautioning them against adopting hate speech codes that intruded on free speech rights.

∽

The hate speech cases were as much about the way the Court handled free speech questions as they were about hate speech. The justices all agreed that St. Paul's ordinance was unconstitutional, but they disagreed about the proper way of thinking about free speech questions. Scalia's opinion reflected his long-standing position that constitutional law required hard-edged rules rather than fuzzy standards or balancing tests that called on judges to exercise judgment. In one area of constitutional law after another, he insisted that the rule of law required a law of rules, as he put it in one of his most cited law review articles.

Liberal law professors initially thought that there had to be some connection between Scalia's political conservatism and his insistence on hard-edged rules rather than standards and judgment. Quite often Scalia's invocation of rules coincided with a conventional conservative position. When liberals urged that the Constitution's ban on cruel and unusual punishments meant that some criminal sentences were excessively harsh and therefore unconstitutional—life sentences for a third minor offense under a three strikes and you're out law, for example—Scalia took the conservative position that the Constitution didn't contain a principle against excessive sentences. When liberals thought that the benefits of affirmative action for racial justice had to be balanced against the costs of such programs to whites, Scalia insisted that the Constitution was color-blind—a rule, that is, that race simply couldn't be taken into account at all, ever.

Eventually constitutional scholars came to understand that rules and standards had no particular political spin in themselves. Scalia's own practice made the point. When conservatives urged that the Constitution limited the size of punitive damages, Scalia took the liberal position that it did not. His invocation of rules in free speech cases was quite protective of speech, which before the 1990s was the liberal position. The flag burning controversy shows how Scalia's interest in rules—or, perhaps better in that setting, his disdain for balancing—led him to support a free speech claim that most conservatives thought frivolous.

The Rehnquist Court decided two flag burning cases, but only the first really mattered. Gregory "Joey" Johnson, a member of the Revolutionary Communist Youth Brigade (a tiny Maoist group), was part of a political coalition that organized a "Republican War Chest Tour" in 1984. The "Tour" culminated in a street demonstration at the 1984 Republican National Convention in Dallas, Texas.

Johnson's group, which included singer Michelle Shocked, marched through the streets, stopping at several businesses they associated with the Republicans and defacing some storefronts with spray-painted graffiti. Someone took a flag from the flagpost at one of those stores and handed it to Johnson. The march ended near City Hall. Johnson set the flag on fire while the group shouted, "America, the red, white, and blue, we spit on you." He was convicted for desecrating the flag.

At the purely doctrinal level, Johnson's case was easy, so easy that the Texas Court of Criminal Appeals, not a hotbed of liberalism, reversed his conviction because the flag desecration statute violated the First Amendment. Johnson burned the flag as part of a political protest, and indeed, no one deliberately burns flags in public except for political reasons. Also, the statute made it a crime to "desecrate" a flag—that is, to do something to the flag that expressed an opinion about what the flag stood for. Anti–flag burning statutes are paradigms of viewpoint-based regulations.

At the emotional level, of course, Johnson's case was not easy for justices who were deeply patriotic. Stevens, a Navy veteran of World War II, wept in outrage during the Court's discussion of the case. Ordinarily classified with the Court's liberals, Stevens wrote a restrained dissent. Rehnquist wrote the main dissent. Beginning with a history of the nation's reverence for the flag, the opinion quoted in full John Greenleaf Whittier's poem "Barbara Frietchie" with its famous lines " 'Shoot, if you must, this old gray head,/ But spare your country's flag,' she said." After that, the dissent was a mishmash. Sometimes it hinted that there ought to be exception to general First Amendment principles for flag protection statutes, a position that Scalia might have accepted. Its main thrust, though, was that a ban on flag burning for political purposes was consistent with those general principles. Relying on the Chaplinsky case, Rehnquist wrote that flag burning was "no essential part of any expression of ideas." Flag burning "conveyed nothing that could not be conveyed . . . in a dozen different ways," something that could be said about just about any political speech. Flag burning was, to Rehnquist, "the equivalent of an inarticulate grunt or roar that, it seems fair to say, is most likely to be indulged in not to express any particular idea, but to antagonize others," which seems inconsistent with his point that Johnson could have "conveyed" his message in a dozen other ways.

Scalia joined Brennan's majority opinion without writing separately, a course he followed the next year when the Court reaffirmed its decision in a follow-up case. The reason seems clear: Scalia found Brennan's application of the First Amendment's rules more acceptable than the confusion of Rehnquist's opinion. Here Scalia's desire for rules in constitutional law led him to join the liberals.

✑

Scalia's concern for rules was his major intellectual contribution to the Rehnquist Court. Beyond that, there's something conventional accounts don't say: Antonin Scalia isn't as smart as he thinks he is. That's not to say that he's not smart. He did graduate from Harvard Law School magna cum laude, a distinction not easily achieved even today. Yet after 1994, and for a while before, he was just above the middle of the Court in terms of sheer brainpower. Rehnquist, Stevens, Breyer, Souter, and Ginsburg all could give him a run for his money in that department. Of course, sheer brainpower isn't the only thing we care about in judges, and it may not be the most important thing. Good judges ought to have good judgment too. On that score Scalia came up short as well.

The vocal admiration Scalia received from conservative legal activists and the politicians they influenced unfortunately reinforced his sense of his superior abilities. He came to believe the notices he received in the press, without understanding that his intellectual peers or superiors on the Court didn't need a claque of admirers to reinforce their public identities. I haven't been able to locate a blog for other justices equivalent to "Ninomania," maintained by a law professor at Regent University (which does have a link to the extremely useful "Justice Clarence Thomas Appreciation Page"), or the "Cult of Scalia" home page. Scalia, though, has built his public identity around the fact, as his admirers would have it, that he was the smartest kid on the block. Neither his admirers nor he can afford to acknowledge that he wasn't.

Measuring brainpower from a distance isn't an exact science. It mattered to Richard Nixon that Rehnquist had served as a law clerk to a Supreme Court justice, and Stevens and Breyer had as well, whereas Scalia hadn't. Scalia's academic appointments were at first-rank law schools, though not as highly ranked as Harvard, where Breyer taught. After practicing law for a "hot" law firm in Cleveland for six years, Scalia started teaching at the University of Virginia Law School. After four years there he left to work in the Nixon administration, beginning as general counsel to the Office of Telecommunications Policy in the White House and ending as head of the Justice Department's Office of Legal Counsel, Rehnquist's old position. At the end of the Ford administration, Scalia parked at the conservative American Enterprise Institute, teaching at Georgetown University Law Center as well. He then moved to the University of Chicago Law School, where he stayed until President Reagan named him to the federal appeals court in Washington, D.C.

The law schools Scalia taught at were in the top tier of law schools, but he wasn't one of either school's superstars. He was at the top of the second rank of law professors in his generation. His specialty was administrative law, not constitutional law. The titles of his major law review articles give some indication of his interests: "Sovereign Immunity and Nonstatutory Review of Federal Administrative Action: Some Conclusions from the Public-Lands Cases"; "The Hearing Examiner Loan Program"; "The ALJ Fiasco—A Reprise." These were good, solid articles about good, solid topics in administrative law, but they didn't transform even that field.

In 1979 Scalia published his only article as a law professor on an issue of constitutional law that had captured public attention, a short critique of affirmative action originally presented as a comment on a lecture by Harry Edwards, a professor at Michigan Law School, soon to become a judge on the court of appeals that Scalia later joined. Scalia called Powell's opinion in the Bakke case "thoroughly unconvincing as an honest, hard-minded, reasoned analysis of an important provision of the Constitution" and criticized it for resembling "an excellent compromise between two Committees of the American Bar Association on some insignificant legislative proposal." He described affirmative action as "racist."

Scalia's comment on affirmative action had the characteristic style he brought to his Supreme Court opinions. It was strongly stated, used catchy examples and phrases, and cast aspersions on his opponents' honesty. He had familiarized himself with that style as a member of the editorial board of the magazine *Regulation*, then published by the American Enterprise Institute. *Regulation*'s articles were designed to catch readers' attention with horror stories about government regulation, then develop a more sustained and slightly more academic critique explaining why those horror stories were typical. The articles' real audience was opinion makers who would read not the articles themselves but the summaries that appeared in leading newspapers, summaries that predictably focused on the horror stories and played down the typically more complicated and qualified academic analysis.

Some law professors and an even larger number of journalists praised Scalia for his literary style. That style isn't as distinctive as it seems at first. Certainly it's distinctive among Supreme Court justices. But everyone has *heard* Scalia's style. It's the sound bite style of *Crossfire*, highly quotable, reducing complex issues to simple—and often misleading—phrases.

Maureen Dowd of the *New York Times* accurately captured the persona Scalia tried to convey in his dissents, in an acerbic and overstated column in 2003. Scalia, she wrote, "fancies himself the intellectual of the Supreme Court, an aesthete who likes opera and wines, a bon vivant who loves poker and plays songs like 'It's a Grand Old Flag' on the piano; a real man who hunts and reads Ducks Unlimited magazine." Scalia's style was an effort to show that he was both erudite *and* a man of the people. So in one dissent he did a riff on Cole Porter. The majority, he wrote, "resuscitates the *ne plus ultra*, the Napoleon Brandy, the Mahatma Ghandi [*sic*], the Celophane [*sic*] of subjectivity, th' ol' 'shocks-the-conscience' test." But Scalia was into more than pop culture (at least the culture that was pop a couple of generations ago, which he, again trying to get noticed for cleverness, referred to as "classical music"). He thought he could impress with seeming erudition. Dowd quoted Scalia's comment to another journalist: "[B]eing tough and traditional is a heavy cross to bear. Duresse oblige." Tough, smart, and honest, in contrast with his opponents, who were, his phrasings suggested, weak, dumb, and dishonest.

Maybe Scalia's sound bites were clever, but it's not obvious how they advanced any argument. Sometimes his search for the sound bite actually got in the way of clear thinking. Scalia began his dissent in a gay rights case, "The Court has mistaken a Kulturkampf for a fit of spite." Molly Ivins once wrote that Pat Buchanan's speech to the Republican National Convention in 1992 probably sounded better in the original German. Scalia's line doesn't, because although he thought he was simply translating the fashionable term *culture war* into German, he's actually got the historical reference backward. The real *Kulturkampf* was German Chancellor Otto von Bismarck's vicious campaign against the Catholic Church, which included the imprisonment of priests who challenged Bismarck's policies. In a sense, then, the original *Kulturkampf* was indeed a fit of spite, and a devout Catholic should have been sensitive to the reference. Scalia, though, went for the sound bite.

His rhetorical choices demonstrated a failure of good judgment. His tone "marginalized" him, according to some observers. Rehnquist sometimes snapped at Scalia's interventions at oral arguments. When Scalia bailed out an attorney who was having trouble making the argument he wanted to hear, Rehnquist suggested, to audience laughter, that the time Scalia took to ask the "question" should be deducted from the lawyer's allotted argument time. In the same case, when Scalia interrupted the answer from the side he didn't favor, Rehnquist intervened to say, "Let her answer." Scalia's colleagues put up with his behavior at oral arguments because they really had no choice, but it didn't make them any friendlier to him

He made misjudgments too even when he was doing a fine job of taking apart the logic of the opinions he disagreed with. Often his strategy was to demonstrate that that logic led to what he regarded as absurd conclusions. But of course absurdity may lie in the eye of the beholder, and what he regarded as absurd might have seemed reasonable to the justices on the other side, although they might have conceded that moving to the logical conclusion of their premises would be premature. This certainly seems the best description of Scalia's observation in the 2003 gay rights case that the majority's logic would lead to invalidating statutes like Alabama's ban on selling sex toys. I can imagine a member of the majority responding, "And your point is?"

Scalia's logical deconstructions could actually undermine litigators who wanted to engage in damage control. The 2003 affirmative action cases held that university affirmative action programs could be justified on the ground that they promoted the important value of achieving diversity in the classroom. Anti-affirmative action litigators might still want to challenge affirmative action programs in other settings, such as government employment. Scalia cut the ground out from under them, saying that the majority's opinion demonstrated that "it is surely no less appropriate—indeed, *particularly* appropriate—for the civil service system" to pursue diversity. If anti-affirmative action litigators tried to attack affirmative action in the civil service, they would now be met with the response that even Scalia believed that the cases of universities and the civil service were indistinguishable. A prudent judge would have refrained from making the point, however well founded it might be. Scalia was more interesting in scoring points than in preserving the ground for later successes.

Still, probably the most troubling thing about Scalia's style is that it *is* just like *Crossfire*. It is filled with assertions that opponents are stupid, as in his description of O'Connor's position as "irrational," or, even worse, liars. Referring in the 2003 gay rights case to the majority's disclaimer that the case at hand didn't involve questions about whether the government had to recognize gay marriage, an accurate enough statement about the case itself, although perhaps not about the holding's implications, Scalia wrote, "Do not believe it." Filling the official reports with statements that your opponents are the equivalent of fools and liars doesn't improve the quality of public discourse.

☙

An early comment on Scalia's affection for rules rather than standards or balancing rooted it in his upbringing. The key was said to be the catechism as taught in the Catholic schools Scalia attended, supplemented by dinner table conversations with his father, a professor of romantic literature who specialized in the study of translations. The law professor George Kannar argued that students learned the catechism as a system of unchallengeable rules and that Scalia transferred that approach to constitutional law. It was "a formalistic vision of how one perceives and evaluates the world, and a particular literalistic view of what one does with texts." Drawing on Garry Wills's discussion of the "experience of growing up Catholic in a pre–Vatican II world," Kannar quoted Wills's description of the "world of quaint legalism" in the Catholic Church.

Scalia's own defense of his insistence on rules resonates with a sense of human frailty—or sinfulness, as a traditionalist might put it. He emphasized the predictability of rules over standards and balancing. Yet predictability isn't quite what Scalia was after. His opinion in the Viktora case shows that rule structures can get really elaborate, and people can get just as lost wandering around in a complex structure of rules as they can while awaiting a decision about what the right balance of considerations is.

Scalia connected his interest in predictability to a deeper commitment to constraint. Rules, he said, limited what lower courts could do. And rules limited Scalia himself, in his view: "If the next case should have such different facts that my political or policy preferences regarding the outcome are quite the opposite, I will be unable to indulge those preferences; I have committed myself to the governing principles." The basic idea here is simple, although the analysis is trickier than Scalia suggested. Consider a judge who is quite confident that she can figure out what justice requires in a particular case—O'Connor, for example. That judge might still worry that other people don't have as good judgment as she does. She might not trust them to get the balance of considerations right. And she might think those other people will come closer to getting it right in more cases if they are given rigid rules to follow.

The same could be true for Supreme Court justices, said Scalia. It's not clear why, though. The rule of law he advocated was a law of rules, in the plural. Presented with a case where a previously stated rule seemed to point to the wrong result, a Supreme Court justice could always articulate an exception to the rule—stated, of course, in terms of a rule rather than a standard. That's precisely how Scalia's opinion in the Viktora case reads.

Beyond theory, there's practice. Scalia said that rules mattered because they constrained what he could do. Here it's impossible to avoid *Bush v. Gore*. On one level the Court's opinion, which Scalia joined, did invoke the idea of rules rather than standards. The Florida Supreme Court had directed the vote counters to determine what the intent of each voter was. The U.S. Supreme Court agreed that this was "unobjectionable as an abstract proposition and a starting principle." But it concluded that the general standard could be made more precise by "uniform rules." On another level, though, the Court's opinion was inconsistent with Scalia's proposition that rules were good because they constrained Supreme Court justices. The reason lies in the Court's notorious unwillingness to commit to any rule beyond the one that awarded the presidency to George W. Bush: "Our consideration is limited to the present circumstances, for the problem of equal protection in election processes generally presents many complexities."

Scalia's willingness to join the majority opinion in *Bush v. Gore* may have been purely strategic. He also joined Rehnquist's separate opinion, which relied on a previously obscure constitutional provision that the chief justice interpreted to limit the degree to which a state court could interpret statutes dealing with presidential elections. That opinion was certainly more rulelike than the majority opinion, although it was a rule so unlikely to be applied in any case in the future—because the circumstances giving rise to the problem weren't likely to recur within several generations, if ever—that the idea that Scalia was constraining himself by following the rule seems fanciful.

In addition to strategy, there's human sinfulness. Scalia's position in *Bush v. Gore* may show why he's right about rules—and right to think that they can never completely solve the problems he worries about.

⌒

The flag burning cases illustrate that method and outcome don't always coincide neatly. The Rehnquist Court's First Amendment decisions tended to support the status quo. They did so mostly through free speech absolutism. But absolutism has some collateral consequences, sometimes favorable to political dissidents like Joey Johnson.

Margaret Gilleo was another dissenter who benefited from the Rehnquist Court's free speech absolutism. Gilleo grew up thinking that "war is really stupid." After her husband died, Gilleo moved to Ladue, a St. Louis suburb, and became an active environmentalist employed by a local project aimed at converting what it described as America's military-based economy into a more peace-oriented one. In December 1990, as Congress was considering whether to go to war against Iraq, Gilleo made a sign on poster board saying SAY NO TO WAR IN THE PERSIAN GULF, CALL CONGRESS NOW and set it up in her front yard. This violated a city ordinance prohibiting homeowners from putting signs in their yards.

Ladue was a conservative community, which had been sued by the Justice Department in 1975 for discriminating against black teachers. The city's conservatism was reflected in the fact that the first sign Gilleo put up was stolen, and the second knocked down. The police told her that they couldn't do anything because the signs violated the city ordinance. Edith Spink dominated the city's politics. In her seventies when Gilleo put up the antiwar sign, Spink had been elected mayor in 1975. She tried hard to preserve Ladue's special character, driving around the city to spot garbage, lawn waste, and other unsightly things, including lawn signs. After the city council turned down Gilleo's request for a variance, she sued in federal court. Testimony at the trial included Spink's statement that she would have been more likely to allow the sign if it said, BRING OUR HOSTAGES HOME or SAY NO TO DRUGS.

The trial court barred the city from enforcing its ordinance. Gilleo, apparently learning from experience that putting up a yard sign was going to lead to an endless round of signs and vandalism, then put a letter-size sign in the second-story window of her house, this one reading FOR PEACE IN THE GULF. The city amended its ban on signs, but not in a way that helped Gilleo, and she continued her lawsuit. The lower courts agreed that even the amended ordinance was unconstitutional.

So did the Supreme Court—unanimously. Stevens's opinion noted the possibility that the city was discriminating against viewpoints it didn't like, but in the end the decision rested on much broader ground. The city's ban, Stevens wrote, "covers even such absolutely pivotal speech as a sign protesting an imminent governmental decision to go to war." The city couldn't "completely foreclose a venerable means of communication that is both unique and important," such as displaying lawn signs on political issues that homeowners care about. Such signs were "an unusually cheap and convenient form of communication," particularly important to people of modest means. Ladue might take "more temperate measures" to avoid visual clutter, but here the city was trying to "suppress too much speech."

Joey Johnson and Margaret Gilleo certainly benefited from the Rehnquist Court's First Amendment absolutism, and so do people like them, outsiders who protest the status quo. (Ladue didn't; its residents defeated a tax increase proposal to fund the nearly five hundred thousand dollars in legal fees the city had incurred defending its ordinance, apparently preferring to see leaves accumulate in the gutters and city roads deteriorate.) In a rough count of the winners of First Amendment claims in the Rehnquist Court, the insiders who win slightly outnumber the outsiders. Johnson, Gilleo, Jews for Jesus, antiabortion protesters, the racist militia movement, and Viktora are among the outsiders who won: twenty-eight cases. The insiders are the major political parties, corporations, and lawyers and other professionals selling their services. They won thirty-five cases.

Each case of course sets a precedent for others, so a simple win-loss count doesn't tell you much about the social consequences of the Rehnquist Court's First Amendment decisions. Some of the decisions protected government workers and contractors against retaliation for campaigning against incumbent local officials. The cases had unique factual backgrounds, but the decisions themselves stated principles that gave significant protection to the large number of people who depend on the government for their livelihoods.

Taken as a group, the cases protecting the status quo through the First Amendment are more important than the ones protecting outsiders. The important point, though, is the fact that the political valence of the First Amendment had certainly changed. At the very least, the First Amendment enforced by the Rehnquist Court gave more protection to the status quo than the First Amendment the Warren Court had enforced. Part of the reason is that conservatives began to see the advantages of First Amendment absolutism—for example, as a way of attacking political correctness—and liberals, at least those outside the Court, overlooked its disadvantages. They might have been making a strategic calculation that absolutism's benefits to the outsiders were more important than its benefits to insiders, or they might not have noticed what had happened. Inside the Court, however, the balancers tried to preserve doctrines, and outcomes, that didn't give quite as many benefits to insiders.

CHAPTER SIX

Anthony Kennedy and
Gay Rights

J ustice Lewis F. Powell, Jr., regret-
ted his vote to uphold Georgia's ban on homosexual sodomy almost
immediately after the Court announced its decision in 1986. Powell
didn't get a chance to do it over, but gay rights advocates did—seventeen years later. The Burger Court rejected gay rights; the Rehnquist
Court embraced the most important gay rights claim it considered.
The Rehnquist Court's acceptance of core gay rights claims is
another indication that social conservatives lost the culture wars
battles inside the Supreme Court—largely because they lost them
outside the Supreme Court as well.

∽

Rehnquist became chief justice right after the Court had rejected a
constitutional challenge to Georgia's law against sodomy. According
to Byron White's short opinion, the right to engage in homosexual
sodomy was not covered by prior decisions protecting families, marriage, and procreation. White, a persistent dissenter in abortion
cases, connected the antisodomy case to those cases. "The Court is
most vulnerable," he wrote, "and comes nearest to illegitimacy when
it deals with judge-made constitutional law having little or no cog-
nizable roots in the language or design of the Constitution." The
Court could enforce fundamental rights that weren't spelled out in
the Constitution only if those rights were "deeply rooted in this

Nation's history and tradition." White thought it obvious that "a fundamental right to engage in homosexual sodomy" didn't fit. Indeed, he wrote, the claim that it did was, "at best, facetious." And to the argument that judgments of immorality weren't enough to justify a statute, White responded that law "is constantly based on notions of morality, and if all laws representing essentially moral choices are to be invalidated . . . , the courts will be very busy indeed."

Gays rightly heard overtones of homophobia in White's opinion; the word *facetious* was particularly insensitive. Burger's separate opinion was even worse. Noting that "Judeo-Christian moral and ethical standards" condemned homosexual practices, the chief justice concluded that protecting gay sodomy as a fundamental right would "cast aside millennia of moral teaching."

Blackmun wrote the main dissent, sounding the theme that prior cases protected sexual intimacy in the home. Stevens also dissented, taking on directly the argument that Georgia could prohibit sodomy simply because its voters thought it immoral. The Court's cases dealing with marital intimacy showed that the state could not, Stevens wrote. "When individual married couples are isolated from observation by others, the way in which they voluntarily choose to conduct their intimate relations is a matter for them—not the State—to decide." The "essential 'liberty' " protected by the Court's cases "surely embraces the right to engage in non-reproductive, sexual conduct that others may consider offensive or immoral." Stevens also developed an analysis that the Court revived in 2003. Georgia couldn't treat gays as having a different "liberty" interest from straights. Stevens invoked the principle that "all men are created equal," saying that although its precise meaning might be unclear, it had to mean that "every free citizen has the same interest in 'liberty' that the members of the majority share."

With precedent and an apparently conservative Court against them, gay rights advocates could well have been discouraged at their prospects. They knew, though, that the public culture was moving in their direction, and they didn't abandon their efforts to protect gay rights. Their primary target at first was not the courts. They focused instead on state legislatures and city councils, getting them to expand existing antidiscrimination laws to cover discrimination against gays.

Their opponents countered by arguing that applying such laws violated *their* constitutional rights. The Supreme Court agreed.

∾

Two New England characters met when David Souter wrote the Court's opinion finding that John J. "Wacko" Hurley, who ran Boston's St. Patrick's Day parade as head of the South Boston Allied War Veterans Council, could keep a gay and lesbian group from marching in the parade. Boston's Irish-American Gay, Lesbian, and Bisexual Group (known as GLIB, the initials being rearranged) started its campaign for inclusion in the parade in 1992. GLIB's leaders saw people marching under the banners of all sorts of groups: politicians, the AFL-CIO, a Boston Baptist organization, even Gruff the Crime Dog. They wanted to parade under a banner identifying them as Irish-American and gay, affirming both aspects of their identity. In 1992 Hurley said no because of "safety concerns." GLIB got a one-time-only court order letting twenty-five members march under a simple banner naming the group. The march went off without any real problems, although some spectators shouted antigay slogans as the group passed. The next year Hurley said no again, this time asserting that GLIB's presence would introduce a "sexual theme" into a parade that focused on "traditional religious and social values." Again GLIB got a court order for that year's parade, allowing it to participate.

Trying to get a permanent order, GLIB sued Hurley in state court, saying that keeping it out of the parade violated Massachusett's antidiscrimination laws, which prohibited discrimination on the basis of sexual orientation in places of public accommodation. GLIB's lawyers argued that the parade, open as it was to almost everyone, was like an amusement park stretched out over a number of city blocks. Amusement parks couldn't discriminate, and neither could the parade's organizers. In December 1993 the trial judge agreed with GLIB. Hurley filed an appeal and canceled the 1994 parade. Massachusetts's supreme court affirmed the trial judge, and Hurley took the case to the Supreme Court.

Hurley based his claim on the First Amendment. A parade was a way of expressing yourself, and forcing the parade's organizers to let in people who had a message they disagreed with—even so bland a message as "I'm Irish and I'm Gay"—violated their right to say what they wanted. GLIB countered that the "message" the parade's organizers sent was so diffuse—because they let so many different groups march under their own banners—that letting it march couldn't interfere with any message Hurley and the other organizers wanted to send.

The St. Patrick's Day parade case was the first case involving gays that Souter heard. The rumors about his sexual orientation hadn't completely died down, giving GLIB's leaders some hope. The oral argument dispelled any optimism they had had, though. Souter, seconded by Scalia, pushed Chester Darling, representing Hurley, to say that the parade's sponsors didn't have to have a very coherent message to be protected by the First Amendment; all they needed was a desire to maintain the parade's "traditions." Darling emphasized that the parade didn't exclude gays as such; gays could march in the parade, but they couldn't carry a banner identifying themselves as gay. So, he said, they weren't discriminating on the basis of sexual orientation itself, just on the basis of the messages people wanted to display. That, Darling finished, was precisely what the First Amendment allowed.

Gay-friendly journalists Joyce Murdoch and Deb Price gave the Court's unanimous decision against GLIB the best spin they could by saying that it was the first time the Court spoke of gays respectfully—indeed, they pointed out, the first time a Court opinion used the word *gay* "except in a formal name or a quote." Still, GLIB didn't get a single vote for its position. Souter's constitutional analysis was straightforward: Real parades were inherently about sending a message, not about "reach[ing] a destination." And, he continued, the message didn't have to be all that clear or precise; after all, he said, Jackson Pollock's paintings and Arnold Schoenberg's music were clearly protected by the First Amendment even though everyone would be hard pressed to say what their messages were. Pushing the musical metaphor a bit too hard, Souter wrote that "like a composer, the [Veterans] Council selects the expressive units of the parade . . . , and though the score may not produce a particularized message, each contingent's expression in the Council's eyes comports with what merits celebration on that day." Souter observed that the point of GLIB's banner wasn't "wholly articulate" either, but at least it would "bear witness to the fact that some Irish are gay, lesbian, or bisexual," and their presence would "suggest their view" that gays and lesbians "have as much claim to unqualified social acceptance as heterosexuals."

The fact that the Massachusetts courts relied on the state's antidiscrimination law didn't change things. The parade organizers weren't keeping gays out of the line of march, so the physical parade couldn't be the "place of public accommodation" the state courts were worried about. Rather, Souter said, the organizers' speech was the public accommodation. But the First Amendment prohibited the government from interfering with a speaker's choice of message, even by calling the interference a way of enforcing an antidiscrimination statute.

GLIB existed to march in the St. Patrick's Day parade, and its defeat in the Supreme Court ended its life. There were some pretty obvious work-arounds. The most important was that state governments could invoke their antidiscrimination laws to eliminate giving Hurley and the parade organizers preference in getting permission to march on St. Patrick's Day. The Constitution certainly allowed the city to give out permits on a first-come, first-served basis, which is how New York adjusted to increasing gay activism on the parade question.

The St. Patrick's Day parade was an important cultural event in Boston and New York but was less important elsewhere. Gay rights litigators used antidiscrimination statutes to take on another important cultural symbol, the Boy Scouts. The Boy Scouts were hardly an inviting target. You could win against them only in states that protected gays against discrimination, and then only if you got the state courts to interpret the statute to make the Boy Scouts a public accommodation (even California's fairly liberal supreme court refused to do that) and even then only if you managed to persuade the courts that the Boy Scouts weren't entitled to the kind of First Amendment protection the St. Patrick's Day parade got. And in the event you won, the possibility of generating a backlash was pretty large; the image of gay Boy Scout leaders evoked homophobic concerns about pedophilic gay men preying on the young boys in their charge out in the woods. Moreover, treating the Boy Scouts as a public accommodation was the kind of stretch that led opponents to talk disparagingly about special rights and a gay agenda.

Evan Wolfson, the chief strategist for the Lambda Legal Defense Fund, the leading gay rights litigating group, saw things differently. Even cases that didn't look good at the start might end up being spun favorably. He thought that taking on the Boy Scouts would actually educate the public about antigay discrimination even if he lost the cases. When James Dale came to Lambda for help, Wolfson was happy to sign on.

Dale was a dedicated Boy Scout who enjoyed the hikes and the camaraderie in the Scouts. After becoming an Eagle Scout, he started to work as an assistant scoutmaster while he attended Rutgers University. He also became copresident of the university's Lesbian/Gay Alliance. In July 1990 he spoke at a seminar for high school teachers about suicide among gay teens, describing his experiences as a teenager, "pretending to be straight while attending a military academy." A number of Scout leaders brought the newspaper report on his talk to the attention of the leader of the local Boy Scout executive committee. Using a policy adopted in 1978 that gays couldn't be Boy Scouts, the Scouts revoked Dale's membership and stopped him from leading his troop (which then disbanded).

Having become comfortable with his homosexuality, Dale wasn't ready to put up with discrimination and sought out Lambda. His lawsuit invoked a recent amendment to New Jersey's antidiscrimination law bringing gays within its protection. It took Dale eight years, but in 1999 the New Jersey Supreme Court agreed with him, finding that eliminating discrimination against gays was a "compelling" interest. The Boy Scouts were a public accommodation, according to the court, because the organization was so large and generally so indiscriminate in whom it admitted.

The Boy Scouts took the case to the Supreme Court. Of course they relied on the Hurley decision, claiming that being forced to admit Dale as a scoutmaster violated their right of free expression. Dale's lawyers thought that the Hurley case was different. As Souter had said, a parade was inherently expressive, not just a way of getting from here to there, but there was nothing particularly expressive about the Boy Scouts. The lawyers also argued that Dale was expelled simply for being gay, not for saying anything at all—not even for making his presentation at the Rutgers seminar. A minor spat later developed among the lawyers in the case over whether it was fair to call Dale a gay activist (at the campus level, he probably was) or to attribute the Scouts' actions to his activism (probably not; he hadn't said anything about the Scouts, or about being a Scout, at the seminar). But in the end what mattered was what the *Scouts* said they were about, not what Dale had done.

The oral argument seemed to go well for Dale. George Davidson, the Boy Scouts' lawyer, fumbled repeatedly when asked whether the Scouts expelled Dale because he was gay or because he had advocated gay rights. Davidson couldn't spell out what the Scouts' policy on gays was because it hadn't been written down until gay rights advocates began to sue the Scouts. Wolfson did better, emphasizing that "a human being, such as Mr. Dale, is not speech," so letting him be a Scout leader couldn't undermine whatever message the Scouts thought they were sending.

Showing that you can't predict outcomes from the tone of an oral argument, Dale lost, getting votes only from the Court's liberals. Rehnquist's opinion, handed down just two months after the case was argued, was crisp and—probably because of its brevity—quite expansive in its doctrinal formulations. Rehnquist relied on a slight variant of free speech, which the Court calls the freedom of expressive association. The core idea is simple. A group of vegetarians get together to swap recipes, reinforce their values, and publicize their beliefs. A law requiring them to admit carnivores would severely limit their ability to do what they want. The right of expressive association protects them against such laws.

The trick in enforcing the right of expressive association lies in identifying what groups are entitled to its protection and which laws interfere with it. Rehnquist's answer to the second question was seemingly simple. Forcing a group to include someone it doesn't want violates its members' rights, he wrote, "if the presence of that person affects in a significant way the group's ability to advocate public or private viewpoints." The Dale case posed two problems under that test. It wasn't clear that the Boy Scouts really did advocate "public or private viewpoints," and it wasn't clear that merely having Dale as a member would affect "in a significant way" the Scouts' ability to advocate whatever viewpoints it had.

As Rehnquist saw the case, the Boy Scouts sought to "transmit" a "system of values," and that was enough expressive activity to qualify for protection. The Scouts didn't have to exist for the very purpose of expression; the organization merely had to engage in expression part of the time. The New Jersey court had examined the Scouts' views on homosexuality and found them fuzzy and confused. But, Rehnquist wrote, that wasn't what a court was supposed to do. Instead, the courts had to accept an expressive association's own claims—its "official position," as Rehnquist put it—about what it was trying to express. The Scouts *said*—in this very lawsuit—that they wanted to express the view that homosexuality was inconsistent with their values, and that was enough.

However, would Dale's presence substantially interfere with the Scouts' ability to express that message? Here too, Rehnquist said, the courts had to "defer" to the organization's own claims about what would "impair its expression." According to Rehnquist, "Dale's presence in the Boy Scouts would, at the very least, force the organization to send a message, both to the youth members and the world, that the Boy Scouts accepts homosexual conduct as a legitimate form of behavior."

Interviewed about the Court's decision, Dale protested, "I'm not a message. I'm not a symbol. I'm not a sign. I'm just a person who happens to be gay." By the time the case was decided, Dale had moved to New York, where he was the advertising director for a gay-oriented magazine, and he was annoyed at what he regarded as media prying into his private life. Still, Dale couldn't control what he had become. The Boy Scouts and the Supreme Court made Dale into a message. In doing so the Court put on the table the question of whether other groups—school boards, in particular—should continue to sponsor Boy Scout troops. Gay-friendly school boards and some mainline churches dropped sponsorship, but the slack seems to have been taken up by an increasing number of troops sponsored by other churches.

The Boy Scouts case provoked an odd gay-friendly defense of the Court's decision. The decision actually promoted the interests of gays, some conservative gays said, by protecting the rights of organizations to define their own missions. Think about gay bars or social clubs in states dominated by the Christian Right, they said; antidiscrimination laws could be turned against gays where the political winds were unfavorable.

The gay-friendly defense of the Boy Scouts decision brings out another point. The St. Patrick's Day parade and the Boy Scouts cases involved gays, but they really weren't about gay rights—except in a way that, ironically, might have helped the cause of gay rights in the end. The Court's decisions give people who don't like gays a First Amendment defense for refusing to associate with them. As gay rights expand, they can say to themselves, "Well, after all, the expansion doesn't affect *me* because I can invoke the First Amendment." The First Amendment cases, that is, may have the effect of reducing the political opposition to expanding gay rights by ratcheting down the threat such an expansion poses to people who don't like gays.

⚯

Cultures clash in Colorado. Conservative Colorado Springs, home of the Air Force Academy and James Dobson's lobbying organization Focus on the Family, counters Denver, the ski resort Aspen, and liberal Boulder, home of the state's university. Conservative Christians mobilized in 1991, when they became concerned that gay rights organizations were about to extend existing antidiscrimination laws to cover sexual preference. Some cities already had done so, and the state's Democratic governor, Roy Romer, had issued an executive order banning discrimination against gays in state employment. Conservatives worried that these protections would become statewide and apply to private employment and public accommodations, which they knew could cover an enormous range of activities.

Conservative activists in Colorado Springs put together Colorado for Family Values. CFV decided to use the state's referendum laws, which allow voters to enact laws directly, and drafted what became known as Amendment 2, aimed at barring what its proponents called special protections for gays and lesbians. They recruited a former senator and the state university's football coach to urge people to sign the petitions to get Amendment 2 placed on the ballot. CFV compiled more than enough signatures, and the proposal appeared on the November 1992 ballot.

Amendment 2 was written in broad and confusing terms. Its heading seemed to say it was limited: "No protected status based on homosexual, lesbian, or bisexual orientation." That sounded as if the targets were typical antidiscrimination ordinances that might be expanded to cover gays and lesbians as protected classes. But its terms were broader. It said that no government entity in the state—the state government, city councils, school boards, libraries—could enact or enforce any statute or policy whereby gay or lesbian orientation or conduct would entitle anyone "to have or claim any minority status, quota preferences, protected status or claim of discrimination." As written, this meant that a library board could refuse to give a library card to gay people and that a police department could adopt a policy of refusing to protect gays against gay bashers, and in neither case could gays challenge the policy as discriminatory.

Colorado's gay and lesbian community couldn't quite believe that *their* state would go for Amendment 2, but as a precaution they put together a legal team to challenge Amendment 2 if it happened to be adopted. Linda Fowler, a leader in the lesbian community, persuaded Jean Dubofsky, who had served on the state supreme court before returning to private practice, to head the legal team. Fowler and Dubofsky assembled a number of potential plaintiffs, including tennis star Martina Navratilova and Richard Evans, an assistant to Denver's mayor.

CFV's campaign for Amendment 2 took as its theme "No special rights." One of its election pamphlets said that child molestation was "a large part of many homosexuals' lifestyle—part of the very life-style 'gay-rights' activists want government to give special class, ethnic status!" Despite their initial optimism, gays and lesbians discovered that they had no sound bite on their side that was nearly as effective as "No special rights," and 53.4 percent of Colorado's voters wrote Amendment 2 into the Colorado Constitution.

Nine days after election day Dubofsky filed a constitutional challenge to Amendment 2 in state court. The trial judge issued an injunction against enforcing the amendment, and the state supreme court agreed. Its theory was that Amendment 2 violated the federal Constitution's guarantee of equal protection because it made it harder for gays and lesbians than for other interest groups to get the state legislature or city councils to adopt antidiscrimination statutes. Before Amendment 2, gays and lesbians simply had to persuade the legislature; after it, they had to amend the state constitution again and *then* persuade the legislature. The state supreme court relied on a U.S. Supreme Court case saying that governments couldn't make it harder for racial minorities to get protective laws adopted. That case, though, relied on the idea that laws adversely affecting racial minorities needed very strong justifications. The Colorado Supreme Court didn't say that legislation adversely affecting gays and lesbians was "suspect" in the same way, but if not, its theory was impossible to defend: Every constitutional amendment makes it harder to enact ordinary laws sought by the interest group the amendment targets.

With the injunction against enforcement in place, the state had to try to show—in the lawyers' jargon—that Amendment 2 was a narrowly tailored way of advancing a compelling government interest. It couldn't, and it lost again when the case went back to the state supreme court. Colorado's attorney general, Gale Norton, then appealed to the U.S. Supreme Court. The core of her argument was simple. The Georgia sodomy case, *Bowers v. Hardwick,* showed that states could make homosexual conduct illegal. Colorado in fact didn't do that, but Norton said that the Constitution allowed it to express its disapproval of homosexual conduct and to try to discourage that conduct by the less severe means of denying gays and lesbians the protections afforded by antidiscrimination laws. She also emphasized that Colorado's voters had taken a position on a highly contentious issue of social policy and that the courts should let such issues be decided by ordinary democratic politics.

Dubofsky responded by pointing out that the state's defense treated Amendment 2 as narrower than it really was. Effectively using the example of a police policy against patrolling gay neighborhoods, she argued that under Amendment 2 as written, "even state actors who irrationally and maliciously discriminate based on sexual orientation are immune from state legislative, executive, administrative or judicial remedy."

Her argument gained powerful support from a brief filed—on their own behalf, not for any identified interest group—by the nation's five most prominent constitutional scholars, Laurence Tribe, John Hart Ely, Gerald Gunther, Philip Kurland, and Kathleen Sullivan. The names of Gunther and particularly Kurland

carried particular weight because they were known to be moderates, even conservatives, on the question of judicial activism. The
law professors' brief described Amendment 2 as a "rare" example of
a "per se" denial of equal protection because it "flatly excludes
some of a state's people from eligibility for legal protection from a
category of wrongs."

The impact of the law professors' brief became clear when Justice
Kennedy's first questions at the oral argument echoed its theme, saying that the amendment was "adopted to fence out" gays and lesbians "for all purposes, and I've never seen a statute like that."
O'Connor too stressed the breadth of Amendment 2's terms, using
the example of the library that refused to lend books to gays.

The justices voted six to three to find Amendment 2 unconstitutional. Stevens, the senior associate justice with the majority, had the
right to decide who would write the opinion, and he astutely chose
Kennedy, who was outraged by Amendment 2's sweep.

Kennedy signaled the importance he gave the case in his opinion's
first sentences: "One century ago, the first Justice Harlan admon-
ished this Court that the Constitution 'neither knows nor tolerates
classes among citizens.' Unheeded then, those words are now understood to state a commitment to the law's neutrality where the rights
of persons are at stake." Kennedy was quoting from Harlan's *dissent*
when the Supreme Court upheld Louisiana's law requiring racial
segregation on trains. The opinion was released almost one hundred
years to the day after that notorious decision had ratified racial segregation, and Kennedy surely appreciated the symbolism of the date
and of his quotation.

Everything after that was pretty much anticlimax. Kennedy went
through Amendment 2 to show how broad it was, concluding that it
couldn't fairly be interpreted to be aimed only at denying gays and
lesbians "special rights." The heart of Kennedy's constitutional
analysis was that Amendment 2 was so much broader than any reason that the state offered for it that the only explanation for its
adoption was sheer hostility to gays and lesbians and that previous
decisions established that this kind of "animus" was never enough
to justify legislation. Kennedy said that it was "central" to "our constitutional tradition" that every unit of government "remain open

on impartial terms to all who seek its assistance." In part to ensure
that O'Connor would join it, the opinion didn't even mention the
Hardwick case, despite the argument Colorado's lawyers had made
that the state could try to reduce homosexuality by a less drastic
method than criminalizing sodomy. Kennedy's opinion ended with
another powerful bit of rhetoric: "A State cannot so deem a class of
persons strangers to its laws."

Scalia's vigorous dissent was shot through with disparaging comments about Kennedy's opinion, which Scalia said was "long on
emotive utterance" and "short on relevant legal citation," "barely
pretend[ed] to" have a "foundation in American constitutional law,"
and invented a "novel and extravagant constitutional doctrine."

As Scalia saw it, Amendment 2 was "a modest attempt by seemingly tolerant Coloradans to preserve traditional sexual mores
against the efforts of a politically powerful minority to revise those
mores through use of the laws." The equal protection claim in the
case was that gays and lesbians were discriminated against simply
because it was harder for them than for others to "obtain preferen-
tial treatment under the laws." If the Court really was buying that
proposition, "our constitutional jurisprudence has achieved terminal silliness."

For Scalia, gays weren't an oppressed minority. In certain cities
they had "high disposable income" and used their political clout to
get local ordinances favoring them. Well and good, but, Scalia continued, people in the rest of the state should be allowed to respond
through politics. The courts had "no business" taking sides in the
culture war over gay rights. When they do, he said, they will "be with
the knights rather than the villains—and more specifically with the
Templars, the views and values of the lawyer class from which the
Court's Members are drawn." At that point Scalia went off on a tan-
gent, mentioning the policy of the Association of American Law
Schools making law school employment services available only to
employers who signed a statement saying that they didn't discriminate on the basis of race, gender, or sexual orientation. Scalia clearly
had a bee in his bonnet about this policy, but to make his point
about the lawyer class, all he had to do was mention the brief supporting the attack on Amendment 2 filed by more than a dozen state
bar associations. Perhaps Scalia felt betrayed not only by the "lawyer

class" of which he was a member but by the "academic class" of which he used to be a member.

∽

As one law clerk put it, the Court's decision in the Colorado case "kind of level[ed] the playing field." It was the first gay rights victory, with a solid majority. The next step was to get a do-over of the antisodomy decision from 1986. Gays and lesbians got their chance when a state prosecutor made the mistake of bringing a case against two gay men for engaging in consensual sodomy at home.

In 1998 Roger Nance called the Houston police and reported that a crazy man was waving a gun in an apartment near his. The police came to investigate. There was no disturbance, but they discovered John Lawrence and Tyron Garner engaged in anal intercourse. They arrested the men for violating Texas's antisodomy law. Lawrence and Garner pleaded no contest and were fined two hundred dollars. (Nance, described in some reports as a disgruntled neighbor and in others as Lawrence's former lover, later pleaded guilty to making a false report to the police and was sentenced to thirty days in jail.)

Lawrence and Garner appealed, represented by Mitchell Katine, a local lawyer who had represented members of Houston's gay community for many years. At first a panel of the appeals court agreed with Katine, whose argument had relied on the equal protection clause and the Colorado case. Texas's statute, unlike Georgia's, made only homosexual sodomy an offense, and the panel agreed that making something a crime when committed by men but not when committed by a man and a woman amounted to discrimination based on gender. Local Republican party officials circulated a letter criticizing the elected judges who reversed the convictions. The full appeals court agreed to rehear the case and then affirmed the convictions.

Gay rights advocates knew that this was a near-perfect case to take to the Supreme Court. They could make the equal protection argument, which would get rid of the Texas statute, but they decided to go for the big win too by asking the Court to overrule the Georgia decision.

It was widely known within the Court for several years before the Lawrence case got there that Justice Kennedy wanted to overrule *Bowers v. Hardwick,* and once the Court took the case the outcome was inevitable. The state's oral argument didn't help its case. Charles

Rosenthal of the Houston district attorney's office made what was widely regarded as the worst oral argument in years, although probably his argument was so bad at least in part because his heart wasn't really in it.

Scalia did his best to help Rosenthal out, to the point where Rehnquist interjected, "Maybe we should go through counsel," when Scalia started to answer a question another justice posed. Rosenthal sometimes seemed not to realize that Scalia was making his argument for him. Scalia pushed Rosenthal to say that public views about homosexuality hadn't changed since the Hardwick decision in 1986, and Rosenthal answered that a number of state legislatures had "changed their position on sodomy" through legislation, showing that public perception had indeed changed, hardly what Scalia wanted to hear.

Decorum in the courtroom usually keeps the audience from openly snickering too often, but Rosenthal's argument was punctuated with laughter—not because anyone had made a joke but because his answers were so inept. The argument deteriorated to the point that one justice managed to ask Rosenthal if he was certain that gays couldn't "procreate children." Spectators laughed as well when Justice Breyer asked Rosenthal for a "straight answer" to one of his questions. (Later Breyer expressed puzzlement about why people had laughed.)

The decision was announced at the end of June 2003. Six justices agreed that the Texas statute was unconstitutional. O'Connor, who had voted with the majority in the Hardwick case, focused on the equal protection question, but Kennedy's opinion for the Court took on the central issue and overruled *Bowers v. Hardwick*. The robust opinion was filled with references to the dignity of gays and their right to treatment as equal citizens of the United States.

It began with a libertarian theme: "Liberty protects the person from unwarranted government intrusion into a dwelling or other private places. In our tradition the State is not omnipresent in the home." Turning to the Hardwick decision, Kennedy wrote that the Court "disclose[d]" its "failure to appreciate the extent of the liberty at stake" when it asked if there was a fundamental right to engage in homosexual sodomy. The Court's earlier formulation "demeans the claim the individual put forward, just as it would demean a married couple were it to be said marriage is simply about the right to have sexual intercourse." What mattered was whether the government's criminal laws allowed people to "retain their dignity as free persons." Kennedy continued, "When sexuality finds overt expression in intimate conduct with another person, the conduct can be but one element in a personal bond that is more enduring." The Constitution, he said, allowed people "the right to make this choice."

After a long and largely unpersuasive explanation of why the historical record didn't show a long tradition of social condemnation of homosexual sodomy, Kennedy turned to "an emerging awareness," which should have been apparent in 1986, that "liberty gives substantial protection to adult persons in deciding how to conduct their private lives in matters pertaining to sex." And after a quotation from Stevens's dissent in the Hardwick case, Kennedy said that Stevens's analysis "should have been controlling then." *Hardwick* "was not correct when it was decided, and it is not correct today," Kennedy concluded.

He then devoted a paragraph to defending against the charge, made by Pennsylvania Senator Rick Santorum (among others) while the case was pending, that ruling for Lawrence would mean that laws against incest, bestiality, and adultery were unconstitutional and would lead to constitutional protection for gay marriages. Kennedy's answers were basically that *Lawrence* didn't involve those problems. It involved "two adults who, with full and mutual consent from each other, engaged in sexual practices common to a homosexual lifestyle."

Kennedy ended with a flourish. The Constitution's authors "knew times can blind us to certain truths and later generations can see that laws once thought necessary and proper serve only to oppress. As the Constitution endures, persons in every generation can invoke its principles in their own search for greater freedom."

Scalia was no more splenetic than usual, perhaps because he knew that the Lawrence case was merely the other shoe dropping after the Colorado decision. The Lawrence decision, he said, cast doubt on state laws "against bigamy, same-sex marriage, adult incest, prostitution, masturbation, adultery, fornication, bestiality, and obscenity" because those laws too rested on the state's judgment that the activities were immoral. (Criticizing a decision for implying that laws against masturbation were unconstitutional doesn't seem likely to win many votes among the public that made *American Pie* a smash hit.)

Scalia concluded by describing the decision as "the product of a Court, which is the product of a law-profession culture, that has largely signed on to the so-called homosexual agenda, by which I mean the agenda promoted by some homosexual activists directed at eliminating the moral opprobrium that has traditionally attached to homosexual conduct." He referred to "the law profession's anti-anti-homosexual culture."

He told readers, "Do not believe it," when Kennedy said that the case didn't raise questions about gay marriage. That was a "bald, unreasoning disclaimer" that couldn't overcome the implications of the Court's earlier references to marriage as one of the personal decisions for which gays "seek autonomy . . . just as heterosexual persons do." The majority's analysis meant that mere moral disapproval couldn't justify limiting gays' rights, but if that was so, Scalia said, "what justification could there possibly be for denying the benefits of marriage" to gays?

This time Scalia translated *Kulturkampf*, writing again that "the Court has taken sides in the culture war, departing from its role of assuring, as neutral observer, that the democratic rules of engagement are observed." One sentence of his opinion was widely quoted in a truncated, and misleading, form. The sentence began, "Let me be clear that I have nothing against homosexuals," which was quoted as showing that he was personally tolerant. The full sentence, though, was: "I have nothing against homosexuals, or any other group, promoting their agenda through normal democratic means." *Homosexuals* wasn't the object of the phrase "nothing against homosexuals"; it was the subject of the phrase *homosexuals . . . promoting their agenda*. Scalia didn't see his job as fighting in the culture war, but there was no doubt on which side he would fight.

&

In a generally admiring portrait of Anthony Kennedy, Jeffrey Rosen said that Kennedy's "only visible personal vice appears to be a weakness for innocent pomp." After the terrorist attacks on September 11, 2001, Kennedy took an active part in educational programs directed at high school and college students to enhance their understanding of democracy. He thought of himself as an academic, priding himself on the summer courses he taught in Europe and his experience as a part-time teacher when he was a lawyer and lobbyist in California, where he occasionally dressed up as James Madison to teach his course in constitutional law. His post–September 11 exercises brought the law school style to younger students. Kennedy asked them to imagine that they were stuck in a very poor country where a charismatic political leader "preaches that the decadent United States should be destroyed." He asked the students "whether it was right to let people in other nations choose dictatorships." Someone who attended one of the sessions rejected the suggestion that his manner was probably unbearably pompous, hesitating before saying that the *unbearably* was perhaps a bit strong.

Kennedy grew into the public pomposity he displayed. He was raised in Sacramento, the middle son of a father whose law practice included a fair amount of lobbying for tobacco and liquor companies. He was a "shy, bookish boy" whose father, joking about Kennedy's restraint, once offered him a prize of one hundred dollars "if he would do something to get arrested by the police." Kennedy took up his father's lobbying practice following his father's death shortly after Kennedy graduated from Harvard Law School. He was, however, "a bashful lobbyist," unlike his gladhanding, backslapping father.

Kennedy responded to an expression of interest by Edwin Meese, then serving as California Governor Ronald Reagan's chief of staff, in locating someone to draft a tax reduction ballot initiative. The initiative failed, but Meese was impressed with Kennedy's work and sponsored him for an appointment to the federal court of appeals in 1975. Reflecting years later on his first judicial position, which he got when he was only thirty-eight years old, Kennedy thought that he had actually been too young to be a good judge because "you don't see real people" as a judge and "you might not recognize your own limitations." The lawyers who practiced in front of him found him "courteous, stern on the bench, somewhat conservative, bright, well prepared, filled with nervous energy" and "hard to peg, an enigma, tends to agonize over opinions."

President Reagan nominated Robert Bork for the vacancy created by Lewis Powell's resignation in 1987. Bork was a hero among conservative constitutional scholars, and his nomination threatened to move the Court sharply to the right. Liberal interest groups mobilized against the nomination, which eventually failed by a vote of 58 to 42. Then Reagan announced his intention to nominate the court of appeals judge Douglas Ginsburg to the Powell vacancy. Ginsburg's main appeal, in addition to his conservative credentials, was his youth (he was only forty-one). Reagan's intention was quickly abandoned after Nina Totenberg of National Public Radio discovered that Ginsburg had smoked marijuana at a party with some of his students at Harvard Law School (and after some conservatives expressed concern that Ginsburg's wife, a doctor, had performed abortions). Kennedy, who had been on the list of potential nominees for several years, was Reagan's third choice.

Kennedy reproduced in Washington the disciplined life he led in Sacramento, arriving early at the office but making time for the embassy party circuit in Washington, which he enjoyed immensely, and for theatergoing. He was something of a Shakespeare freak, organizing excursions to performances of Shakespeare's plays. He once commented that one performance was too homoerotic for his taste, indicating both that he was an attentive viewer of the performance and that he was a cultural conservative.

The invitations to embassy parties fed into Kennedy's growing sense of his own public importance, although he remained quite unpretentious when he was not onstage. The party circuit in itself didn't change him. He met people from all over the world, and thought them "fascinating conversationalists," but what they had to say only confirmed for him his confidence in the correctness of America's values. Still, the simple fact of his being invited to embassy parties showed Kennedy how important he was, as did all the news stories emphasizing his key position on a divided Supreme Court.

⁂

In *Lawrence*, Kennedy relied on international authority to rebut Burger's contention in the Georgia case that governments had regulated homosexual conduct "throughout the history of Western civilization" and that "condemnation of those practices is firmly rooted in Judaeo-Christian moral and ethical standards." Kennedy referred to a major decision of the European Court of Human Rights in 1981, holding that bans on consensual homosexual conduct were violations of the fundamental human rights in the European Convention on Human Rights. That decision, he wrote, was "at odds with the premise . . . that the claim put forward was insubstantial in our Western civilization."

The reference signaled the Court's increasing interest in constitutional developments outside the United States. Ginsburg, whose first job after law school involved a study of Swedish procedural law, was sympathetic to drawing on those developments. She opened her opinion in the Michigan affirmative action cases with a paragraph observing that the majority's insistence that affirmative action have some end point "accords with the international understanding of the office of affirmative action," citing the International Conventions on the Elimination of All Forms of Racial Discrimination and of Discrimination Against Women. Rehnquist himself gave several speeches asserting that "it is time that the United States courts begin looking to the decisions of other constitutional courts to aid in their own deliberative process."

Scalia strenuously objected to this development. He called the discussion of the European Court of Human Rights's decision "meaningless dicta." When anti–death penalty activists argued that the international condemnation of the death penalty for people who were under seventeen when they committed their crimes showed that the death penalty was cruel and unusual punishment, Scalia insisted that the Constitution embodied "*American* conceptions of decency," not international ones.

When the Court struck down the death penalty for persons with mental retardation because the practice was inconsistent with an American consensus about who should be eligible for capital punishment, Stevens's opinion for the majority contained a modest footnote simply observing that "within the world community, the imposition of the death penalty for crimes committed by mentally retarded offenders is overwhelmingly disapproved." Scalia again derided the effort: "[T]he Prize for the Court's Most Feeble Effort to fabricate 'national consensus' must go to its appeal (deservedly relegated to a footnote) to the views of . . . the so-called 'world community.' " That community's views were irrelevant, he observed, adding that its "notions of justice are (thankfully) not always those of our people."

Despite Scalia's sarcasm, the justices became more sensitive to the world's community of constitutional judges as the Rehnquist Court ended. Anne-Marie Slaughter, the dean of Princeton's Woodrow Wilson School, observed that the international community was increasingly characterized by cross-border networks of activists and government officials. The Supreme Court's justices were part of a network of constitutional judges that was invigorated by the expansion of constitutional courts around the world in the 1990s.

Calling these arrangements networks may suggest that they are more formal than they really are. Constitutional court justices get together at conferences regularly sponsored by New York University Law School and Yale Law School. Some foreign justices, notably Aharon Barak of Israel and Dieter Grimm of Germany, are distinguished participants in general discussions of judicial review. In 2003 the justices' law clerks had an organized meeting with the young men and women who were serving as law clerks to the justices of Canada's Supreme Court. In that same year, for the first time a U.S. Supreme Court justice took as his law clerk someone whose prior experience was as a law clerk on the Canadian Supreme Court.

The effects of these networks were barely visible in the Rehnquist Court's later years. Still, the fact that several U.S. justices regularly hung out with constitutional court judges from other nations was bound to have some influence, if only because the justices wanted to preserve the reputation of the U.S. Supreme Court as the world's preeminent constitutional court. The interest within the Court in comparative constitutional law was likely to grow.

৩৩

Kennedy's concern for his public persona is suggested by the views of a former Kennedy law clerk, recounted by Rosen: Kennedy "would constantly refer to how it's going to be perceived, how the papers are going to do it, how it's going to look." For a while he appeared to have entertained thoughts of being promoted to chief justice when Rehnquist retired, but his part in abortion rights, school prayer, and gay rights cases disqualified him among Republican legal activists.

But neither career aspirations nor the Greenhouse Effect explain how Kennedy approached his work. He did what he did, and voted as he did, because he thought that was what a judge applying the Constitution should do.

Conservatives were initially uncertain about Kennedy, primarily because they had lost their hero Bork and didn't know what they had gotten instead. "Bork was perfect," one said, "Kennedy is merely good." His first years on the Court reassured conservatives. As one conservative activist put it in 1989, "Anthony Kennedy's performance on the Supreme Court is what all those raving lunatics who opposed Bob Bork deserve. What's so wonderful about it is that he is so young and healthy." Their enthusiasm wouldn't last.

No one knows yet exactly where Kennedy got his commitment to gay rights from. During Kennedy's nomination hearing, Tom Stoddard, a highly respected gay rights litigator, said that it would be "very difficult for any gay person to read Judge Kennedy's opinions and depart with anything other than distress and some degree of anger." Perhaps the opinions Stoddard read concealed a more tolerant attitude Kennedy had picked up while living in California. Louis Michael Seidman suggested that Kennedy's "moderate Republicanism was characterized by the kind of genial openness and sensible good will exemplified in the personality of [California's] Earl Warren himself."

The difficulty for conservatives was that Kennedy's conservatism centered on a moderate libertarian streak, about which he himself was somewhat conflicted, complemented by a vague optimism about the good sense of the American people. The libertarian streak inclined him to be suspicious of laws that licensed the government to intrude on people's private lives. That led him to a strong position in favor of free speech.

Yet Kennedy's libertarian streak conflicted with his optimism about the American people. That optimism meant that he wanted to uphold the judgments the people made through their governments, which no libertarian could do. Kennedy also understood, probably because of his work as a lobbyist, that the libertarian yearning for a sharply reduced government was entirely utopian. Big government was here to stay, and Kennedy knew it. Finally, his years of teaching constitutional law taught him about the limits on the role of judges. The limits were practical; if judges went too far, the political system would slap them down. The limits were rooted in democratic theory as well; a sensible people ought to be allowed to make their own decisions without the close supervision of judges enforcing the Constitution. Reconciling all this into a coherent jurisprudence was impossible. Instead, Kennedy reverted to rhetoric alone.

Kennedy's pomposity was mostly harmless. It affected the rhetoric he used, though. His opinion in the flag burning case, like many of his opinions, was written to be quoted, not analyzed. Its confusion is almost transparent. Unlike Scalia, Kennedy felt compelled to add something to what Brennan said because, he wrote, the case "exacts its personal toll." Here are three sentences that come one after the other in Kennedy's opinion: "The outcome can be laid at no door but ours. The hard fact is that sometimes we must make decisions we do not like. We make them because they are right, right in the sense that the law and the Constitution, as we see them, compel the result." So, to get this right, he's saying, "Letting Joey Johnson go free is our decision, ours alone, and we have to take responsibility for it. But of course we don't really take responsibility for it because the Constitution compels us to do it." This is not a really attractive description of heroic Supreme Court decision making, although at the time Kennedy pretty clearly thought it was. Later Kennedy speculated that he hadn't made the right choice in publishing the opinion, because of "this hand-wringing thing." He continued, "I thought you were supposed to defend the speech clause. . . . Why all the crybaby stuff?"

Kennedy didn't like the *Crossfire* style, saying that "it destroys a sense of community and a sense of mission and a sense of purpose." Then, reaching, he connected the "fractious" and "adversarial tone" of the *Crossfire* style to what he thought was a deeper truth, adding, "And a nation has to have a sense of purpose." But Kennedy's own efforts to elevate discourse took the form of writing phrases that weren't sound bites but were designed as "Quotes of the Day" for the *New York Times*. The phrases sound as if they mean something when you first read them, but a moment's reflection—reflection that ordinary citizens ought to be expected to engage in—leads to the discovery that they actually don't.

Designed to connect the Supreme Court through the persona of Anthony Kennedy to the ordinary citizens the justices never really see face-to-face, Kennedy's rhetoric actually distanced the above-it-all orator from the people more often than it should have. But as the character named Grandfather says in the movie *Little Big Man*, sometimes the magic works. The Castro District is in the center of San Francisco's gay community. For years there's been a huge rainbow Gay Pride flag flying over the neighborhood's main intersection. The day after Kennedy's opinion in the Texas gay rights case was released, the rainbow flag came down, to be replaced (for a day) by a huge American flag.

CHAPTER SEVEN

The Religious Right's Agenda —Symbols and Money

Santa Fe, Texas, was a suitable battleground on one front in the culture wars. With a population of about ten thousand, the town, incorporated only in the late 1970s, was a working-class suburb on the outskirts of Galveston. In 1981 the Ku Klux Klan held a cross burning in Santa Fe, and in 1997 some teenagers surrounded a busload of African Americans who had come to Santa Fe for a basketball game and threatened them with lynching. Not surprisingly, the 1990 census found only nine African Americans living there. At the end of the decade there was only one Jewish child in the town's schools, and he was regularly threatened and harassed, once being told that Hitler had "missed one" and later, "We're going to hang you, you dirty Jew."

In 1995 two parents—one Catholic, one Mormon—became disturbed by the religion they saw pervading the public schools. Some children were called un-Christian when they refused to accept free Bibles. A teacher berated a Mormon student for being a cult member. Prayers were said at school graduations and football games. Anticipating a suit, the school board changed some of its policies and reprimanded the teacher who called Mormonism a cult. Still, harassment of Catholics and Mormons continued. Objecting to the board's policy changes, one parent said, "Catholics aren't Christians anyway."

The two parents sued the Santa Fe school board, listing eleven school activities they said violated the Constitution's ban on establishments of religion. One was that the school board arranged for prayers to be said at high school football games. The women filed the lawsuits as Jane Doe #1 and #2 because they feared retaliation against them and their children if their names became known. The anonymity didn't help a lot. Because some ministers exhorted their congregations to find out who the plaintiffs were, every Catholic and Mormon became the object of speculation, and some were harassed.

Federal Judge Sam Kent separated the football game prayer issue from the others. He said that such prayers would be constitutional if they weren't religious "sales-pitches." The school board didn't like the restriction, so it changed its policy. Instead of sponsoring the prayer itself, it allowed students to vote on two questions. Should there be "an invocation and/or message" at the start of football games, and who should deliver it? (Later the board rephrased the first election issue, dropping the word *invocation*, but everyone knew that in Santa Fe an elected speaker would indeed deliver a prayer.) The board thought this would change the constitutional contours of the issue. Parents who objected might be seen as interfering with the rights of the students to express themselves, violating their right of free speech, rather than as objecting to the school board's establishment of religion.

Judge Kent eventually ruled against the school board in the larger lawsuit. The board appealed but suffered a worse loss in the court of appeals, which said that the board couldn't allow prayers at high school football games, which, the judges wrote, "are hardly the sober type of annual event that can be appropriately solemnized with prayer."

Marian Ward was the deeply devout daughter of a Baptist minister in Santa Fe. She was outraged at what she saw as the courts' effort to take religion out of school. "If I'm given a public platform," she said, "I must glorify God, even if the courts say otherwise." Her schoolmates voted in favor of having a speaker at football games and then elected a Catholic girl as speaker. Probably overreacting to the lawsuit, the school principal, Gary Causey, kept at the elected speaker, repeatedly pointing out that she couldn't deliver a prayer or even mention God. If she did, Causey said, she might be expelled. Eventually the elected speaker decided that it wasn't worth the hassle to continue and withdrew.

Marian Ward had come in second in the election, and she wasn't one to be deterred. Causey was as aggressive with her as he had been with the first speaker. He met with her several times in the days preceding the first football game, and her teachers told her that Causey might lose his job if she delivered a prayer. Ward and her parents decided to take the initiative. They hired a lawyer who got federal Judge Sim Lake to bar the district from punishing Marian if she delivered a prayer at the football game. Marian got word of the order as she was dressing in her band uniform just before the game started.

The crowd roared as Marian approached the microphone. "Lord, thank you for this evening," she said. "I pray that you watch over each and every person here tonight, especially those involved in the game, that they will demonstrate good sportsmanship, Lord, and that we'll have safety." She ended with the traditional "In Jesus' name, I pray. Amen."

∽

Marian Ward's prayer was part of the Religious Right's response to the Warren Court, which held that public school teachers could not direct their students in organized prayer because that violated the Constitution's ban on laws "respecting an establishment of religion." To religious conservatives, the Warren Court's decisions took God out of the schools. They mobilized to put God back in, trying a variety of techniques for getting public endorsement of religious symbols: graduation prayers, displays of the Ten Commandments, and more.

The Warren Court's desegregation decisions had a more complicated relation to the rise of the Religious Right. White southerners opposed to desegregation initially organized private schools for their children. The Internal Revenue Service eventually started to threaten these so-called white academies with loss of their tax-exempt status, important in keeping their tuitions relatively low. The segregation academies were gradually transformed into religious schools, offering prayers and curricular approaches, such as teaching creationism rather than evolution, that were unavailable in the public schools. The Religious Right then began to seek public support for these private schools. It urged state legislatures to adopt school voucher programs, giving public money to parents for tuition at private schools.

Warren Court precedents suggested that making vouchers available for use at religiously affiliated schools violated the establishment clause. The Religious Right had to combine its campaign for legislation allowing school vouchers with a campaign in the courts to make sure that vouchers would be held constitutional.

The Religious Right pretty much lost its battles in the Rehnquist Court over religious symbols in public life. It pretty much won its battles for public money to support religion. This combination of outcomes posed interesting political problems for the Religious Right. You can never run out of symbolic battles to fight, but taxpayers can run out of money. The Religious Right's defeats over symbols left it on the field of battle, with new symbols replacing the ones the courts had taken out of public life. Its victories in cases involving public money meant that it could *try* to get more money for more expansive school voucher programs. Suburban taxpayers, happy with the schools they sent their children to, were unlikely to support voucher programs large enough to satisfy the Religious Right's demands. Its constitutional victories, then, were likely to turn to ashes in its mouth, while its defeats allowed its supporters to continue to mobilize against the courts.

This combination of results was pretty good politically for the Republican Party, because the Religious Right could be mobilized to support Republican policies in favor of vouchers and against overreaching federal judges. The results had a political downside, though. At some point the Religious Right might realize that Republicans weren't delivering on their promises of victories over symbols or on their promises of voucher programs that actually were extensive enough to support the religious schools attended by the children of the Religious Right's most active supporters.

⊘

The Warren Court said that schools couldn't open their days with prayers conducted by teachers. Some states responded by enacting moment of silence laws, which ordered teachers to start the school day by directing students to take a minute or two in silence. The Burger Court struck down one moment of silence law, which specifically said that the moment of silence could be used "for meditation or silent prayer." It did indicate that pure moment of silence laws didn't violate the Constitution, and many school systems used moments of silence to substitute for prayer.

The school prayer cases became one of the building blocks for *Lemon v. Kurtzman*, decided by the Burger Court in 1971, which the Religious Right took as a major target. According to Burger, the school prayer cases showed that state laws that had the purpose of "advancing" religion were unconstitutional. That's clearly correct. The problem, though, is that it's easy to come up with nonreligious purposes for all sorts of practices that advance religion anyway. A prayer at the beginning of the school day calms the kids down and brings home to them the seriousness of the tasks that they face; posting the Ten Commandments in classrooms is a way of educating children in the historical sources of contemporary legal codes. Yet there's some awkwardness when defenders of religion in public life have to argue that the practices they support actually don't have the purpose of advancing religion.

Overstating the importance of *any* so-called test, the Religious Right mistakenly thought that the Lemon test stood as a real obstacle to accomplishing its goals. The details of the Lemon test are irrelevant, however, because the Rehnquist Court never relied on it to find a statute unconstitutional. A majority of the justices on the Rehnquist Court said—in different cases—that they disagreed with the Lemon test, although no Court opinion formally repudiated it. The test was, as Justice Scalia said in 1993, something like "a ghoul in a late-night horror movie that repeatedly sits up in its grave and shuffles abroad, after being repeatedly killed and buried." The only people the Lemon test frightened were members of the Religious Right. No one on the Rehnquist Court thought that the Lemon test mattered.

The Burger Court dealt with other symbols. In one of its most derided opinions, it upheld the display of a crèche by the city of Pawtucket, Rhode Island. The display did not violate the Constitution, according to Burger, because it had to be considered in its "proper context," which included a Santa Claus display, complete with reindeer and sleigh, candy-striped poles, and other of the ordinary commercial accoutrements of commercialized Christmas in the United States. One secular conservative called Burger's opinion "sleazy" because it "demean[ed] the religion of those who erected it."

O'Connor used the crèche case to articulate her own approach to establishment clause questions. The government, she said, couldn't make "adherence to a religion relevant in any way to a person's standing in the political community." That meant that the government couldn't "endorse" religion because doing so "sends a message to nonadherents that they are outsiders, not full members of the political community." Most constitutional scholars think that O'Connor is on to something important here, but they are skeptical about whether courts can actually implement the endorsement approach sensibly. O'Connor herself said that no reasonable person would regard the crèche as an endorsement of Christianity, an assertion that came as a surprise to many Jews who thought they were reasonable in doing so.

The Religious Right started a Hang Ten campaign to get the Ten Commandments displayed on public property all over the country. Lower courts tried to figure out whether that was an endorsement of religion. They ended up with some peculiar distinctions: Displays that had been on public property for a long time weren't endorsements of religion according to some courts, but new ones were. The difficulties with O'Connor's endorsement test made other doctrinal options attractive.

Kennedy came up with one that, like O'Connor's, made sense in the abstract but was hard to apply in practice. According to Kennedy, the government couldn't coerce people into religious activities. That's certainly a large part of what the history of the establishment clause is about, and the anticoercion principle is generally uncontroversial. Applying it is another matter.

Daniel and Vivian Weisman, trained as social workers, were so proud of engaging in quixotic quests that they used "The Impossible Dream" from the musical *Man of La Mancha* as the first song at their wedding reception and later bought a sculpture of Don Quixote to put in their yard. Vivian Weisman was a plaintiff in a 1982 suit challenging a crèche in their hometown of Providence, Rhode Island. Four years later the Weismans were at their daughter Merith's graduation from the Nathan Bishop Middle School. A Baptist minister ended the graduation prayer by asking everyone in the audience to stand up and observe a moment of silence to thank Jesus. Daniel Weisman, a nonobservant Jew, later said that though he did stand up, he felt "absolutely humiliated." He complained to the school's principal, then forgot about it—until three years later, when a second Weisman daughter was about to graduate from Nathan Bishop. Weisman sent a note to Robert E. Lee, the school's principal, mentioning his concerns about prayer at the graduation.

Lee came up with what he thought was a compromise, inviting Rabbi Leslie Gutterman to deliver the invocation and benediction at the graduation ceremony. He also gave Rabbi Gutterman some "Guidelines for Civic Occasions," developed by the National Conference of Christians and Jews. The Weismans thought that Lee hadn't quite got the point of their concern. Providence, they observed, had a diverse student population, and its Christian students and their families might be offended by a prayer offered by a rabbi, its Jewish students and their families offended by a prayer offered by a Christian minister, and its Buddhist students and their families—from the city's growing Asian community—offended by any prayer at all. The Weismans filed suit four days before the graduation. Without time to consider the case fully, the judge allowed Rabbi Gutterman to participate in the graduation ceremony.

The rabbi did his best. His prayers were about as bland as they could be. The invocation thanked the "God of the Free, Hope of the Brave" for "the legacy of America," including diversity and protection of minority rights. His benediction began, "O God, we are grateful to you for having endowed us with the capacity for learning which we have celebrated on this joyous commencement" and ended, "We give thanks to You, Lord, for keeping us alive, sustaining us and allowing us to reach this special, happy occasion." Nonsectarian indeed, although also clearly religious in content.

The lower courts held that having a religious component in school graduations violated the establishment clause. The Providence school board hired Charles Cooper, a prominent conservative attorney, to prepare its appeal to the Supreme Court, and the George H. W. Bush administration came in on the board's side as well.

The administration hoped to use the case as a vehicle to overturn the Lemon case. At first five justices voted to allow graduation prayer without dealing with that precedent. Justice Kennedy was the least sure of his vote, and Rehnquist assigned the opinon to him in the hope that, as Kennedy wrote, he would get more convinced. Instead,

Kennedy changed his mind, telling his colleagues that his attempt to uphold the prayer "looked quite wrong" when he actually wrote it down. Religion, according to Kennedy's final opinion, was "committed to the private sphere," and the establishment clause gave the government a "duty to guard and respect that sphere of inviolable conscience and belief which is the mark of a free people." It violated that duty when it subjected high school graduates to "subtle coercive pressure" by having Rabbi Gutterman say the prayers at the graduation ceremony. The government was coercing the graduates by placing them in a position either to go along with the prayers or to demonstrate their disagreement in the face of obvious peer pressure to conform. True, students who didn't want to pray could just stand silently, but most people who saw them doing that would think that they were agreeing with the prayer. True, attending graduation was entirely voluntary, and students who objected to the prayers didn't have to go to the ceremony. But, Kennedy said, it was "formalistic in the extreme" to say that a teenager had "a real choice not to attend her high school graduation," which was "one of life's most significant occasions" in American society and culture.

The football game prayer case again raised the question of formalism. The Santa Fe school board of course appealed to the Supreme Court. The appeal raised broad challenges to the appeals court's decision, but the Supreme Court, following a practice it used more and more over the Rehnquist years, rewrote the questions it wanted to hear, limiting the case to whether the football game prayer was constitutional.

The American Center for Law and Justice, founded in 1990 by Pat Robertson, is one of the leading groups litigating for the Religious Right. It adopted its name, abbreviated ACLJ, to evoke the initials of its frequent adversary, the American Civil Liberties Union. By 2000 the ACLJ had a budget of more than ten million dollars, from direct-mail contributions from small donors and grants from the Alliance Defense Fund, a coordinating group for Religious Right litigation. It had a network of over three hundred volunteer attorneys. Its legal director was Jay Sekulow, who converted from Judaism to Christianity as a college student. After his successful tax practice collapsed in the late 1980s because of tax reforms and the end of Atlanta's real estate boom, Sekulow was rescued by Jews for Jesus, which hired him to represent the organization in a successful Supreme Court challenge to a policy that barred the group from distributing pamphlets at the Los Angeles airport.

According to Sekulow, the center monitored the Santa Fe case in the lower courts. The town's school board first asked him to make a presentation after the Supreme Court decided to hear the case and then asked him to represent it in the Court. The Does had Anthony Griffin, an African American lawyer for the American Civil Liberties Union who had been in the national news before. The Texas branch of the NAACP had fired Griffin as its chief outside lawyer after he insisted as an ACLU volunteer lawyer on defending the Ku Klux Klan's right to keep its membership lists secret.

Supreme Court observers had a field day with the football game case. Any fool would know, they said, that football games were part of Texas's religion. Griffin emphasized that high school football games in Texas were "big public events" and, to laughter, that they were "really not all that different from the Inauguration, really."

Stevens wrote the decision finding the prayer unconstitutional, on the ground that the government set up the process by which the student delivering the invocation would be chosen, against a background in which it was clear that the student would give a religious invocation. The establishment clause, he said, was designed "to remove debate over this kind of issue from governmental supervision and control." There was coercion in the case because some students—football players and cheerleaders, for example—had to attend and, more important, because of the "immense social pressure" on other students to attend.

Stevens's point was made even more effective because of a mistake Scalia had made during the oral argument. Scalia jumped on Griffin as soon as he began his argument for the Does, asking why the plaintiffs didn't have the courage to sue under their real names. Could anyone who's "ashamed" of suing "for one reason or another" sue under an assumed name? he asked. Griffin knew an opportunity when he saw one. The trial judge had the power "to protect the plaintiffs . . . from any threat," he replied. Scalia continued: "What was the threat?" Kids had been pushed, Griffin answered, and he hinted that some plaintiffs had received death threats. Scalia subsided for the moment, but he had damaged his cause.

Scalia derided his colleagues in the graduation case for relying on their psychological intuitions about how dissenting high school students would feel when faced with a religious invocation. "[I]nterior decorating is a rock-hard science compared to psychology practiced by amateurs," he wrote. To him, the students certainly weren't coerced into praying. All they had to do was stand silently. "We indeed live in a vulgar age. But surely 'our social conventions' have not coarsened to the point that anyone who does not stand on his chair and shout obscenities can reasonably be deemed to have assented to everything said in his presence." Standing in silence could just as easily be interpreted by reasonable observers as demonstrating simple respect for the religious views of other students, not as agreement with those views. And, Scalia said, being "coerced" to show respect—even if it occurred, as he doubted—didn't violate the Constitution. Scalia's strictures on amateur psychology notwithstanding, "coercion" is inevitably a psychological phenomenon (even a person being tortured can choose to die rather than confess, after all), and most observers thought that the Court's analysis of the psychology of high school graduations and football games in Texas was about right.

The Religious Right didn't give up on trying to get prayers back into the schools. Lower courts struggled with cases in which commencement speakers gave highly sectarian speeches, to the point of urging listeners to become Christians, but had been chosen to speak as class valedictorians, not because of their religious commitments. Other football game cases arose. Some teams said a prayer in a visible huddle just before the game started. Elsewhere students ignored the Court. In one Texas town a student simply seized the microphone and delivered a prayer at a football game. In another, students brought in a portable public-address system and used it to broadcast a prayer.

The Religious Right's campaign over symbols degenerated into farce in 2003. Roy Moore started out as a trial judge in Alabama. He rose to political prominence when lawyers challenged his display of the Ten Commandments in his courtroom. Moore eventually complied with an order that he move the display out of the public courtroom into his private office. The controversy gave him a political base among Alabama's religious conservatives. He used that base in his successful campaign to be elected to the state's supreme court—

as chief justice, no less. Chief Justice Moore ordered that a two-ton granite tablet inscribed with the Ten Commandments be displayed outside the state supreme court's courtroom.

This display was no less unconstitutional than the one in his trial courtroom had been, and the federal courts had no difficulty directing that the display be removed. Moore used the order as an occasion to defy the courts. His supporters threatened to surround the monument and prevent its removal. In the end workers managed to get the monument out of the courthouse's public areas. Moore took the case to the U.S. Supreme Court, which was having nothing to do with his defiance and refused to hear his case. His colleagues on the state supreme court, embarrassed by Moore's antics, supported his removal from the bench on the ground that his defiance of a court order showed that he was unfit to be a judge. No one expected that Moore was gone from Alabama politics, though.

The jokes in the football case raise questions for the Religious Right. Prayers opening the school day, common in the 1950s, might be more or less serious religious exercises (although, as one cartoonist put it, "As long as there are pop quizzes in math, there will be prayer in the schools"). As prayer was pushed out of schools, the Religious Right tried to get it back in by working on the margins—commencement addresses and athletic events. The campaign came close to trivializing the religious content of the prayers they wanted said. Even Jay Sekulow managed to make a joke about religion at football games. Responding to one justice's suggestion that it would obviously be unconstitutional for the prayer opening the game to be a Hail Mary, Sekulow replied that a Hail Mary at a football game would "probably be appropriate."

Scalia said in the graduation prayer case that the Pledge of Allegiance, with its reference to "one nation under God," was "the next project for the Court's bulldozer." Indeed, a lower court did plow the pledge under, a decision that reached the Supreme Court in 2004. Symbols, it seems, are inexhaustible.

℘

The Religious Right's cases had less and less real religious content as their lawyers tried to adapt to the Court's decisions. A crèche wasn't really religious because it was part of a commercialized Christmas;

graduation prayers were all right if they were nonsectarian; prayers at football games—well, no one could take them seriously. The Rehnquist Court's cases about money also ended up turning on ignoring the distinctively religious aspects of religious practices.

Many lawyers for the Religious Right shared the Santa Fe school board's instinct that it would help their cause to convert cases about religion into cases about speech. They believed that the American public, and certainly Supreme Court justices, had deeper commitments to free speech than they did to religious practices and indeed that many elite lawyers were actively hostile to religion's involvement in public life. Presenting their cases as free speech cases made it more likely that they could win the cases.

The Santa Fe case suggested the strategy. Present the religious exercise as a speech made by an individual, not as one endorsed by the government. Then point out that the school—or some other government body—let people say something political, or nonreligious, or sometimes even antireligious. Surely the government couldn't discriminate *against* religious speech.

The only answer governments could give was that they were trying to avoid violations of the establishment clause. But when lots of school clubs used schoolrooms for their meetings, it was hard to see how anyone would be coerced into going to a meeting of a prayer group and equally hard to see how any reasonable person could interpret the fact that the prayer group met in a schoolroom as government's endorsement of the group.

The doctrinal arguments for the Religious Right were clear and compelling. It had to identify some government program that distributed benefits—access to classrooms after school and, eventually, money—to a wide range of speakers without regard to what the recipients wanted to do with the benefits. It could then require that the government distribute those benefits to religious speakers as well because the government can't discriminate against speech on the basis of the speaker's viewpoint. Also, it could defeat the government's establishment clause defense by noting that the very neutrality it was seeking from the government eliminated concerns about coercion or endorsement.

This strategy led to repeated successes for the Religious Right in the courts, culminating in 2002 with a decision upholding a voucher program that included religious schools. It did have a downside, which some in the Religious Right noted. The lawyers' strategy was to minimize the religious content of religious symbols and to treat religion as one of many "viewpoints" rattling around in American society. More serious adherents of religion wanted to infuse public life with real religion, which wouldn't happen under the lawyers' strategy. The lawyers had the upper hand in the internal struggle within the Religious Right, though.

The most important case arose at the University of Virginia. The student activities fee was used to fund student newspapers and magazines. The school's rules said that the money could be used to support magazines that took political positions. The school wouldn't allow the money to be used for "religious activities," which were defined as activities that primarily promoted "a particular belief in or about a deity or an ultimate reality."

With two friends, Ronald Rosenberger, a devout Christian, founded Wide Awake Productions in 1990, to publish a "magazine of philosophical and religious expression." They were bothered by the way other campus publications treated Christianity. *Wide Awake* magazine included stories about the Christian author C. S. Lewis, crisis pregnancy, eating disorders, and Christian missionary work, all treated from a Christian perspective. Rosenberger wanted to use student activities fund money to pay the printer of *Wide Awake*, but the school refused. It was entitled, it said, to make its own decisions about what type of speech to subsidize. Moreover, even if the free speech clause required it to subsidize *some* publications, the establishment clause allowed it to refuse to subsidize a religious magazine like *Wide Awake*.

Rosenberger went to the Rutherford Institute, one of the Religious Right's litigating groups, based in Charlottesville near the university, to see if it would support a legal challenge. The institute refused, and Rosenberger went ahead using his own lawyers. By the time the case was ready for the Supreme Court, though, Rosenberger's lawyers were, according to one Religious Right lawyer, "out of steam." The Alliance Defense Fund stepped in to help finance the Supreme Court appeal. The network of Religious Right lawyers got Michael McConnell, probably the most respected academic associated with the Religious Right, to argue the case in the Supreme Court.

The Court supported Rosenberger. Kennedy's opinion agreed that the university had the power to decide what *it* wanted to say, but, he wrote, it had created a "limited public forum" by setting up the student activities fund. The university wasn't speaking in that forum; its students were. And the university couldn't discriminate in access to that forum on the basis of the viewpoints magazines took.

Here Kennedy relied on well-established doctrine. For free speech purposes, public forums are places like public streets and parks. The Court has held that governments have to make these places available for demonstrations and the like. It can't pick and choose who can use the spaces on the basis of some judgment about what they want to say. Limited purpose forums are different. Here the doctrine is the same as that in Viktora's hate speech case. Governments can restrict access to limited public forums on the basis of the general type of speech potential users plan to make, but they can't restrict access on the basis of the viewpoints being expressed.

Was *Wide Awake* a magazine with a particular subject matter, religion? If it was, maybe the university could refuse to pay the magazine's printer from the activities fund. Or was it a magazine that addressed a lot of different subjects from a particular viewpoint, a religious one? If so, the university couldn't refuse to pay the printer's bill.

Kennedy said that *Wide Awake* offered a religious viewpoint on general subjects. Souter's dissent argued that this distorted the idea of *viewpoint*: It would be unconstitutional to prohibit Christian advocacy but not Jewish advocacy, but, he said, the university could prohibit *all* religious advocacy. Kennedy responded that the university would be skewing its students' access to perspectives if it paid for printing magazines offering secular viewpoints on crisis pregnancies but not those offering religious ones. That seems right, but it's worth noting that the effect is to blur distinctions among religions, which, as the disparagement of Mormons in Santa Fe shows, are really important to people who take their own religions seriously. Again, the constitutional doctrine needed to advance the Religious Right's immediate goals weakened the public support for the specific religious commitments of people in the Religious Right.

That weakening was precisely what made subsidizing *Wide Awake* constitutional under the establishment clause. What mattered to the majority was that the student activities fund was "neutral" in making money available to magazines, no matter what their perspectives. Prior cases did say, Kennedy noted, that there were special "dangers" when the government made money available directly to religious institutions. Here, though, the university wasn't paying a church to do anything; it was just paying *Wide Awake*'s printer: "[N]o public funds flow directly to [*Wide Awake*'s] coffers." As long as the university made its facilities, including its money, available "to a wide spectrum of student groups," it wouldn't violate the establishment clause. As Kennedy concluded, "There is no Establishment Clause violation in the University's honoring its duties under the Free Speech Clause."

The *Wide Awake* case laid the groundwork for the Religious Right's most important victory: getting the Court to approve school voucher programs that included religious schools.

A Rehnquist opinion in 1983 set the Court's course toward approval of vouchers, although it took two decades to arrive at the destination. Rehnquist upheld a Minnesota statute giving parents a tax deduction for tuition, textbooks, and transportation costs of sending their children to school. Parents with children in public schools could also claim the deduction, but it really mattered only to parents sending their children to private schools, most of which were affiliated with religious institutions. Over 90 percent of the financial benefits went to those parents.

That didn't matter to Rehnquist. What did matter was that the statute made its benefits available to everyone who chose to use them. Its purpose was to promote education generally, not to promote education in religious schools, and the fact that as it happened, most of the benefits went to parents who sent their children to such schools didn't mean that the statute's "primary effect" was to advance religion. According to Rehnquist, a program "that neutrally provides state assistance to a broad spectrum of citizens is not readily subject" to constitutional challenge. "Facial neutrality" mattered a lot; so did the fact that parents made the decisions about where they sent their children to school and therefore about whether they would benefit from the deductions.

"Not readily subject" turned out to be an understatement. Over the next decades the Court considered a series of challenges to statutes that provided financial assistance to students and—with one exception, later overruled—rejected them all. Larry Witters was allowed to use vocational rehabilitation money from Washington's state program to assist the blind to pay his tuition at the Inland Empire School of the Bible, to prepare for a career as a pastor. Larry Zobrest was able to use federal funds from the Individuals with Disabilities Act to pay the salary of a sign language interpreter who accompanied him to his high school classes, including classes in theology. Both programs were general ones that distributed funds neutrally, without regard to what sort of education the recipient chose to pursue.

These decisions should have made the issue of school vouchers easy. Antivoucher lawyers said that the cases were different because vouchers involved money paid for *general* education at religious schools, unlike the targeted programs in the Witters and Zobrest cases. Still, the trend in the Court's decisions was clear.

Thomas made a misstep in the march toward approving vouchers in a 2000 case involving a Louisiana program that "lent" computers and library books to private schools. The amount of the loans was measured by the schools' enrollment. Thomas relied on O'Connor's endorsement test, saying that any program that was neutral, providing money to private schools whether they were religious or nonreligious, would be constitutional because no one could think that the religious schools were acting on the government's behalf. Even direct grants to nonpublic schools would be constitutional, he wrote.

Thomas overreached, "losing" the Court, with O'Connor writing a separate opinion agreeing that the statute was constitutional but disagreeing with Thomas's analysis. O'Connor, joined by Breyer, was troubled by Thomas's "near-absolute position with respect to neutrality." She was also bothered by the way Louisiana distributed the money. Giving schools money on the basis of their enrollment relied on parents' choices *indirectly*, but, she said, aid based on enrollment "differs meaningfully" from programs—like true voucher programs—that give money "directly to individual students who, in turn, decide to use the aid at . . . religious schools." When schools used government money doled out in proportion to enrollment to teach religion, she wrote, observers would reasonably think that the government endorsed the religious education. She upheld the Louisiana program, though, because the state had in place accounting measures to make sure that the computers and books weren't used for religious education itself.

◇

Breyer's agreement with O'Connor's opinion in the Louisiana case was part of his attempt to forge an alliance that might move her more consistently in a liberal direction. In the 2003 affirmative action cases, he was the only justice who agreed entirely with O'Connor in finding one affirmative action program unconstitutional and upholding another similar one.

Born and raised in San Francisco, Breyer was a first-rank student and scholar. After attending Stanford University, he was a Marshall Scholar at Oxford University in England. Returning to the United States, he attended Harvard Law School and graduated near the top of his class in 1964. After clerking for Justice Arthur Goldberg, Breyer started teaching at Harvard Law School in 1967. He wrote important articles on copyright law and administrative law. In 1974 he worked as special counsel to the Senate Judiciary Committee, and he returned as chief counsel to the committee in 1979. Senator Edward Kennedy promoted his appointment to the federal court of appeals in Boston, and he had so impressed the Republicans on the Judiciary Committee that they were willing to confirm him as a judge in December 1980, *after* Ronald Reagan had defeated Jimmy Carter. Bill Clinton considered appointing Breyer to the Supreme Court in 1993 but eventually settled on Ginsburg.

When Blackmun retired a year later, Breyer got the nod, although not without some dithering by the White House. Clinton considered naming George Mitchell to the Court, but Mitchell told Clinton that he should stay in the Senate to handle the president's health care initiative. Clinton looked at some other judges, including one Hispanic and a longtime friend from Arkansas. From a political point of view, Breyer's main qualification was his work in the Senate.

Breyer strongly supported national power and technocracy. His scholarship supported his technocratic inclinations. A year before his nomination to the Supreme Court, he published a book on modern regulation, *Breaking the Vicious Circle: Toward Effective Risk Regulation*. The book gave liberals the only misgivings they had about his appointment. Breyer expressed great skepticism about the effectiveness of modern regulation, arguing that it often resulted from the overestimation of risks by ordinary people and the legislators who represented them. He proposed to substitute a small group of technically skilled civil servants to make the key decisions about risk and its regulation.

Breyer looks a lot like Mr. Burns, the owner of the atomic power plant on *The Simpsons*. He retains the air of a somewhat eccentric academic, quoting literary classics with a flourish while simultaneously hinting by his body language that he knows he can't be taken too seriously. Sitting on the bench, he often cradles his head in his hand, as if he had to keep his brains from bursting out of his head because of the high intellectual pressure inside.

His questions to lawyers arguing before the Supreme Court are the bane of their existence. They are complex and long-winded. Often he's trying to help the side he leans toward by serving up softball questions, but they are so convoluted that it's often hard to see their point. Even more, Breyer seems completely unaware of how much the questions eat into the advocate's time for argument. And some of his questions are, as he himself once put it, "weird" law school hypotheticals. In one intellectual property case involving whether a product's shape alone can indicate to consumers who made it, Breyer asked the lawyer to "imagine you made a hair brush in the shape of a grape" and then rambled on about other products the company might make, "a grape comb, a grape hair curler, and a grape—you know, et cetera." The lawyer got out of the exchange as gracefully as possible, but he had lost valuable time.

In another case Breyer drew on Lewis Carroll to explain his views on statutory interpretation. He began simply enough: "I learned the second year of law school that when you have a text which says 'all,' that there are often implied, not-written exceptions. All animals in the park. 'No animals in the park' doesn't necessarily apply to a pet oyster, okay, and so—" at which point another justice interrupted to observe, "Well, it's not an animal." Breyer continued: "An oyster in my course in biology is an animal, all right. Maybe in yours it was a rock, or a vegetable or a mineral. But regardless, you see my point, and my question, of course, is that since that's how I read statutes— not everybody—is that I find exceptions implicit in statutes where to fail to read that exception is to destroy the purpose of the statute, and is not backed by anything in respect to what the people wrote it want." It's easy to imagine the frustration of the lawyer who was standing there waiting to say something to advance the ball, listening to Breyer's riff on walking his pet oyster in the park.

When Breyer is hitting on all cylinders, his questioning can be devastating. In the 2003 cross burning case, he toyed with the defendants' lawyer, Rodney Smolla, himself a professor of constitutional law. Breyer began by getting Smolla to agree that "the First Amendment doesn't protect words. It protects the use of words for certain purposes" and that it doesn't protect "a symbol when used for symbolic purposes." Smolla then agreed with Breyer that the First Amendment protects the words *I will kill you* when they're used in a play but not when they are a true threat. "So," he continued, "it doesn't protect the burning of the cross when used as a threat and not as a symbol." Again, Smolla agreed. "And now we have a statute," Breyer went on, "that says you can use it as a symbol, but you can't use it as a threat." To Breyer's final question, "What's your response?" Smolla could only stumble, to the audience's laughter: "Your Honor, that—that everything you said up until the very end, we would not accept. I have a hunch to at least say that much."

Breyer's effort to develop an alliance with O'Connor may have come out of his experience working with senators who knew how to develop compromises that advanced good public policy. That kind of compromise was not entirely welcome in the Rehnquist Court, though. In *Bush v. Gore*, Breyer offered O'Connor a trade: He would agree that the Florida recount procedure violated the equal protection clause if she would agree to give the state more time to conduct a proper recount. O'Connor rarely wanted to compromise, and her position on the Court meant that she didn't have to. She refused Breyer's trade, leaving him with an embarrassing opinion that, by acknowledging the possibility that the recount procedure did violate the Constitution, allowed conservatives to say that even a liberal like Breyer thought the state courts were out of control.

In the run-up to the crucial voucher case, Breyer and O'Connor joined in rejecting Thomas's more hard-edged approach. But in the end O'Connor endorsed school vouchers, and Breyer didn't.

❦

O'Connor signaled what she required in a voucher program when she wrote in the Louisiana case that it wasn't a "true private-choice program." The Minnesota tax deduction case was, as were the programs in the Witters and Zobrest cases. Individual parents and students decided where to use public money, and as long as the program was neutral in allowing them to choose nonreligious schools or religious ones, no one could take their decisions to indicate that the government endorsed religion. A "true private-choice program" from Cleveland gave the Court its chance to say that voucher programs were perfectly constitutional.

The idea for school vouchers came from the libertarian economist Milton Friedman, who believed that the government had no business running schools. Acknowledging that eliminating the public schools was politically impossible, he proposed to create competition in education by giving parents, not schools, the money spent on education. Parents could then choose to send their children to whatever school they thought best, "public" or private, religious or secular.

Some Republicans and many on the Religious Right were attracted to the idea of education vouchers, but proposals as wide-ranging as Friedman's were still politically unrealistic. Suburban parents were happy with their children's schools and were unwilling to support programs that threatened to take money away from those schools as some parents shifted from public to private schools.

Voucher proponents scaled back their proposals even more. They developed plans for limited voucher programs, which would be available to only a small number of children. More important, they proposed voucher programs that would be confined to inner-city schools, thereby allaying any fears suburban parents might have. In doing so, voucher proponents capitalized on a sense, increasingly widespread in the 1980s and 1990s, that inner-city public schools were failing to offer even a minimally adequate education.

Polly Williams, an African American Democratic state legislator from Milwaukee, Wisconsin, became the leading public advocate for inner-city vouchers. Working with Wisconsin's Republican governor, Tommy Thompson, Williams got the state legislature to adopt a voucher program. The program was tiny at first, and it was limited to private nonreligious schools within Milwaukee's boundaries. However, to voucher proponents, it might be the opening wedge for more expansive programs that would include religious schools.

While litigation challenging the Milwaukee program was pending, Ohio's conservative Republican governor George Voinovich proposed a similar program for Cleveland, where the public schools were so bad that a federal court had put the state in charge of reconstructing the system. Voinovich did not try to gather bipartisan support for his proposal, instead making it a symbol of innovative Republican policies for dealing with inner-city problems.

Cleveland's voucher program had several elements. The city operated ordinary public schools; charter schools, with closer contacts to the local community and less regulation by the city's school bureaucracy; and magnet schools, specializing in particular subjects, such as the arts or science. Ohio paid $4,000 for each student in a public or magnet school, $4,500 for each one in a charter school. Parents could also receive money to pay for tutorial assistance for their children in public schools.

More important, the state gave parents who sent their children to private schools checks to cover either 90 percent of tuition up to a limit of $2,500 for poor parents or 75 percent of tuition up to a limit of $1,875 for everyone else. These amounts didn't cover the full cost of educating children at most private schools, so parents still had to pay *some* tuition, and private schools that accepted children from poor parents often ended up subsidizing the students themselves. A large majority of the private schools receiving vouchers were religious schools, and over 90 percent of the children whose parents used vouchers went to religious schools. The state took the case to the Supreme Court after lower courts held the program violated the establishment clause.

For Rehnquist and O'Connor, the Cleveland voucher case was just like the Minnesota tax deduction case and its successors. As Rehnquist put it, using O'Connor's words from the Louisiana case, the Cleveland program was one of "true private choice." Parents could choose between religious and nonreligious private schools, and—important to O'Connor—they also could choose between regular public schools and charter or magnet schools within the public school system. The range of options was large enough, she said, to ensure that parents really did have a choice.

Breyer wrote a short dissent, emphasizing that making public funds available to religious schools threatened to create real political divisions centering on religious differences, which was, he argued, one of the primary reasons for including the establishment clause in the Constitution. He pointed out that the Ohio statute required officials to deny the use of vouchers at schools that "advocate or foster unlawful behavior or teach hatred of any person or group on the basis of race, ethnicity, national origin, or religion," and he wondered if there could be any more divisive chore than trying to decide whether a religious school was teaching "a view of history that casts members of other religions in the worst possible light." Souter's version of the point was more direct:

> Not all taxpaying Protestant citizens, for example, will be content to underwrite the teaching of the Roman Catholic Church condemning the death penalty. Nor will all of America's Muslims acquiesce in paying for the endorsement of the religious Zionism taught in many religious Jewish schools, which combines "a nationalistic sentiment" in support of Israel with a "deeply religious" element. Nor will every secular taxpayer be content to support Muslim views on differential treatment of the sexes, or, for that matter, to fund the espousal of a wife's obligation of obedience to her husband, presumably taught in any schools adopting the articles of faith of the Southern Baptist Convention.

By counting Cleveland's alternative public schools within the range of choices, O'Connor overlooked the fact that the voucher program was created because the legislature believed that Cleveland's public schools had failed. Souter wrote the main dissent. He challenged O'Connor over whether the city's charter schools were half decent. He said that the charter schools were not much better than the failed public schools. O'Connor replied that they were good enough, even if not terrific, to provide some "real choices" for parents who did not want to send their children to private schools. Focusing only on private schools, the dissenters had a decent argument that nearly all parents had no real options other than religious schools. True choice, it seems, may have been as formalistic as real neutrality was.

℘

Clint Bolick hailed the Cleveland decision as a contemporary *Brown v. Board of Education*, holding out the promise of real improvements in education for the nation's African American children mired in distressed inner-city schools. *Brown* didn't produce integration, though, and the Cleveland voucher decision might not help education much either.

The Religious Right's support for voucher programs goes beyond interest in aiding inner-city children. Its members want voucher programs that allow support for the religious schools—often in the suburbs—to which they send their children, or would send them if the parents could afford the cost. Suburban parents not associated with the Religious Right do not favor expansive voucher programs, which have not fared well in the political arena. As two scholars point out, "Every proposal to provide for vouchers on a large scale has failed." Voucher proponents blame teachers' unions and the ACLU for the failures. Suburban parents are more important factors in blocking large voucher programs. A large-scale voucher program whose benefits are available to suburban parents will almost inevitably reduce public expenditures on public schools. But suburban parents typically have paid extra for their homes because of the quality of public education in the suburbs. Suburban parents also fear the educational and social effects of an influx of minority children into suburban schools. The Ohio program authorized inner-city parents to use vouchers at any suburban public school that would accept them, but no suburb did, because accepting students from Cleveland's inner-city schools would, suburban parents thought, reduce the quality of education in the suburban schools.

Suburban indifference or opposition to large-scale voucher programs means that voucher programs are likely to be confined to failing inner-city schools. That in turn means that the Religious Right's more expansive hopes are likely to be defeated. Legislatures may enact programs for inner-city schools but go no further, and eventually the Religious Right's supporters may decide that they aren't getting what they expected and themselves abandon support for limited voucher programs.

❧

The Religious Right's victories in the Rehnquist Court were larger than those social conservatives won on other issues. Still, the victories were ambiguous. To win, the Religious Right had to insist that all they sought was government neutrality, thereby draining any specifically religious content out of the programs they supported. And in the end politics was more likely to determine how well the Religious Right did than was the Supreme Court. As the nation became more religiously diverse, the Religious Right's agenda became harder to achieve.

The Religious Right's constitutional agenda was not going to go away, though. They might lose the cases involving symbols, but they could always come up with new symbols to fight over. They might not get large-scale voucher programs adopted, but they could always blame teachers' unions and secularists rather than suburban parents. The justices certainly didn't intend to do so, but their decisions probably helped keep the Religious Right tied to the Republican Party.

CHAPTER EIGHT

Holding the Line on Abortion

Antonin Scalia was furious at Sandra Day O'Connor. It was late June 1989, just days before the Court's Term was to end. Two months earlier the Court had heard oral argument in a case giving it the chance to overrule *Roe v. Wade*, its 1973 decision protecting women's right to choose to have abortions. Scalia abhorred that decision. A devout Catholic, he opposed abortion on moral grounds and believed that abortions were indeed murders. As a legislator Scalia would have voted against laws making abortions easily available, but that position on policy didn't drive his position on what the Constitution means. The Constitution he read contained not a word protecting a right to choose abortion. And when the Constitution doesn't say anything about a subject, legislatures, and the people of each state, have the right to decide what to do.

Scalia thought that the case the Court was considering would be the one in which the Rehnquist Court overruled *Roe*. He knew that he, Rehnquist, and Byron White, who had dissented in 1973 from the Roe decision, wanted to overrule. And he believed the Court's other Reagan-appointed justices, O'Connor and Anthony Kennedy, were on his side on that question.

The Bush administration had appeared in the case, filing an amicus brief urging that *Roe* be overruled. Solicitor General Charles Fried's oral argument hadn't gone all that well. He said overruling *Roe* wouldn't threaten more popular decisions like the one finding it unconstitutional for Connecticut to make it a crime to use contraceptives, because abortion was different from those cases, which involved "quite intimate intrusions into the details of marital intimacy." Striving for a rhetorical effect, but missing, Fried opened his argument by saying, "I would like to make quite clear how limited that submission is. First, we are not asking the Court to unravel the fabric of unenumerated and privacy rights which this court has woven. . . . Rather, we are asking the Court to pull this one thread." Frank Susman, arguing against the statute, knew an opening when he saw one. The first sentence of his oral argument was: "I think the Solicitor General's submission is somewhat disingenuous when he suggests to this court that he does not seek to unravel the whole cloth of procreational rights, but merely to pull a thread. It has always been my personal experience that when I pull a thread, my sleeve falls off. There is no stopping. It is not a thread he is after." Still, oral arguments rarely change votes, and Scalia thought the votes were there to overrule *Roe*.

The case the Court was considering involved several provisions of a Missouri statute. Pro-choice advocates were particularly upset about the statute's preamble, which declared that life begins at conception. But for the justices, that was merely an abstract statement that had no legal consequences. More important to them was a provision that required doctors to perform "medically appropriate" tests to determine the fetus's viability when the doctor believed that the fetus was twenty or more weeks since conception.

The number twenty made a real difference in the constitutional law of abortion. *Roe* divided pregnancy into three periods. During the first trimester the government basically couldn't regulate abortion at all (except to require that abortions be performed by physicians); during the second, the government could impose regulations aimed at protecting the pregnant woman's health. After the fetus was viable (meaning that the woman, without extraordinary intervention, could be expected to deliver a reasonably healthy baby), the government could adopt regulations aimed at protecting the fetus itself. In 1973—and perhaps even today—for technological and physical reasons viability occurred roughly around the end of the second trimester.

On its face, the Court's third holding meant that the government could ban abortions where the fetus was viable. The Court added an important qualification, though. The government couldn't ban abortions, even in the third trimester, if the pregnancy endangered the woman's life or health. The Court then defined *health* so broadly that virtually any pregnant woman who wanted an abortion in the third trimester, a number that is unknown but believed to be relatively small, could fairly claim that carrying the pregnancy through to delivery would endanger her health as the Court defined it.

Still, within *Roe*'s framework, it mattered whether a pregnant woman was in the second or third trimester of her pregnancy. Missouri's testing law couldn't possibly be justified as protecting the woman's health. So under *Roe* it was unconstitutional—*if* it was a second-trimester regulation. And because each trimester is roughly twelve weeks long, by ordinary calculations, twenty weeks is in the second trimester.

The Court could have upheld the testing requirement in several ways. Of course it could have overruled *Roe*. Or it could have treated the requirement as a second-trimester regulation but said that even before viability, the Constitution placed less strict limits on regulation than *Roe* had said and that the Missouri law did not violate those relaxed limits. Scalia preferred the first, a decision straightforwardly overruling *Roe*. He could live with the second, a substantial relaxation of the constitutional limits facing legislatures that wanted to regulate abortions. It turned out, though, that O'Connor came up with a third course, and her defection from the anti-*Roe* camp infuriated Scalia.

At the Court's discussion of the case, Rehnquist said that he "disagrees with *Roe v. Wade.*" Five justices, including Kennedy and O'Connor, took the same position, but O'Connor seemed to prefer a decision limiting rather than overruling *Roe*. Rehnquist took the case for himself and within a month circulated a draft saying that the case did not require the Court to overrule *Roe*. Instead, he proposed to change the constitutional standard. The right to choose an abortion was indeed a liberty interest protected by the due process clause, but states could regulate abortions without violating the Constitution—or impairing the woman's liberty—if a regulation "reasonably furthers the state interest in protecting potential human life."

Stevens immediately responded with a letter pointing out that

Rehnquist's approach gave "no weight at all" to "the woman's interest in making the abortion decision." Stevens came up with several regulations that he said, accurately, should survive under Rehnquist's test. "[A] tax on abortions, a requirement that the pregnant woman must be able to stand on her head for fifteen minutes," and "tests of the woman's knowledge of Shakespeare or American history"—all would advance the state's interest in protecting potential human life by disqualifying some women from getting abortions.

White, Scalia, and Kennedy promptly joined Rehnquist's draft, and then things hung fire. O'Connor apparently had misgivings about the draft. Three weeks later Blackmun circulated a draft dissent. Then came O'Connor's bombshell: She couldn't agree with the way Rehnquist discussed the testing requirement. Instead, she proposed to uphold the requirement, on a new theory. Noting that determinations of fetal age were always somewhat inaccurate, she said that doctors thought there was roughly a four-week margin of error when they estimated fetal age. So the testing requirement was actually a *third*-trimester regulation and, because it was aimed at determining fetal viability, was indeed within the scope of third-trimester regulations under *Roe* itself. Drawing on a suggestion made in the solicitor general's amicus brief, O'Connor did propose a new constitutional standard—a regulation would be unconstitutional if it imposed an "undue burden" on the woman's right to choose—but that standard would pretty clearly produce greater restrictions on the ability of states to regulate abortions than Rehnquist's state interest test would.

O'Connor's position deprived Rehnquist of a majority for a substantial reworking of the constitutional standard for evaluating abortion regulations. Worse, from Scalia's point of view, he knew that O'Connor's late defection meant that Rehnquist wouldn't publish a strong opinion saying that *Roe* should be overruled. Once Rehnquist had a draft, that basically was it. He might tinker with it to get votes, but he wouldn't scrap it and start over. Things might have been different if O'Connor had let Rehnquist know her thinking earlier. Then he might have drafted an opinion directly challenging *Roe*, knowing and accepting that it would end up as a plurality opinion. Instead, as Scalia saw it, O'Connor had led Rehnquist down the garden path, where he ended up with a plurality opinion anyway.

Scalia took it upon himself to attack *Roe*—and O'Connor. He described four courses the Court might have taken: "to reaffirm *Roe*, to overrule it explicitly, to overrule it *sub silentio*, or to avoid the question." The fourth, he said, was "the least responsible," and he "strongly" dissented from "the manner" in which the decision to uphold Missouri's law "had been reached." His primary target was O'Connor. He criticized her undue burden test as failing to provide the kind of guidance the law should and described another part of her analysis as "similarly irrational." He said that O'Connor's statement that judicial restraint required the Court to refrain from reconsidering *Roe* in a case where the regulation could be upheld anyway could not "be taken seriously." His most pointed attack on her went to his understanding of *her* self-understanding as the Court's moderate and stateswoman: "The outcome of today's case will doubtless be heralded as a triumph of judicial statesmanship. It is not that, unless it is statesmanlike needlessly to prolong this Court's self-awarded sovereignty over a field where it has little proper business since the answers to most of the crucial questions posed are political and not juridical." As Supreme Court opinions go, this was venomous.

Scalia's attack on O'Connor solidified her drift away from a strong anti-*Roe* position. She did think of herself as the Court's stateswoman, and she didn't think highly of the way in which Scalia expressed himself. The next year the Court took up two more abortion cases. Mostly it upheld the regulations. But in one O'Connor voted to strike down an abortion regulation for the first time. That vote was more important as a signal for the future than it seemed at the time. Minnesota required a minor seeking an abortion to notify *both* her parents even if she was living with only one of them; it allowed minors to avoid getting parental permission by going to court. O'Connor voted with the other anti-*Roe* justices to uphold the judicial bypass provision, but she voted with the Court's liberals to strike down the two-parent notification provision. Stevens's opinion on the two-parent notification provision emphasized factual findings made by the lower courts about how the provision worked in practice. He discussed the "harmful effects" the provision had. When the parents were separated, notification of the noncustodial parent led to tension. Worse, often when the parents remained together, the family was pervaded by violence, and notification simply increased the chance of violence. The requirement, Stevens wrote, "does not reasonably further any legitimate state interest." O'Connor appreciated Stevens's attention to the facts and—it turned out—his focus on family violence as well.

O'Connor had jumped ship in 1989, but three years later Scalia thought he could topple *Roe* without her. Thomas, a sure vote against *Roe*, and Souter, a possible one, had joined the Court. With Rehnquist, White, and Kennedy still on board, Scalia counted five, or even six, on his side.

It didn't happen. Souter never was on board, and more important, this time Kennedy jumped ship. The case involved abortion regulations from Pennsylvania: that a woman seeking an abortion be provided with information about the procedure at least twenty-four hours before it was performed; that a minor seeking an abortion get the consent of one parent (or get a court's permission); and that a married woman seeking an abortion certify that she had notified her husband of her intention. The Court had invalidated informed consent requirements when in the majority's view, the information provided was designed to push the woman away from getting the abortion she initially sought. And although it had struck down a requirement that a married woman get her husband's *consent* to an abortion, it hadn't yet considered a case involving only a notification requirement. As in the earlier cases, the Court could have upheld Pennsylvania's statute by overruling *Roe* or by modifying the constitutional test.

Pro-choice advocates decided to go for broke. They filed their petition for review two months before they had to and presented only the single question they wanted the Court to consider: "Has the Supreme Court overruled *Roe v. Wade*, holding that a woman's right to choose abortion is a fundamental right protected by the United States Constitution?" The lawyers described their decision as a "high stakes game of chicken" with the Court: Either overrule *Roe* or reaffirm it, and do so before the 1992 elections. The case was argued on the last possible day to get an opinion out before the elections.

The pro-choice lawyers centered their argument on the proposition that the Pennsylvania regulations could not be upheld unless the Court repudiated *Roe*. Kathryn Kolbert, a lawyer with substantial experience in the American Civil Liberties Union, represented

Planned Parenthood of Eastern Pennsylvania, which had brought
the case to the Court. She began her argument with an extended, and
surprisingly uninterrupted, defense of *Roe*. O'Connor was uncomfortable with Kolbert's all-or-nothing approach and eventually
broke in to ask her to address the particulars of Pennsylvania's
statute. Kolbert gestured in the direction of dealing with specific
provisions, but her position was that those provisions were unconstitutional because they were inconsistent with *Roe*.

Pennsylvania's attorney general, Ernest Preate, defended the
state's statute but didn't directly challenge *Roe*. Stevens and
O'Connor peppered him with questions about the spousal notification provision, pointing out that lots of women would notify their
husbands even without the statute, so the statute affected only those
women who, for whatever reason, decided to get abortions without
notifying their husbands. Scalia helped Preate out by suggesting
that whether the provision placed an undue burden on the right to
choose was basically a question about policy and values rather than
one about facts. "What law books do I look to?" Scalia asked. After
Preate said that the test required a "quantitative analysis," Scalia
went on: "I suppose it depends on how important I would think it is,
that a husband of a wife know before a fetus that he co-generated be
destroyed. Would that be part of it?" Preate of course agreed.

Kenneth Starr, the solicitor general, also appeared. He too did not
ask that *Roe* be overruled, but only that the Pennsylvania statue be
tested against the reasonable regulation standard Rehnquist had
developed in the Missouri case, rather than O'Connor's undue burden standard. Starr got a series of really hostile questions from
Stevens, and then Souter jumped in. Under the reasonable basis
standard, he asked, wouldn't a complete prohibition on abortion be
constitutional? Starr replied that a statute without an exception for
the life of the mother "could raise very serious questions." Pressed
further by Souter, Starr dodged, and Souter was a bit exasperated:
"You're asking the Court to adopt a standard and I think we ought
to know where the standard would take us." Starr never got a chance
to give a satisfactory answer, if he had one, to the question of
whether a complete ban on abortions would be a reasonable way of
advancing the interest he insisted the government had in "preserving
fetal life at all times during pregnancy."

When the justices voted, only Blackmun and Stevens stuck with *Roe*. The seven others wanted to change the law of abortion, and it appeared as if five, including Kennedy, were willing to adopt the position Rehnquist set out in the Missouri case: The right to choose abortion was a liberty interest, but not a fundamental one, and therefore could be limited by reasonable regulations (just as the right to work as a barber was a liberty interest that could be limited by reasonable regulations). Rehnquist took the opinion for himself and drafted one along the lines of his Missouri opinion.

David Souter hadn't dealt with abortion before. He was acutely uncomfortable with the prospect of a decision overruling *Roe*, which he believed would be taken by the public to demonstrate that the Court's decisions were affected by politics acting through the appointment process and not by law. O'Connor continued to prefer her undue burden approach to Rehnquist's. Souter and O'Connor got together and then approached Kennedy with the idea of collaborating on an opinion that would preserve what they called the "core holding" of *Roe*—that states couldn't make abortion a criminal offense—but also allow for a wider range of regulations than *Roe* did. Kennedy was sympathetic to the idea, resolving the conflict between his Roman Catholic religious beliefs and his mildly libertarian political and constitutional views in favor of the latter.

The three justices divided work on what ended up as a joint opinion. (Although it's sometimes described as a plurality opinion, technically it wasn't. To be a plurality opinion, an opinion has to have more votes than any other, and in the Pennsylvania case Rehnquist's opinion got four votes to the joint opinion's three. The joint opinion's undue burden rule is what matters today, though, because Blackmun and Stevens, who dissented, clearly agreed more with the joint opinion than with Rehnquist's.)

O'Connor drafted a section that modified *Roe* in two ways, both foreshadowed by her opinion in the Missouri case. It abandoned the trimester framework and substituted a line drawn at viability. Doing so, the opinion said, respected the government's "profound interest in potential life." That interest existed throughout pregnancy and hadn't been given enough weight in *Roe*'s rules about the first trimester.

The viability line, it turned out, didn't matter that much. *Roe* barred essentially all first-trimester regulations, but O'Connor didn't mean to carry *that* rule over to stop states from regulating before viability. Here her second innovation came in, the undue burden standard. Now states could adopt regulations applicable before viability, if the regulations didn't impose an undue burden on the choice of abortion. And undue burdens were those that placed "a substantial obstacle in the path of a woman seeking an abortion of a nonviable [that is, not yet viable] fetus." The opinion then said that the rule *Roe* developed for the third trimester—that abortions could be regulated and even prohibited unless the procedure was necessary to preserve the woman's life or health—would now apply to all postviability abortions.

O'Connor then applied the undue burden test. She thought that a mandatory twenty-four-hour waiting period was troublesome because of its practical effects on women who had to travel to obtain abortions. But ultimately she concluded that the waiting period didn't impose an undue burden, although exactly why wasn't clear. Then, following up on her concern about domestic violence, O'Connor wrote a section striking down the spousal notification provision. Quoting copiously from the lower court's fact findings, she emphasized the point made in oral argument that the notification mattered only when a woman wouldn't tell her spouse about the abortion on her own and that women who withheld that information from their spouses usually had good reasons, rooted in fear of violence, for doing so.

Souter drafted the joint opinion's discussion of why the Court shouldn't overrule *Roe*. He carefully mentioned that "some of us" might have "personal reluctance" for "affirming *Roe*'s central holding." But, he said, the demands of adhering to precedent in constitutional law overrode any such reluctance. He made some standard points about overruling: It was easier to do when the earlier decision turned out to be "unworkable," but that wasn't true of *Roe*. Lots of people didn't like the decision, but courts had no real problems figuring out what its core holding was. Nor had later cases cast doubt on that core holding. These were straightforward commonplaces.

Other parts of Souter's discussion of overruling were more unusual. Standard accounts of overruling say that it's a bad idea when people have relied on the prior decision to order their affairs.

Souter picked up on that idea but transformed it. He conceded that women don't rely on *Roe* and the possibility of obtaining an abortion when they engage in intercourse. But, he said, the idea of reliance was broader. He referred to the feminist revolution: "[F]or two decades of economic and social developments, people have organized intimate relationships and made choices that define their views of themselves and their places in society, in reliance on the availability of abortion in the event that contraception should fail. The ability of women to participate equally in the economic and social life of the Nation has been facilitated by their ability to control their reproductive lives." Clearly Souter was on to something here. *Roe* had made a difference in the way women understood their place in society. It's just that forcing the point into the framework of "reliance" doesn't work particularly well.

Souter also had some difficulty dealing with the obvious fact that the Court *does* overrule cases. Sometimes the cases are minor, but some overrulings deal with cases as important as *Roe*. According to Souter, the Court acted properly in abandoning important doctrines when time had shown that the older cases rested on false factual assumptions. That argument works, sort of, for *Brown v. Board of Education*, which repudiated the separate but equal doctrine. There the Court did indeed say that time had shown that separate educational facilities could not be equal, as the earlier cases had assumed. But treating *Brown* as a case about facts pretty clearly understates the importance that changed values, a new vision of what racial equality meant, had in the Court's decision. Souter's treatment of *Lochner v. New York*, which struck down state labor regulations, as a case involving mistaken factual assumptions is almost impossible to defend. Souter said that the Court in *Lochner* adopted "fundamentally false factual assumptions about the capacity of a relatively unregulated market to satisfy minimal levels of human welfare." That's not a terribly accurate description of that Court's premises, which were far more about the moral dimensions of human choice than about micro- or macroeconomics. Moreover, the adjectives *relatively* and *minimal* show that the Court's factual assumptions, whatever they were, were inextricably tied to normative judgments.

The final section of Souter's contribution was the most questionable. It argued that overruling *Roe* "would seriously weaken the

Court's capacity to exercise the judicial power." Souter built his argument in stages. The Court's power, he said, rested on its "legitimacy," which he described as "the people's acceptance of the Judiciary as fit to determine what the Nation's law means." That in turn meant that the Court's decisions had to rest upon—and be seen to rest upon—honest assessments of what the law required, "not as compromises with social and political pressures having, as such, no bearing on the principled choices that the Court is obliged to make."

But, Souter continued, the public belief that the Court acted on principle would be shaken if it overruled *Roe*. When the Court decides a case as "intensely divisive" as *Roe*, "its decision has a dimension that the resolution of the normal case does not carry." This was "the dimension present whenever the Court's interpretation of the Constitution calls the contending sides of a national controversy to end their national division by accepting a common mandate rooted in the Constitution." *Brown* and *Roe* were the only modern examples of such decisions. They showed that precedent had to have a particularly strong effect because of the "inevitable efforts" to overturn decisions addressing the kinds of controversies those decisions dealt with. Overruling such decisions required exceedingly powerful justifications because otherwise it would look as if the overruling were "a surrender to political pressure." Souter concluded: "[T]o overrule under fire in the absence of the most compelling reason to reexamine a watershed decision would subvert the Court's legitimacy beyond any serious question." As Scalia pointed out in dissent, this was an argument that the more wrong the Court was about a really important matter, the more it should balk at acknowledging its error.

Kennedy took on the task of defending *Roe*'s "core holding." He noted, "Some of us as individuals find abortion offensive to our most basic principles of morality, but that cannot control our decision." After recounting the Court's efforts in a number of areas to define the liberties the Constitution protected, Kennedy concluded that the Constitution defined "a realm of personal liberty which the government may not enter." How to identify that realm? By using the "same capacity which by tradition courts always have exercised: reasoned judgment." This was not a mechanical task, of course. According to Kennedy, the Court's cases recognized an important sphere of personal autonomy. Decisions about "the most intimate and personal choices a person may make in a lifetime" were "central to personal dignity and autonomy" and equally "central to the liberty protected by the Fourteenth Amendment." In a passage that his critics derided, Kennedy concluded, "At the heart of liberty is the right to define one's own concept of existence, of meaning, of the universe, and of the mystery of human life."

He then turned to the state's interest in regulating abortion. He described abortion's consequences for the woman and, "depending on one's beliefs, for the life or potential life that is aborted." These consequences meant that the woman's "suffering is too intimate and personal for the State to insist, without more, upon its own vision of the woman's role." The "destiny of the woman," he wrote, "must be shaped to a large extent on her own conception of her spiritual imperatives and her place in society."

He also wrote the joint's opinion's sonorous—and almost meaningless—opening and closing sentences. The opinion began: "Liberty finds no refuge in a jurisprudence of doubt." Justice Oliver Wendell Holmes might have responded that liberty finds refuge *only* in a jurisprudence of doubt. In a famous free speech dissent, Holmes wrote, "If you have no doubt of your premises or your power and want a certain result with all your heart you naturally express your wishes in law and sweep away all opposition." The joint opinion ended by describing the Constitution as "a covenant" running from the founding to the indefinite future. "We accept our responsibility not to retreat from interpreting the full meaning of the covenant in light of all of our precedents. We invoke it once again to define the freedom guaranteed by the Constitution's own promise, the promise of liberty." That might work as the conclusion of a president's State of the Union address, where we don't expect anything but platitudes. But exactly what it means remains entirely unclear.

Kennedy was nervous about his participation in the joint opinion. As he became committed to the joint opinion's approach, he went to Rehnquist and apologized for depriving him of a majority yet again. The affable Rehnquist reportedly told Kennedy that he "had to do what he thought was right." The same reports indicate that Scalia was so upset at Kennedy's defection that he "walked over to Kennedy's nearby house . . . to upbraid him." On the day the decision was released, Kennedy allowed a journalist into his office and enhanced the self-dramatization of the event by telling his guest, "Sometimes you don't know if you're Caesar about to cross the Rubicon, or Captain Queeg cutting your own tow line," and then excused himself, saying, "I need to brood" for the ten minutes before the Court convened.

At the end of the Court's Term, the law clerks staged a skit and used the theme from the television program *Flipper* as Kennedy's signature song. Why had Kennedy jumped ship? Conservatives had a conspiracy theory. Michael Dorf, one of Kennedy's law clerks that year, had worked closely with the pro-choice constitutional scholar Laurence Tribe. Conservatives suggested that Tribe had successfully used his protégé—and another, Peter Rubin, who was clerking for Souter—to lobby Kennedy. Others referred to the Greenhouse Effect. Yet another story was that Kennedy, who had initially been taken under Scalia's wing to the point that the law clerks referred to Kennedy as Nini, or little Nino, gradually was "put off by Scalia's fanged personal attacks on O'Connor" and found "Souter's low-key manner . . . a welcome contrast to Scalia's intensity."

Conservatives certainly overstated the influence of Rubin and Dorf, and Tribe even more; law clerks don't have much impact on the important decisions made by justices with strong self-images, like Kennedy. As Peter Keisler, a reliable Federalist Society lawyer who clerked for Kennedy, said, "No justice is going to abdicate" to a law clerk on an issue like abortion. The other things they identified may have played some role. In the end it's almost certain that Kennedy joined the joint opinion because he thought it offered a better interpretation of the Constitution—his interpretation and, to some degree, O'Connor's—than Rehnquist's.

The joint opinion gave Scalia a large target to shoot at, and he didn't miss. He wrote that he had to "respond to a few of the more outrageous arguments" in the opinion, "which it is beyond human nature to leave unanswered." He organized his dissent in sections headed with quotations in bold type from the joint opinion. Against the joint opinion's invocation of "reasoned judgment," Scalia noted that the best it could do was "rattle off a collection of adjectives that simply decorate a value judgment and conceal a political choice." It was not "reasoned judgment that supports the Court's decision; only personal predilection."

He went after the joint opinion's "august and sonorous" first sentence with particular vigor. *Roe*'s rule, however wrong, was clear and free from doubt. It was, however, "really more than one should have to bear" to be told that the joint opinion's new undue burden standard avoided, rather than created, a jurisprudence of doubt. For Scalia, "the standard is inherently manipulable and will prove hopelessly unworkable in practice," hardly a model for clarity in legal rules. He called the joint opinion's effort to clarify the standard a "verbal shell game" that concealed "raw judicial policy choices" of what the judges decided was "appropriate" abortion legislation. Even the opinion's attention to facts didn't help, because it described the facts its authors thought important and then simply asserted that the facts showed that the regulation was or wasn't an undue burden.

The Court's real role in solving national controversies was, to Scalia, "unrecognizable" in the joint opinion's description. *Roe* hadn't resolved a national controversy about abortion; it had "destroyed the compromises of the past, rendered compromise impossible for the future, and required the entire issue to be resolved uniformly, at the national level." It had also "eliminated the moral opprobrium" attached to abortion and "obscured with its smoke the selection of Justices to this Court." Saying that *Roe* settled the question was "nothing less than Orwellian."

"The imperial judiciary lives," Scalia replied to the joint opinion's "Nietzschean vision of us unelected, life-tenured judges—leading a Volk who will be 'tested by following.' " He couldn't "sit still" for a "lengthy lecture on the virtues of 'constancy,' " delivered by two judges, Kennedy and O'Connor, who, "in order thus to remain steadfast, had to abandon previously stated positions." He was "appalled by" the joint opinion's argument that the strength of opposition to an erroneous Court decision was a reason for adhering to the decision rather than for overruling it. For him, "the notion that we would decide a case differently from the way we otherwise would have in order to show that we can stand firm against public disapproval is frightening," a position of "almost czarist arrogance." According to Scalia, the Court should be distressed at the fact that there were annual marches to the Supreme Court protesting *Roe* on its anniversary but should worry more about the cause of the marches than the mere fact that they occurred. The cause, he said, was "a new mode of constitutional adjudication that relies not upon text and traditional practice to determine the law, but upon what the Court calls 'reasoned judgment,' which turns out to be nothing but philosophical predilection and moral intuition."

Much of this was persuasive. The idea that opposition to a wrong decision is a reason for adhering to it is indeed weird. Scalia ended his opinion with what he thought was a rhetorical flourish, which actually weakened the dissent by descending into bathetic reference to Chief Justice Roger Taney, the author of the notorious Dred Scott opinion, in 1857, holding that African Americans could not be citizens of the United States and had "no rights the white man was bound to respect." Antiabortion legal activists regularly drew an analogy between that statement in the Dred Scott case and *Roe*, which similarly held, they said, that there was a class of human beings—unborn children—who had no rights under the Constitution. Scalia wrote that the Court's decisions brought "vividly to mind" a portrait of Taney:

> He is all in black, sitting in a shadowed red armchair, left hand resting upon a pad of paper in his lap, right hand hanging limply, almost lifelessly, beside the inner arm of the chair. He sits facing the viewer and staring straight out. There seems to be on his face, and in his deep-set eyes, an expression of profound sadness and disillusionment. Perhaps he always looked that way, even when dwelling upon the happiest of thoughts. But those of us who know how the lustre of his great Chief Justiceship came to be eclipsed by *Dred Scott* cannot help believing that he had that case—its already apparent consequences for the Court and its soon-to-be-played-out consequences for the Nation—burning on his mind. I expect that two years earlier he, too, had thought himself "calling the contending sides of national controversy to end their national division by accepting a common mandate rooted in the Constitution."

Scalia said that "we should get out of this area, where we have no right to be, and where we do neither ourselves nor the country any good by remaining." Blackmun of course wanted the Court to stay in. As he had in the Missouri case, he welcomed the fact that *Roe* was not overruled. But he too could not resist the pull of bathos. The approaches taken by the joint opinion and the dissenters were, he wrote, "worlds apart," while the distance between them was "but a single vote." His opinion ended: "I am 83 years old. I cannot remain on this Court forever, and when I do step down, the confirmation process for my successor well may focus on the issue before us today. That, I regret, may be exactly where the choice between the two worlds will be made."

∽

The Casey decision succeeded in taking the abortion issue largely off the Supreme Court's agenda. The authors of the joint opinion were right about that, and Scalia was wrong. Having lost the battle to overrule *Roe*, antiabortion activists turned to new tactics, including demonstrations at facilities where abortions were performed. In legislatures they began to develop an essentially cultural strategy to discredit the theories they believed underpinned public acceptance of abortion, the idea that abortion was an ordinary medical procedure and the belief that fetuses weren't really human beings. They initially focused on a couple of extremely gruesome procedures for aborting a fetus, which doctors sometimes called intact dilation and evacuation and dilation and extraction. Doctors performed these procedures relatively late in pregnancy and usually because they were at that point the only techniques that didn't threaten a woman's life. The techniques involved dismemberment of the fetus, sometimes after it had begun to emerge from the womb. Antiabortion activists called these techniques partial birth abortions. That label served important public relations purposes and stuck in the public's mind in a way that the more desiccated medical terminology did not.

Antiabortion activists pushed state legislatures to adopt statutes banning these procedures, emphasizing in their publicity campaigns how violent the procedures were. Their strategy was that by showing how gruesome *these* procedures were, they would condition the wider public to begin to accept the idea that *all* abortions were gruesome. States adopted bans on partial birth abortions, but the lower federal courts generally found them unconstitutional under the approach taken by the joint opinion in the Casey decision. So did the Supreme Court. Having jumped the conservative ship in *Casey*, Kennedy got on again in the partial abortion case, but his vote was no longer needed.

Writing for a five-justice majority, Breyer found a Nebraska ban on partial birth abortions unconstitutional for two reasons. The Nebraska statute tried to describe the medical technique at which it aimed, but its language could reasonably be understood to cover the much more common technique of ordinary dilation and extraction, used in most abortions. Doctors who did "ordinary" abortions might be afraid of being prosecuted under the Nebraska statute and stop doing abortions entirely. Perhaps that was what the statute's sponsors wanted, but the effect, Breyer wrote, was to place an undue burden on the woman's right to choose abortion.

Breyer acknowledged that the difficulty could be remedied by statutory language expressly saying that it didn't ban ordinary abortions. The second constitutional hurdle was much harder—indeed, politically impossible—for antiabortion legislators to overcome. The difficulty, Breyer said, was that the Nebraska statute didn't allow doctors to perform the prohibited technique when they determined that doing so was necessary to preserve the woman's life or health. The "life" exception is simple, and even some antiabortion activists concede its merit in principle. Where continuing a pregnancy really does threaten the woman's life, the only decision is, Which life will be sacrificed, the woman's or the fetus's? There's no reason from a pro-life point of view to prefer one over the other.

The exception for threats to the woman's health was different. The Casey decision, Breyer wrote, "made clear that a State may promote but not endanger a woman's health when it regulates the methods of abortion." The majority in the Nebraska case was satisfied that sometimes the technique the state prohibited was the only way a woman could have an abortion without risking ruptures of the uterus and other serious medical conditions. That was enough to convince the majority that Nebraska's ban was unconstitutional because it didn't contain an exception allowing the technique to be used to avoid threats (from other abortion procedures, not from continuing the pregnancy) to the woman's health.

Antiabortion activists feared that the courts would treat exceptions to protect the woman's health too broadly, so that almost anything would count as a threat. Roe itself required states to make exceptions to abortion regulations in the third trimester when continuing the pregnancy threatened the woman's health, and it included in the category of threats to the woman's health the physical stresses of pregnancy and child care and the psychological stresses of unwanted pregnancies. Enacting a statute with an exception for the woman's health, where that category was as large as *Roe* suggested, wouldn't accomplish anything, in the eyes of the activists.

One possibility was to get the Court to define the scope of the required exception for the woman's health more narrowly than *Roe* had. To do that, however, a legislature had to enact a statute with such an exception, and antiabortion activists weren't willing to run the risk that the Court would uphold the statute *and* read the exception's language broadly. Their real hope was that the Court would overrule *Roe*, but the Casey decision showed that the Rehnquist Court wasn't going to do that. Only a Court with new appointees would.

Meanwhile, antiabortion activists pursued their culture conditioning strategy. They endorsed prosecutions for child endangerment of pregnant women who abused drugs. They supported prosecutions of people who assaulted pregnant women for injuring, and sometimes killing, the fetuses. If existing statutes didn't allow that sort of prosecution, they pushed legislatures to adopt new ones that did. The idea was that each one of these prosecutions and statutes showed that *sometimes* the wider public thought of fetuses as human beings. Eventually, antiabortion activists hoped, others would realize that treating a fetus as a human being when it was killed during an assault on the pregnant woman implied that *all* laws should treat fetuses as human beings entitled to protection from murder, whether by strangers who beat their mothers, by their fathers who beat their mothers, or—in the case of abortions—by their mothers alone. This was essentially a strategy for cultural change, indeed, for reversing the cultural changes that had occurred in the years leading up to *Roe* and, as the joint opinion in the Casey decision emphasized, in the years after *Roe* as well.

The joint opinion in *Casey* succeeded as an act of statesmanship, no matter its deficiencies as a matter of legal analysis. It basically took the abortion issue off the Supreme Court's agenda for more than a decade. The Court's pro-choice members were happy to get rid of the issue; the others weren't ready to risk another major defeat. Edwin Meese called "the Court's failure to overrule *Roe v. Wade*" the Reagan administration's "most disappointing loss," and the conservative legal community remained committed to overruling *Roe*. A united Court might overrule *Roe*, yet doing so might well produce the kind of backlash—this time from the pro-choice side—that generated the Court's divisions in the first place.

CHAPTER NINE

Race, Affirmative Action, and Crime

The story of race in the Rehnquist Court is simple. The Warren Court saw the status of African Americans as *the* central issue in constitutional law; the Burger Court saw it as an important issue; the Rehnquist Court did not see it as an issue at all. The Rehnquist Court worried not that public policy treated blacks unconstitutionally but that it treated whites unconstitutionally. For all practical purposes, concern over the status of African Americans in the law disappeared.

∽

Brown v. Board of Education was the defining moment in mid-century constitutional law. By the time Earl Warren retired as chief justice in 1969, the Court had, after a long period of quiescence, strongly encouraged lower courts to adopt desegregation plans that would, in Justice William Brennan's words, create systems "without a 'white' school and a 'Negro' school, but just schools." The lower courts tried their best. Within a few years federal courts were ordering school boards to redraw the lines for assigning children to particular schools and, even more, requiring them to assign children to schools away from their homes. These orders led to an uproar over school busing, an issue exploited by Richard Nixon and other Republicans in their political campaigns.

The Burger Court endorsed the power of the federal courts to require school busing. It also made it clear that segregated schools weren't a problem only in the South. Dealing with a case from Denver, the Court held that school boards violated the Constitution if they consciously adopted policies, such as drawing "neighborhood" school lines in ways that effectively separated blacks and whites, that resulted in schools that were white or black, not "just schools." It also held that federal courts could enter orders affecting an entire district even if the school board's policies had created segregation in only a part of the district.

Given the racial realities of urban America in the 1970s, these decisions meant that lower courts had the power to require any urban school district to adopt extensive busing programs. Many did. The Burger Court was plainly uncomfortable with how aggressive lower courts became and reined them in a bit. The most important decision involved Detroit and its suburbs. Stephen Roth, a conservative federal judge, was persuaded by the evidence that the Detroit school board had purposefully segregated the city's black children in separate schools for generations. Over time, though, the city had more and more blacks, fewer and fewer whites. Judge Roth realized that a desegregation order limited to the city's borders wouldn't help much. Most of the city's schools would still be "racially identifiable," as the jargon had it, and white parents might well accelerate their departure to the suburbs, making a difficult job of desegregation into an impossible one. Judge Roth responded by ordering an "interdistrict remedy"—that is, he ordered that Detroit and its suburbs cooperate in desegregating the schools. The plan he adopted ingeniously sliced the city and the suburbs into districts shaped like pie pieces, so children wouldn't ride buses for much longer than children in a Detroit only plan would have.

The Supreme Court balked. Writing for a sharply divided Court, Burger said that Judge Roth's interdistrict remedy punished the suburbs for Detroit's sins. A few years later Burger tried to repair the damage in an opinion holding that federal judges could order *educational* "remedies" to alleviate the inadequacies of segregated schools, but the initial Detroit decision meant that the Supreme Court had withdrawn from the project of achieving integrated schools in urban areas.

The desegregation case from Kansas City, Missouri, gave the Rehnquist Court the chance to cut back on the use of educational measures in such cases. Barred from pulling the city's suburbs into a desegregation plan, the federal district judge Russell Clark ordered the city and the state to increase their investments in the city's schools, directing them to reduce the average class sizes in the city's schools, to create specialized programs in science and the arts, to renovate run-down schools, and to install computers and—in a provision conservatives delighted in criticizing—swimming pools.

Judge Clark had two theories for what he did. As the city's schools got better, whites would move back into the city, making it easier to achieve integration without including the suburbs. Rehnquist said that magnet schools were one thing; a "magnet district," another. To Rehnquist and the Court's majority, Judge Clark was improperly trying to achieve effects outside Kansas City, the equivalent, Rehnquist said, to the interdistrict remedy the Court had disapproved for Detroit.

Judge Clark's second theory was that African American children in Kansas City's schools couldn't get an education equal to that available in integrated districts and so should get something else to compensate for that lack. The majority didn't take up this theory, but Justice Thomas did. He challenged Judge Clark's implicit assumption, as he saw it, that "anything that is predominantly black must be inferior." Judge Clark, according to Thomas, was "experiment[ing] with the education of [Kansas City's] black youth," trying out untested theories about what improved educational quality without any basis for thinking that the students weren't able to get a good education under the ordinary, predominantly black conditions in the city's schools.

The Rehnquist Court's retreat went further. It encouraged lower courts to get out of the business of trying to integrate the schools. In a case from Oklahoma City, it said that federal judges could stop supervising school districts when they found that the districts weren't violating the Constitution anymore and weren't likely to start up again. Then, in a case from Atlanta, the Court told judges to withdraw from supervision step by step. As soon as a school district showed that it was complying with the Constitution in one regard—no longer discriminating in assigning teachers to particular schools, for example—the judge could stop monitoring that part of the desegregation order even if the district still was violating the Constitution in some other way—for example, by drawing neighborhood school district lines to keep the races apart.

After 1995 the Rehnquist Court didn't hear a single case involving desegregation. A benign view of the Court's actions is that it adopted the strategy Senator George Aiken suggested for getting out of the hopeless Vietnam War. Seeing that integrating the nation's urban schools was impossible, the Rehnquist Court declared victory and went home.

∽

The Rehnquist Court saw the question of racial justice through the lens of affirmative action and its effects on whites. For generations liberals had quoted the dissenting opinion in the notorious 1896 case upholding racial segregation, in which Justice John Marshall Harlan (the grandfather of the Justice Harlan who served on the Warren Court) said, "The Constitution is color-blind." Affirmative action programs, conservatives said, were color-conscious. They quoted Martin Luther King's famous "I Have a Dream" speech, in which one of the things King dreamed of was a world where his children would be judged not "by the color of their skin but by the content of their character." Affirmative action programs, conservatives said, judged people by the color of their skin.

The term *affirmative action* goes back to the New Deal's labor laws, but it came into its own in the 1960s. President John F. Kennedy directed that federal contractors take "affirmative action to ensure that applicants are employed without regard to race." Lyndon Johnson strengthened the enforcement of this requirement by creating an office that monitored employment patterns and threatened to take federal contracts away from employers who didn't act affirmatively enough.

The real breakthrough for modern affirmative action came under Richard Nixon. In 1969 Nixon directed that federal contracts for construction in Philadelphia be held up until employers and unions agreed to set and meet goals for the employment of African Americans. His motivations were complex. The Philadelphia Plan, as it was known, was a way of appealing to African Americans, a counterbalance to Nixon's southern strategy of opposing school busing for desegregation. It also divided the traditional Democratic coalition of labor unions and African Americans.

Affirmative action had its start in employment, but it expanded to college admissions, and the legal standards were the same in both areas. As affirmative action took hold, the justifications its proponents offered expanded. Affirmative action was first a way of making sure that employers and colleges didn't discriminate against racial minorities. It was also a way of remedying what its proponents called societal discrimination, the pervasive effects of race on the opportunities available to African Americans, even when you couldn't point to some specific act of discrimination that denied a particular African American a job or a place in college. Finally, in some contexts, particularly education, affirmative action promoted diversity in groups that might benefit from learning about people from other racial groups.

By the time Rehnquist became chief justice the Court had set the fundamental outlines of the constitutional law dealing with affirmative action. In employment, the stage at which affirmative action programs kicked in mattered. Affirmative action was easier to justify when people were hired, harder to justify when they were promoted, and most difficult when they were fired. Affirmative action programs might set "goals," but they couldn't use strict numerical quotas, although no one was ever quite sure how you could distinguish between a goal and a quota when it mattered. But a government couldn't defend its affirmative action programs by pointing to societal discrimination, and the diversity justification seemed limited. Basically, then, the Court said that affirmative action was constitutional in employment only if it was adopted by a government trying to eliminate the effects of discriminatory actions in the past, whether by government itself or by private employers.

In higher education, the famous Bakke case set the standard, or more precisely, Justice Lewis F. Powell's opinion in *Bakke* set the standard. The case involved an admissions program at the medical school of one of the branches of the University of California. The medical school operated a two-track admissions program, reserving sixteen seats in its one-hundred-person class for racial minorities. Agreeing that the two-track system was unconstitutional, Powell rejected the broader argument that race could never be used in admissions decisions and concluded that universities could use affirmative action to achieve the educational benefits flowing from having a diverse student body.

The law of affirmative action wasn't stable, though. The Reagan administration strongly opposed affirmative action, and the Rehnquist Court ate away at its foundations. Powell had been a key figure in working out the Court's intermediate position, accepting affirmative action in principle but placing some ill-defined limits on it. His retirement in 1987 opened the way to reconsidering its constitutional status.

The first inroad occurred in 1989, when the Court struck down a program from Richmond, Virginia, that was modeled on federal affirmative action programs for construction. The Richmond City Council, which Justice O'Connor's opinion for the Court noted had an African American majority, set aside 30 percent of the amount of city contracts for minority-owned businesses. The city council showed that, over the preceding five years, less than 1 percent of the city's construction contracts had gone to minority-owned businesses in a city with a 50 percent black population. The council adopted the federal definitions of who qualified for the program, meaning that Richmond included "Eskimos or Aleuts" in the program, giving conservatives a rhetorical hook to disparage the program's silliness. But of course the program's point was to provide contracts for African American businesses.

O'Connor stated the tough standard affirmative action programs had to meet. The lawyers' jargon is *strict scrutiny*, which means, again in the jargon, that affirmative action programs have to be *narrowly tailored* to meet a *compelling state interest*. As O'Connor put it, strict scrutiny was needed when a "highly suspect tool" like racial classification was used so that courts could " 'smoke out' illegitimate uses of race." Addressing problems caused by societal discrimination had already been ruled out as a justification, so the only constitutionally permissible reason the city could have for its program was its own prior discrimination. And, O'Connor said, there simply wasn't enough evidence of such discrimination. The statistics were misleading, she wrote, because they compared the number of contracts awarded with the city's population as a whole. The real comparison had to be between contracts awarded and available minority-owned businesses. Maybe there weren't that many minority-owned businesses qualified for the contracts, or maybe minorities weren't interested in going into the construction business, O'Connor said.

The Court held open the possibility that some affirmative action programs might survive its strict scrutiny. Its next confrontation with affirmative action petered out, but along the way Scalia and Thomas stated their strong opposition to all forms of affirmative action. Scalia was pretty sure that no affirmative action program could ever be constitutional. "Government can never have a 'compelling interest' in discriminating on the basis of race in order to 'make up' for past racial discrimination in the opposite direction." He concluded, "In the eyes of government, we are just one race here. It is American." Thomas, writing his first opinion on affirmative action in 1995, also took a strong position. Racial classifications, he said, "ultimately have a destructive impact on the individual and our society." Affirmative action programs weren't at all "benign," as their defenders said. Rather, they "stamp minorities with a badge of inferiority and may cause them to develop dependencies or to adopt an attitude that they are 'entitled' to preferences," and that was unequivocally a bad thing.

In the 1990s the Court didn't uphold a single affirmative action program. In 1997 liberals were afraid that Sharon Taxman's case was going to give the Court the chance to slam the door on all affirmative action programs. Taxman had taught business classes in Piscataway, New Jersey, for nine years when the school board, facing drops in business class enrollment, decided to let one teacher go. The school board used seniority as the basis for keeping teachers on. But when it consulted its lists, the board discovered that Taxman and Deborah Wilson had been hired on the same day. Other tie breakers didn't help. Taxman and Wilson were just about equal in their teaching evaluations. Taxman had two more years of teaching experience than Wilson, but Wilson had a master's degree. In the past the school board had flipped a coin to decide whom to let go when there was a tie. This time it relied on race. Wilson was the only African American teacher in the high school's ten-person business department, in a system where 50 percent of the students were African American.

The school board rehired Taxman in 1992, when another teacher retired, but she sued for the wages she had lost between 1989 and 1992. The lower courts held that the school board violated the Constitution by choosing to let Taxman go solely because of her race, rejecting the board's argument that the race-based decision was justified because of its interest in ensuring that the school's African American students had a role model in the business department to look up to. The board decided to appeal to the Supreme Court, which agreed to hear the case.

Opponents of affirmative action regarded Taxman as an extraordinarily attractive "victim" of affirmative action and hoped that the Supreme Court would use her case to say that race could never be used in making employment decisions. Supporters of affirmative action feared that their adversaries were right. They cobbled together a group of organizations that raised over $300,000 to donate to the Piscataway school board. The board voted five to three to settle the case by paying $433,500, $186,000 in back pay to Taxman, the rest to her lawyers.

The settlement generated a spate of peculiar comments by columnists, who somehow thought it was wrong for interest groups to buy their way out of a case they thought might end up badly for them. Conservative Linda Chavez called Jesse Jackson a "bagman" for delivering the three hundred thousand dollars to the school board. Clint Bolick of the Institute of Justice said that the settlement "demonstrates panic within the civil rights establishment," which was, he thought, desperate to avoid "a knockout blow for racial preferences."

It's hard to see what was wrong with settling the case. Taxman wasn't an ideological crusader; as her lawyer said, "She just wants to be a teacher. She doesn't want to be a lightning rod for affirmative action." In addition, the school board was in a financial hole again, happy to avoid spending any more money for lawyers to brief and argue the case in the Supreme Court. The Supreme Court, in a routine order, dismissed the school board's appeal.

Opponents of affirmative action continued to hope that the Supreme Court would weigh in on their side. Some lower courts did. The federal court of appeals that handled cases from Texas, Louisiana, and Mississippi ruled that universities within its jurisdiction couldn't use race in making admissions decisions. Louisiana and Mississippi were able to continue their affirmative action programs because they were under federal court orders to do so. Texas modified its affirmative action program, which gave the Supreme Court a reason for ducking the case when the state tried to get a review. Voters in California and Washington adopted amendments to their state's constitutions barring their universities from engaging in affirmative action. Florida's governor Jeb Bush directed his state's universities to stop their affirmative action programs too. Affirmative action, in education at least, seemed to be on its last legs.

Then came the University of Michigan affirmative action cases.

⁂

Most accounts of the Supreme Court's 2003 decision upholding the principle of affirmative action in higher education begin with the plaintiffs, Jennifer Gratz and Barbara Grutter. The real story begins, though, not in Michigan but in Washington and not with applicants to the university but with conservative litigating groups.

After successful challenges to affirmative action in Texas and California, conservatives were looking for a way "to put the consideration of race beyond the reach of the state." Michael Greve and Michael McDonald, who had worked at the Washington Legal Foundation, founded the Center for Individual Rights in 1989. They wanted to focus on litigation taking the conservative side in free speech and civil rights controversies. After a decade they moved on, but the center continued. In 2003 it was headed by Terence Pell, with a budget of about $1.5 million, just under half coming from three major conservative foundations: the John M. Olin, Lynde and Harry Bradley, and Scaife Family foundations. Like other conservative litigating groups, the center had a small staff, and rather than engage in large-scale litigation, its leaders were "very choosy," deciding to "tell the story through someone who had experienced it firsthand." They canvassed the nation for people who would present the challenge to affirmative action in the most sympathetic light.

The center made its interest in generating a lawsuit against affirmative action widely known. Some Michigan legislators who had heard complaints from constituents that their children had not gotten in to the state's university because of affirmative action began to send it names of possible plaintiffs. The center picked Gratz and Grutter. Having located them, the center turned the actual litigation over to lawyers from a Minneapolis law firm who contributed their time to the case without asking for payment. The center remained involved in the publicity campaign that accompanied the litigation.

The daughter of a police officer and a hospital systems analyst, Gratz attended Southgate Anderson High School, in Detroit's southern suburbs. She had a good high school record and was something of a fanatical follower of the University of Michigan football team. She applied in 1995, hoping to become a doctor but wasn't admitted. Instead, she attended the university's branch at Dearborn and, saying that her rejection discouraged her, majored in math rather than premed. After graduating from the Dearborn campus, Gratz married and moved to San Diego, where she became a project manager and software trainer for a management consulting firm. She sued the University of Michigan in October 1997.

Barbara Grutter was a forty-three-year-old mother of two teenagers, running a health care consulting business from her home in Detroit's suburbs, when she applied to the University of Michigan's law school. Grutter had graduated from Michigan State University with a 3.8 grade point average and got a 161 on the Law School Admissions Test, putting her in the eighty-sixth percentile. These scores set her in the large middle group of applicants to Michigan's law school, and her experience in health care wasn't enough to get her in, although she was put on the school's waiting list. She was admitted to Wayne State University's law school in Detroit but decided against attending because it didn't have a health law concentration. (The University of Michigan Law School's Web site in 2003 showed that the school has a health law "curriculum interest area," which is a fairly small assemblage of courses touching on health care; the Wayne State Web site suggests that Grutter could have reproduced the "concentration" on her own there, although the offerings were a bit thinner.) Grutter filed her suit against Michigan's law school in December 1997.

The plaintiffs and defendants weren't the only important players in the litigation. As it turned out, former President Gerald Ford may have played the most important part. In 1999 Ford was having dinner with James Cannon, an old friend who had worked for him in the White House and then gone on to write his biography. A loyal alumnus of the University of Michigan, Ford talked with Cannon about the lawsuits against the university's affirmative action programs. Cannon, who had been chair of the board of visitors at the U.S. Naval Academy in Annapolis, mentioned how important affirmative action had been there. Ford had just published an op-ed in the *New York Times* defending the university's affirmative action program, and he and Cannon agreed that limiting affirmative action would be a "real handicap" to the school. Ford and Cannon decided to see if they could do something to help.

Cannon took on the job. He met with Lee Bollinger, then the university's president, to see what might be done. Cannon thought that it might help the case if he could line up a brief from people involved in military affairs that would explain how important affirmative action had been in creating the modern armed forces. He initially hoped that the Department of Defense itself would weigh in on the university's side, but the Bush administration was still struggling to develop a position in the case when Cannon had to get the brief put together. He put together a group of former military officers and civilians involved in military affairs, including retired General Norman Schwarzkopf and former Secretary of Defense William Cohen.

Marvin Krislov, the university's inside counsel, who had worked in the Clinton White House, contacted Joe Reeder, undersecretary of the army in the Clinton administration and in 2002 the managing partner at a large Washington law firm, to locate a lawyer who could write the military brief. Reeder in turn got in touch with Maureen Mahoney, whom the university had retained to argue the law school part of the case at the Supreme Court. Mahoney was a Republican, a former law clerk to Rehnquist (during the oral argument, Rehnquist once addressed her as Maureen), who had been nominated to the federal court of appeals by George H. W. Bush. The nomination died with Bush's defeat in 1992, and Mahoney continued to work in Washington as one of the city's leading appellate and Supreme Court practitioners. Mahoney recommended that Reeder contact Carter Phillips, who agreed to write the military amicus brief. Cannon and Reeder continued to line up military leaders to sign the brief. It was filed under the name of twenty-nine prominent leaders.

Ford and the military amicus brief showed where the establishment was on the issue of affirmative action. Any remaining doubts were dispelled by a brief filed by a group of Fortune 500 companies, also defending the importance of affirmative action in developing their work forces for what they described as the needs of their global operations.

As Justice Stevens told his colleagues, the question for the Court was whether the nine of them should decide or whether the Court should rely on "the accumulated wisdom of the country's leaders," as reflected in the amicus briefs. It takes a strong Supreme Court to resist when the establishment is so heavily on one side. The Rehnquist Court didn't.

The Court did strike down the affirmative action program the university had used when Gratz applied (which the university itself had modified before the case reached the Supreme Court), but its more important holding was that the law school's program was con-stitutional. Strikingly, seven justices agreed that the programs were exactly the same in constitutional terms; four thought both of them were unconstitutional, three that both were perfectly constitutional. Justices O'Connor and Breyer swung the case in favor of affirmative action by finding the law school program constitutionally permissible even if the undergraduate one was not.

Michigan's undergraduate admissions office had to process more than twenty thousand applications a year. To handle the volume, the office developed a point system. Applicants who got 100 out of a possible 150 points were admitted; those with lower point scores were deferred or denied admission. Applicants got points for their high school grades and their scores on admissions tests. They also could get a few points for being from Michigan, for writing an espe-cially good personal statement in the application, for personal achievements in the arts, and for being the child of a Michigan alum-nus. There was also a "miscellaneous" category. Applicants in that category—racial minorities and athletes the school wanted to recruit—got 20 points, a much larger number than was available for the other subjective categories. Basically, the undergraduate system meant that an applicant from a racial minority (or an athlete) who met minimum academic standards would be admitted, while others who had no more than that going for them would be rejected.

The law school's admissions process was different—on the sur-face. Dealing with a smaller number of applications, the admissions office looked at each application as a whole. Its staff would take aca-demic qualifications into account in deciding whether to admit the applicant. The staff was also guided by a faculty decision to seek a class that had what the university called a critical mass of minority students. The idea was that a class had to have enough minority students in it for everyone in the class to benefit from the perspectives those students brought to their classes. The critical mass was a goal for the admissions office to reach. It wasn't a quota, if a quota means a numerical goal to be met no matter what and never to be exceeded. There was some variation from year to year in the percentage of minority students admitted to the law school. But the record in the case strongly suggested that the variation was the natural result of competition among law schools for well-qualified minority students. The law school's director of admissions monitored the results of the admissions decisions, sometimes receiving daily reports, the only purpose of which was to ensure that "enough" minority applicants were being admitted to guarantee that the school would meet its goals. That in turn meant that if admissions decisions were going badly from that perspective, the weight to be given minority status might well vary depending on the time of year. In a "bad" year, minority status might count for a lot more later in the admissions season than it had earlier.

O'Connor wrote two opinions. One, for a five-justice majority, upheld the law school's "holistic" admissions process. The other, which Justice Breyer joined, agreed with Rehnquist's opinion striking down the undergraduate program. The difference, for her, was that the law school's program promised individualized consideration to every applicant, while the undergraduate process was too rigid, giving too much obvious weight to an applicant's race.

O'Connor took Powell's opinion in the Bakke case as her touchstone. She recited the governing legal standards: strict scrutiny, compelling interest, narrow tailoring. Achieving a racially diverse student body, she wrote, was indeed a compelling interest because it provided educational benefits through enhancing the quality of classroom discussions. The point of having a critical mass was to reduce the stereotype that all minority students thought alike. But in some tension with that idea, she also stressed that "one's own, unique experience of being a racial minority in a society, like our own, in which race unfortunately still matters," was "likely to affect an individual's views." The critical mass was needed, it seems, to dispel the idea that all racial minorities thought alike, but race could be taken into consideration because the mere fact of being one of a racial minority shaped each minority student's "unique" experience. Exactly how these two points could be reconciled is unclear.

According to O'Connor, racial diversity in universities had broader benefits. Citing the brief filed by the Fortune 500 companies, she said that "the skills needed in today's increasingly global marketplace can only be developed through exposure to widely diverse people, cultures, ideas, and viewpoints." And quoting important passages in the military brief, she endorsed the view that the military needed to be both selective and race-conscious in developing its leadership corps. Diversity in law schools was particularly important because of the role lawyers played in the nation's leadership. She concluded, "In order to cultivate a set of leaders with legitimacy in the eyes of the citizenry, it is necessary that the path to leadership be visibly open to talented and qualified individuals of every race and ethnicity."

She then turned to the question of narrow tailoring. The law school passed the test because it considered each applicant's file as a whole in a reasonably flexible way. The goal of achieving a critical mass and the daily monitoring of results didn't convert the system into an impermissible quota. Nor were there other ways to achieve the critical mass. The law school couldn't admit students by lottery because it wanted to maintain its status as an elite, selective law school. To get "enough" minorities through a lottery system, the school's standards would have to be lowered, and even then the chances of getting a critical mass weren't that great because there would be more white applicants included in the lottery as the pool expanded. A percentage plan, admitting a specified percentage of students from a range of undergraduate schools, wouldn't work for a law school drawing applicants from all over the country.

O'Connor's opinion was a nearly complete victory for proponents of affirmative action. The only concession she made to opponents was her insistence that affirmative action programs had to "have a logical end point," which could be met by "sunset provisions" in particular plans and periodic reconsideration of the need for affirmative action by every school that used it. She ended her opinion by noting the Court's expectation "that 25 years from now, the use of racial preferences will no longer be necessary."

Each dissenter wrote a separate opinion. Rehnquist's criticized

O'Connor's deference to the law school's judgments about what was needed to achieve its educational goals, a deference that he argued was inconsistent with the very idea that strict scrutiny was needed, as O'Connor herself had said in the Richmond case, to "smoke out" impermissible racial discrimination. He also criticized the critical mass idea. The problem he identified was that the law school lumped Hispanics and African Americans into the single "minority" group but then seemed to reject some Hispanics with better academic credentials than some admitted African Americans. This indicated, he said, that the school "capped out" Hispanic enrollment—imposed a quota—to ensure that the entering class would have a critical mass of African Americans.

Thomas wrote the most interesting and substantial dissent. Despite some rhetorical excesses, it made powerful points against the elite endorsement of affirmative action. Thomas observed that some states got along perfectly fine without having a law school at all, suggesting that operating a law school wasn't a compelling state interest. Even more, he argued, there wasn't anything particularly important about operating a *selective* law school. Abandon selectivity, and there would be no need for affirmative action. Indeed, he observed, many states that *did* operate law schools didn't define their schools' mission to be an elite institution of the sort that the University of Michigan Law School was. Thomas also noted that the law school's heavy reliance on the Law School Admissions Test generated its "need" for affirmative action, because everyone knew of the "poor performance" of African Americans, "relatively speaking," on the LSAT. The school could give up on the test *and* on affirmative action, but it couldn't continue to use a test with a racially disparate effect without accepting "the constitutional burdens that come with" doing so.

Thomas was exercised as well at the impact of the law school's programs on the minority students it admitted. It "tantalizes unprepared students," who "take the bait" of admissions, "only to find that they cannot succeed in the cauldron of competition." There was no evidence, he said, that minority students who attended the Michigan law school and were graduated low in the class got a better education than minority students who went to "a less 'elite' law school for which they were better prepared" and in which they might have done better. He was bitter that proponents of affirmative action "will never address the real problems facing 'underrepresented minorities,' instead continuing their social experiments on other people's children." Those real problems included the "crisis of black male underperformance," reflected in the fact that the law school had forty-eight black women students and twenty-eight black men, and the "racial gap in academic credentials" resulting from the inadequate academic resources available to racial minorities at the college and even the elementary and secondary school levels.

Striking down the undergraduate program was small cheese after O'Connor's opinion in the law school case. Souter and Ginsburg dissented anyway. Ginsburg's opinion recited evidence showing that "large disparities" between the races persisted in the United States and insisted that race could be used as a means of promoting inclusion rather than exclusion. Because the "stain of racial oppression is still visible in our society," she wrote, we could expect universities to try to "maintain their minority enrollment." Better "candor" than "camouflage," she said. Souter made the same point. He was "tempted to give Michigan an extra point of its own for its frankness. Equal protection cannot become an exercise in which the winners are the ones who hide the ball."

Scalia's dissent in the law school case sketched a road map for future challenges to university affirmative action programs: Disappointed applicants could say that the school hadn't given them enough individualized consideration, or that the school's critical mass really was a quota, or that the school wasn't really committed to diversity in the classroom if it "talk[ed] the talk of multiculturalism and racial diversity in the courts but walk[ed] the walk of tribalism and racial segregation . . . through minority-only student organizations, separate minority housing opportunities, separate minority student centers, even separate minority-only graduation ceremonies." The litigation he described wasn't likely, and not just because the Court discouraged it with its tacit approval of affirmative action for a generation. It wasn't likely because it was going to be expensive. The Center for Individual Rights had the resources to finance one big lawsuit that might have knocked out affirmative action everywhere. It didn't have the resources to support scores of lawsuits against affirmative action programs that, as

Souter and Ginsburg noted, weren't likely to be transparent in the way they operated. Michael Greve called the decisions "a complete wipeout" and observed, "What happens in the litigation community? It becomes harder to drum up money for this and harder to persuade people this is a righteous fight." Curt Levey of the Center for Individual Rights did say that the group would soldier on, but he also said, "We have to pick good targets," or as others suggested, the fight would turn away from the courts to legislatures and ballot initiatives. The Rehnquist Court, though, took itself out of the picture for a while.

⚬⫯⚬

Questions of racial justice were directly raised in the segregation and affirmative action cases. The Warren and Burger Courts got into trouble when they took those questions seriously. The Warren Court got into even more trouble when it connected racial justice and the administration of criminal justice. That Court's boldness in constitutionalizing the law of police behavior was driven in large part by the justices' perception that the enforcement of the criminal law was tightly bound up with the nation's racial divisions. Many of the cases that shaped those justices' understanding of what law enforcement meant on the ground arose out of racially charged confrontations. The Rehnquist Court lost any sense that criminal justice issues were closely tied to issues of race, separating the constitutional law of law enforcement from the constitutional law of race, even as Rodney King's beating by Los Angeles police officers confirmed for many observers that the Warren Court's perception was more accurate than the Rehnquist Court's.

The Rehnquist Court took up the relation between race and criminal justice most extensively in a death penalty case in 1987. After that, it decided two important cases with racial overtones the Warren Court's justices would have noticed immediately, and in both the Rehnquist Court saw neither the specter of race nor any serious constitutional problem. Probably the most remarkable thing about one of those cases is that it was unanimous. Even the Rehnquist Court's liberals, that is, were not liberals in the Warren Court mold.

In the death penalty case Warren McCleskey presented the Rehnquist Court with a fully developed challenge to race-based

imposition of the death penalty. McCleskey had been convicted of
killing a police officer who walked in on a robbery. McCleskey's
lawyers hired social scientists to examine *when* juries returned capital
sentences. It turned out that the common intuition—that African
Americans received death sentences more often than whites did—
didn't stand up to examination once everything else about the crime
was taken into account. But there *was* a racial element in the administration of the death penalty. If you put aside the most egregious
murders, in which entire families are massacred, for example, and
those in which the killing is almost understandable, as when an
abused wife stabs her husband, there's a large middle category of bad
but not stomach-churning murders. When you look at cases in that
category, you find that African Americans who killed whites were
more than four times as likely to receive a death sentence as African
Americans who killed other African Americans. It's easy enough to
see this as an example of a structure of race discrimination. The "system" values African American lives less than it does white lives, not
because it executes African Americans more readily but because it
doesn't care as much about African American victims.

McCleskey's case was in the middle category. (You might think
that cases in which police officers were killed would be in the
"almost always impose the death penalty" category, but in fact
McCleskey was the only defendant in Fulton County, Georgia, who
received the death penalty for killing a police officer, out of seventeen cases from 1973 and 1979.) McCleskey's attack on the death
penalty was based on the racial disparities the social scientists had
discovered. Inside the Court Justice Powell was skeptical about the
statistical evidence, writing his colleagues, "No study can take all . . .
individual circumstances into account." He "couldn't decide criminal cases on statistics alone," he told them. Instead, his opinion
rejecting McCleskey's challenge said, McCleskey would have to show
that the particular jury that sentenced him to death took race into
account when it made its decision. That of course was an impossible
standard for defendants to meet. Any other rule, according to
Powell, would bring "into serious question the principles that under-
lie our entire criminal justice system." McCleskey had to show that
racial prejudice—by a prosecutor, by the jury, by someone—infected
his particular case, although Powell didn't say how he could do that.

Brennan's dissent began: "At some point in this case, Warren McCleskey doubtless asked his lawyer whether a jury was likely to sentence him to die. A candid reply to this question would have been disturbing. . . . The story could be told in a variety of ways, but McCleskey could not fail to grasp its essential narrative line: there was a significant chance that race would play a prominent role in determining if he lived or died."

Brennan, an old-fashioned liberal on these matters, saw the connection between race and criminal justice differently from his colleagues in the majority. Their concern that McCleskey's argument, if accepted, would undermine the entire system was right, but, Brennan wrote, the concern suggested "a fear of too much justice." By the end of the Rehnquist era, though, the connection between race and criminal justice had basically disappeared from the liberals' jurisprudence of constitutional law except for racial profiling, where liberals and conservatives might well agree anyway.

Michael Whren, a drug dealer in Washington, D.C., was typical of the people whose cases raise important issues about police practices. Gail Atwater was not at all typical; she was a soccer mom who ran a bed-and-breakfast outside Austin, Texas. Warren Court liberals would have known what the Whren and Atwater cases were about—the relation between American's police officers and its racial minorities—even though race was not directly involved in either case. Their cases involved the Fourth Amendment, which protects against unreasonable searches and seizures and requires probable cause for arrests. (This is an oversimplification of a complex body of law, but presenting the complexities wouldn't clarify the problems in the Whren and Atwater cases.) Fourth Amendment law in the Rehnquist Court suppressed the racial dimension of the practices Whren and Atwater challenged.

On a June evening in 1993 James Brown was driving his car in southeast Washington, with Whren as a passenger. He stopped at a stop sign but didn't pull into the intersection quickly enough for Efrain Soto, an undercover police officer in an unmarked police car that made a turn in front of Brown's car. Soto saw the driver glancing at his passenger's lap. As the unmarked police car continued slowly down the block and made a U-turn, Brown suddenly turned at the intersection without signaling and sped off. Suspicions aroused, Soto drove next to Brown's car and directed him to put the car in neutral. Looking in the window, Soto saw Whren with two large plastic bags that Soto believed to contain cocaine. Whren yelled, "Pull off, pull off," and tried to hide the bags. Soto yanked the car door open, dived across Brown, and grabbed one of the bags from Whren's hands.

Good police work, you might think. The problem was that police can't stop drivers simply on a hunch that something bad is going on. They have to have probable cause to believe that a crime is happening. While what Soto saw was undoubtedly suspicious, it almost certainly wasn't enough to amount to probable cause to believe that Brown and Whren were dealing drugs.

Not to worry. The officers did have probable cause to believe that Brown was indeed violating the law—not the drug laws but the traffic laws. Brown had made a turn without signaling and—my favorite—stopped too long at a stop sign, violating the traffic code provision requiring drivers to "give full time and attention to the operation of the vehicle." Obviously, *every* driver violates that provision: Make a call on a cell phone or change the channels on your car radio, and you're not devoting full attention to the car's operation.

There's one more piece of the picture. Soto was in an unmarked police car, and the police department's regulations directed that undercover officers in unmarked cars shouldn't make routine traffic stops. And for good reason. When you see someone in an unmarked car signal you to pull over, you don't know whether it's an unmarked police car or a couple of criminals about to rob you or steal your car. Letting undercover officers in unmarked cars make traffic stops is a recipe for disaster; people will drive away in fear, causing accidents as they flee, or criminals will impersonate police officers to get access to their victims. The police department's rules let everybody in the city know that they shouldn't stop when someone in an unmarked car told them to—a good rule for the police and for everyone else.

So on the level of criminal justice *policy*, Officer Soto's actions actually weren't good police work. They were dangerous to the community. The problem faced by Whren's lawyers was to translate this policy concern into a constitutional one. Using the probable cause rule alone wasn't enough because Soto did have probable cause to arrest Brown for the traffic violations. So the lawyers pointed out the obvious: Soto used the traffic violation as a "pretext" for stopping somebody he suspected—without probable cause—of violating the drug laws. They argued that such pretextual searches should be unconstitutional because particularly in light of the ease of finding probable cause that a car's driver was violating some traffic law, they were a way police officers could get around the real point of the probable cause requirement, which was to limit the extent to which police officers can intrude on ordinary people's lives.

The Supreme Court unanimously disagreed. Scalia's opinion focused on precedents that seemed to say that once the police had probable cause, that was the end of it. *Why* they went after somebody was irrelevant, as long as they had probable cause to think that their target was indeed violating the law. The Court's decision was not out of line with the cases Scalia relied on. There's nothing particularly troubling, even, in the fact that the Court's liberals joined the opinion. What does deserve notice is that no one even thought it necessary to write a separate opinion pointing out the way pretextual searches could be—or were likely to be—used by police officers in minority communities (where every car with a broken taillight might become the pretext for a search). Scalia's opinion mentioned the fact that the defendants' lawyers argued that allowing pretextual searches meant that officers "might decide which motorists to stop based on decidedly impermissible factors, such as the race of the car's occupants." But in the end his opinion said that whatever problem there might be, it should be handled as a problem of race discrimination, not one involving the probable cause rule. Still, other Rehnquist Court decisions, such as Warren McCleskey's, make it hard for defendants to establish that the police engage in selective enforcement, taking race into account in targeting their enforcement efforts. Scalia didn't mention those decisions either. The distance from the Warren Court era was immeasurable.

The Whren case was about *when* the police can arrest you. Gail Atwater discovered what they could do afterward. Atwater's case never went to trial, so the facts the Supreme Court relied on were only her allegations about what happened. Those facts, Justice O'Connor said, gave her the "perfect case." There's some reason to

believe that the real events were a little more complicated than
Atwater alleged, but as it turned out, five justices were willing to
reject even a perfect case.

Atwater lived in Lago Vista, Texas, a suburb of five thousand people north of Austin. She had worked as a nurse, but after marrying
her doctor husband, she started to run a bed-and-breakfast on Lake
Travis outside Austin. Atwater said that on May 26, 1997, she was
driving her children, six-year-old Anya and four-year-old Mac, back
from soccer practice when one of the kids noticed that a favorite
plastic toy vampire attached to her pickup's window by suction cups
was missing. She figured that the toy might have fallen out of the car
somewhere on the way home, so she turned around and started driving slowly back over the route she had just taken. She told the kids to
unbuckle their seat belts and look out the car window to see if they
could spot the toy.

Police officer Bart Turek saw Atwater's kids and remembered
that he had stopped her a couple of weeks earlier for letting Mac
ride without a seat belt. He was wrong then, but this time he was
sure he had her. Turek had been a patrol officer for three years. The
city's mayor said that Turek was "not exactly a graduate of the
school of good manners," and his gun and badge gave "him a sense
of imagined importance." Turek stopped Atwater and asked for her
license and proof of insurance. She told him that she didn't have
them because her purse had been stolen a few days before. Turek
then arrested her for violating the seat belt law. According to
Atwater, Turek screamed at her, although Turek never accepted that
allegation. He arrested and handcuffed Atwater. A bunch of neighbors and kids watched Atwater's arrest, and one of her neighbors
took Anya and Mac home after Turek took her to the police station.
(According to the city, Turek waited to make sure that someone
took care of the children before he left with Atwater.) At the station
Atwater was booked and photographed and held in a jail cell for an
hour before she was released. Later she paid fifty dollars for the seat
belt violations.

Some of Lago Vista's citizens were upset about the city's police
department. They hired Charles Lincoln, who filed five lawsuits
challenging arrests that Turek and other officers had made. The
city's mayor, who lived down the block from Atwater and her hus-

band, called Atwater "an independent 'free spirit' who is very protective of her rights." Atwater agreed that she deserved to be stopped and fined, but she said she "didn't deserve to be arrested."

Lincoln argued that Officer Turek had violated the Constitution by taking Atwater into custody for a minor traffic violation, which carried no possible jail sentence but only a fine of fifty dollars. Lincoln wasn't highly regarded in the local legal community. Judge Sam Sparks, who heard Atwater's case, told Lincoln to stop practicing in his court a week before he decided the case, and Lincoln later was disbarred for taking money from clients' accounts. Judge Sparks threw out all of Lincoln's cases against Lago Vista. The seat belt law said that violators could be arrested and taken into custody, and Judge Sparks held that the Constitution didn't stop a state from deciding that an offense that might seem minor could be the basis for taking someone into custody, if only for a short period. Cases like Atwater's (or maybe Lincoln's) are "the bane of the American legal system," Sparks said.

Atwater had a different lawyer when the case got to the Supreme Court. The outcome was the same, though. O'Connor did indeed join the liberals. Unfortunately for Atwater, Souter didn't. He wrote an opinion joined by Kennedy and the Court's other conservatives, saying that the Constitution allowed the police to arrest someone for a minor criminal offense like Atwater's seat belt violation even if the "crime" couldn't result in a jail sentence. Souter's opinion referred to learned scholars of English law, who didn't have a settled understanding of what the police—or constables, to use the old-fashioned term—could do in the eighteenth century. Constables could arrest people for "cozening with false dice," Souter wrote, quoting one of the authorities. Indeed, his opinion seems designed to list as many archaic terms and crimes as it could. The upshot was that when the Fourth Amendment was drafted, there was no understanding that the police couldn't arrest a person whom they saw committing a minor crime. Souter concluded that nothing had changed since then: Federal and state courts upheld the power of police officers to arrest people for minor offenses.

He acknowledged that Atwater presented a sympathetic case and said that if the Court could come up with "a rule exclusively to address the uncontested facts of this case, Atwater might well prevail." He agreed that handcuffing Atwater and taking her to the police station were "merely gratuitous humiliations imposed by a police officer who was (at best) exercising extremely poor judgment." Kennedy had said at oral argument, "It's not a constitutional violation for a police officer to be a jerk." Basically, Souter agreed.

Atwater said there should be a rule against arresting someone for a fine only crime, but Souter responded that an officer might not know immediately which kind of crime he had seen. Penalties varied for crimes that looked a lot alike: a fine for a first conviction for driving while intoxicated, jail for a second offense; a fine for possessing a small amount of marijuana, jail for possessing a gram more than the minimum. The only clear rule that would work was one allowing the police to arrest whenever they saw someone violating the law, no matter how minor. Souter pointed out that some states had prohibited their officers from arresting people for minor offenses and suggested that a legislative solution to the problem, such as it was, was better than a constitutional one.

O'Connor's dissent ignored history to focus on Fourth Amendment policy. The Fourth Amendment required that arrests be reasonable, and to O'Connor and the three liberals who joined her, Officer Turek's actions simply weren't reasonable. She agreed with Atwater that the police shouldn't be allowed to take someone into custody for an offense whose only penalty was a fine; issuing a citation would be good enough to serve the state's interests and would avoid humiliations like those Atwater had experienced.

The aftermath of the case for the participants was generally unhappy. Turek resigned from the police force. The lawsuit put strains on Atwater's marriage. She and her husband had to pay a hundred thousand dollars to their lawyers, and they had to sell their house and close the bed-and-breakfast business, converting it into their home.

The implications for the rest of the country were clear as well. Souter's opinion observed that when he asked Robert DeCarli, Atwater's lawyer, at oral argument, "How big is the problem?," Atwater's lawyer had been able to point to only a single incident, a young girl taken into custody for eating french fries on the Washington, D.C., subway. The country, Souter concluded, was "not confronting anything like an epidemic of minor-offense arrests."

The problem wasn't the country as a whole, though. As DeCarli observed, "If the city's position is accepted by the courts, anyone who receives a ticket—no matter how small the infraction—could be handcuffed and hauled off to jail." Coupled with the Whren decision, *Atwater* might allow *anyone* driving a car to be hauled off to jail. But as the Texas director of the American Civil Liberties Union said, "We know who will be most affected if the city wins—Latino and African American men."

O'Connor's dissent referred to the decision's "potentially serious consequences for the everyday lives of Americans." It also referred to "the recent debate over racial profiling," which, she said, demonstrated that "a relatively minor traffic infraction may serve as an excuse for stopping and harassing an individual." As she delicately put it, the Whren decision put police officers' subjective motivations outside the courts' purview, making it all the more important to place some limits on what officers did after they stopped someone. It's hard to avoid the suspicion that the fact that Atwater was a soccer mom made it easier for O'Connor to see the implications of the case for racial minorities.

The Whren and Atwater decisions together licensed racist police officers to act on their impulses, leaving victims with legal remedies that were available in theory but unavailable in practice. The Warren Court's liberals would have been more sensitive to the racial implications of these cases even though the cases weren't formally about race at all.

℘

O'Connor's attempt to put a twenty-five-year sunset on affirmative action in the Michigan law school case was legally a fantasy. Twenty-five years are an eternity in constitutional law; the Court reconsidered its abortion decision nineteen years after *Roe v. Wade* and overruled its sodomy decision after only seventeen years. The sunset provision was a signal, not a holding or a doctrine. O'Connor was telling everyone, including those who might be appointed to the Court over the next few years, that it was done with affirmative action for the foreseeable future. Technically, new justices could reopen the issue, but O'Connor's opinion meant that they would have to confront not only the issue of affirmative action itself but the preliminary issue of stare decisis.

The sunset provision symbolized the Court's withdrawal from the arena of racial justice. The time might come again when the Court reentered it. But for the next few years it would await the developments in politics and culture that might create a permanent united majority on issues of racial justice.

CHAPTER TEN

The Federalism Revolution

Linda Greenhouse, the longtime Supreme Court correspondent for the *New York Times*, finally persuaded her editors to give her space on the front page for an analysis of the Supreme Court's federalism revolution. Greenhouse thought that the Rehnquist Court had dramatically repudiated a central feature of the Constitution as it had developed since the New Deal, the ability of the national government to do pretty much whatever it wanted under the guise of regulating the national economy.

The problem Greenhouse faced was that no one really cared about the federalism revolution. People care about what government can do; federalism is about which government can do it. One of the Rehnquist Court's decisions stopped the national government from prosecuting a high school student who brought a gun to school, but the majority agreed, indeed emphasized, that the state could prosecute the student for the very same offense. The issue of how much power the national government has and the related question of states' rights were important in the past. States' rights were the constitutional bulwark of slavery and, later, of segregation. The consolidation of national power over civil rights transformed the issue of federalism. By the end of the Rehnquist Court era, states' rights was the rallying cry for people who simply wanted a smaller national government and who didn't realize that limiting national power did nothing to limit *government* power or thought that they could stop state and local governments from acting more easily than they could stop the national government from acting.

The question for liberals was how to address the federalism revolution. In Washington jargon, the liberal challenge to the federalism revolution didn't have legs. Liberal activists tried to get Democrats in Congress to understand that the federalism revolution was a real threat to congressional power generally. They discovered that members of Congress cared about particular issues—gun control, the rights of the disabled, and more—but rarely cared about the questions of political theory raised by the Rehnquist Court's federalism decisions.

The Rehnquist Court did revolutionize federalism doctrine. What it didn't do was revolutionize the actual scope of national power. Instead, the Rehnquist Court opened the door for a later Court to do that without dramatically changing the doctrine handed to it in 2004.

෧

What *is* federalism, and why should anyone care about it? From a constitutional point of view, the rules of federalism describe the things the national government *can't* do even if there's a national majority in favor of them.

To James Madison and other framers, federalism was important because it allowed the national government to act on matters requiring coordinated national action while ensuring that the national government wouldn't be so powerful that it threatened liberty. Madison said that the national government's powers were "few and defined" precisely to guarantee that it wouldn't be able to threaten Americans' freedoms.

There was a serious difficulty with treating federalism as a protection of liberty. Madison may not have been disingenuous in saying that the powers given the new national government were few and defined, but he certainly was mistaken. Of course some of Congress's powers are limited; you can't get a whole lot of mileage out of the provision giving it the power to "provide for the Punishment of counterfeiting the Securities and current Coin of the United States." Other provisions, though, were open to much wider use. Two turned out to be central to constitutional development. Congress was given the power to "regulate Commerce with foreign Nations, and among the several States," and the power to "lay and collect Taxes . . . to pay the Debts and provide for the common Defence and general Welfare of the United States." The so-called interstate commerce clause drove the expansion of the national government's power from the middle of the nineteenth century through the twentieth. It was supplemented from the middle of the twentieth century by widening use of the power to spend money raised through national taxes. As the nation expanded, so did national power, and federalism's role in protecting liberty became increasingly problematic.

From 1789 to the Civil War the question of national power was inextricably bound up with the slavery question. Southerners feared national actions the constitutionality of which might rest on theories that would authorize Congress to regulate slavery in the South and in the nation's new territories to the west. They worried that the commerce clause might be used to regulate or even abolish slavery, which was, after all, a system that involved commercial transactions, often crossing state lines, in the sale and purchase of human beings.

The North's victory in the Civil War eliminated slavery as the focal point of concerns over expansive exercises of national power, although the southern interest in preserving segregation through states' rights continued to shape the discussion of the scope of national power. The Civil War also showed that national power could in fact be used effectively to advance important social goals and to protect rather than to threaten liberty. Three constitutional amendments adopted after the Civil War—eliminating slavery, protecting rights against state governments, and banning race discrimination in voting—also rested on the idea that national power could protect liberty.

Perhaps more important, national economic expansion spurred Congress to exercise its power to regulate interstate commerce. Here the railroad was the engine of change. Railroads created a national economy, linking farmers in the Midwest to consumers in the East. They were also dangerous: They derailed; they blew up; they crushed workers when cars jostled one another. Political pressure to regulate railroad rates and railroad operations increased. In 1887 Congress enacted the Interstate Commerce Act, which is generally taken to be the start of the modern era of constitutional expansion of national power and erosion of state power.

Congress took advantage of the constitutional opportunities provided by the new economic order. It enacted one statute after another, regulating food and drugs, worker safety, and more. The Supreme Court sporadically attempted to stem the tide by saying that Congress had acted beyond the scope of the "few and defined" powers the Constitution gave it. For example, in 1918 the Court held that Congress didn't have the power to ban interstate shipment of goods made by children. Its interventions did little to stem the expansion of national power, though.

Everything came to a head with the Great Depression. Franklin Roosevelt argued that the economic emergency demonstrated that only action on a national level could preserve economic stability, ensure economic growth, and in general promote the general welfare. For a brief period the Supreme Court resisted the New Deal's economic initiatives, but its resistance collapsed after 1937, when the justices gave up in the face of Roosevelt's assault, or they came to realize the implications of some of their pre–New Deal doctrines, or the justices who distrusted the exercise of national power were replaced by justices favorable to it, depending on which historian you read. In a case that became the stalking horse for the Rehnquist Court, the Supreme Court upheld a statute giving Congress the power to fine a wheat farmer for growing too much wheat, the excess of which the farmer planned to use on his own farm without selling it to anyone. The Court's theory was that Farmer Filburn's home consumption of his own wheat stopped him from buying someone else's wheat, and his actions, taken together with those of all the other farmers who raised wheat for on-farm consumption, thereby depressed the national market for wheat.

From 1937 to the Rehnquist Court federalism meant nothing as a restriction on Congress's power. The Rehnquist Court's federalism revolution consisted of replacing that zero with something more than zero. But not much more. The Court's traditional Republicans believed that the exigencies of the modern economy and the needs and desires of the American people required more of the national government than its more modern Republicans did.

❦

The Rehnquist Court had several weapons to use in conducting its federalism revolution, although it turns out that counting the weapons is itself a bit tricky. Two constitutional amendments seem to protect federalism by their own terms. But on close examination, the constitutional text can't do much work. Liberal critics of the Rehnquist Court pointed out that justices who made the Constitution's text central to their jurisprudence should have been at least a little embarrassed by carrying out a federalism revolution with weapons crafted outside the text.

Probably the least important weapon in the federalism revolution was the Eleventh Amendment. It says that "the Judicial power of the United States shall not be construed to extend to any suit . . . against one of the United States by Citizens of another State. . . ." The amendment, the first one added after the adoption of the Bill of Rights, was the states' outraged response to one of the Supreme Court's earliest decisions. The former colonies had gotten into a lot of financial difficulty during and after the Revolutionary War, and a key political issue in the nation's early years was whether the states were going to have to pay their debts. In England the idea that the king could do no wrong or, more precisely, that all the courts were technically the king's courts generated the idea of sovereign immunity, that the government couldn't be held responsible in its own courts for its wrongdoing.

The new states were confident that they could invoke sovereign immunity to bar suits attempting to collect state debts in *state* courts, even though the idea of sovereign immunity was in some tension with the idea that governments were now to be responsible to the people. Unfortunately for them, the new national government had its own courts, and the theory that generated sovereign immunity wasn't obviously applicable to suits against states in the new national courts. Even worse, the Constitution gave those courts the power to decide cases "between a State and Citizens of another State," language that would seem to allow a South Carolina cloth merchant to sue Georgia to collect unpaid bills for clothing supplied to Georgia's soldiers during the Revolution, exactly what happened in *Chisholm v. Georgia* (1793). The states rejected the Court's decision, and the Eleventh Amendment moved rapidly through

Congress, got the needed ratifications quickly, and then—for reasons no one quite understands—wasn't proclaimed to be part of the Constitution until 1798.

By protecting the states against some lawsuits, the Eleventh Amendment is indeed one weapon to use in a federalism revolution. The text, however, isn't all that helpful. It says that a state can't be sued by someone from *another* state. But of course today what really matters is a suit by one of the state's own citizens. The Eleventh Amendment doesn't speak to that at all. The Supreme Court in the late nineteenth century gave the Rehnquist Court what it needed in a series of cases holding that despite the Eleventh Amendment's express terms, what it really meant was that states couldn't be sued in the national courts by anyone (other than other states and the national government). This new-fashioned, nontextual "Eleventh Amendment" became part of the Rehnquist Court's federalism revolution. Its reach is nevertheless limited because it deals only with how you can go about making sure that states comply with national laws and doesn't deal with the scope of the national government's power.

The Tenth Amendment might seem more promising. It says, "The powers not delegated to the United States by the Constitution . . . are reserved to the States. . . ." This picks up on Madison's idea that the national government's powers were few and defined. The difficulty here, though, was captured by Justice Harlan Fiske Stone's observation in 1941 that the amendment "states but a truism." It says that if Congress doesn't have a power, the states do. The issue in federalism cases, however, is whether Congress has the power in the first place.

What's left is the list of powers delegated to Congress in the Constitution. To adapt Madison's term, the trick lies in defining the specific powers so that the list both gives Congress the power to do what's important for the nation and limits that power to ensure that states still have an important role. The Court has tried two methods of definition, and neither generated satisfactory constitutional doctrine over the medium to long run.

The first method was to give the term *commerce* (and the other terms used in the list of congressional powers) a meaning that preserves some domain for state governments to act. But the limiting definitions that the Court's been able to come up with stop Congress from doing things that too many people, including

Supreme Court justices, think ought to be done. In 1895, for example, the Court said that manufacturing wasn't interstate commerce and blocked the government from stopping the creation of a monopoly over the manufacture of refined sugar. By the 1930s, if not earlier, that decision seemed out of line with what regulating a modern economy required.

The Rehnquist Court's federalism revolution focused on the other method of defining the scope of the listed powers. It's sometimes called the enclave theory. The idea is to identify areas where regulation by the states, rather than by the national government, is so important that the national government has to stay out. The difficulty here lies in figuring out what those areas are. The usual candidates are family law, land use regulation, ordinary criminal law, and elementary and secondary education. Yet Congress has intruded on each of these areas, sometimes extensively and in ways that many people, including some conservatives, think is entirely justified.

None of the textual weapons available to the Rehnquist Court were terribly effective for conducting a federalism revolution. The Court did have one additional weapon, and it may have been the most important: focus on the Constitution's overall structure rather than on the words of particular provisions. The Constitution is pervaded by the assumption that states exist and have an important role in our government. The New Deal constitutional transformation basically rejected that assumption. It treated the states as administrative units that Congress could use if it wanted to and could bypass whenever it chose. The Rehnquist Court could appeal to a perfectly defensible sense that in our system of government states had to amount to something. It couldn't explain what that something was or, even more, why anyone should care. This was the revolution's strength. The Rehnquist Court could get away with a dramatic change in constitutional doctrine. It was also the revolution's weakness: The dramatic change in doctrine had essentially no effects on the actual exercise of congressional power.

॰৶০

Rehnquist set the long fuse for the federalism revolution shortly after he joined the Court, in a case challenging the constitutionality of one of Richard Nixon's antiinflation measures. Nixon got

Congress to adopt a statute freezing wages and setting up a pay board that limited wage increases. Ohio's legislature, then quite susceptible to pressure from public employee unions, enacted a statute raising state wages by more than the pay board allowed. Ohio thus challenged the federal statute. The Burger Court found no constitutional problems and ordered Ohio to limit its wage increases. Rehnquist was the only dissenter. He thought it was a "danger to our federal system" to allow the national government to prescribe wages for state employees. For him, each state had "an affirmative constitutional right, inherent in its capacity as a State, to be free from such congressionally asserted authority." He referred to both the Tenth and the Eleventh Amendments but acknowledged that their words were not what mattered to him: "Both Amendments are simply examples of the understanding of those who drafted and ratified the Constitution that the States were sovereign in many respects, and that . . . Congress was . . . not free to deal with a State as if it were just another individual or business enterprise subject to regulation." There were, he agreed, "gray areas" and hard problems of drawing lines, but he thought that the wage freeze was clearly on the wrong side of the line.

Rehnquist prevailed a year later, when the Court again confronted questions about Congress's power to set wages for state employees, but his victory was short-lived. The case involved applying federal minimum wage and overtime laws to employees of state and local governments. Most local governments were willing to pay the federal minimum wage, and many paid well above that. What mattered to them were the overtime provisions, particularly for their police and fire departments. The difficulty was that national laws limited the ability of local governments to require their first responders to accept compensatory time off, at a premium rate, when they had to do overtime work. These comp time requirements were a convenient tool for working out the staffing requirements for first responders, much better than paying a premium wage for required overtime. A sharply divided Court held that Congress couldn't require states to comply with the federal minimum wage and overtime provisions, for employees performing "traditional governmental functions."

It turned out, though, that the category of "traditional governmental functions" wasn't at all easy to identify. Over the next decade the Court confronted a series of cases that tested its ability to draw a sensible line between those functions and everything else a local government did. By 1985 Justice Blackmun, a member of the majority that gave state and local governments immunity from the federal minimum wage laws, had had enough. Writing for the Court, he overruled the earlier decision, saying that the traditional governmental functions test had turned out to be "unworkable." The difficulty, he said, was that a federal system had to let states figure out what they wanted to do; there was no fixed category of functions that states did or did not have to perform.

Justice O'Connor brought her perspective as a former state legislator to the case and dissented. Using a martial metaphor appropriate to someone who would participate in the Rehnquist Court's federalism revolution, she began her opinion, "The Court today surveys the battle scene of federalism and sounds a retreat. . . . I would prefer to hold the field and, at the very least, render a little aid to the wounded." The expansion of national power because of economic growth, she believed, required the Court to develop complementary restrictions on Congress's power to regulate state and local governments.

That, though, was the problem. As had Rehnquist, O'Connor noted the difficulty of "craft[ing] bright lines defining the scope of state autonomy." But she didn't really say what even fuzzy lines would look like. Rehnquist dissented too but said, "I do not think it incumbent on those of us in dissent to spell out further the fine points of a principle that will, I am confident, in time again command the support of a majority of this Court." O'Connor joined him in this prediction.

The aftermath of this decision casts some doubt on O'Connor's insistence that only the federal judiciary could effectively carry out whatever responsibility the national government had to implement limits on Congress's power, so that state interests would be protected. After the Court acted, Congress amended the federal wage and hour laws. It allowed public employers, but not private ones, to substitute comp time for overtime pay, limited to about three months for first responders and about six weeks for other employees. This seems a sensible compromise between the conflicting interests, and it's not likely that the courts could have developed as complex a solution.

By 2004 the Court still hadn't revisited the wage and hour question, much less overruled the decision from which Rehnquist and O'Connor dissented. Perhaps indicating that the "fine points" mattered more than the unspecified general principle of federalism, O'Connor in 2003 wrote for a unanimous Supreme Court an opinion endorsing the view that attempting to draw constitutional lines on the basis of whether a state's activity was "traditional" or "integral" to its operation was "unsound in principle and unworkable in practice," a phrase she quoted from the Blackmun opinion from which she had dissented over fifteen years before.

∽

Alfonso Lopez, a good student at Edison High School who had already enlisted in the Marine Corps, certainly didn't expect to inaugurate a constitutional revolution when he carried a gun to his school in San Antonio, Texas, on March 10, 1992. Acting on a tip from the mother of another student at the school, the school's principal brought Lopez to his office, where a school police officer questioned him. Lopez said he had been paid forty dollars to bring the gun to school and give it to another student, who planned to use it in a gang war. Later in the day a federal agent arrived at the school and interviewed Lopez. City police officers took the teenager to jail. The United States attorney initially refused to prosecute Lopez, so the local prosecutor charged the student with firearm possession on school grounds, a third-degree felony under Texas law, carrying a sentence of two to ten years in prison. A day later the U.S. attorney, apparently feeling some pressure from headquarters in Washington, changed his mind. He charged Lopez with violating the national Gun-Free School Zones Act of 1990 and then held a press conference with Senator Phil Gramm to announce a get tough policy on guns in schools. The Gun-Free School Zones Act, the brainchild of Wisconsin Senator Herbert Kohl, treated possession of a gun near a school as a misdemeanor, although one that could be punished by up to five years in prison. Lopez had no defense, of course, and was sentenced to six months' imprisonment.

John Carter, Lopez's lawyer, worked for the federal public defender's office. He decided to challenge the constitutionality of the Gun-Free School Zones Act, on the ground that it didn't fall within any of the powers given Congress in the Constitution. Carter knew that the Supreme Court had not held a single statute unconstitutional on that ground since the New Deal, but he had to do something to salvage the life of a decent kid who had made one bad mistake. After the court of appeals struck the statute down, Carter found himself standing in front of the justices, arguing that Congress had simply gone too far when it enacted the Gun-Free School Zones Act.

By the time Carter stood up, though, he had won his case. The solicitor general was Drew Days, a Yale Law School professor who had headed the Civil Rights Division in Jimmy Carter's Justice Department. The key exchanges came early in Days's argument. O'Connor asked him, "What is there that Congress could not do under this rubric, if you are correct?" Days evaded answering: "Justice O'Connor, that certainly is a question that one might ask, but this Court has asked that question in a number of other circumstances. . . ." This wasn't much of a response, and Rehnquist returned to the issue a few moments later: "What would be an example of a case which you couldn't reach?" Again Days had no answer: "Well, Your Honor, I'm not prepared to speculate generally." Also, when asked if his position meant that Congress could make all violent crime a federal offense, Days conceded that it could. The questions disconcerted Days so much that he later told Justice Kennedy defensively, "It's not an argument that I concocted." An exchange near the end of Days's argument showed how deep a hole he found himself in:

Question: What would be a case that would fall outside . . . ?
DAYS: I don't have—
Question: Don't give away anything here. (Laughter)
DAYS: Your Honor, I—
Question: General Days, could I ask—
DAYS: —the Court has never looked at this in the abstract. It's not an abstract process. It's been viewed by the Court as an empirical process.

The justices who questioned Days were looking for some limiting principle, and he offered them nothing. Rehnquist's opinion for the Court ran through its decisions, slotting them into three boxes:

Congress could regulate "the use of the channels of interstate commerce," the "instrumentalities of interstate commerce," and "those activities that substantially affect interstate commerce." The only box for the Gun-Free School Zones Act was the third one. But, Rehnquist said, if you looked at the cases, you would see that every time the Court dealt with a problem in the third box, it was dealing with an "economic activity." Possessing a gun near a school wasn't an economic activity.

Days had tried to argue that possessing guns near schools had a substantial effect on interstate commerce because possessing guns near schools threatens the educational climate, impairing the education children get and thereby producing less well-educated and less productive graduates. Rehnquist said that with this theory, *anything* could substantially affect interstate commerce: "Congress could regulate any activity that it found was related to the economic productivity of individual citizens." His examples hinted at the enclave theory: ordinary criminal law, "family law (including marriage, divorce, and child custody)," and education. If Congress could regulate guns near schools because their presence affected the quality of education and, through education, economic productivity, surely Congress could "mandate a federal curriculum for local elementary and secondary schools. . . ." According to Rehnquist, the government's "rationale lacks any real limits because, depending on the level of generality, any activity can be looked upon as commercial."

It wasn't clear what doctrine emerged from Lopez's case. As Rehnquist acknowledged, defining what was a commercial activity wasn't always going to be easy. The opinion demonstrated hostility to making it possible for Congress to make ordinary street crime a federal offense. But it's hardly a stretch to say that an ordinary robbery or a purse snatching is an economic activity, the involuntary transfer of wealth from the victim to the criminal.

Congress responded to the Lopez decision by reenacting the Gun-Free School Zones Act in a slightly modified form, inserting what constitutional scholars call a jurisdictional trigger. Under the new statute it was a federal crime to possess near a school a gun *that had once crossed a state line*. Senator Kohl's theory was that after all, Congress was now simply regulating "the use of the channels of interstate commerce"—that is, the shipment of guns across state lines. Federal prosecutors haven't brought any prosecutions under the new statute, as far as I've been able to determine. Maybe they have constitutional qualms about it. They might have other reasons too. Questioned in 2001, a federal prosecutor in San Antonio said that these cases "are not worth the time and money spent on them."

Alfonso Lopez went into the Marine Corps and stayed out of trouble.

℘

Rehnquist didn't like one part of the Violence Against Women Act, adopted by Congress in 1994 with both the House and Senate dividing along partisan lines. The act, known as VAWA, provided money for shelters for abused women and for educational programs about violence against women. It made it easier to enforce orders restraining abusive men from approaching their victims by making it a federal crime to cross state lines to harm a person protected by a restraining order. VAWA also had a civil remedy provision, allowing people—mostly women, of course—attacked by others on the basis of their gender to sue the attackers in federal court for damages.

Rehnquist had raised policy-based concerns about VAWA's civil remedy provision almost from the time it was proposed. Speaking in 1991, he referred to a policy position taken by the federal Judicial Conference, composed of judges he had appointed, that said the civil remedy provision "could involve the federal courts in a whole host of domestic relations disputes." VAWA's sponsors modified the proposal to deal with some of the Judicial Conference's objections, and the conference took no position on the final version of the civil remedy provision. Rehnquist still didn't like that part of VAWA. In 1998 he included it on a list of statutes that inappropriately expanded federal jurisdiction.

Rehnquist got his chance to get rid of the provision when a case challenging its constitutionality came to the Supreme Court in 2000. The case involved Christy Brzonkala, a student at Virginia Polytechnic Institute, and two players on Virginia Tech's football team, Antonio Morrison and James Crawford. Brzonkala alleged that Morrison and Crawford had raped her and that Virginia Tech had protected its football program by covering up the rape and administering only a slap on the wrists to Morrison and no punishment at all to Crawford. Virginia Tech sided with the football players, but no court or jury ever determined the facts. Rehnquist's opinion for the Supreme Court stopped Brzonkala's claim against Morrison and Virginia Tech from going forward, and a grand jury in Virginia decided not to indict Morrison for sexual assault.

Brzonkala was walking with a friend outside her dormitory in September 1994, a few months after she had started school at Virginia Tech, when Crawford and Morrison called to them from a third-floor window of the dormitory, one floor above Brzonkala's room. She and her friend, who didn't know either man at the time, went to the men's room. After about fifteen minutes of conversation Crawford and Brzonkala's friend left the room. According to Brzonkala, Morrison then "immediately requested intercourse." When she refused, Morrison raped her. Crawford returned to the room and raped her too. Again according to Brzonkala, Morrison then raped her a third time, after which he said, "You better not have any fucking diseases," and followed her to her room on the floor below. (Rehnquist's report of the allegations omits the expletive.) Morrison's story was different: They had had voluntary intercourse. So was Crawford's: He had had nothing to do with any sexual intercourse with Brzonkala.

In the months after the event Brzonkala stopped attending classes and attempted suicide by taking an overdose of thyroid pills. In October (or—again the facts are unclear—in January) she told her roommate that she had been raped but gave no details. Although Morrison and Crawford lived only one flight above Brzonkala in the dormitory, she did not identify them as her attackers until February 1995. In April Brzonkala filed a complaint against the men under the school's sexual assault policy. She hadn't reported the assault to the police because, she said, she thought prosecution would be impossible without physical evidence. Nor did Virginia Tech report it; the school's policy was to report all violent felonies *except* sexual assault to the local police. Virginia Tech held a three-hour hearing, after which it took no action against Crawford because of lack of evidence. The committee did find Morrison guilty of sexual assault and suspended him for two semesters. The dean of students rejected Morrison's appeal.

That wasn't the end of the matter, though. Morrison threatened to sue the school. His position was that he had been "convicted" of an offense that wasn't included in the student disciplinary code. The school did have a sexual assault policy, formally released in July 1994, two months before the events, but it hadn't been widely publicized, and it wasn't printed in the student handbook. Virginia Tech officials were worried that Morrison's suit might succeed. So, in July 1995, two Virginia Tech officials drove to Brzonkala's home, which was four hours from the school. They told her about Morrison's lawsuit and that the school wasn't willing to defend its actions. They said that the school would hold another hearing, where the prior disciplinary policy would be applied. According to Brzonkala, the school officials assured her that they believed her story and that the new hearing was just a technicality. She said, however, that the new hearing was a sham: Morrison had access to the prior testimony, but she didn't; Morrison was given enough time to get affidavits from supporters, and she wasn't; and she was told that she couldn't refer to Crawford's participation because he had been absolved in the earlier proceeding.

Morrison was convicted again, but this time of "using abusive language." Although the formal offense was much less serious than the sexual assault, he again was suspended for two semesters. This time his appeal was successful. The school's provost upheld the conviction but reduced the punishment to "deferred suspension until graduation" and a requirement that Morrison go to a one-hour educational session on acceptable behavior. The school didn't inform Brzonkala that the suspension had been lifted and that Morrison would be returning to school in the fall. Brzonkala believed that the outcome was designed to protect the school's football program.

Brzonkala sued Virginia Tech under one federal statute and Morrison and Crawford under VAWA. Virginia Tech settled its suit by paying her seventy-five thousand dollars. The lower courts dismissed her VAWA suit, and she took the case to the Supreme Court, supported by the solicitor general, who has a statutory obligation to defend the constitutionality of federal laws.

Writing for the same five justices who were the majority in the Lopez case, Rehnquist found the civil remedy portion of VAWA unconstitutional. His opinion had the structure typical of his opinions near the end of his career. It recited the facts and summarized the relevant precedents. He compared Brzonkala's arguments to those rejected in the Lopez case and found them essentially identical. A few passages and footnotes addressed the dissenters' position, saying, in effect and accurately enough, that their quarrel was really with the Lopez decision, which couldn't fairly be distinguished from this one.

Gender-motivated crimes, Rehnquist said, were not economic activities. He acknowledged that Congress had made extensive findings that sexual assaults on women seriously affected their participation in the nation's economy. Women didn't take some jobs that would have been available to them because they were afraid of being assaulted, and they didn't travel from one state to another because of their fears. But, Rehnquist wrote, the Court's new doctrine wouldn't allow Congress to regulate a noneconomic activity on the theory that the aggregate effects of such activities on interstate commerce was substantial, and that was all that Congress's findings showed. If that approach were allowed, "Congress might use the Commerce Clause to completely obliterate the Constitution's distinction between national and local authority. . . ." Somehow the Court had to maintain a line "between what is truly national and what is truly local," and the ban on justifying regulation by aggregating the effects of noneconomic activities did that.

Breyer wrote a dissent that showed how little the Court's decision might actually mean. He suggested that the majority's approach would allow Congress to reenact the civil remedy provision by "limiting" it to noneconomic activity "taking place at economic establishments." He asked, "Can Congress save the present law by including it, or much of it, in a broader 'Safe Transport' or 'Workplace Safety' act?" His most pointed observation was that under the Court's theory, you could have two activities, one economic and the other noneconomic, with precisely identical effects on the national economy, and Congress would have the power to regulate the first and not the second, a result Breyer thought entirely inconsistent with the idea underlying the commerce clause. (Indeed, Congress could regulate an economic activity such as selling dried mangoes if its effects on the national economy were less than the effects of some noneconomic activity like violence against women, which seems really peculiar.)

In 1996 Crawford was indicted for participating in a gang rape of another Virginia Tech student. He pleaded guilty to attempted aggravated sexual assault and received a suspended sentence of a year in prison. He lost his football scholarship and went back home to Florida. Morrison was suspended from the football team after he was involved in a bar fight. He spent one semester at Hampton University, then returned to Virginia Tech, from which he graduated in 1999 with a degree in human nutrition, foods, and exercise. His lawyer explained Morrison's difficulty in getting a job as an athletic trainer by referring to the lawsuit: "How's he going to get hired by a college once people realize he's the guy all the stuff has been written about? His good name has been completely trashed." Brzonkala dropped out of Virginia Tech when she found out that Morrison would be returning there in the fall of 1995. She enrolled in a school in northern Virginia but did not graduate. After moving to the District of Columbia, she began working as a waitress at a yuppie bar.

VAWA's supporters pointed out that only about fifty cases had been filed invoking the statute's civil remedy provision, hardly the flood of "domestic relations" cases Rehnquist feared from the statute. It turns out that the courts dismissed about half those cases for failing to establish a VAWA claim, suggesting that the civil remedy provision added little to the protection women had against abuse. Congress reauthorized the Violence Against Women Act in 2003, without the civil remedy provision. It did, however, substantially increase the amounts it made available to support shelters for abused women. Even conservative Republicans stumbled over one another in claiming credit for the new VAWA. A statute that had divided the parties in 1994, when it was first enacted, received bipartisan support. Perhaps the Court's decision in Christy Brzonkala's case made it important for Republicans to demonstrate that they too supported action against those who abused women.

※

The Constitution gives Congress power over more than commerce among the states. The North's victory in the Civil War produced three constitutional amendments. The most important turned out to be the Fourteenth Amendment. Section One of that amendment provides, "No State shall . . . deprive any person of life, liberty, or property without due process of law." Section Five provides, "The Congress shall have power to enforce, by appropriate legislation, the provisions of this article." From the New Deal through the Warren Court the Supreme Court made the due process clause the vehicle for enforcing the Bill of Rights against state legislatures. Congress rarely invoked its power under Section Five, because the Supreme Court was doing all the work Congress might have wanted done.

The Court changed more quickly than Congress did. That opened up a space for Congress to use its Section Five power to protect what it thought were constitutional rights even if the Court hadn't expressed a view—or even when the Court had said that the states *weren't* violating the due process clause. The idea underlying congressional action in the face of a contrary Supreme Court decision is that the Constitution's meaning isn't transparent. Members of Congress can reasonably disagree with the justices' interpretation of some particular provision. They might then try to "enforce" their interpretation.

At this point questions of federalism blend together with questions about judicial supremacy. Technically what's at stake is whether Congress has the power to require states to do something to avoid violating their citizens' rights. Underneath this, though, is the question of whether the states are violating constitutional rights when the Supreme Court has already said that they aren't.

These problems were largely theoretical until late in the Rehnquist Court. The closest Congress came to confronting the Court was a minor provision of the Voting Rights Act of 1965. In 1959 the Supreme Court held that states didn't violate the Constitution when they imposed literacy requirements for voting. One provision in the Voting Rights Act said that states had to allow voting by people who became literate in Spanish in Puerto Rican schools but weren't literate in English. On its face this provision seems inconsistent with the Court's 1959 decision. The Court upheld the Voting Rights Act provision anyway.

Justice Brennan's opinion developed two arguments for the statute. The first didn't pose a theoretical problem about the relation between Congress and the Supreme Court, although it was something of a factual reach. According to Brennan, Congress might have been concerned that state and local governments, not being concerned about getting the votes of people who were literate in Spanish but not in English, wouldn't provide services to those people and so would violate their right to equal protection of the laws. Here the predicate for Congress's action is a real constitutional violation, although not one the courts had already ruled on.

Brennan's second argument came to be known as the substantive interpretation of Congress's power. According to this argument, Congress has a power, independent of the courts, to specify what rights the Constitution protects. The substantive interpretation won't cause any problems when Congress and the Court are in sync. All it means it that Congress might protect some rights before the courts do. But which interpretation prevails when Congress and the Court are out of sync?

The Supreme Court set the stage for a confrontation in 1990, when it substantially modified its interpretation of the free exercise clause, which, applied to the states through the due process clause, says that states cannot prohibit the free exercise of religion. From 1963 to 1990 the Court said that state laws imposing substantial burdens on religious exercise were constitutionally permissible only if they were justified by some compelling interest. For example, a state couldn't deny unemployment compensation benefits to a woman who couldn't get a job because her religious beliefs prevented her from working on Saturday in a community where the only available jobs required such work.

The Court didn't apply the compelling interest test with much vigor, though, and in 1990 Justice Scalia wrote an opinion abandoning it. Like all states, Oregon denies unemployment compensation benefits to people who are fired from their jobs for good reasons. Alfred Smith was a Native American and recovering alcoholic who worked as a drug and alcohol counselor. He also was an adherent of the Native American Church. He used peyote as part of that church's rituals. But under Oregon law peyote was an illegal drug. Smith's employer fired him when it learned that he used peyote. Smith tried to get unemployment compensation, but the state took the position that he had been fired for cause—that is, because he had violated the state antidrug laws. He responded that the state law making peyote use illegal violated his rights under the free exercise clause, and that was the claim the Supreme Court considered.

Scalia replaced the compelling interest test with one far more generous to state regulations. A state could enforce "neutral laws of general applicability" no matter what their impact was on religious exercise. A law was neutral if it didn't refer to religion and hadn't been adopted in order to penalize religious exercises, and it was of general applicability if there were lots of nonreligious activities it penalized along with the religious ones. Oregon's antidrug laws easily satisfied the Court's new test.

The decision evoked a storm of protest from a wide range of religious and civil liberties organizations. They assembled a coalition to support the enactment of a federal statute that would direct the courts to use the compelling state interest test again. Congress responded with the Religious Freedom Restoration Act of 1993 (RFRA, pronounced riff-ra).

RFRA says that its goal is to "restore the compelling interest test set forth" by the Supreme Court in cases before the peyote case. It provides that government—defined to include the federal government and state and local governments—shall not substantially burden a person's exercise of religion, even through the enforcement of a neutral law of general applicability, unless the government demonstrates that "application of the burden" advances "a compelling government interest" and is "the least restrictive means" of doing so.

The Supreme Court got its chance to decide on RFRA's constitutionality in a case from the city of Boerne (pronounced bernie), Texas. The city, a bedroom suburb thirty miles northwest of San Antonio, in 1992 created a historic preservation district, hoping to attract tourists and provide the right atmosphere for local antiques dealers. St. Peter Catholic Church, erected in 1923 and modeled on a Spanish mission church in San Antonio, is within the historic preservation district and is a prominent feature on the hillside as drivers approach Boerne. Phillip Bell, the chair of the city's Historic Landmark Commission, called the church "a drawing card for the whole city."

As San Antonio's population grew, so did its suburbs, and, more important, so did the congregation at St. Peter. The church seated about 230 people, but by the early 1990s another 40 to 60 people regularly attended mass, a number that Archbishop P. F. Flores of San Antonio expected only to increase. Archbishop Flores authorized the parish to expand the church. At the end of 1993 the church applied for a building permit. Under the church's proposal, the church's façade would be preserved, but 80 percent of the structure behind it would be demolished and seven hundred seats added for the congregation. The landmark commission refused to approve the plans after a public hearing, and the city council voted to deny the application, with Bell saying, "We would like you to build a new church, but don't touch a rock of the old one." The church's architect estimated that following that course would add five hundred thousand dollars to the project's cost.

The archbishop sued the city in federal court, arguing that the permit denial violated RFRA because it imposed a substantial burden on the church and was not justified by any compelling interest. The city replied that RFRA was unconstitutional.

The city's claim raised questions of federal and judicial supremacy. Federalism means that Congress has only those powers listed in the Constitution. The question in the Boerne case thus becomes, What is appropriate legislation enforcing the provisions of Section One of the Fourteenth Amendment?

Section One in turn says that states may not deprive people of liberty without due process. But the peyote case held that a neutral law of general applicability did not deprive anyone of a right to free exercise of religion. RFRA purported to require state and local governments to have only compelling reasons for the burdens they placed on free exercise, even though the peyote case held that Section One did not require them to have such reasons. How, then, can RFRA be said to be a statute "enforcing" rights protected by Section One?

Justice Kennedy wrote the Court's opinion that RFRA was unconstitutional. He started with Section Five's text. It clearly means that Congress can enforce the right to free exercise of religion. But, Kennedy said, Congress can only enforce Section One rights, not define them. The line between *enforcing* and *defining* might be difficult to locate, and "Congress must have wide latitude in determining where it lies," but the line must be respected. According to Kennedy, the line is determined by a test of congruence and proportionality. RFRA couldn't possibly satisfy that test. Its supporters had identified lots of cases where neutral laws of general applicability created real problems for religious exercise, but no more than a handful of situations in which laws were specifically targeted at religion or were administered to discriminate against religion.

The Boerne case may be the poster child for the late Rehnquist Court's view of Congress. Sometimes the Court's disdain for Congress was almost palpable. The Lopez case treated the Gun-Free School Zones Act for what it was: an effort by a few members of Congress to grandstand and put themselves forward as champions of law and order. Sometimes the disdain was a bit below the surface. Rehnquist's constitutional opinion in the Brzonkala case mirrored the policy objections he had voiced to Congress about the Violence Against Women Act, which Congress seemed to ignore.

Sometimes the disdain operated on a highly theoretical level, as in the Boerne case. Here perhaps it's better to say that the Rehnquist Court had an exalted view of its own position in the constitutional scheme of things rather than that it had a view of Congress as an institution that couldn't really be trusted. But the overall effect was the same: to advance a very strong view of judicial supremacy.

In an important passage summarizing the Court's analysis of Section Five's meaning, Kennedy wrote: "Legislation which alters the meaning of the Free Exercise Clause cannot be said to be enforcing the Clause. Congress does not enforce a constitutional right by changing what the right is. It has been given the power 'to enforce,' not the power to determine what constitutes a constitutional violation. Were it not so, what Congress would be enforcing would no longer be, in any meaningful sense, the 'provisions of [the Fourteenth Amendment].' " Some of the words used here open the way to a deeper understanding of what was at stake. Kennedy says that RFRA alters the meaning of the free exercise clause; this phrasing assumes that the Court's decision in the peyote case determined that meaning. He says that Congress changed the right to free exercise of religion; this phrasing assumes that the Court's decision in the peyote case is unalterable except by the Court itself. The deepest issues in the Boerne case deal with the relation between the Court and Congress in determining what the Constitution means.

The entire Rehnquist Court's commitment to a strong vision of judicial supremacy is reflected in the fact that neither Kennedy nor anyone else on the Court seemed interested in engaging those issues.

All the justices appear to have thought that it went without saying that they had to have the last word on interpreting the Constitution.

While litigation proceeded, the church held mass in a nearby gymnasium. Some city residents said that the lawsuit divided the city, pitting "friend against friend, relative against relative." Negotiations produced a proposal that would have allowed an expansion at the church that would have left 75 percent of the building intact. After the Supreme Court's decision in the city's favor, the parties agreed on a plan that preserved 80 percent of the church building, while allowing an increase in seating to eight hundred.

The coalition that supported RFRA assembled again in response to the Boerne case. In 2000 Congress passed the Religious Land Use and Institutionalized Persons Act. RLUIPA (pronounced raloopa), like RFRA, requires that courts apply the compelling interest and least restrictive means tests to statutes that substantially burden religious practices, but it confines itself to land use and imprisonment, areas where the coalition's members found the most extensive examples of state actions they thought inappropriate. RLUIPA limits its reach to situations in which the burden "is imposed in a program or activity that receives Federal financial assistance," in which the burden—or its removal—affects interstate commerce, or in which the burden arises in connection with a land use program in which the government has in place a system for making "individualized assessments" of proposed land uses. These jurisdictional triggers aim to get around the federalism problems the Court found with RFRA. RLUIPA provides, in addition, that "[n]o government shall impose or implement a land use regulation in a manner that treats a religious assembly or institution on less than equal terms with a nonreligious assembly or institution." The Rehnquist Court hasn't had a chance to decide whether RLIUPA was constitutional.

✑

Doctrines dealing with the immunity of states from suit were also a weapon in the Rehnquist Court's armory for its federalism revolution. (The Rehnquist Court developed another weapon, the so-called anticommandeering principle, which barred the national government from dragooning state legislatures and executive officials into doing Congress's bidding. It used the weapon twice, and going through the details of the cases and their problems wouldn't add much to the story here.)

The immunity doctrines are almost unbearably arcane. Law professors write extremely long articles about the Eleventh Amendment. Reading them brings to mind the fabled (and perhaps apocryphal) medieval debates about how many angels can dance on the head of a pin. Supreme Court justices appear to believe that they have to write unbearably long and elaborate opinions in these cases, starting almost with the creation of the world—or at least the creation of the nation—and working painstakingly up to the present.

State governments have to comply with national law, including both the Constitution and federal statutes (other than those that are unconstitutional under the Lopez analysis or the anticommandeering principle). How can we make sure that they do? Ordinarily, by making them liable in court for their failures. The sovereign immunity doctrines limit that possibility. You can't sue a state government or one of its component units, like a department of public safety, in federal court.

Because the doctrine is one of *state* immunity, none of these rules apply to cities or counties. More important, you *can* sue individual employees. You can get money damages for their misconduct, but the employees can defeat your claim if they're able to show that they had a reasonable and good faith belief that they weren't violating the law when they acted. You also can get an injunction directing them to comply with the law in the future, and that injunction will apply to the employees in what lawyers call their official capacities, meaning that an injunction against the official currently holding office will continue to apply to that person's successors.

It's hard to get these rules out of the language of the Eleventh Amendment. Before the Rehnquist Court's federalism revolution, it was an open question whether Congress could override the states' constitutional immunity by specifying in a substantive law, which applied to the states, that the states could be sued for violating the law in the federal courts. In 1996 the Court said no.

The easiest way to understand the Rehnquist Court's position is to notice that the Eleventh Amendment was an *amendment* to the original Constitution. So you might say that it limited what Congress could do under its power to regulate interstate commerce, a power granted in the original Constitution.

The Rehnquist Court worked out the solution to the Court's inattention to the Constitution's language when it held that Congress couldn't override the states' immunity from suit by using the powers it got in the original Constitution. State immunity from suit, the Court said, was an unstated presupposition of the entire constitutional scheme. It went without saying. The decision that produced the Eleventh Amendment as a reaction ran contrary to this presupposition. Congress and the states responded with an amendment addressing the precise problem the case presented, but this action simply restored the situation to what it should have been under the more general presupposition.

The implications of this analysis became clear when some Maine probation officers sued their employer *in state court* for failing to comply with the overtime provisions of the federal minimum wage law. Obviously the Eleventh Amendment didn't apply in state court, but the Rehnquist Court majority said that the constitutional presupposition allowed states to hold themselves immune from suit in their own courts if they wanted to.

At first glance, these sovereign immunity decisions look as if they really might immunize states not simply from lawsuits but from complying with federal law entirely. A closer look reveals a more complicated, and less disturbing, picture. Consider the Maine probation officers' case. Their problem was that the state was treating them as professional employees who weren't entitled to the minimum wage but was also saying that if they were covered by the federal law, they should be treated as police officers, who could be required to work overtime and get compensatory time off rather than time-and-a-half wages. By the time the Supreme Court decided the case, a federal court had entered an order directing that in the future Maine treat the probation officers as regular, nonprofessional employees, allowing the state to treat them like police officers. Maine didn't appeal *that* decision. Generally, the availability of such orders means that you can get the states to comply with national law on a going-forward basis.

The Rehnquist Court's majority emphasized a number of other reasons why its decisions didn't really undermine the effectiveness of national law. The national government can recover money damages from states under the federal minimum wage laws and then transfer the proceeds to the workers. Still, the enforcement staffs of the national government are not large enough to police state compliance with national law all that effectively.

More important, perhaps, is voluntary state compliance with national law. Public employees are well organized in politics, and it's not hard to understand why state politicians would be willing to pay up when they're told that they've violated national law. Going-forward remedies are always available. Of course such remedies are helpful only if you're still employed by the state. Money damages are usually much more important in age and disability discrimination cases because the victim of the state's failure to comply with national law probably isn't going to be working for the state in the future. Even here, though, there are some possibilities. State laws often parallel federal ones. Those laws might not provide quite as extensive a set of protections as the national age discrimination law did, but they aren't completely toothless either. Finally, the idea of sovereign immunity, deriving as it does from notions of royal prerogative, has become increasingly discredited in the past fifty years. Many state courts have abandoned the doctrine. Maine might join the ranks of those other states, where public employees can sue their employer in state courts.

What about Congress's power to enforce the Fourteenth Amendment? The Fourteenth Amendment comes after the Eleventh, so Congress *can* use its Section Five power to override the states' immunity from suit. If Congress wants to, it can make states defend against claims that they violated rights protected by the Fourteenth Amendment. But under the Boerne decision Congress's power to enforce that amendment is limited by the requirement that enforcement statutes must be proportional to the constitutional violations Congress identified.

The Rehnquist Court showed what this meant in cases involving discrimination by state employers—against people with disabilities, against older workers, and against women. That sort of discrimination *can* violate the Constitution, but only if the employer's decision is completely unreasonable. Congress investigated discrimination and thought it had come up with a decent number of examples of impermissible discrimination by state employers. In the disabilities and older workers' cases the Supreme Court went through the congressional material with a fine-tooth comb and disagreed. There were too many anecdotes and not enough data. Discrimination by cities and counties didn't count, for example. Neither did employment decisions that, while perhaps unwise and unfair, nonetheless had some minimum justification. The age discrimination statute, the Court said, was "an unwarranted response to a perhaps inconsequential problem."

To the surprise of many, in 2003 Rehnquist himself wrote the Court's opinion *allowing* men and women to sue state employers for damages they suffered when the states violated the federal Family and Medical Leave Act, which requires employers to give their workers up to twelve weeks of unpaid leave to take care of ailing family members (or newborn children). William Hibbs, who worked for the Nevada welfare department, requested leave to take care of his wife, who had been injured in a car accident. Because of some confusing communications between Hibbs and the department, it mistakenly thought that Hibbs had used up his FMLA leave, ordered him to come back to work, and fired him when he didn't. Rehnquist's opinion for the Court upholding the statute said that federal laws aimed at overcoming gender discrimination were different from those aimed at discrimination based on disability or age. It was harder for states to justify gender discrimination, and so it should be easier for Congress to come up with enough evidence to justify overriding the states' immunity.

For all the hoopla over the Rehnquist Court's immunity decisions, no one seems to have tried to find out how many state probation officers aren't getting the minimum wage or how many people with disabilities who are subjected to unlawful discrimination don't get any remedy at all. My guess is that the numbers are low.

❧

Kennedy and O'Connor were attracted to using rhetorical flourishes to frame and emphasize their federalism opinions. In one, O'Connor began the final paragraph of her opinion, "Some truths are so basic that, like the air around us, they are easily overlooked." Presumably until the smog gets too thick—that is, until Congress does something to draw our attention to those truths. The problem is that this sentence doesn't help identify what the truths are. The same can be said of Kennedy's most notable rhetorical move in these cases. Joining the Court's liberals in holding unconstitutional state efforts to limit the terms of members of the national House of Representatives, Kennedy used an arresting metaphor. The framers, he wrote, "split the atom of sovereignty." In some ways that's the best description of federalism in the Court's recent cases, but it's only a metaphor and doesn't get you far toward figuring out, so to speak, what the neutrons, electrons, and protons actually do.

Probably the most celebrated, and troubling, rhetorical move was the first sentence of another O'Connor opinion: "This is a case about federalism," she wrote. The case involved Roger Keith Thompson's desperate attempt to get a federal court to hear his claim that he hadn't committed the rape and murder for which he had been sentenced to death. (Coleman's supporters thought that the evidence clearly showed that he was actually innocent; others found the evidence more ambiguous, although everyone seemed to agree that Coleman had raised some serious questions about the evidence against him.) The Virginia Supreme Court refused to hear Coleman's appeal because his lawyer filed the appeal papers three days too late. The result of this "case about federalism" is that Coleman, possibly innocent of rape and murder, lost his chance to show that his constitutional rights were violated during his trial and was executed. Federalism, O'Connor once wrote, existed "for the protection of individuals." One can see how Alfonso Lopez's liberty was protected by federalism, but it's harder to see how Roger Coleman's was. Blackmun's dissent charged the majority with losing "sight of the animating principles of federalism," and perhaps he was right.

∞

What can we make of the federalism revolution? The starting point has to be that Congress didn't respond angrily to the Court's "revolution." One reason is the availability of easy work-arounds. Another is that interest groups don't care much about federalism either. They care about substance, and they can get what they want through the work-arounds or by lobbying at the state level. In fact, no one besides the justices really cares about federalism.

The Court's disdain for Congress is also part of the picture. Roger Coleman's case suggests a complication. The Court decided his case in 1991. Five years later Congress enacted a comprehensive revision of the habeas corpus statute. The new statute endorsed a lot of what the Court had been doing about habeas corpus over the prior decades, including the rule it adopted in Coleman's case, and went even further in restricting the access convicted criminals had to federal courts. The Republican majority in Congress after 1994 had views about national power more in line with the Court's than with Great Society Democrats' views. Some of what the Court did involved statutes adopted before Republicans took over Congress. Basically the Court was striking down statutes that the Congress of the late 1990s wouldn't have enacted anyway. In some ways the Court was moving *with* the Congress that existed in the 1990s rather than against it. It "dissed" the Congress controlled by Democrats, and it's not surprising that the Republican Congress did not take up arms against the Court's disparagement of "Congress."

Scholars of real revolutions would be amused by the Rehnquist Court's federalism revolution. Not a single central feature of the New Deal's regulatory regime was overturned in that revolution, nor were central elements of the Great Society's programs displaced. The federalism revolution snipped off some stray excesses in Congress's actions and suggested that perhaps the Great Society's rights revolution had gone too far. It did little to rein in *that* revolution, though.

Clarence Thomas was the Court's true revolutionary. He wrote a concurring opinion in the Lopez case showing where the revolution might lead. As a good originalist Thomas went back to the Constitution's language and the understandings of that language prevalent in 1787. According to Thomas, in 1787 the term *commerce* was used "in contradistinction to productive activities such as manufacturing and agriculture." He made the nice textual point that it was hard to replace the term *commerce* in the commerce clause with the words *agriculture* and *manufacturing*. You can't say that Congress had the power to regulate manufacturing among the several states or agriculture among the several states. He also pointed out, accurately, that the modern broad interpretations the Court had given to the commerce clause—and left untouched by the rest of the majority in the Lopez case—made a lot of the rest of the Constitution's list of congressional powers redundant. Define *commerce* broadly, and there's no point in giving Congress the power to "Establish Post Office and Post Roads," the power to "fix the Standard of Weights and Measures," or even the power to "coin Money."

This is the voice of a true revolutionary. Thomas's approach would indeed overturn New Deal and Great Society regulations wholesale. Kennedy and O'Connor responded by saying that the Supreme Court's history of dealing with the commerce clause "counsels great restraint before the Court determines that the Clause is insufficient to support an exercise of the national power." The federalism revolution would stay within narrow bounds as long as the Court's conservatives were divided. Thomas showed where new justices might take the Rehnquist Court's decisions.

CHAPTER ELEVEN

The Takings Project

Richard Lazarus knew he had lost his case when Justice O'Connor asked, "My goodness, why not give this poor, elderly woman the right to go to court to have her takings claim heard?" Lazarus, a professor at Georgetown Law School and one of the nation's leading environmental lawyers, was representing the Tahoe Regional Planning Agency against Bernadine Suitum. This issue was fairly technical, dealing with when a person would be allowed to challenge land use regulations as a "taking" of her property without the constitutionally required compensation. The Suitum case's technicality masked its significance as part of a sustained litigation effort by developers and business interests to limit the reach of the modern regulatory state through the Constitution's takings clause.

Mrs. Suitum and her husband sold their Sacramento house in 1972 and bought a half acre residential lot in a development about half a mile from the shore of Lake Tahoe, planning to build a retirement home there. Mr. Suitum became ill, and the couple's financial difficulties made it impossible for them to start building the house until 1989, when their lot was one of the last undeveloped lots in the subdivision. All the neighboring lots had small houses like the one the Suitums planned to build, and the subdivision was a typical suburban one, with "modest homes fitted with basketball hoops, snow-covered lawn chairs and trailers on blocks."

Development in the area was regulated by the Tahoe Regional

Planning Agency, created by Congress in 1969. Congress told the agency to adopt a regional plan that barred development from exceeding "environmental threshold carrying capacities." The agency's 1987 plan listed some vacant lots as suitable for development, but not others. After her husband's death Mrs. Suitum applied for a permit to build her house in 1989. The lot bordered on a small stream, which her lawyers described as a "foot-wide ditch that runs along the back of her land . . . from a waste treatment plant to the water." The agency denied the permit because the lot was in a "Stream Environment Zone," protected because it carried surface water into Lake Tahoe.

The agency did give Mrs. Suitum what it called marketable credits or transferable development rights. She could sell these credits to another developer, who would then purchase additional credits from other sellers and gradually assemble enough land to build a house. Mrs. Suitum got a land credit amounting to 1 percent of her lot's area (about 183 square feet), but she refused even to try to sell it. Instead, she sued the agency, seeking real money for its restrictions on her ability to use her property. The lower courts dismissed her claim, saying that she couldn't try to get compensation until she tried to sell the land credit.

Justice Souter's opinion for a unanimous Supreme Court gave Mrs. Suitum the chance to try to get compensation immediately. A year later Mrs. Suitum was "blind, bedridden, and living with her daughter in Sacramento," receiving Social Security benefits and her husband's military pension. The case was settled two years after the Supreme Court's decision, with Mrs. Suitum getting six hundred thousand dollars for the government's taking of her property.

♔

The Suitum case was simply one of a large number of challenges to modern regulations mounted by land developers and business interests. The Supreme Court had seen such challenges before. Through the 1920s businesses used the due process clause as their preferred constitutional vehicle. It says that governments can't take people's property "without due process of law." Reading the words, you might think that the clause dealt with *processes*, the ways in which governments went about imposing regulations, by giving people hearings, making factual findings, and the like. The Supreme Court, though, came up with the idea of substantive due process, a phrase a leading constitutional scholar likened to "green pastel redness," a contradiction in terms. The idea was that the due process clause limited *what* the government could do, not just *how* the government did it.

The term *due process* dates back to the Magna Carta, where it appears as "the law of the land." Over time the idea of due process became coupled with two others: Governments could act arbitrarily—and violate due process—if they went beyond traditional methods of regulating (what constitutional lawyers of the nineteenth century called the government's police powers), and one way governments could act arbitrarily was by acting on behalf of narrow interest groups instead of in the public interest.

The Supreme Court in the first years of the twentieth century used the idea of substantive due process to strike down a significant number of popular reforms. The most notable was *Lochner v. New York*. Progressive reformers fulminated at the Court's substantive due process decisions, and when Franklin Roosevelt's justices gained control of the Supreme Court, they repudiated the idea as thoroughly as they could.

The Court's privacy and abortion decisions revived the idea of substantive due process. Conservatives who opposed those decisions couldn't use them to bring back the earlier cases limiting government regulation. They turned instead to a different constitutional provision, the takings clause.

The takings clause says that governments can't take your property unless they give you "just compensation" for it. It means that the government can buy your property from you even if you don't want to sell it and can pay you a fair market price rather than the price you would charge if you *did* want to sell. Government takings are most familiar in connection with the power of eminent domain. The government has a project it wants to pursue—build a convention center, for example—and it needs to assemble the land for the project. It wouldn't be fair for the government simply to seize the property it wanted because that would give the whole city or state the benefit of getting the convention center at the expense of the individual property owner. So the government has to pay for the land it takes. But we can't run a government that assembles land for projects by allowing property owners to set their own prices for the property. The convention center has to be built at a particular place, and the landowners, particularly the owner of the very last piece of land needed for the project, could blackmail the city into paying outrageous prices for the parcels. That's why the government has the power to take property over an owner's objection, why the government has to pay something for the property, and why the price is the fair market value and not what the landowner might like to bargain for.

The example of taking land for a convention center through the power of eminent domain illustrates both the historical core of the takings clause and its common sense. Traditional cases cropped up occasionally on the Rehnquist Court's docket, but they really didn't matter much to real estate developers and business interests. Developers were much more concerned with modern land use regulations. Historic preservation statutes blocked the projects they wanted to pursue, and some towns and cities forced developers to give up some of their property to create parks and other recreation areas in exchange for permission to develop subdivisions. As the Suitum case illustrates, developers were concerned about environmental regulations too. Moreover, as the modern environmental movement matured, states and cities began to adopt smart growth programs that imposed additional limits on real estate development. Business interests were more generally concerned about extensive regulation, the modern versions of the regulations their predecessors had challenged as violations of substantive due process.

The traditional idea of the takings clause didn't help in these cases because the government wasn't taking a chunk of land for its own purposes but was "simply" limiting what property owners could do with their property. All sorts of regulations—zoning rules for land, rules saying that dangerous drugs can't be sold directly to the public without prescriptions—limit what a property owner can do with her property. It was hard to describe regulations limiting the use of property as a taking requiring compensation.

Hard, but not impossible. Rattling around in constitutional doctrine since at least the 1920s was the idea of a regulatory taking. Justice Oliver Wendell Holmes articulated the doctrine most clearly in a 1922 case. Pennsylvania had a statute aimed at protecting homes from collapsing when underground coal mines ate away at the ground supporting the houses. The statute said that mineowners who bought the right to mine under a person's property, a subsurface right, had to ensure that the mining operation didn't undermine (literally) the house's foundation, even if the homeowner had not written such a provision into the contract giving the mineowner a right to work the veins beneath the surface. Pennsylvania mineowners claimed that this statute took away the property right, the right to mine, they had acquired when they bought the subsurface right without limitation. The Supreme Court agreed. It conceded that the government's police power gave it the ability to impose regulations to serve the public interest in safety and security and that the Pennsylvania statute, aimed at keeping houses from collapsing, did serve that interest. But, Holmes wrote, some regulations could be takings requiring compensation if they "go too far."

The Supreme Court's rejection of substantive due process spilled over into the doctrine of regulatory takings too. The justices understood that a robust doctrine of regulatory takings could be a complete substitute for the discredited doctrine of substantive due process. From the 1940s through the 1970s the justices didn't take the idea that a regulation could "go too far" at all seriously, rejecting challenges that looked a lot like the one the Court accepted in the coal case. Indeed, in 1987 the Court upheld a newer Pennsylvania statute that accomplished pretty much the same thing that the earlier one had tried to do.

Still, the earlier coal mining case did make it clear that regulations could be takings, and that is all that real estate developers and business interests needed to mount their challenges to modern regulations.

Ironically, the idea of regulatory takings has no foundation whatever in the original meaning of the takings clause. Legal scholars have established that the drafters and ratifiers of the takings clause in the eighteenth century were worried only about the permanent physical occupations of land covered by the traditional idea of eminent domain. They knew that regulations could sometimes severely limit the value of someone's property, but they clearly understood as well that the takings clause wouldn't apply to such regulations. The framers, and several generations of their successors, believed that the takings clause was entirely irrelevant when the government exercised its police powers over health, safety, and morals.

Even Justice Scalia, an enthusiastic proponent of the regulatory takings doctrine, agreed with this originalist view of the takings clause. Buried in a footnote in one of his takings cases is an acknowledgment that the takings clause, as originally understood, didn't apply to regulatory takings. But, Scalia wrote, the understanding as of 1791 didn't matter when the Court dealt with *state* regulations. The takings clause is in the Fifth Amendment, part of the Bill of Rights adopted in 1791. According to well-established constitutional doctrine, the Bill of Rights imposes limits only on the national government. State governments have to comply with the Constitution, of course, but the reason they do is the Fourteenth Amendment, adopted in 1868. And, Scalia said, by 1868 the idea that a regulation could be a taking was well embedded in constitutional understandings.

The conservatives' struggle to reconcile a doctrine they like—regulatory takings—with the originalist constitutional theory they also like is not the only irony in the takings area. Equally ironic, the idea of regulatory takings emerged from *progressive* challenges to legal theory in the first part of the twentieth century. The takings clause was originally about the power of eminent domain, a state's power to take property for a fair market price and use it for public purposes. Through the nineteenth century legal theorists treated regulation as something deriving from an entirely separate source of government power, the police power to control the *uses* of private property so that the property wouldn't harm public interests in health, safety, or morals.

Early in the twentieth century progressive legal thinkers mounted a strong challenge to what they described as the mere conceptualism of traditionalist lawyers. Justice Holmes, the author of the Pennsylvania coal case, was one of those progressives. Holmes looked at cases involving police power regulations and saw that those regulations could have exactly the same effect on the value of private property as did eminent domain. The distinction between eminent domain and the police power, that is, was exactly the kind of mere conceptualism that the progressives rejected. So, in the Pennsylvania coal case, Holmes held that police power regulations could become takings if they went too far.

For several generations, though, the Supreme Court always found that challenged regulations didn't go far enough to become takings.

The Court's most important decisions involved zoning. Traditionally governments could exclude businesses from some areas if they were what lawyers called public nuisances, which were often described as businesses that were entirely legal if conducted in an appropriate area but became nuisances in the wrong place. As Supreme Court Justice George Sutherland put it in 1926, "A nuisance may be merely a right thing in a wrong place, like a pig in a parlor instead of the barnyard." Most zoning could be said to involve things similar to such nuisances, limiting housing to some areas, businesses to others, restricting the sizes of lots in one area and requiring large lots in others, and the like. The Supreme Court upheld modern zoning in a decision only four years after the Pennsylvania coal case. Zoning, it seems, was a police power regulation that didn't go too far.

Or at least traditional zoning didn't go too far. Real estate developers sometimes found traditional zoning economically beneficial to their projects, and sometimes they simply adapted to zoning requirements. The rise of middle-class social movements concerned about preserving the legacies of the past—both in the natural environment and in human constructions—changed the economic picture for developers. Historic preservation laws sometimes posed severe obstacles to development; if a developer couldn't tear down a historic building, it might be nearly impossible to build the project the developer wanted. Some environmental regulations had almost the same effect. Laws aiming at the preservation of beaches from erosion or of wetlands from destruction sometimes made it impossible to build anything on a beachfront or on wetlands. Developers might be able to comply with other environmental regulations, but only by eating into their profits.

The Supreme Court first confronted challenges to modern zoning regulations in a case involving New York's Grand Central Terminal. The city adopted a historic preservation law in 1965. Like many such laws, it created a commission to designate particular buildings and districts as historical landmarks. The owners of landmark buildings have to keep their exteriors in good repair and can change the exterior appearance only with the commission's permission.

New York made the façade of Grand Central Terminal a historic landmark. Facing economic difficulties, the terminal's owner, the Penn Central Railroad, wanted to generate income by building an office on top of the terminal. New York's commission refused to allow the construction, saying that putting a fifty-five-story office tower "above a flamboyant Beaux-Arts façade seems nothing more than an aesthetic joke." Penn Central said that the landmarking amounted to a taking of its property right to develop its own land. The question for the Supreme Court was whether the historic preservation law went too far.

Rehnquist said that it did. Historic preservation laws, he wrote, were different from the traditional zoning laws the courts had upheld against takings clause challenges. Those laws, he said, simultaneously decreased the value of a particular piece of property by limiting its use and increased the value of that same piece of property by ensuring that a neighborhood as a whole would be residential or commercial. Historic preservation laws, though, singled out a few buildings to benefit the entire city but didn't give the building owners anything in return.

But Rehnquist was writing a dissent. Justice Brennan wrote a majority opinion that upheld New York's historic preservation law but opened the way for continuing challenges to modern environmental and other regulations. He rejected a lot of Penn Central's challenges but did take seriously the possibility that a land use regulation could go too far. He developed a balancing test for deciding when it did: The courts had to examine the economic impact of the regulation on the property owner, particularly its impact on investment-backed expectations—in effect, not on what the owner hoped to do if things turned out right but on what the owner had already put up some money for, either in the price paid for the property or in other investments anticipating development. They also had to examine the "character" of the government's action. The more the regulation looked like a traditional exercise of the police power, the less likely it was to be a taking.

Applying this test, Brennan upheld the landmarking. It wasn't enough that landmarking reduced Grand Central Terminal's economic value to its owner. Penn Central could still use the terminal as it had for more than sixty years and would continue to get what it had expected to be a reasonable return from using the terminal as a terminal rather than as the site for an office building.

Brennan's opinion was strategically designed to hold the votes of the more conservative justices Lewis Powell and Potter Stewart. As a liberal Brennan thought that the people acting through their representatives were regulating businesses pretty much as much as they wanted. But Brennan, a consummate judicial strategist, needed to get the votes of some more conservative justices. Flatly saying that regulations could never be takings wouldn't do. Instead, he conceded that *some* regulations might be takings. Early in the opinion, Brennan stuck in a footnote saying explicitly that "we do not embrace the proposition that a 'taking' can never occur unless government has transferred physical control over a portion of a parcel." This divided the world of takings into two areas: One involved permanent physical occupations—the classical uses of eminent domain—and the other involved regulations that went too far.

Brennan certainly hoped that his multipart test for determining when a regulation went too far would lead courts to invalidate few regulations indeed. And so it has. Yet the test Brennan wrote did give real estate developers and other businesses the opportunity to increase the costs of *attempting* to regulate. They could deploy his test against any regulations they found burdensome. They might not win, but they could make it expensive for governments to try to regulate them.

✑

The Suitum and Grand Central cases didn't get to the Supreme Court simply because a particular individual or corporation had a lot at stake. They were, instead, part of what two liberal critics called the Takings Project. Brennan in the Grand Central Terminal case beat back the first assault on regulatory takings, but to salvage a victory, he had to concede that sometimes regulations could amount to takings. This gave more conservative justices their chance. They argued that regulations went "too far" when they deprived landowners of the right to *any* economically beneficial uses of their property.

Grand Central Terminal of course was economically viable even after its designation as a historic landmark. Environmental regulations were sometimes a different matter. Preserving wetlands might mean keeping marshes from any development, even in areas with expanding populations. Regulations might indeed deprive the wetlands' owner of any economically viable use of the land.

The Court used a beach erosion case to announce that finally it had discovered a regulation that deprived the landowner of any economically viable use of his property. David Lucas, a burly, full-bearded developer and building contractor, was a conservative Republican activist in South Carolina politics. He was involved with some of the state's major developers and Republicans in the Wild Dunes development project on the Isle of Palms, a barrier island east of Charleston, South Carolina. The Isle of Palms is a millionaires' retreat. In 1986 Lucas paid $975,000 for two lots in Wild Dunes, where he planned to build one house for his family and another for resale. Lucas's houses would fill in some blank spaces on the map; there were houses on nearly all the nearby lots, including one on the lot between the two Lucas bought.

There was a problem, though. The Atlantic Ocean tides regularly changed the contours of the Isle of Palms, eating away at some beaches and expanding others. In 1988 South Carolina adopted a beachfront management act prohibiting development in many parts of the Isle of Palms, including on Lucas's two lots, to protect against damage to the beaches resulting from houses in areas where the tides were eroding the island. Lucas sued, claiming that the regulation barring development amounted to a taking because it deprived him of the land's entire economic value. After losing in the South Carolina Supreme Court, Lucas contacted the Pacific Legal Foundation, which offered to take his case to the U.S. Supreme Court. Lucas decided to use some South Carolina attorneys, although they welcomed the support the participants in the Takings Project offered in amicus briefs.

Scalia, writing for the Court's five conservatives, agreed with Lucas's argument. Quoting a medieval British author, Scalia wrote, "For what is the land but the profits thereof?" Taking all the value of property away from the owner is "the equivalent of a physical appropriation." When the government does so, it's hard to see how it's simply "adjusting the benefits and burdens of economic life," a phrase Scalia took from the Grand Central Terminal case. The government defended its regulation as necessary for environmental preservation or—invoking traditional terms—as necessary to eliminate "harmful or noxious uses" of property. But, Scalia said, "confiscatory regulations" could be justified only by "the restrictions that background principles of the State's law of property and nuisance already place upon land ownership." Traditional public nuisances, like the pig in the parlor or land uses that led to flooding a neighbor's land, were one thing; the government's power to limit *them* was indeed part of the background law. Innovative regulations like the one against beachfront erosion were another thing altogether. Scalia emphasized that the owners of the lots near Lucas's had already built houses and weren't being asked to tear them down, indicating that the limitation on Lucas's rights wasn't already part of the law.

Scalia's opinion was characteristically hard-edged, looking for a rule courts could apply rather than invoking a balancing test, seeking some rule that could be applied "on an objective, value-free basis." Justice Stevens, dissenting, thought that "[a]rresting the development of the common law" was "profoundly unwise" because it ignored the fact that the "human condition is one of constant learning and evolution—both moral and practical." (Of course Scalia's entire way of thinking rejected the idea of moral evolution.) Blackmun's dissent was even more critical of Scalia's refusal to examine "the particular circumstances of each case." For him, what mattered was simply whether the use caused harm.

The Court sent the case back to the state courts for them to decide whether building a house on Lucas's lot was barred by "background principles of nuisance and property law." They said it wasn't, giving Lucas his victory. When the case ended, South Carolina paid Lucas $850,000 for his land and another $725,000 in interest and attorneys' fees. Lucas, whose development business had run into trouble when the second-home market collapsed, used the proceeds to pay his attorneys and the banks that held his loans and ended up with about $10,000 in his pockets. The state realized $730,000 by selling the lots for development, relaxing its previous restrictions. One property rights supporter said that this showed that "it's no fun regulating if it's not for 'free.' " But the economic and political dynamics surrounding the Isle of Palms had changed, and the state's decision to sell the property might have made as much economic sense then as regulating it had made earlier. In 1994 coastal erosion did indeed undermine a house built on one of Lucas's lots, and sandbags had to be used to protect the house. Lucas himself continued to work as a developer, on projects in Mexico and Poland, and published a book about his case.

℘

Lucas's case opened up a lot of possibilities. One was what lawyers involved in this area called the denominator problem. Stevens's dissent in the case opened the way to identifying the problem. Under the Court's approach, said Stevens, "[a] landowner whose property is diminished in value 95% recovers nothing, while an owner whose property is diminished 100% recovers the land's full value." But of course it's easy enough to say that the first landowner lost 100 percent of 95 percent of her property, a complete deprivation of a *part* of the property rather than a partial deprivation of the entire property.

An easy version of the denominator problem is this. Suppose Lucas bought two lots for $500,000 each, one on the beach and one directly behind it on the landward side of the island, and suppose the state law prohibited development only on the seaward lot. Lucas would have lost all economically viable use of *that* lot, but he could still build a $750,000 house on the landward lot. Does the regulation take his property? Yes, it does if the denominator is the value of the seaward lot and the numerator is the value of what he can build on that lot (zero divided by $500,000 is zero). No, it doesn't if the denominator is the value of both lots and the numerator is the value of what he can build on them ($750,000 divided by $1 million isn't zero, or a complete deprivation of all economically viable uses). You might want to say that Lucas has indeed lost all use of the seaward lot, which he purchased separately from the landward one. But suppose he simply bought one big lot but was barred from developing half of it. What's the denominator there: the entire lot or the part on which he can't build?

The denominator problem is the key to the Takings Project, because of the way lawyers have come to think about property. Most people have land, houses, cars, or computers in mind when they think about property. Property is *stuff*, or things. Lawyers have come to know better. Property may be about stuff, but the *law* of property is about *rights* to use the stuff. And a lot of different rights are bound up with everything we have. We "own" a house, but the bank that's lent us money has the right to take it from us if we don't keep up with our mortgage payments. We "own" our land, but a neighbor may have a right to use the driveway that's on our land if it's the only way to get to his door. Lawyers have come to think of property rights as a bundle of sticks rather than as a thing.

Put the bundle of sticks idea together with the rule that depriving someone of all economically viable use of property is a taking, and the implications for the Takings Project are clear. All you have to do is identify the right to use the property in the way barred by regulation as one of the sticks in the bundle, and the government has to compensate for *every* regulation it adopts. This approach to the takings clause would stop modern regulation in its tracks. Precisely for that reason, the Rehnquist Court wasn't about to take it.

The way to get out of the bundle of sticks problem is to control the manipulation of the denominator. In *Lucas* Scalia suggested that the solution to the denominator issue would "lie in how the owner's reasonable expectations have been shaped by the State's law of property." The idea here is the one opponents of the Takings Project like. Suppose you're thinking about buying a piece of property and check out what the law says you can do with it. Nobody's going to sympathize with your claim that the government has taken away some right you had to build a mansion if you find out that laws already in existence say that you can't build a mansion on the land. Similarly, for Scalia, if the government tells you that you've bought two pieces of property, you're going to expect that you've got two denominators to work with. Finally, if the law has already recognized something as an identifiable stick in the bundle of sticks, you're going to have reasonable expectations about what you can do with that stick; the denominator will be that stick. But if the government hasn't separated out some interest as an individual stick, the denominator will be the whole bundle.

⁂

How the denominator problem would be solved would determine how successful the Takings Project would be. In the end the Rehnquist Court didn't quite solve the denominator problem, but it fuzzed up the answer enough to impede challenges to all but the most extreme forms of regulation. At the end of the road the

Takings Project was back where it started, with a complex balancing test that courts could use to uphold virtually any regulation.

The decisive case came from Westerly, Rhode Island, which had become a major summer resort area for the Northeast. Atlantic Avenue provides access to Westerly's main beach area. The street is something of a commercial strip at its western end, but it becomes more residential toward the east. Anthony Palazzolo, the son of Sicilian immigrants and the owner of a junkyard, ended up owning a large parcel of land near the eastern end of Atlantic Avenue, which he wanted to develop as an investment for his six children. How he got the property is a complex story, with some bearing on the outcome. The land started out as an eighteen-acre tract. It was divided into three parcels in 1939. All three were sold in 1949 to Natale and Elizabeth Urso. Ten years later the Ursos proposed to develop the land into eighty lots, and the city's zoning board approved. Palazzolo joined the Ursos in the project, setting up a corporation to develop the land. The Ursos then sold their shares to Palazzolo, who ended up owning sixty-nine lots.

Most of Palazzolo's land was wetlands, but in the 1960s Rhode Island had no wetlands regulations, and indeed, one observer wrote, "everyone was filling and dredging back then." In 1962 Palazzolo applied for a permit to dredge part of the wetlands and use the material to fill the marsh and make it useful for development. (It turned out that Rhode Island law in 1962 might not have required Palazzolo to get a permit at all. The litigation that followed might have been avoided if he had simply dredged the pond and waited to see if anyone sued him.) The state returned the application to him for more detail. He provided it, explaining that he wanted to fill the entire eighteen acres. A year later Rhode Island adopted a modest wetlands protection law. In 1966 Palazzolo applied again for approval to dredge the pond and fill the marsh for "a recreational beach facility." In April 1971 the state's regulators approved the plan, as well as an earlier plan to fill in the marsh, giving Palazzolo the choice of projects. The regulators thought again and revoked the permit in November.

Palazzolo put his project on hold. Meanwhile Rhode Island's environmentalists continued their efforts to regulate wetlands. In 1971 the state created a Coastal Resources Management Council, which adopted regulations in 1977 that prohibited filling coastal wetlands like Palazzolo's without special permission. In 1978 the corporation Palazzolo had set up was shut down by the state for failing to pay corporate income taxes. Its property was transferred automatically to Palazzolo himself. In the 1980s land prices in Westerly soared, and Palazzolo renewed his efforts to develop the land, so that, he said, he could pay college tuitions for his children. He submitted new applications to develop his land, which the regulators rejected because they were "vague and inadequate for a project of this size and nature." In the end he came up with a proposal for a beachfront facility on eleven acres of the property, with room for "fifty cars with boat trailers, a dumpster, picnic table, and barbecue pits." The Supreme Court observed acerbically that "the details do not tend to inspire the reader with an idyllic coastal image," although Palazzolo responded that the whole area was heavily developed, with vacation homes and a public beach with parking spaces for nearly three thousand cars nearby.

Palazzolo sued after the state denied this application. He was the kind of plaintiff conservative litigators loved. He was a crusty man in his sixties when the lawsuit began. He was in the case as a matter of principle, willing, he said, to "fight for my rights as long as I do no harm." Palazzolo told one reporter, "You think those guys fighting the Revolutionary War wanted us to have to ask the next person, 'Can I do this with my land?' [Expletive] They were tough." To another, he said, "This land had rights . . . after the sweep of a pen, it had no rights. Where did they go to? The state got them. How much did it pay for them? Zero." He walked his property with a state official, trying to persuade the state to let him do something with his land. According to Palazzolo, the official said that he could do "nothing" with the land. Palazzolo replied, "Wait a minute. This isn't going to end because you say 'nothing.' Well, now it's a battle."

The Rhode Island Supreme Court ruled against Palazzolo, using a theory that would have been a major victory for environmentalists. It said that he got the property *after* the state had adopted its comprehensive wetlands regulations, so he couldn't have expected to use the property for development. In the language of the Lucas case, state regulations in existence when someone bought land were background rules of state law. As Kennedy put the argument, "by

prospective legislation the State can shape and define property
rights and reasonable investment backed expectations." Later purchasers can't complain because they got the property knowing of the
limitations the state imposed on its use.

The Supreme Court rejected that theory, which environmentalists
initially treated as a serious defeat. Kennedy tried to turn a phrase by
writing, "The State may not put so potent a Hobbesian stick into the
Lockean bundle." An owner's notice that the state had the right to
regulate couldn't by itself defeat a takings claim because that rule
would allow the state "to defend any action restricting land use, no
matter how extreme or unreasonable." Fair enough. But remember,
the Grand Central Terminal case said that one element of the test for
determining whether something was a regulatory taking was how
much the regulation affected investment-backed expectations.
Exactly what could a property owner expect to do with land that an
existing regulation said he couldn't develop?

Kennedy didn't say anything about that question, but O'Connor
and Scalia did. For O'Connor, the regulations in place "help . . .
shape the reasonableness" of the expectations. They should "inform
the analysis." Otherwise, someone who bought property could
unfairly "reap windfalls" by getting compensated for being unable to
do something she should have known she couldn't do. Scalia
responded by sniping at O'Connor for articulating an unintelligible
approach. The windfalls she criticized were, he said, "not much different from the windfalls that occur every day at stock exchanges or
antique auctions, where the knowledgeable (or the venturesome)
profit at the expense of the ignorant (or the risk averse)." Maybe
there was something unfair when a sharp buyer got land at a bargain
price from a seller, then turned around and got more money from
the government because the regulations went too far. That, though,
was an unfairness between the buyer and the seller. For Scalia, "there
is nothing to be said" for giving the windfall to the government—
that is, "giving the malefactor the benefit of its malefaction." He proposed a simple rule: The existence of regulations was entirely
irrelevant to determining whether a taking occurred.

The stakes here were fairly large. Scalia's approach would have
allowed many more successful challenges to regulatory takings than
O'Connor's. More important, O'Connor explicitly argued that the

test for a taking could not "be reduced to any 'set formula.' " That type of approach, an all-things-considered balancing test, was the kind of test that set Scalia's teeth on edge. O'Connor's balancing test made it easier for regulators to defeat challenges to their actions. As one environmental lawyer put it, her approach "likely means that most long-established environmental and land use regulations will be largely immune from takings challenges. And they should become increasingly immune from challenge as properties change hands and additional time passes."

The denominator problem surfaced in the Palazzolo case as well. As the case had been developed in the lower courts, Palazzolo appeared to concede that he could still build a two-hundred-thousand-dollar house on part of the larger tract. That was enough for the Court to say that he hadn't been deprived of all economically viable use of the tract as a whole, significantly limiting the extent of his victory. He tried to persuade the Court that the denominator should be just the marshland subject to regulation, but it rejected that argument on procedural grounds. Kennedy did say that the denominator problem was a "difficult, persisting question."

In the end the Palazzolo case only looked like a defeat for environ-mentalists and regulators. Four justices dissented, and they certainly would choose O'Connor's approach—more generous to regulators— over Scalia's. The Court had rejected the approach most favorable to regulators, but O'Connor's wasn't all that bad from their point of view, although it certainly was confusing. It's not at all clear how you can take the existence of a regulation barring development into account without making it dispositive on the question of whether the regulation affected investment-backed expectations. Still, regu-lators could live with O'Connor's approach. It could mean that only "rare and unusual" regulations go too far.

☙

Modern city planners thought up an ingenious device to make sure that developers paid for civic improvements—what's known as the exaction. Developers need a city's permission to build their projects: permission to close roads or permission to have more square feet of space in a building than the general zoning rules allow. Cities grant permission, but only on condition: The developer will have to maintain some area as a public park or will have to devote some part of the project to a walkway. In essence, the developer absorbs some of the costs of civic improvements as part of the project's cost. This seems like a good deal all around. The city gets the park, and the developer gets the project. But of course the developer pays, by not having as large a project as it initially wanted.

Scalia wrote the Court's opinion imposing some limits on exactions. James and Marilyn Nollan owned beachfront property in California, between two public beaches. They wanted to tear down a ramshackle bungalow on their property and replace it with a three-bedroom house. California law required them to get permission from the state Coastal Commission for beachfront development. The commission told the Nollans that they could build their house, but only if they gave the public permission to walk along the beachfront from one public beach to the other (what lawyers call an easement). The commission's theory was that replacing the bungalow with the house would create a "wall" of houses blocking the ocean view. People on the highway above the beaches wouldn't realize that they could get to two public beaches. Giving people permission to walk along the beach in front of the Nollans' house would increase public access to the beaches.

Scalia began by noting that an order directing the Nollans to give the public permission to walk along their beachfront would undoubtedly have been a permanent physical occupation and therefore a taking. The harder question was whether giving an easement could be required in exchange for permission to build the house. According to Scalia, exactions were constitutional if they had a reasonable relation to the problems granting permission to develop would cause. So, he wrote, the Coastal Commission could limit the height of houses on the beach to ensure that the public would be able to see the ocean. But there had to be some "nexus" between the problems and the exaction: "[U]nless the permit condition serves the same governmental purpose as the development ban, the building restriction is not a valid regulation of land use but 'an out-and-out plan of extortion.' " Scalia couldn't understand how letting people walk along the beach on the Nollans' property would make it easier for people on the highway to appreciate that somewhere down below there was a public beach: "It is quite impossible to understand how a requirement that people already on the public beaches be able to walk across the Nollans' property reduces any obstacles to viewing the beach created by the new house. It is also impossible to understand how it lowers any 'psychological barrier' to using the public beaches. . . ."

The Coastal Commission's position in the Nollans' case does seem extreme, and even the dissenters struggled to explain how letting people walk across the beach addressed the problems caused by blocking the ocean view. The Court's next exaction case, though, should have been harder.

Florence Dolan owned a small hardware store in downtown Tigard, Oregon, with a gravel parking lot for customers. A small creek flowed along the parking lot's boundary. Mrs. Dolan wanted to double the store's size and pave the parking lot. Her plans involved tearing down the old hardware store and building a new one that would include additional businesses. Following its general city plan, the city required Mrs. Dolan to donate a strip of land along the creek as a pedestrian walkway and bikeway and to dedicate another part of the property for a storm drainage system. The effect was to take about 10 percent of the property. The city said that the walkway and bikeway were related to the store's expansion because some of the customers would walk or bike to the store and that paving the parking lot would increase problems of drainage, meaning that the storm sewer condition was also related to the new building. Rehnquist wrote the Court's opinion. It agreed with the city that there was a nexus between the development and the conditions the city imposed. But, he said, the city had failed to show that the exaction was "roughly proportional" to the burdens development created. The city had failed to provide enough evidence that it needed to obtain the land for the drainage system (rather than leave it with Mrs. Dolan subject to regulation) or that enough people would walk or bike to the new store to justify forcing Mrs. Dolan to give up her land for the walkway and bikeway.

Tigard's requirements were obviously more related to Mrs. Dolan's project than were the Coastal Commission's requirements in the Nollans' case. Rehnquist said that he was choosing a middle path between state courts that had required only the most general statements of a connection between a development and the exaction and state courts that demanded "a very exacting correspondence." Yet the Dolan case pretty clearly ratcheted up the requirements for evidence supporting exactions. The Takings Project seemed well along. And then the project subsided without having done much to dismantle the regulatory state.

☙

One reason the project ebbed was precisely its ambition. The Rehnquist Court's takings cases were decided by the usual five to four votes, and the Court's moderate conservatives were not about to return the nation to a world of unregulated businesses. They would work on the margins, but faced with challenges going to the heart of modern regulation, they hesitated.

Ask mainstream economists during the Rehnquist years for examples of misguided economic policies, and you'd be overwhelmed by their agreement on two: minimum wage laws and rent control ordinances. Mainstream economists believed that minimum wage laws kept employers from hiring less skilled workers whose contribution to production, while positive, didn't match the minimum wage. They believed that rent control ordinances kept decent housing from poor people who happened to live outside the city and benefited only the better-off people who happened to live in rent-controlled apartments and refused to leave them because after all, they were getting a terrific deal.

Conservatives knew that mounting constitutional challenges to minimum wage laws would be political suicide and would truly signal their interest in revolutionizing constitutional law. Rent control laws were another matter altogether. They existed in only a few cities, so challenging them would not raise political red flags. Moreover, their burdens on people who would like to move into the apartments kept off the market by rent control laws were fairly easy to describe.

The takings clause was a promising vehicle for an attack on rent control laws. Lawyers didn't have to manipulate the idea of a bundle of sticks at all to point out that the right to transfer your property to someone else—that is, to rent it to whomever you wanted—was clearly one of the most traditional property rights in the bundle. Many rent control ordinances limited that right pretty substantially.

And at least on the metaphoric level, the tenants who liked the deal they had were physically occupying the apartments as permanently as they could. The metaphor of permanent physical occupation could be brought into play as part of the atmospherics of a constitutional attack on rent control.

The attack failed. Not surprisingly, the two challenges the Court considered came from California. The first involved a rent control ordinance in San Jose that allowed annual rent increases of up to 8 percent. A tenant could object if the increase was more than that. A hearing board would decide if the extra increase was reasonable, and one ground for rejecting the increase was that the particular tenant was simply too poor to afford it. Scalia and O'Connor thought that this was unconstitutional: Landlords who charged tenants what was needed to keep the apartment building in decent condition weren't different from grocers who charged market prices to people who bought food. To them, it simply wasn't fair to force landlords to subsidize these tenants; the public generally should bear the costs of poverty programs through the taxes they paid to provide public assistance to the poor. Scalia's opinion invoked standard economic theories of the political process to point out that the rent control ordinance transferred wealth from landlords to tenants, but without real public visibility.

The majority disagreed and upheld the ordinance. The fact that Rehnquist wrote the Court's opinion suggests that the Takings Project might be overreaching. His opinion demonstrated some modest sympathy for the landlords, acknowledging that someday some landlord might be able to show that the provision for subsidizing poor tenants was particularly harsh in a specific case. But the opinion rejected the challenge to the subsidy overall, in the typically crisp Rehnquist manner. It hurt the challenge that the landlords hadn't even come up with an example of a single use of the hardship clause to force a subsidy. The Court concluded that the rent control ordinance was "a rational attempt to accommodate the conflicting interests of protecting tenants from burdensome rent increases while at the same time ensuring that landlords are guaranteed a fair rate of return on their investment."

The second attack on rent control was an even larger defeat for the Takings Project, with a unanimous Court rejecting a challenge that tried to capitalize on the metaphor of permanent physical occupation. Escondido, California, regulated rates charged by mobile home parks. As O'Connor's opinion for the Court indicated, calling the home mobile is something of a misnomer. The homes in mobile home parks sit on concrete pads, are connected to city gas and electric services, and, notably, almost never move; according to O'Connor, only one out of a hundred "mobile" homes ever leaves the mobile home park. When the home's owner wants to move on, she sells the home to someone else. California state law gives mobile home owners substantial protections from eviction and, more important, allows the homeowner to sell her mobile home to whomever she wants, without getting any permission from the owner of the mobile home park.

Technically the mobile home owner rents the pad from the owner of the mobile home park. Escondido regulated the rental fees for the pads. Its ordinance rolled back rental fees by two years and then allowed mobile home park owners to increase their fees only if they persuaded the city council that the increases were "just, fair and reasonable." The ordinance listed nearly a dozen factors for the city council to take into account in making that decision.

John and Irene Yee owned a mobile home park in Escondido. They argued that the ordinance, taken together with the state law, took away a whole bunch of sticks: They couldn't set the fees they charged for the pads they rented out, and they couldn't even decide who would occupy the pads because the mobile home owners did that when they sold their homes. As the Yees saw it, the ordinance and the state laws in effect transferred an interest in land—the right to occupy a pad at a regulated rate—from them to their "tenants." The economics were simple: If the value of mobile home housing increased, the Yees couldn't capture the increased value by increasing their rents; instead, the owners of the mobile homes would, by selling their homes at a higher price.

O'Connor suggested that the metaphor of permanent physical occupation was too cute. No one in the government, she wrote, forced the Yees to rent their property to anyone; the tenants were "invited" by the Yees, "not forced upon them by the government." She also addressed the economic argument against rent control. First she noted that every land use regulation transfers wealth from the landowner who is regulated to someone else, including neighbors, whose homes end up being worth more because the landowner can't use the land as he wishes. She acknowledged that the Escondido ordinance transferred wealth from the Yees to the people who happened to own mobile homes in their park when the ordinance was enacted and didn't benefit future occupiers of the pads. The incumbents would pay below-market rents as long as they occupied their homes and would sell the homes to new buyers at a premium that reflected the below-market rents, which the new buyers would then continue to pay. In short, the Escondido ordinance simply took wealth from current owners and gave it to current incumbents, in contrast with traditional rent control ordinances, which transfer wealth from landlords to all tenants, incumbents and future ones as well. But, O'Connor said, this didn't make any difference on the question of whether the ordinance forced a permanent physical occupation.

The Yees' case was the Rehnquist Court's last confrontation with the issue on which standard economics supported the Takings Project most strongly. The Court's refusal to bite indicates the limits of the project's success.

෯

At the end of the Rehnquist era, what had the Takings Project accomplished? On the surface, not much. The Rehnquist Court didn't force governments to pay substantially for any modern environmental, wetlands, or historic preservation regulations—if the governments proceeded carefully enough. However, the qualification is important. Before the Rehnquist Court got hold of the takings clause, environmentalists thought all they had to do was persuade legislatures to adopt regulations they liked. Today, though, businesses and developers can credibly threaten to tie regulation up in court with takings clause challenges unless the regulations are to their liking. The cases indicate that the challenges are almost always going to lose, but defending against them costs money that cities and states don't have. The Takings Project may have failed to wipe regulations off the board, but it succeeded in limiting the reach of regulations by increasing the costs of adopting them. And of course the point of the takings clause itself is to increase costs by making governments pay. So, paradoxically, what looks like the failure of the Takings Project might actually be its success.

CHAPTER TWELVE

Big Business's Constitution

Once upon a time the First Amendment was about Eugene V. Debs and Martin Luther King, Jr., rebels and rabble-rousers. The Rehnquist Court transformed it. Now it is about Lorillard Tobacco and Ted Turner: money and marketing. Or as one observer writing in 2003 said, the Rehnquist Court was preoccupied with money and sex (and the cases involving sex were about money too). The Court's First Amendment docket shifted from cases dealing with protest demonstrations and defamation to cases dealing with commercial speech and pornography.

Once upon a time liberal heroes like Justices Hugo Black and William Douglas insisted that the First Amendment was an absolute and fought their more conservative colleagues who argued that First Amendment cases always involved a host of considerations that had to be balanced carefully against one another. The Rehnquist Court saw the players shift sides. Its conservatives insisted that the First Amendment protected speech absolutely, brooking no exceptions, and rejected the arguments offered by its liberals that First Amendment cases involved considerations that had to be balanced against one another.

Once upon a time the due process clause protected the right of employers to insist on setting the terms of employment for their workers. The New Deal Court abandoned the doctrine that the Constitution protected a general liberty of contract. The idea of due process lived on, but it morphed into a doctrine protecting privacy and the right to choose abortion. Conservative legal theorists derided the idea of substantive due process in the abortion cases, but they rediscovered how convenient the idea was when they too wanted to protect rights they couldn't locate anywhere else in the Constitution. The due process clause morphed again, adding a branch that revived some of the economic protections the Court had invented a century earlier.

Why this happened is a complicated story. It involves the conservative commitment to a free market, in ideas as well as cars. It involves the suspicion some modern liberals have about "ordinary" people. It also involves what one law professor called ideological drift, the changing political valence of ideas and arguments as circumstances change.

✑

A month after it decided the fighting words case in 1942 (Chapter Five), the Supreme Court added commercial speech to the category of words outside the First Amendment. Captain F. J. Chrestensen, a retired naval officer, bought a decommissioned Navy submarine and set it up as a tourist site in New York, charging adults twenty-five cents (this was the 1940s, after all) and children fifteen cents for admission. To attract tourists, he printed up handbills for distribution on the city's streets. At first the handbills simply had a picture of the submarine and its description, along with information about how to get to the site. Chrestensen modified the handbill when he was told that distributing commercial handbills violated a city ordinance. He reprinted them, but this time when readers turned the flyer over, they found a statement criticizing "the 'almost unbelievable' action of 'dictatorial' subordinates of 'a mayor who is one of the outstanding liberals of the United States.'" The city threatened to prosecute Chrestensen, but he got the federal courts to bar any prosecution.

The Supreme Court, though, unanimously said that the city's ordinance was perfectly all right. Devoting only two paragraphs to legal analysis, the Court said that the Constitution did not place any limits on the government's ability to restrict "purely commercial advertising" on city streets. It treated as a gimmick Chrestensen's effort to bring his handbill inside the First Amendment by including the protest against the city's action.

The Court's lack of interest in protecting commercial speech came under stress in the 1970s. Justice William O. Douglas, who had gone along with the majority in the Chrestensen case, dissented on First Amendment grounds in 1973, when the Court upheld a Pittsburgh ordinance barring newspapers from publishing job advertisements labeled as "for women" or "for men," and three other justices agreed that the ordinance was unconstitutional. (Ruth Bader Ginsburg had signed the ACLU's brief supporting the city's ordinance.)

Two years later the Court began to bring commercial advertising within the First Amendment. The case involved Virginia's prosecution of John C. Bigelow, the editor of the weekly "underground" newspaper at the University of Virginia, for publishing an advertisement for abortion services available in New York. This, the Virginia Supreme Court said, violated a state statute against "encouraging" abortions. By 1975 nothing much was at stake—except Bigelow's $150 fine—because the Court had already decided the abortion cases, and Virginia had already repealed its statute and now banned only encouraging *illegal* abortions. Justice Blackmun, the author of the abortion decisions, used the Bigelow case as the vehicle for casting doubt on the idea that commercial advertising was outside the First Amendment. He pointed out that Bigelow's advertising "contained factual material of clear 'public interest' " and emphasized that the Chrestensen case was "distinctly limited." Rehnquist, who had dissented in the abortion cases, dissented here as well. The only other dissenter was Justice White, the only other dissenter in the abortion cases as well, perhaps suggesting that they saw Bigelow's case as an abortion case, not as a free speech one. Still, Rehnquist expressed a general concern about the Court's willingness to give First Amendment protection to commercial advertising, a concern he continued to express as the Court expanded that protection over the next decades.

The decisive step came in 1976, when the Court struck down Virginia's ban on advertising prices for prescription drugs. Blackmun again wrote the opinion. Even speech that simply proposed a commercial transaction was within the scope of the First Amendment, he said. After all, he said, the consumer's interest in knowing that prices for prescription drugs varied at different pharmacies might be "as keen

[as], if not keener by far, than his interest in the day's most urgent political debate." He observed that knowledge of drug prices was particularly important to people with limited incomes, who have to figure out where to spend "their scarce dollars."

The opinion pointed out, "So long as we preserve a predominantly free enterprise economy, the allocation of our resources in large measure will be made through numerous private economic decisions," and there was a public interest in seeing that those decisions were "intelligent and well informed." Blackmun also criticized the "highly paternalistic approach" Virginia took. The state defended its statute by saying that advertising would undermine professional standards. But, Blackmun said, the state was really arguing that people would be better off if they were "kept in ignorance." Through these maneuvers, the marketplace of ideas came to include the marketplace pure and simple.

Again Rehnquist dissented, this time alone. Observing that the Court's criticism of paternalistic regulation couldn't logically be limited to price advertising but had to cover general advertising too, he presciently described the appearance of consumer-oriented drug advertising, inventing an advertisement of a sort that later became common: "Pain getting you down? Insist that your physician prescribe Demerol. You pay a little more than for aspirin, but you get a lot more relief."

The Virginia drug price advertising case led to a series of decisions, generally striking down state regulations while occasionally upholding a regulation that the Court thought really did address problems of fraud. The Court's commercial advertising decisions didn't adopt free speech absolutism, though, probably because the justices understood that there is a huge amount of advertising regulation. The Federal Trade Commission regulates "deceptive" advertising, while the Food and Drug Administration regulates the claims drug manufacturers can make about their products. The Court's general approach involves a balancing test, although in practice there's a pretty heavy thumb on the scales weighing against the state's regulatory interests.

By the 1990s many justices seemed ready to decide that the First Amendment placed fairly severe limits on government regulation of even purely commercial advertising. The first sign of the more absolutist approach came in another price advertising case, this one involving Rhode Island's ban on advertising liquor prices. Within the Court the justices debated whether to adopt an entirely new approach to regulations of commercial advertising. Its proponents wanted to say that commercial advertising was fully protected by the First Amendment and could be regulated only if the regulation really did advance truly important public interests. Stevens and Thomas were the strongest voices for the new approach, arguing that the Court should strike down any regulation of commercial advertising that rested on paternalistic assumptions about the ability of ordinary consumers to assess the validity of what the advertising said. The push for a new approach was highly divisive, however, largely because other justices weren't at all sure what the new approach meant for well-established forms of consumer protection regulation. The result was that although every justice agreed that Rhode Island's restriction on liquor price advertising was unconstitutional, there wasn't an opinion for the Court, and there were a slew of separate opinions.

Twice more during the Rehnquist years, the Court tried to settle the question of whether commercial speech deserved the highest level of protection, and each time it could not. The question, it turned out, was much harder than the Court's absolutists believed. But, then, that was what balancers had said about the questions Black and Douglas tried to answer through absolutism two generations earlier.

The Clinton administration's interest in health care policy led it to take a vigorous stand against smoking. Its path was eased by increasing public disdain for the tobacco industry, fueled by revelations about the lengths to which industry officials went to cover up their knowledge of smoking's health risks. Smoking became a major public health issue. The Clinton administration tried to act against smoking through the Food and Drug Administration, proposing an extensive set of regulations of cigarette advertising and distribution. The Supreme Court's five conservatives blocked the initiative, though, finding that Congress had specifically barred the FDA from regulating tobacco.

That decision couldn't foreclose state efforts to regulate tobacco use. Democratic activists saw tobacco regulation as a good government issue that might help them win votes too. Massachusetts (no surprise here) adopted comprehensive regulation of tobacco advertising. The state's attorney general, Scott Harshbarger, issued the regulations as, Justice O'Connor carefully noted, "one of his last acts in office" after losing a race for governor.

The Court dealt with First Amendment challenges to several regulations. One prohibited outdoor advertising within one thousand feet of public playgrounds and schools; this, the tobacco industry said, eliminated the possibility of outdoor advertising in about 90 percent of Boston and made it impossible to use outdoor advertising in some other cities in the state. Another regulation barred advertising placed lower than five feet above the ground in places where tobacco products were sold. The point of the regulations, according to Massachusetts, was to prevent or at least limit tobacco use by children, but the industry said that they severely limited its ability to provide "truthful information" to adults who wanted to use a lawful product.

The language of O'Connor's opinion invalidating Massachusetts's regulations indicates why free speech absolutists *and* proponents of regulation might be nervous about a balancing test. According to O'Connor, the "broad sweep" of the regulations showed that Massachusetts hadn't done a careful weighing of speech interests against the public health concerns it had. Harshbarger had simply picked up the thousand-foot rule from the failed FDA proposals without considering its effect in specific locations, but the impact of regulations would vary from place to place. In addition, she wrote, banning all signs "seems ill suited to target the problem of highly visible billboards." Similarly, because "not all children are less than 5 feet tall, and those who are certainly have the ability to look up and take in their surroundings," the ban on low signs where tobacco products were sold "does not seem to advance" the goal of discouraging tobacco use by young people.

The words *seems* and *seem* in these sentences are what raises questions. O'Connor's judgments, expressed so tentatively, are those we would ordinarily expect to come from legislators, not judges. The regulators are legislators, of course, and O'Connor's use of balancing doesn't explain why she's better at making this sort of tentative, empirically driven assessment than they are. Free speech absolutists

don't have to worry about empirical judgments; that's the strength—
and the weakness—of their position.

The absolutist position draws a line against government regulation. To absolutists, the government can't stop political candidates
from making false claims about their own backgrounds or their
opponent's policies, and neither can the government stop advertis-
ers from making false claims about their products or their competi-
tors'. In both areas, the absolutists said, it was better to rely on the
marketplace—of ideas, in politics, and of goods, in the market—to
correct false statements than to let the government try to sort things
out. Skeptics about the market for consumer goods found that a difficult argument to accept.

The balancers had their own problem, though: distinguishing
between truly commercial speech and political speech. The Rehnquist
Court's final confrontation with the problem of commercial speech
posed the problem in a form that turned out to be surprisingly difficult to deal with.

In the tobacco advertising case Thomas pointed out that free
speech absolutism had the advantage of eliminating difficult
inquiries into whether words published by someone trying to make
money were commercial speech, subject to a balancing test, or political commentary, subject to the absolutist approach. The antiglobalization movement of the early 2000s generated a case showing why
Thomas was right. In the end, though, the case fizzled out, largely
because a majority of the justices came to understand that the problem of regulating commercial speech to prevent consumer deception
and unfair trade practices was a lot harder than the absolutists
thought it was.

Nobody really needs to be told that Nike makes shoes. When the
company began operating, its market strategy was to undersell com-
petitors by designing shoes that could be made in low-cost Asian factories—by the 1990s, in Indonesia, Thailand, Vietnam, and mainland
China. Antiglobalization activists focused on labor conditions in
these factories, which they described as sweatshops. Nike developed
a code of conduct for its contractors, requiring them to certify that
they were complying with local minimum wage laws, child labor
laws, occupational safety and health laws, and more. The company
implausibly claimed that it had employees monitoring the contrac-

tors on a daily basis. More plausibly, it hired Ernst & Young, the accounting and consulting firm, to inspect the factories in unannounced visits. One of the Ernst & Young audits was leaked to the press. It said that the Vietnamese factory it had inspected had between 6 and 177 times the allowable limits of one toxic chemical and that nearly all the workers were working longer hours than local law allowed. Nike responded to its critics through letters to newspaper editors and letters to university athletic directors who had been targeted by campus activists because of the firm's endorsement arrangements with the universities.

Marc Kasky was one of Nike's critics. Kasky managed a community theater in San Francisco and ran marathons and took part in labor and antiglobalization activism on the side. He had stopped buying Nike shoes in the early 1990s because of reports about the sweatshops, but he said he had been "heartened" by Nike's code of conduct. His hopes were dashed when he read a *New York Times* story about the Ernst & Young report. He decided to do something about it.

Kasky was familiar with California's consumer protection law, which allowed *anyone* to sue a company for unfair trade practices, including the making of misleading statements designed to induce consumers to buy the company's products. He had sued Perrier for falsely claiming that its water was "spring water" and Pillsbury for labeling vegetables harvested in Mexico "San Francisco style." This time he claimed that Nike's responses to its critics violated the consumer protection law. He noted, for example, that one of Nike's letters to the editor said that the contractors provided "free" meals and health care, but its own response to its critics said only that the contractors "typically" provided "subsidies for" meals and health care.

The lawsuit had two central elements. First, Kasky said, accurately, that some of Nike's statements were straightforward factual claims. Second, he said that the company made those claims to persuade consumers to buy its shoes; they were targeted at potential buyers who might be reluctant to purchase shoes made in sweatshops. Seen in that light, the case really wasn't much different from an ordinary false advertising case. Suppose consumers thought that shoes made with real rubber were better than other shoes. If Nike shoes didn't have any rubber in them an advertisement that said, "Our shoes are made with genuine rubber," is false advertising: It contains a false statement, and it's made to persuade people to buy the shoes. Then suppose a newspaper columnist picked up the story and wrote a column saying that Nike shoes didn't have any rubber. A letter to the editor—or to college athletic directors—saying, "Your columnist is wrong; our shoes are indeed made with rubber," doesn't seem different, in terms of ordinary false advertising law, from the advertisement itself. Like the advertisement, the letter is false and aimed at persuading people to buy Nike shoes. As Kasky's lawyer put it, Nike's letters were not efforts to solve "the great moral dilemmas of the world." Nike was "trying to sell you a pair of shoes." The trial judge who handled the case disagreed, holding that Kasky didn't present the courts with a claim that deserved even a factual hearing.

The California Supreme Court, in its turn, agreed with Kasky and said that he deserved a trial at which the facts could be examined. It said that at least some of the statements Nike made in its letters to editors and athletic directors were factual assertions, that at least some of them might be inaccurate, and that at least some of the inaccuracies might have helped persuade readers to buy Nike shoes. It said that Kasky ought to have a chance to prove the essential elements of his claim in a trial court. The chances of his doing so, though, were really slim. Saying that the factories provided "free" meals rather than "subsidized" meals, for example, might be inaccurate, but Kasky would have a hard time showing that someone who would be persuaded that Nike didn't operate sweatshops because it provided free meals would be persuaded that Nike *did* operate sweatshops because it provided only subsidized meals.

The business community and its advertising companies went ballistic at the California Supreme Court's decision. So did the media. So did traditional civil libertarians. Nike's supporters suggested that the California decision threatened every corporation that published some sort of statement about how its policies showed it was a good corporate citizen because someone in California might sue the corporation for misleading readers by failing to provide a complete picture of the corporation's activities.

Nike's petition for Supreme Court review got the support of several amici, and thirty-one—quite a large number by Supreme Court standards—filed briefs supporting the company after the Court decided to hear the case. Their argument was simple: Nike's letters were part of an ongoing public debate about globalization. They were really *political*, not commercial, statements, even if they were made by a corporation aiming to protect its market. Nike and its supporters made some supplementary points. They wondered why Kasky, who hadn't even bought a pair of Nike shoes, should be allowed to sue. They pointed out that California's false advertising statute would allow Kasky to win if Nike's statements were misleading even if, when read literally, they were accurate.

Kasky did get some support, though, from elements of the antiglobalization movement and—more important—from government agencies like the Federal Trade Commission, whose mission includes enforcing laws against false advertising. The agencies were afraid that a broad decision favoring Nike would make it much harder to go after "ordinary" false advertising.

Neither side had an easy time at oral argument, although most of the justices seemed to want to rule against Kasky. Breyer said that Nike's statements were both commercial and political and, adopting a point made by the company's lawyers, added, "I think the First Amendment was designed to protect all the participants in a public debate, and a debate consists of facts. Once you've tied a party's hands behind his back with respect to facts, you've silenced him." The idea here was that Kasky could make lots of outrageous factual statements about Nike, and it couldn't win a lawsuit against him unless it showed that his statements met the stringent standards of defamation law, whereas Nike would be liable for *its* false statements under a much looser standard. Paul Hoeber, Kasky's lawyer, had to acknowledge O'Connor's point that Nike's statements weren't "advertising in a true sense," and when he tried to say that the Court couldn't draw a line between "real" advertising and something else because it would get into trouble with "a lot of promotions and representations consumers rely on," Kennedy picked up on the problem, saying, "If it's very difficult to define commercial speech, isn't it true that companies will be chilled in speaking?"

Laurence Tribe, arguing for Nike, didn't get off scot-free either. Ginsburg said that "the problem with this case is that it comes to us at such a preliminary stage," before any determination of whether any of Nike's statements were inaccurate or misleading. Tribe went for rhetoric rather than analysis in replying that a trial would be a "show trial" aiming to put a "scarlet letter" on Nike. When Theodore Olson, the solicitor general, argued that the flaw in California's system was that anyone "with a whim or a grievance and a filing fee," not just a person injured by Nike's alleged misstatements, could "become a government-licensed censor," Breyer disparaged the point, saying that "in five minutes, they'll find someone who bought Nike shoes."

The justices were clearly engaged with the problem, but in the end they discovered that they couldn't deal with it. The procedural messiness of the case was one part of the difficulty. How could they resolve an important and, it turned out, complicated First Amendment case without knowing if Nike's statements were inaccurate and misleading? Finding out, though, would require the very trial that Nike was trying to avoid. Even more important, there still was no majority for treating commercial speech exactly like political speech. The Court dropped the case. In insider jargon, the Court DIG-ged the case, that is Dismissed it as Improvidently Granted.

The Court doesn't explain its reasons for DIG-ging, but in the Nike case Stevens gave the reasons he, Ginsburg, and Souter had for it. For them, the case was particularly difficult "because the speech at issue represents a blending of commercial speech, noncommercial speech and debate on an issue of public importance." The state's interest in protecting consumers "from being misled" by factual misstatements was "of the highest order." But so was the interest in ensuring that "knowledgeable people" could take part in debates about important public issues like globalization "without fear of unfair reprisal" or "the prospect of expensive litigation." According to Stevens, the Court would be in a better position to figure out what to do when the speaker was the corporation itself from "the study of a full factual record" that a trial would produce.

Breyer, joined by O'Connor, responded that the whole point of Nike's claim was that it shouldn't have to go through a trial and that the Court didn't need any additional information to work out the right answer. Nike's behavior had already been affected by the mere fact that it would face a trial: It cut down on social responsibility advertising, didn't release its annual report on its corporate responsibility, and refused invitations to send speakers to discussions of corporate responsibility.

Breyer acknowledged that sorting out the commercial from the noncommercial might sometimes be difficult but was confident that he (at least) could do it right. He thought that Nike's statements, blending commercial and "public-issue-oriented" elements, were "predominantly" noncommercial. They weren't in the form of traditional advertisements, didn't directly propose to sell shoes, and concerned a matter of "significant public interest and active controversy"—that is, Nike's labor policies.

For Breyer, the statements deserved "a form of heightened scrutiny." This was his balancing test. California's law did advance "legitimate, traditional, and important public objectives" in maintaining "an honest commercial marketplace." The state could advance those objectives through traditional methods of regulation, as the federal government did with the Federal Trade Commission. But allowing anyone to sue imposed a "disproportionate" burden on speech. "The delegation of state authority to private individuals authorizes a purely ideological plaintiff, convinced that his opponent is not telling the truth, to bring into the courtroom the kind of political battle better waged in other forums." The disparagement of ideological plaintiffs sounds odd coming from Breyer, except that it fits—in this case—with his technocrat's skepticism about the ability of ordinary people to do a good job in regulating industry. So he contrasted ideological plaintiffs with public enforcement agencies, who have "legal and practical checks" that keep them "focused upon more purely economic harm."

We don't know how Stevens, Ginsburg, and Souter would have come out if they *had* decided the constitutional question. A majority in Nike's favor, though, would have had to have the votes of Breyer and O'Connor, and their insistence on a balancing test was presumably the reason the absolutists preferred DIG-ging the case to getting another mushy ruling on commercial speech. Resolving the question of the degree to which the First Amendment protected commercial speech remained for another day.

Two and a half months after the Court ducked the case, Nike settled with Kasky. The company agreed to pay $1.5 million to a public interest group, the Fair Labor Association, that monitors corporate labor practices.

∽

The emergence of conservative free speech absolutism on the Rehnquist Court had the effect of entrenching the free market in goods by means of extending the free market in ideas. Liberal activists in the ACLU may have thought that the collateral benefits of absolutism in cases like flag burning and individual dissent were worth the costs to regulation of the market. Or they may have failed to notice that the political terrain had shifted under their feet. Absolutism, once the liberals' darling, had become their challenger on many issues that mattered to their constituencies.

The absolutist opposition to paternalistic regulation of commercial advertising meant that aggressive marketing tactics had substantial constitutional protection. Libertarian-leaning scholars could take the rhetoric of antipaternalism even further. If paternalism was so offensive as the basis for regulating speech, why wasn't it equally offensive as the basis for regulating conduct? Instead of keeping people from getting their hair cut by unlicensed barbers, why not let people decide whether they get good enough haircuts from barbers without licenses? The libertarian's dream is that antipaternalism would extend all the way through the field of regulation—back to the 1905 case of *Lochner v. New York*. The Court's commercial advertising cases said that limiting the information consumers could get on the ground that they might make bad choices once they had the information was offensively paternalistic. Libertarians rightly pointed out that it was just as paternalistic to say that informed consumers—and workers—couldn't make certain choices because they were bad ones. Antipaternalism couldn't easily be confined to free speech law.

Business interests got the Rehnquist Court to adopt one of the major items on their agenda for tort reform, a restriction on the use of punitive damages. People who are injured by defective products or harmed by the way businesses operate can recover the amounts by which they were injured (if, of course, the businesses were at fault in what they did). In addition, people can sometimes recover punitive damages to punish the businesses for particularly egregious wrongdoing. During the Rehnquist years tort reformers focused a great deal of attention at what they described as arbitrary and excessive awards of punitive damages by local juries biased against businesses from outside the area. They compiled a list of what they described as outrageous punitive damages awards, the most famous of which was a jury award of $2.7 million to a woman burned by hot coffee that spilled out of a cup nestled between her legs as she was driving away from the McDonald's where she had bought the coffee. Academic researchers showed that many of the anecdotes were inaccurate or exaggerated, that punitive damages awards were rare, that there were usually pretty good reasons when juries awarded such damages, and, surprisingly, that judges awarded punitive damages more frequently—and for higher amounts—than juries did. (In the McDonald's case the judge reduced the punitive damage award to $480,000, and McDonald's had a terrible history of ignoring burns caused by their coffee.) None of this had much impact on the public perception of the punitive damages problem, though.

The Supreme Court sidled up to the punitive damages problem. Its first decision dealing with excessive punitive damages was highly fractured, but seven justices did agree that the Constitution limited punitive damages. The case involved a dispute between two oil and gas companies in West Virginia. TXO, the larger one, engaged in a variety of "nefarious" activities to force the smaller one to accept a low royalty rate. A jury awarded the smaller company nineteen thousand dollars in actual damages, and ten million dollars in punitive damages. Stevens wrote for four justices that the Constitution did prohibit "grossly excessive" punitive damages awards but concluded that on the facts of the case the jury's award was not unreasonable. Kennedy agreed with that conclusion but wanted the Court to provide more guidance than "reasonableness," and O'Connor, along with White and Souter, thought that the punitive damages award was unreasonable.

What constitutional provision made excessive punitive damages awards unconstitutional? Stevens's opinion cited several cases from the Lochner era in which the Court said that excessive damage awards violated the due process clause. This revival of substantive due process set Scalia off. Substantive due process was anathema to him because it was the basis of the Court's abortion decisions and because it let justices enact their visceral reactions to the cases they saw, with no tether to the Constitution's language.

The due process clause, he wrote, was not "the secret repository" of unenumerated rights.

The TXO case upheld a jury verdict where the punitive damages were 546 times the actual damages, although Stevens emphasized that the damages were so small only because TXO's scheme to defraud the smaller company was found out and that if TXO had gotten away with it, the smaller company would have lost about a million dollars. Three years later the Court for the first time struck down a punitive damages award as unconstitutionally excessive. The case did not have a sympathetic plaintiff, and it came from Alabama, which had achieved the reputation as harboring an "epidemic" of punitive damage awards. Dr. Ira Gore, a Birmingham oncologist, bought a black BMW for $40,750. Nine months later he took the car to a detailer to "make the car look snazzier." The detailer noticed that the car's finish seemed to have been repainted. Dr. Gore was outraged: He had bought the car new and had been assured that it was in original, mint condition. In fact, about a thousand BMWs were repainted before their first sale, because their finishes faded while they were exposed to acid raid as they were shipped from Germany, where they were made, to the United States. BMW had a policy of selling cars as used if the cost of repairing original defects was over 3 percent of the sales prices. Repainting Dr. Gore's car cost only $600, or about 1.5 percent of the price, so BMW's policy was to sell the car as new and not tell purchasers about the repainting. Dr. Gore's witnesses testified that a car with a repainted finish was worth about 10 percent less than a car with a new finish, so Dr. Gore's actual damages were about $4,000.

Dr. Gore sued BMW for consumer fraud—that is, for its failure to disclose the fact that the car had been repainted. He also sought punitive damages. The jury awarded four million dollars in punitive damages, pretty clearly multiplying the four-thousand-dollar damages Dr. Gore suffered by the thousand BMWs that had been repainted. The Alabama Supreme Court reduced the award to two million dollars, figuring that about half the BMW sales occurred in states where the failure to disclose the repainting wasn't regarded as consumer fraud.

This time Stevens reversed the jury's verdict. He agreed with the state supreme court that Alabama couldn't include in its punitive damage calculations BMW's actions in states where what it had done wasn't regarded as wrong enough to justify awarding even compensatory damages. Even so, the two-million-dollar award was too big. Stevens set out three "guideposts." BMW's behavior, while wrongful under state law, wasn't truly reprehensible. The repainting didn't affect the car's performance or safety, and Dr. Gore himself hadn't even noticed that the finish had been repainted. BMW hadn't shown "reckless disregard for the health and safety of others" and hadn't even made any "deliberate false statements" about the car's condition. Second, the disparity between the four-thousand-dollar actual damages and the two-million-dollar punitive damages was simply too large. Stevens noted that earlier cases had suggested that punitive damages that were four times actual damages were "close to the line" and that the TXO case upheld an award that, properly understood, was ten times actual damages. The punitive damage award to Dr. Gore, though, was five hundred times the actual harm to him (and thirty-five times the actual damage to everyone who bought a repainted BMW in Alabama), and that was far too much. Finally, civil penalties for consumer fraud in Alabama and elsewhere, ranging from about two thousand to around ten thousand dollars, were a tiny fraction of what the state supreme court awarded. And those civil penalties were what state legislatures thought were appropriate to punish and deter consumer fraud like BMW's.

Again Scalia dissented, saying that supervising punitive damages awards was none of the Court's business. He said that the decision was "dressed up as a legal opinion" but was "really no more than a disagreement with the community's sense of indignation or outrage expressed" by the jury and the state supreme court. Ginsburg dissented too. Her opinion began, "The Court, I am convinced, unnecessarily and unwisely ventures into territory traditionally within the States' domain, and does so in the face of reform measures recently adopted or currently under consideration in legislative arenas." This invocation of federalism got Rehnquist to join her in dissent.

The Court wrapped things up in 2003, with an opinion pinning down the rules even more carefully. Punitive damages more than ten times actual damages would almost certainly be unconstitutional (unless the defendant's behavior was particularly egregious). Smaller ratios would sometimes be required: A plaintiff who recovered a "substantial" award of actual damages might be able to no more than double that amount with an award of punitive damages. The single digit ratio came from some of the Court's earlier decisions; the one to one ratio was, as far as anyone could tell, simply made up, confirming Scalia's misgivings about the entire enterprise.

⤜⤛

Ginsburg's dissent in Dr. Gore's case had an appendix listing "recent state legislative activity regarding punitive damages." States had adopted caps on punitive damages, systems whereby some parts of punitive damage awards were paid to the state rather than to the plaintiff, and systems for trying the underlying question of wrongdoing separately from the question of how large the punitive damage award should be. The Rehnquist Court's own tort reform efforts were preempting legislative reforms, the very thing conservatives had spoken strongly against in so many other settings. Here, though, the Court was collaborating with business interests promoting tort reform.

Still, the Rehnquist Court's record on economic regulation was mixed. The positions of Stevens, Breyer, and Scalia in the punitive damages cases show that ordinary lines between conservatives and liberals don't entirely capture what was going on. The Takings Project clearly tilted constitutional law away from the most enthusiastic proponents of environmental and other forms of modern regulation, but it did not revolutionize the constitutional law of regulation. The Rehnquist Court's divisions limited how far it could go to advance the agenda of business supporters of the Republican Party.

CHAPTER THIRTEEN

A Supreme Court United?

C an the divided Supreme Court become united? It depends on who is nominated and confirmed to Court vacancies. Writing in mid-2004, I find it necessary to canvass all the possibilities, although the November elections will have eliminated some.

Potential Supreme Court nominees fall into three categories:

- DEMOCRATS. If a Democratic president gets to nominate a justice, the models will be Ruth Bader Ginsburg and Stephen Breyer, not Earl Warren, William J. Brennan, or Thurgood Marshall, the classic judicial activists. Most Democratic judges would describe themselves as against judicial activism. But in some ways Democratic nominees would have a free ride: They could reject Warren Court–like activism on Rehnquist's issues of economic regulation and federalism and remain activist on the social issues, defending themselves by using the activism of O'Connor and Kennedy on those issues to show that *that* kind of activism isn't a reversion to the Warren Court. A Court with some new justices appointed by a Democratic president would place tight limits on challenges to economic regulations and continue to limit government power over social agenda issues.

The Court's gay rights decision in 2003 and a decision by Massachusetts's highest court pushed the issue of gay marriage to the fore. A Court with new Democratic nominees wouldn't find a constitutional right to gay marriage anytime soon, although it wouldn't interfere with state decisions to recognize gay marriage and might try to limit Congress's power to restrict states that do so. The most likely course for such a Court would be to stay away from gay rights issues, waiting for a deeper social consensus to emerge, which it could then endorse, just as the Rehnquist Court endorsed a consensus about antisodomy laws in 2003.

What else might we expect of a new Democratic-dominated Court? It might limit the scope of school voucher programs, perhaps by finding that the school systems involved were so bad that parents didn't have the "real choice" that the Rehnquist Court's voucher decision seems to require. It might focus a lot of attention on the administration of capital punishment: the quality of the lawyers who represent defendants in death penalty cases; the attention trial judges pay to mistakes prosecutors make; aggressive tactics by prosecutors even when cautioned by judges. Democratic nominees to the Supreme Court would be a bit more skeptical about police initiatives to control crime and a bit more concerned about protecting privacy. But they would not be interested in recasting criminal law through the Constitution. Beyond that, there's not a lot to anticipate from such a Court.

That itself is interesting. A remade Court would not engage in any bold initiatives using judicial power to address the existence of racial division in the country or to reduce inequalities of wealth. The most that can be said about a remade Court is that it might advance liberal social agenda issues a bit more rapidly than the Rehnquist Court did.

· MODERATE REPUBLICANS. The more moderate Republicans on the Court, the more the Court's "new" path will look like the Rehnquist Court's old one: modest restrictions on government's power to regulate; modest revisions of the scope of Congress's power over the national economy; small steps forward on the liberal social agenda, probably no smaller than the ones a Court with new Democratic appointees would take.

The story of the Delhi Sands flower-loving fly suggests what a Court controlled by moderate Republicans might do. A few hundred flies are all that's left. They live on sand dunes in Colton,

California. In 1993, just as the city was about to develop a medical complex, environmentalists persuaded the federal government to bring the fly under the protection of the Endangered Species Act. The effect on economic development in Colton was dramatic. The federal government designated parts of the city as a fly preservation zone, and neither developers nor the city could do anything that put the fly's continued existence in jeopardy. Anyone planning economic development in Colton had to come up with a plan to preserve the fly's habitat. The effect was to stop economic development in its tracks; by one account, the fly's preservation cost the city as much as three hundred million dollars in investment and more than seven hundred jobs. The city's hospital stands isolated, rather than surrounded by ancillary medical offices. Garbage accumulates along the city's highways because the trash-collecting equipment threatens the fly's habitat. Amid economic growth in California's Inland Empire, Colton, a city with a mostly Hispanic population, has languished.

Congress enacted the Endangered Species Act by using its power to regulate interstate commerce. Sometimes the connection between interstate commerce and endangered species is clear. Defenders of the act can point to ecotourism, for example, to explain why protection of what aficionados call charismatic species, like the bald eagle and bighorn sheep, falls within Congress's power to regulate interstate commerce. But of course no one travels to Colton, California, to watch the Delhi Sands flower-loving fly hover like a hummingbird while it sucks nectar from flowers.

Environmentalists have come up with other reasons why the Endangered Species Act really is a regulation of interstate commerce—because it preserves species that in the future might generate important scientific advances, for example. It wouldn't be hard for moderate Republicans to say that although a lot of what's covered by the act is within Congress's power to regulate interstate commerce, the attempt to preserve the habitat of the fly exceeds that power. They would be bothered by the fact that there don't seem to be many economic benefits to people outside California from doing so and large economic costs imposed on the people there.

Moderate Republicans might extend the Rehnquist Court's decisions on takings a bit, finding some smart growth initiatives too intrusive on private property. Notably, though, moderate Republicans have been at the core of the Rehnquist Court's decisions on social issues like abortion and gay rights, and there's no reason to think that new moderate Republican appointees would think any differently. They won't find gay marriage required by the Constitution, but they won't overrule *Roe v. Wade* either.

• CONSERVATIVE REPUBLICANS. A united Court dominated by conservative Republicans is what liberal legal activists fear and conservative legal activists dream of.

The central issue for conservative Republican appointees will of course be abortion, with gay rights coming in second. Certainly conservative Republican appointees will want to overrule *Roe v. Wade*, probably by overruling the Rehnquist Court's decision invalidating limits on partial birth abortions with an opinion that makes it clear that it would uphold quite severe restrictions on the availability of other abortions.

It's worth noting the political consequences of overruling *Roe v. Wade*. Most political observers think that doing so would be a disaster for Republicans on the national scene. Too many suburban women, and men generally, think that what the Casey opinion called the core holding of *Roe v. Wade* is right. Most observers think that such voters would retaliate against a party that took *Roe* away from them. *Roe* may present conservative Republicans with an issue they would be better off avoiding, yet the attack on *Roe* has been so central to conservative Republican constitutional thought that it's hard to imagine how a conservative appointee could keep from overruling *Roe*, no matter what the political consequences.

Gay rights present a similar, but less pressing, problem for conservative Republicans. Here their difficulty is that the political system isn't likely to generate much for them to do. A new conservative Court might well find local gay rights laws unconstitutional when they require people with religious objections to rent to gay couples, but that's not a huge advance for the conservative social agenda.

The voucher decision of 2002 suggests another line along which conservative Republicans could develop constitutional law. First, it could invalidate state constitutional provisions that limit the power of state legislatures to make vouchers available to parents who choose to send their children to religious schools. Many of these restrictions originated in an anti-Catholic movement in the 1870s, and some conservatives have argued that these discreditable origins mean that the restrictions violate the national Constitution's prohibition of laws that impose disadvantages on religious activities simply because they are religious. Conservatives can also argue that the Constitution's ban on discrimination based on religion means that governments can't create general programs like voucher systems and then refuse to allow religious organizations to participate in the programs. A Rehnquist opinion in 2004 upheld a Washington state scholarship program that barred students pursuing degrees in "devotional theology"—training to be ministers—from getting state money. The establishment clause gave states some flexibility, particularly in connection with support for ministers, historically at the heart of the antiestablishment principle. That decision might be an obstacle to extending voucher programs, but it could easily be distinguished from them because of its focus on how closely the exclusion was tied to history and ministers.

A trickier problem, at least politically, is presented by standard conditions included in voucher programs. Legislators who support voucher programs generally want private schools to accept all comers or at least not to discriminate against applicants on the basis of their races or even their religions. Skeptics about vouchers combine with proponents of equal employment to insist that schools that accept vouchers do not discriminate in hiring either. And of course proponents and skeptics typically think that schools accepting vouchers have to teach their students things that matter. Voucher programs usually deny vouchers to schools that teach racial or religious hatred, for example, and it's easy to imagine a legislature prescribing a broader range of curricular requirements for such schools.

At the same time it's easy to see why the operators of some schools might object to these conditions. Some Christian funda-

mentalist schools, for example, might not want to hire mothers
with small children, on the basis of their belief, derived from their
religion, that women with children should devote their time to
their own children. Other schools might want to teach the superi-
ority of particular religions to others, which the government
might construe as teaching religious hatred, or even the superior-
ity of one race to another. (The paired bugaboos here are schools
organized by the militia movement and by the Nation of Islam.)
Many schools run by Christians would object to a requirement
that they teach evolutionary theory in their biology classes.

A conservative Court might invalidate the application of
nondiscrimination rules and curricular requirements to private
schools that accepted vouchers. Curricular choices are what
voucher programs are all about, and excluding schools from a
voucher program just because the government doesn't like what
the schools are teaching—or would rather have them teach something else—can readily be described as an impermissible discrimination based on the viewpoint the schools offer their students,
something the Rehnquist Court's *Wide Awake* decision prohibits.
The constitutional challenge to discriminatory employment policies would be based on the right of expressive association the
Rehnquist Court recognized in the Boy Scouts case. A conservative Court might well hold that barring schools from participating in voucher programs because of their policies, which,
remember, are based on their values and views, violates their right
of expressive association.

Farther down the line would be a decision *requiring* governments to create voucher programs. Public education, conservatives say, is a system that uses taxes to subsidize the cost of
education for children who attend public schools. Some parents
send their children to private schools because they don't like
what's being taught in public schools. In particular, they don't
like the fact that the public schools are too secular. The government gives a subsidy to parents who accept the messages in the
public schools, and it doesn't subsidize parents who reject those
messages. Standard First Amendment doctrine requires the government to refrain from discriminating against people because of
their views, particularly when those views are religious in nature.

But, the argument goes, giving parents who send their children to public schools subsidies denied to parents with children in private schools skews parental choice in precisely the way the First Amendment bars. As one law professor puts it, "neutrality between religious schools and public schools clearly requires that religious schools be apportioned a share of the tax dollars that currently fund only public education; if most schools receive government aid, then religiously neutral funding requires that religious schools be eligible to receive it, too."

Antidiscrimination law raises other possibilities for a conservative Republican Court. Here are three, put in the starkest terms: Sexual harassment law is unconstitutional in substantial part because it violates the First Amendment, federal antidiscrimination statutes are unconstitutional because they do not deal with an economic activity, and state antidiscrimination statutes are unconstitutional because they violate the right of expressive association. Again, there's no reason to think that conservative Republican appointees would reach the most radical conclusions immediately, but the doctrines of constitutional law they have begun to develop would allow them to move toward these conclusions.

The issue of sexual harassment is the easiest. Verbal expressions form an important component in many sexual harassment cases. Supervisors and coworkers use disparaging terms to refer to their female colleagues; sexually explicit materials are distributed in the workplace in an attempt to discourage female workers from staying on the job. Sexual harassment law imposes penalties on employers that fail to control these verbal expressions. But of course outside the workplace the First Amendment bars the government from imposing penalties on people who express disparaging views about women and their capacity to do a good job. Conservative judges sensitive to claims about political correctness might be willing to hold that a statute that induces employers to regulate their employees' expression in the workplace violated the First Amendment as well.

The Supreme Court's federalism decisions open the way to an attack on national antidiscrimination laws. Congress enacted the present set of antidiscrimination laws by using its power to regulate interstate commerce. The Court upheld these statutes by pointing out that discrimination against African Americans adversely affected the national economy because, for example, it led African Americans to take fewer vacations in states where they anticipated discrimination. But according to the Rehnquist Court's commerce clause decisions, Congress has the power to regulate interstate commerce based on aggregate effects only if the regulated activity is itself economic in character. So far the Court hasn't had to specify the boundaries of the "economic" category, and its moderate Republicans indicated that they weren't about to place substantial limits on that category. But a conservative Republican Court might develop the idea of the "economic" to refer to activities that provide inputs to the production of goods and services for purposes of making money. Maybe acts of discrimination aren't "economic" even though they're connected to economic activities; they're morally bad, not economically harmful.

Of course Congress has the power to enforce the Fourteenth Amendment even with respect to noneconomic activities. Here, though, the problem with federal antidiscrimination law is that it goes too far. The Fourteenth Amendment gives Congress the power to enforce nondiscrimination rules against the states. The relevant language is: "No State shall deny. . . ." Federal nondiscrimination law bans discrimination in private employment and in private hotels and the like, plainly well beyond state actions that discriminate.

Conservative Republican justices might focus first on one part of antidiscrimination law. Federal civil rights statutes ban two kinds of discrimination. First, an employer can't refuse to hire or promote someone *because of* race or gender. The second category involves what lawyers call disparate impact discrimination. It occurs when an employer has some hiring criterion that doesn't refer to race or gender but that blocks more African Americans than whites, or women than men, from getting the job. Some written tests might do that; so can minimum height requirements. Employers can use criteria with disparate impacts only if they can show that doing so is a business necessity, a fairly stringent standard.

Consider first disparate impact discrimination by state or local governments. The Rehnquist Court established the rule that Congress can use its power under Section Five of the Fourteenth Amendment to ban practices that violate constitutional rights and to ban practices that aren't such violations if the ban is congruent with and proportional to such violations. It also held that disparate impact alone doesn't violate the Constitution. So a ban on disparate impact discrimination is constitutional only if it's congruent with and proportional to actual, intentional discrimination by state and local governments. There may have been a lot of that sort of discrimination when Title VII was enacted in 1964, so a ban on disparate impact discrimination might have been constitutional then. What about *now*? Certainly the amount of unconstitutional intentional discrimination by state and local governments has decreased a lot. A conservative Supreme Court might conclude that the ban on disparate impact discrimination was no longer proportional to existing constitutional violations.

That argument affects only state and local governments. But there's more. The Rehnquist Court's decisions on race discrimination set out a series of rules. Statutes that use racial classifications are generally unconstitutional, whether the classifications are designed to disadvantage African Americans or to benefit them. Statutes that don't use racial classifications are generally constitutional, unless they have been adopted in order to achieve race-related ends—again, whether they aim to disadvantage or benefit African Americans. A ban on disparate impact discrimination by private employers might be said to use a racial classification, but even if it doesn't, that sort of ban usually is adopted in order to benefit African Americans. It's a form of affirmative action and so might be challenged by conservative Republican justices for the reasons they have for challenging affirmative action programs.

Finally, what of state and local antidiscrimination laws and ordinances? Here, once more, the right of expressive association might come into play. Lester Maddox was one of the central figures in the demonology of 1960s antidiscrimination law. Maddox operated the Pickrick restaurant in Atlanta, Georgia, where he openly displayed his racist views—to the point of distributing ax handles to his patrons to encourage them to fight off African Americans who had the temerity to try to eat there. Indeed, the vehemence with which he defended segregation at his restaurant provided the initial basis for his political career, which led him eventually into Georgia's statehouse as governor. For Maddox, that is, excluding African Americans from his restaurant *was* an expressive act. But beyond the specifics of Maddox's case there's the broader point, made by the law professor Richard Epstein, that all organizations have corporate cultures that communicate something to the public about the kinds of organization they are. Any organization that objects to the application of antidiscrimination law can find in the right of expressive association the argument that forcing it to comply with that law would interfere with its ability to communicate to the public the distinctive nature of its corporate culture. To those who object, that is, antidiscrimination law violates their right of expressive association.

So far I've moved from what a conservative Republican Court might do—on the basis again, of existing law—in connection with today's social issues, such as gay rights and school vouchers, to what such a Court might do in connection with Great Society commitments to antidiscrimination principles. What about moving even farther back, to the core constitutional commitments of the New Deal?

The New Deal itself was about using the national government to regulate the economy to ensure stability and promote growth and to provide a social safety net for people in need. Times change, and the definition of who is needy does too, but—at least through the Rehnquist Court—no Supreme Court justice seriously questioned the national government's power to pursue the New Deal's goals. Except, of course, Justice Thomas. He would confine Congress's power to regulate commerce to the regulation of transactions that themselves cross state lines. One of the New Deal's great cases upheld the application of the National Labor Relations Act to a major steel manufacturing plant in Pennsylvania. Thomas says that that case involves manufacturing, not commerce as the framers understood the term, so Congress can't regulate it. A second great New Deal case upheld the constitutionality of the national Fair Labor Standards Act, which prescribes a national minimum wage. Thomas would invalidate it too, as applied to workers who weren't themselves involved in transporting goods across state lines.

A united Court with new justices who agreed with Thomas could radically transform the constitutional law dealing with Congress's power to regulate the national economy.

∽

A Supreme Court united under conservative Republican control is a conservative Republican's dream and a liberal Democrat's night-mare. It makes sense, now, to turn back to politics, which will deter-mine whether the dream (and nightmare) will occur. The Supreme Court operates in a larger political system, in which presidents have to decide whom to nominate and the Senate has to decide whom to confirm. The politics of nomination and confirmation will deter-mine whether the Court remains divided or becomes unified.

The most important thing to keep in mind when thinking about the politics of judicial nominations is that the politics of judicial nominations is politics. Politics structures who gets picked by the White House and how the Senate deals with nominations. Moreover, what you get in judicial nominations is the kind of politics you get elsewhere. In 1870 what mattered—for setting tariffs, for reforming the civil service, whatever—was striking a balance among party fac-tions. In the 1960s what mattered was paying off traditional interest groups. Today what matters is interest group mobilization, energiz-ing the base, in contemporary political jargon, and doing what you can to weaken the energized base on the other side.

Political scientist David Alistair Yalof has laid out the patterns of how Supreme Court nominees are selected. During the Truman years nominees were basically cronies of the president. Dwight Eisenhower's Department of Justice reacted against that cronyism. Eisen-hower's first Supreme Court nomination was a blockbuster: Earl Warren as chief justice. The nomination was a political payoff; Eisenhower had promised Warren the first Supreme Court nomina-tion in response to Warren's crucial support for Eisenhower's candi-dacy. (Eisenhower tried to renege on the deal when it turned out that the first vacancy was the chief justiceship, but Warren held him to his promise.) Eisenhower basically delegated the choice of other nominees to the northeastern Republicans who ran the Department of Justice and who chose nominees because of their good profes-sional credentials, although William Brennan's religion (Catholic) and party affiliation (Democratic) played a minor role in his selection as part of the run-up to Eisenhower's reelection campaign in 1956. John F. Kennedy and Lyndon Johnson returned to using Supreme Court nominations to reward political allies and personal friends. Byron White had played an important part in Kennedy's election campaign; Arthur Goldberg filled the Jewish seat and had been the architect of the merger of the two major labor federations into the AFL-CIO in 1955; Abe Fortas was a close adviser to Johnson; Thurgood Marshall was the first African American to sit on the Supreme Court.

The picture changed subtly with Richard Nixon's nominations and more dramatically with Ronald Reagan's. Nixon saw how Supreme Court nominations could serve the long-range goals he set for the Republican Party. His nominations combined a straightforward appeal to the South with a more sharply ideological set of criteria for selection. He fumbled the southern strategy a bit with the nominations of Clement Haynsworth and G. Harrold Carswell, but the other component of his strategy had more lasting effects in the Republican selection process. Nixon deliberately used Supreme Court nominations as part of his law and order campaign against the Warren Court and decided that he wanted "young conservative nominees from 'the meat-and-potatoes law schools' located in areas of the country Nixon thought of as his core constituency: the South, the Midwest, and the Far West."

To succeed Earl Warren, Nixon chose Warren Burger, a graduate of the St. Paul College of Law, who had come to the attention of conservative politicians because of his attacks on the liberal decisions of the District of Columbia Court of Appeals, on which he sat with celebrated (and, among conservatives, reviled) liberals David Bazelon and J. Skelly Wright. And of course Nixon placed William Rehnquist on the Supreme Court. With Ronald Reagan, the Republican selection process became dominated by ideology.

Supreme Court nominations might seem to begin in the White House and the Department of Justice. Actually, though, in the past few decades (and perhaps for even longer) at least some people actively campaign to bring themselves to the attention of those who select nominees. Campaigns to be put on the list take different forms. One is the road show at the Federalist Society conference, something like the out-of-town preview of a Broadway show, where ambitious conservative lawyers strut their stuff.

Another form is the campaign to become a federal appeals court judge in anticipation of promotion to the Supreme Court. Republicans and some Democrats now think that it's important for a Supreme Court justice to have prior judicial experience, so people who think they might want to be justices put themselves forward as potential nominees for lower court positions. The chance that any particular federal appeals court judge will be nominated to the Supreme Court is tiny; the politics surrounding a nomination are unpredictable, so the fact that you got to be a judge ten years ago has almost no bearing on whether you'll be nominated and confirmed for the Supreme Court, and in the meanwhile, you actually have to be a federal appellate judge, spending your time deciding whether someone should get Social Security disability benefits or whether a trial judge sentenced a defendant to too many years in prison.

Ideology and experience aren't enough, of course. A potential nominee has to get through the Department of Justice and the White House and, within the White House, has to satisfy both the lawyers in the counsel's office and the political operatives concerned with the president's wider agenda, including a possible reelection campaign. As a *New York Times* reporter put it, from the Reagan administration on Republican presidents "essentially turned over the privilege of selecting judges to lawyers in the conservative wing of the Republican party," lodged in the Department of Justice. These conservative activists are one important component of the Republican electoral coalition, but not the only one. The White House, in contrast, has to worry about the entire coalition and especially about attracting support from outside what has come to be called the base.

This sets up real possibilities for conflicts within the administration over whom to choose and makes it important to know which "high administration official" is leaking names to the press. People in a Republican Department of Justice are going to push quite conservative ideologues because that's their job and because nominating a conservative ideologue does provide the president with some political benefits. People in the White House have additional concerns. They have to figure out what's going to happen once the nomination occurs: Will there be a large political battle over it? Can the president win such a fight? Will the president be able to make some political points even if he loses the nomination fight? The political operatives in the White House also have to consider the effects of the nomination, and any confirmation battle, on the next campaign: Will this nominee's selection mobilize the Republican base? Will it mobilize the Democratic base in opposition in a way that's going to cause more trouble than the gains the president gets from mobilizing his base? Finally, most obviously, are there constituencies *other than* conservatives who care about constitutional law to whom the nomination might appeal? (For Republicans in the early 2000s, this meant Hispanics.)

I have outlined the politics of judicial selection mostly on the Republican side. During the Rehnquist years Democrats had only two nominees. The party was visibly in transition—or in disarray—so it's even harder than usual to capture the underlying politics of judicial selection on the Democratic side. Ideology and organization matter, except that the Democrats didn't have either a strong ideology or a network of concerned liberal activists who mattered to Bill Clinton—or any other Democrat who aspired to the White House.

For Republicans, legal ideology matters because it has provided a rallying point for different components of their core constituencies. Rein in liberal judges, and you won't get decisions finding the reference to God in the Pledge of Allegiance unconstitutional, you won't get decisions restricting the limitations on abortions, and so on down the list of matters of concern to important, and to some extent different, components of the Republican electoral coalition.

On the Democratic side, only two constitutional issues have ideological significance: abortion rights matters for the organized women's movement that supports Democrats and affirmative action matters for the party's African American constituency. So far at least, liberal constitutional theorists haven't been able to put those two issues together into an appealing package. That provides the hook for Republican rhetoric. They prefer to call the ideology of *their* judges a judicial philosophy and think that judicial philosophy is a fine criterion for nominations and appointments. They disparage Democrats for the Democrats' attention to judicial ideology, though. In this rhetoric *ideology* refers to a set of outcomes in specific cases without any unifying theme. The Republican criticism has some bite precisely because present-day Democrats have positions but don't have anything resembling a unifying approach to constitutional decision making.

The Democrats' vision of the future consists of nostalgia for the past. Attend a conference of liberal lawyers, and what you hear are expressions of hope that somehow someone will figure out some way to revive Earl Warren, William Brennan, and Thurgood Marshall. But to paraphrase Bruce Springsteen, those jobs are gone, and they're not coming back.

What might emerge on the liberal side remains unclear. Democrats needed some way to persuade the public that ideology should play exactly the same role in the confirmation process that it plays in the selection of nominees. The politics of confirmations, however, are much more visible than the politics of selection, which placed the Democrats in a difficult position. As the Rehnquist years neared their end, the Democrats hadn't quite figured out what to do. Their efforts did transform the confirmation process, however.

℘

For conservative legal activists, it all began with the defeat of Robert Bork's nomination to the Supreme Court in 1987. They can quote by heart Senator Ted Kennedy's statement on the Senate floor minutes after Bork's nomination was announced: "Robert Bork's America is a land in which women would be forced into back-alley abortions, blacks would sit at segregated lunch counters, rogue police could break down citizens' doors in midnight raids, schoolchildren could not be taught about evolution." Politicians, both Democrats and Republicans, thought at the time that Kennedy's statement was extreme and unfair to Bork. So did editorial writers. For liberal activists, though, Kennedy's speech helped by giving them a chance to slow down the inevitable momentum accompanying a presidential decision and to use the time to mobilize their constituencies against Bork.

Conservatives invented the term *to bork* to describe what happened in 1987. One online dictionary defines it as meaning "To attack a political opponent in a particularly vicious, partisan manner." Conservatives cite the disclosure of the list of videotapes Bork rented to show the lengths to which his opponents went in attempting to discredit him.

Liberal Democrats see the picture differently. For them, Kennedy's speech, while perhaps a bit overheated, wasn't an entirely distorted version of the *consequences* of Bork's constitutional views. True, there was no reason to think that he actually favored a world in which there were back alley abortions, but to liberal activists, a world in which abortion was illegal, a world that Bork thought perfectly constitutional, would indeed be one with back alley abortions. As for segregated lunch counters, liberals pointed to an article Bork had written opposing the Civil Rights Act of 1964, which outlawed such practices. According to Bork, the act rested on "a principle of unsurpassed ugliness": that "if I find your behavior ugly by my standards, moral or aesthetic, and if you prove stubborn about adopting my view of the situation, I am justified in having the state coerce you into more righteous paths."

Liberal interest groups actually had nothing to do with the rental list's discovery, which came to light because of the efforts of an enterprising reporter for the *City Paper*, Washington's weekly semi-underground newspaper. (Congress eventually passed a statute making it a crime to disclose video rental lists.) The opposition to Bork, from their point of view, wasn't particularly vicious. It was, instead, what had to be done if they were to stop conservatives from taking over the Supreme Court completely.

Democrats thought they had seen borking before, from Republicans who filibustered Abe Fortas's nomination to be chief justice in 1968. Democrats thought that their opposition to Bork, resting as it did on objections to his constitutional philosophy, was much more serious than opposition to some nominees in the past. They were, as they saw it, doing nothing new.

Oddly, both the Republicans and the Democrats were right. Democrats were right in saying that there was nothing new about partisan politics surrounding around judicial nominations. Republicans were right in saying that there was a new feature of judicial nomination politics, the role of modern interest groups.

The Bork nomination wasn't quite the first appearance of interest group mobilization to defeat a Supreme Court nomination. Civil rights groups had worked hard to defeat the nominations of Haynsworth and Carswell in 1969 and 1970. There the mobilization was mostly "inside the Beltway," with leaders of the major civil rights organizations speaking directly to senators about their concerns rather than generating massive outpourings of letters and telephone calls from their members. The Bork nomination was the first in which the liberal interest groups moved outside the Beltway.

The liberal campaign against Bork was built on the model of grass roots lobbying on legislative proposals. Interest group leaders met in Washington, assembled a coalition, parceled out tasks, developed ideas about helpful tactics, like "freezing" Senate action on the Bork nomination until grass roots efforts got under way, and contacted sympathetic staff members in the Senate who worked with, and on, their senators to implement the tactics. They did background research on Bork's positions, compiling what one activist called the book of Bork, and developed talking points distributed to members of the anti-Bork coalition. In short, the anti-Bork campaign *was* modern interest group lobbying.

It differed from earlier efforts because the nature of interest groups had changed. During the New Deal and the Great Society interest groups played a big part in national policy making. But the major liberal interest groups were labor unions and the National Association for the Advancement of Colored People (NAACP). These were membership organizations. They had a self-perpetuating leadership, true, but the leaders could fairly say that they spoke for their members. By the 1980s and 1990s interest groups had changed. They were fund-raising entities, with "members" who wrote checks—in effect endorsing what the leaders did—but otherwise had almost no ongoing contacts with the leadership. Energizing the base, for these interest groups, means striking enough fear in the hearts of contributors to ensure that they'll get out their checkbooks.

A final component of the modern politics of nominations is technology. In 1970 it took some serious reporting effort to dig up the fact that Harrold Carswell had made a speech supporting segregation in 1948 and that he had helped a city golf course avoid desegregation in the 1950s. It takes almost no effort these days to go on the Internet and find essentially everything a nominee has said about anything at all. If there's a smoking gun to be found, someone will find it—and find it quickly enough for it to be used in a nomination battle.

Liberal interest groups used the Bork model in their opposition to Clarence Thomas's nomination as well. The sexual harassment allegations that emerged late in the proceedings blur our memory. The liberal interest groups had already mounted a substantial campaign against Thomas before those allegations surfaced. This time, though, they failed because Republican strategists figured out how to weaken the liberal mobilization by playing the race card.

Republicans had learned from the Bork nomination that it sometimes helped to treat nominations as they would treat legislation. Clarence Thomas met with Kenneth Duberstein, an effective Republican lobbyist, shortly after his nomination, to work out a strategy to ensure confirmation. They made his personal history the focus of their efforts, deflecting attention as best they could from his ideology. Republicans lined up support from African American interest groups early on, getting the NAACP to refrain from opposing the nomination before the liberal interest groups were able to get their ducks in a row and push the NAACP into taking a firm stance against Thomas. Notably, the White House coordinated a grass roots lobbying campaign supporting Thomas's nomination that paralleled in form the anti-Bork lobbying campaign.

Nomination politics under Presidents George H. W. Bush and Bill Clinton show that nomination politics depends on how the president expects the Senate to react to a nomination and how it changes when the same party controls the presidency and the Senate. Senate Republicans promised a big fight against Bruce Babbitt as a nominee, and President Clinton, examining his agenda as a whole, decided not to expend any political capital on a tough confirmation battle. But lacking control of the Senate, Republicans had few weapons to deploy once a nomination was made and did nothing when Clinton nominated Ginsburg and Breyer.

One reason for Republican silence on the Clinton nominations was a principled aversion to borking, at least in the early 1990s. During the early Rehnquist years, conservative interest groups didn't have to mobilize their constituencies much on judicial nominations. They were blindsided by the Bork mobilization. It took them some time to figure out that the politics of judicial nominations had changed. Still, they probably lacked the votes in the Senate to defeat President Clinton's nominations of Ginsburg and Breyer. Even a substantial mobilization of the conservative base probably wouldn't have made much difference in the outcome. It might have galvanized some constituencies, but by methods the Republicans, remembering the Bork experience a few years earlier, found distasteful. By the end of the Clinton presidency Republicans had indeed borked some of Clinton's nominees for lower courts, but they didn't have a chance to show what they would do about a Supreme Court nomination.

☙

Liberals developed one brilliant rhetorical strategy during the Bork nomination and hope to continue to use it in the future. Everybody knew that the liberal interest groups' constituencies cared about preserving *Roe v. Wade*. Everybody also knew that attacking Bork for his opposition to *Roe v. Wade* wasn't a winning strategy, because too many people, including senators, had misgivings about the Court's abortion decisions. The liberals hit upon shifting the discussion to the constitutional right of privacy and focused on *Griswold v. Connecticut*, decided in 1965. There the Supreme Court held unconstitutional a Connecticut statute prohibiting people from *using* contraceptives. Even in 1965 this was, as one of the dissenting justices put it, an "uncommonly silly law." By 1987 it was easy to persuade the public that the law was not only uncommonly silly but obviously unconstitutional.

Bork's problem was that *Griswold* rested on a constitutional analysis that he couldn't possibly accept. The Court in *Griswold* didn't say anything about original understanding, it relied on the metaphor that specific constitutional rights had "penumbras" (a metaphor that conservatives had been making fun of for decades), and it invoked a constitutional "right to privacy" that had no obvious source in the Constitution's text (and that was to become the basis of the abortion decisions a few years later). Liberals used the right to privacy to deflect attention from abortion. Because Bork couldn't support a right to privacy (meaning, primarily, that he thought *Roe v. Wade* should be overruled), he couldn't support *Griswold* either.

Bork understood his problem and desperately wanted to figure out some way to say that he did indeed think that *Griswold* had been correctly decided. His testimony on the matter was almost painful to watch. He said, in 1987, that although he thought that *Griswold* might have been right, he hadn't, in the twenty years since the decision, figured out why, and he said, in effect, that if he went home and thought about it some more, he might come up with a good answer.

Future conservative nominees are going to have to figure out how to deal more effectively with the Democrats' clever rhetorical strategy.

Republicans countered the Democratic rhetorical advantage on privacy with their own advantage on the term *judicial activism*. Ever since the Warren Court conservatives had been criticizing the Court for its judicial activism. That language became increasingly remote from reality as conservatives gained control of the Court. Liberals began to think that they could turn the tables and start criticizing the conservatives using the conservatives' own rhetoric.

In 2002 the Federalist Society and the University of Colorado Law School held conferences on conservative judicial activism. The academics there and two conservative judges—J. Harvie Wilkinson and Frank Easterbrook—basically agreed that the term *activism* didn't have any useful content. *Liberal judicial activism* meant something, of course, and so did *conservative judicial activism*, but the political labels, not the term *activism*, did all the work. Wilkinson defended conservative judicial activism in his opinion in the Violence Against Women Act case. For him, the Warren Court's liberal activism was bad because it dealt with civil rights (and didn't work out very well, in his view). The current Court's conservative activism was all right because it didn't come out on the side of any particular interest group in protecting states. Conservative judicial activism, Wilkinson wrote, "removes no substantive decision from the stage of political debate." Liberal interest groups could still work for laws improving the protection of women against violence; they just had to do it on the state and local level.

Conservative scholars and judges might be willing to abandon the rhetoric of judicial activism, or they might be able to come up with defenses of their version of judicial activism. Still, we can be pretty sure that the liberal attempt to turn the tables won't work. Part of the reason is that *judicial activism* just *means* "liberal judicial activism," as a result of years of rhetoric from conservatives. It would take a very long time for liberals to strip the word *liberal* from that definition.

Even more, though, in the immediate aftermath of the Rehnquist Court liberals aren't going to be able to charge conservatives with hypocrisy for attacking judicial activism for one simple reason: The Rehnquist Court was a conservative activist court on issues that the public basically doesn't care much about—federalism and property rights—and was a moderately liberal activist court on the social issues that attract public attention—abortion and gay rights, for example. Conservative politicians could keep bashing the courts as activist, referring to the issues that the public paid attention to and wouldn't have to defend their own conservative judges against a parallel charge because the charge of conservative judicial activism simply didn't resonate with the public.

Lamenting the Court's behavior, conservative legal scholar Lino Graglia wrote in the *National Review* that he had given up on transforming the Supreme Court: "Not only has the present Court not rescinded prior liberal victories, but it has continued to hand down major positive liberal victories, as in its recent decisions on term limits, the Virginia Military Institute, special rights for homosexuals, and the restriction of pornography on the Internet." He's right, of course, but he's speaking as a conservative legal activist with an ax to grind, not as a Republican politician who has to figure out how to win elections. The divided Court's behavior allowed Republicans to continue to use their well-honed rhetoric about judicial activism to beat up on liberals, even as the Rehnquist Court's divisions made the term *activism* almost useless as an analytic tool.

More important, the Republican side recites the mantra of "qualified, and in the mainstream, and that's all that matters." From their point of view, this has two advantages. It takes a serious breakdown within the White House and the Department of Justice for the president to nominate someone who can't fairly be called qualified. The second advantage for conservatives is that the mainstream has shifted to the right over the past thirty years. Democrats would love to savage the lower court judges J. Harvie Wilkinson and J. Michael Luttig for being out of the mainstream in finding the Violence Against Women Act unconstitutional. But it's hard to make that case after the Supreme Court has agreed with them.

What conservatives don't appreciate, though, is that the "qualifications/mainstream" mantra sets up the dynamics that lead to the borking they purport to hate. The reason is simple: Tell people who don't want a nominee to be confirmed that confirmation is inevitable if the nominee is qualified and in the mainstream, and they're going to rummage around to find reasons for saying that the nominee is unqualified—usually, reasons connected to some aspect of the nominee's actions outside his or her work as a lawyer—or for saying that the nominee is out of the mainstream, usually by giving the nominee's views the least charitable interpretation possible. This *is* a formula to generate borking.

Borking happens when nominees give opponents some ammunition that they use in ways the nominee's supporters think unfair. Confined to attacks on qualifications and to asserting that the nominee's views are out of the mainstream, the opponents have to characterize reasonable views about what the Constitution means as outside the mainstream. Perhaps, though, Republicans are less concerned about borking than they say. Forcing their adversaries to bork nominees may, they may think, lead voters in the middle to think less well of liberals, enhancing the distaste for Washington politics that has helped conservatives gain political power. In any event, seeing one of their own being borked may itself energize the conservative base, even beyond what a conservative nomination would do.

Borking has another advantage for Republicans. It can fail or it can succeed. If it fails, the Democrats are faced with a life-tenured judge likely to be embittered by the confirmation experience. If it succeeds, the replacement nominee is likely to be more moderate. But moderate Republican judges serve Republican partisan interests nearly as well as—maybe even better than—really conservative Republican judges. Borking can mobilize the Democrats' base *during the nomination battle*. Moderate Republican judges then demobilize the Democrats' base *at election time*—by denying the Democrats the opportunity to run against Republicans for nominating judges who undermine the Democratic base's commitment to abortion and privacy rights. Yet those very same moderate Republican judges help mobilize the Republican base at election time—by perpetuating the possibility of running against "activist" judges who enforce abortion and privacy rights. All in all, borking works better for Republicans than for the Democrats who have practiced it.

The politics of judicial nominations in the post-Rehnquist years is likely to be quite unattractive if Republican presidents calculate that their party will benefit from strongly conservative nominations or if there is a Democratic president. Modern interest group politics makes borking an appealing political strategy, although it degrades our civic life.

♋

Politics doesn't end with confirmation battles. Suppose the next Court was a unified conservative Court. Someday it might find itself confronting a hostile Congress and president if the Democrats took control. The Democrats might find even modest initiatives blocked by a conservative Court's doctrines. A constitutional crisis like that of the late 1930s might ensue, with the Democrats challenging the very idea of judicial review that has become so embedded in the nation's constitutional culture.

Although it seems pointless today to think about the prospect of a united *Democratic* Court, the Warren Court's activism *does* illuminate an important point about how the Supreme Court fits into national politics in the longish run. What's most striking about the Warren Court's activism, in retrospect, is how compatible it was with the activism of Lyndon Johnson's Great Society programs. The Warren Court at its height wasn't at odds with the national government; it was a collaborator in creating liberal programs with Congress and the president.

Obviously the Rehnquist Court rejected the Great Society's vision of equality. But the possibility of collaboration between the Court and the other parts of the political system remained open. For almost the entire period of the Rehnquist Court, the national government was divided, with the presidency held by one party and Congress, or one House of Congress, held by the other, making collaboration impossible.

Other courses of action were open, though. Justices during a period of divided government might do things that they might hope would end the period of divided government by creating a unified government to their liking, with which they might then collaborate. In some ways that might be the real meaning of *Bush v. Gore*, an effort by the Court's conservatives to ensure unified conservative government for the foreseeable future.

In turn that might be an important source of Democrats' discomfort with *Bush v. Gore*. By making George W. Bush president, the Supreme Court made it more likely that conservative justices would be nominated to the Court over the succeeding four years, and per-haps longer. That concern led some prominent Democratic legal academics, most notably the Yale law professor Bruce Ackerman, to propose that the Senate refuse to confirm any nominees to the Court until after the 2004 elections. Democratic opposition to con-servative nominees certainly hardened after *Bush v. Gore*, to the point where they filibustered some lower court nominations even after they lost control of the Senate in the 2002 midterm elections. The prospect of a bitter nomination fight may have influenced some jus-tices to delay their resignations, and in fact Bush didn't get a chance to nominate a new justice before the 2004 elections.

The Rehnquist Court's caution might itself be a form of collabo-ration. A collaborative Court signs on to the central project of Congress and the president. During divided government there seems to be no central project. Maybe there is, however. It is a project of modest and small initiatives that manage to get bipartisan approval. The Rehnquist Court's modesty might be the form collaboration took during divided government.

❧

Thinking about the possibility of a collaborative Court suggests that who is on the Court may matter less than what's going on in the political process—and not just because politics affects who gets nominated and confirmed.

Politics matters for two other reasons:

· THE COURT'S AGENDA. In most areas you can complain only about something a government has done, not about what it has-n't done. In a world of divided government legislative initiatives are likely to be small. The Rehnquist Court's takings decisions might be developed in ways that limited expansive environmental programs, but divided governments are unlikely to generate such programs. Instead, they'll produce modest "smart growth" initia-tives, which will be much harder to challenge on constitutional grounds. In a world of divided government the Supreme Court will not have anything to collaborate with, but it won't have much to use as a vehicle for challenging governments either.

This doesn't mean that the Supreme Court in a world of divided government will go out of business. The Rehnquist Court's decisions interpreting the Americans with Disabilities Act show what such a Court can do. Congress adopted the ADA in 1990, with bipartisan support; President George H. W. Bush regarded the act as one of the major legislative accomplishments of his administration. The Rehnquist Court, though, was extremely grudging in its interpretation of the ADA. It used statutory interpretation to narrow the scope of a statute enacted before the shift in national power that occurred in the 1990s. There's no chance that an expansive ADA could be enacted today, so the Court is in a position to make its narrow interpretation stick. The Supreme Court in a world of divided government can invalidate *old* statutes or give them narrow interpretations, knowing that today's Congress will not be able to respond with a corrective statute.

Now combine this observation with my earlier one: The Supreme Court can do what it wants with old statutes, and Congress in a world of divided government won't give the Court much new for it to invalidate or interpret. Whatever the inclinations of new justices, then, they won't be able to move far on their own. A unified conservative Court needs a unified government to collaborate with.

· THE COURT AND POLITICS. Robert Dahl, one of the nation's leading political scientists, observed in 1957 that Supreme Court decisions never got out of line for very long with what the national political consensus was. The law professor Michael Klarman exhaustively examined the Supreme Court's actions involving race relations in the twentieth century and confirmed Dahl's insight. The Warren Court experience challenged Dahl's observation a bit, although the real story of the Warren Court was that it got ahead of the political consensus for a while and then the consensus caught up. As the nation turned more conservative, so did the Burger Court—and the Rehnquist Court.

The stories of the Rehnquist Court are entirely compatible with Dahl's observation as well. The Court's division between economic issues and social issues mirrored what was happening in politics generally: Conservatives were winning the economic war—getting tax cuts, scaling back the size of government, privatizing some government programs—but as conservative leader Paul Weyrich put it in 1999, "I no longer believe that there is a moral majority. I believe that we probably have lost the culture war." Public opinion supported modest restrictions on the availability of abortion, but not criminalizing it again, and so did the Supreme Court. Public opinion moved dramatically in the direction of toleration of gays and lesbians, and so did the Supreme Court.

The mechanism by which the Supreme Court gets in line with the rest of the political system—and gets in a position to collaborate with it as well—is obvious: the nomination and confirmation process. Of course a president can miscalculate—or make a really smart move—by choosing a nominee who's out of line with the current political consensus in the hope that the consensus will move, perhaps with the nominee's assistance, in the direction the president wants. Depending on circumstances, the Senate might also go along with such a choice. Similarly, justices themselves can make mistakes about what the country will put up with. That's probably what happened near the end of the Warren Court period and even partway into the Burger Court era.

Serious miscalculations of either sort can lead to crises for the Court and the country. But in general, presidents and justices know where the nation is and what it will tolerate. That means that despite all the attention Supreme Court nominations attract, over the medium run what happens to the Court will depend on what the people choose when they elect a president and a Senate. That, again, is one reason liberals were so dismayed by *Bush v. Gore*. It seemed to them to allow a president not chosen by the people but by the Rehnquist Court to determine the path of constitutional law in the future.

✢

The terrorist attacks of September 11, 2001, changed American politics. They have not—yet—changed constitutional law. Anyone who confidently asserts *anything* about the Court's likely response to the cases that will reach it is blowing smoke, but it's worth mentioning some problems that it is likely to face.

One set of problems will arise from the fact that war generally leads to an increase in the national government's power, relative to the states, and to an increase of the president's power relative to Congress. The points are obvious when the war is conducted entirely overseas. State governments can't carry out that kind of war, and military operations can't be commanded by a Senate committee. The points are less obvious when the war comes to American soil. During the Civil War, though, the national government got more power, and so did President Abraham Lincoln.

Conservative libertarians would not want to see power centralized in the national executive, but other kinds of conservatives might not worry—at least as long as they thought they were going to control a national government facing a crisis of national security. Today's conservative constitutional thought was shaped by the experience of the New Deal, the Great Society, and the Warren Court, not by war, and there's not much in that thought that has strong implications for wartime centralization of power. Today's conservatives could, as some already have, remold their constitutional thought to take the wartime conditions into account and make centralized executive power (appropriately confined to wartime issues) fit comfortably.

On a deeper level, the terrorist attacks have begun to raise questions about the nature of American nationality and citizenship in the world today. Liberal scholars of constitutional law have begun to develop some answers to those questions, but the work is only beginning. We can be sure that the Supreme Court after Rehnquist will flesh out ideas about nationality and citizenship, but it would be foolish to speculate about which ideas will take hold. We should not take seriously any claims about what the Court will, or should, say about nationality and citizenship because no one knows. Here the cliché "The future lies ahead" is about as much as anyone can reasonably say.

EPILOGUE

The End of the Rehnquist Court

Constitutional law never stands still. The preceding chapters were completed early in 2004. Since then the Court has completed another term, Chief Justice Rehnquist died, John Roberts was confirmed as his replacement, and Justice Sandra Day O'Connor announced her intention to retire as soon as her replacement was confirmed—an event still in the future when this epilogue was written. Rehnquist's death and, more important, O'Connor's imminent departure meant that the Rehnquist Court was no longer. The changes in the Court's membership presaged the effective end of divisions among the Court's Republicans and the consolidation of control in its modern Republicans.

The Court's decisions in 2004–5 confirmed that the conservative judicial revolution had at least taken a pause. In one area after another, the Court confronted and rejected arguments that recent precedents should be extended. Although some of the decisions might later be seen as steps back from the threshold of a large transformation of constitutional law, actually the Court remained poised there. The reason was the division among the Court's Republicans.

Judge John Roberts's nomination to replace Justice O'Connor, and then to replace the Chief Justice, signaled the continuing possibility that some time relatively soon the Court would cross into new constitutional territory. A law clerk to then-Justice Rehnquist and a prominent member of the Department of Justice under Presidents Reagan and George H. W. Bush, Roberts appeared to be a quintessential modern Republican. His modest self-presentation indicated that he might encourage a march toward constitutional transformation—but at a stately pace. The mechanism most observers anticipated was that Roberts's affable personality would pull Justice Anthony Kennedy back toward the Court's modern Republicans.

And yet there were some hints that a Chief Justice Roberts might pursue a different doctrinal course. His professed adherence to the view that courts should be restrained suggested that he would hold that the Constitution placed few limits on what elected officials could do. That sort of deference would support the exercise of substantial presidential power in the war on terrorism. But it would also mean that the Court would uphold expansive exercises of national regulatory power, ending the "Federalism Revolution," and allow Congress and the states to regulate private property as extensively as legislators wished, ending the "Takings Project."

Judge Roberts's performance at his confirmation hearings provided no clues as to what he would do as Chief Justice—or, perhaps, provided too many clues. No matter what their views, listeners could take comfort in Judge Roberts's words, finding support in them for their own positions. And yet, like the prophecies of the oracle at Delphi, whatever happened in the future—rampant conservative activism, complete deference to legislatures, or activism on some issues and deference on others—would be consistent with what Judge Roberts had said. Would the Court remain at the threshold of constitutional transformation, move gradually across it, or leap into the future? The Rehnquist Court's legacy remained ambiguous to the end.

⁄∂

In 2004 the Federalism Revolution's cases involved some apparently attractive litigants: a woman who found that marijuana was the only effective treatment for her persistent severe pain and a paraplegic defendant who was charged with failing to appear at his prosecution when he refused to crawl up the courthouse stairs. In the end, though, doctrine—the limits of the Federalism Revolution—played a larger role than the facts of the cases.

In 1996 California's voters adopted the Compassionate Use Act in a referendum. The act lifted the state's ban on marijuana use for people who, their doctors said, needed the drug for medical treatment. Angel Raich suffered from fibromyalgia and a brain tumor and many other conditions, which caused her severe pain that she found untreatable except through marijuana use. Unfortunately for her, California's law did not immunize the state's residents from prosecution for violating the *national* drug laws. So, Raich said, she sued the federal government "to save my life" by allowing her to get the eight pounds of marijuana she used each year from her local "caregivers," two friends who raised marijuana for her but otherwise did not deal in the drug. Her argument was straightforward: The marijuana she used was grown in California, it was used there, she did not pay for it, and eight pounds per year was hardly enough to have a significant impact on the interstate market for illegal marijuana. Raich and her lawyers argued that Congress could not use its power to regulate interstate commerce to prohibit the private consumption of locally grown marijuana.

Justice John Paul Stevens wrote the Court's opinion rejecting Raich's claim, and even Justice Scalia agreed with that result. For Justice Stevens, the New Deal case involving home-grown wheat was still good law, and dictated the outcome. Maybe Raich's own use did not have much impact on the interstate market for marijuana, but, he wrote, Congress certainly could think that home-grown production for private use would leak into the commercial market, thereby having a substantial effect on interstate commerce. Perhaps Raich's own use was not itself "commercial" because she paid nothing for her marijuana. But, according to Justice Stevens, the earlier Federalism Revolution cases acknowledged that Congress could regulate noncommercial activity like that as long as the regulation was part of a more comprehensive system for regulating commercial activities.

Justice O'Connor wrote a dissent that Chief Justice Rehnquist and Justice Thomas joined. She said that Raich had identified a discrete form of marijuana use—under medical supervision in a state where such use was lawful, with home-grown marijuana donated to the user—that had no real impact on the commercial trade in marijuana. Justice Stevens said, though, that carving out an exception from the general prohibition on marijuana use was a policy decision for Congress to make.

It will take some time to know exactly what the medical marijuana decision means. It might mean that the Federalism Revolution is over, and that the cases involving the Gun Free School Zones Act and the Violence against Women Act are derelicts in the law. It might mean that the Federalism Revolution has a small gap: If Congress passes a statute dealing with something that has some connection to commerce, and a majority of the Supreme Court thinks that the statute is important, the Court will uphold the statute.

Chapter Thirteen pointed out that cases involving the use of the Endangered Species Act to block development to protect what environmentalists call "non-charismatic" species were the best candidates for extending the Federalism Revolution. Writing before the medical marijuana decision, as a court of appeals judge, John Roberts indicated that the Court's Federalism Revolution did indeed cast some doubt on those applications of the act. Still, the Raich decision means that extending the Federalism Revolution into a full-scale assault on the legacy of the New Deal and the Great Society will take more doctrinal work—and more time—than might have seemed necessary before.

The same could be said about the Rehnquist Court's challenges to statutes enforcing constitutional rights against state governments. The Court followed up its decision upholding the application of the Family Medical Leave Act to state governments by doing the same for some applications of the Americans with Disabilities Act. News stories about the case offered the image of wheelchair-bound George Lane arriving at a county courthouse for a hearing on a charge of reckless driving, finding that the courthouse had no elevator, and attempting to crawl up the thirty steps to the second-floor courtroom—and then having insult added to injury when he was charged with failing to appear at the hearing after he abandoned the effort. The real story was more complicated: courthouse employees said that Lane refused their offers to help him up the stairs and rejected the judge's offer to move the trial to the ground floor because, Lane said, he "wanted to be treated like everyone else."

Equal treatment was what the Americans with Disabilities Act was about. Tennessee argued that the statute was unconstitutional, relying on the Court's decision that the federal law banning employment discrimination against those with disabilities could not constitutionally be applied to state employers because it was not a way of enforcing constitutional rights. The Court disagreed with Tennessee. The earlier case, Justice Stevens wrote, dealt with employment, which had no constitutional overtones. Lane's case, though, lay at the intersection of the right of access to the courts, itself protected by the Constitution, with the rights of people with disabilities. This combination meant that Congress's response was proportional to the problems of access to the courts its investigations had disclosed, particularly because Congress required only that states make "reasonable" accommodations to the needs of those with disabilities. The Court was far more generous in its treatment of Congress's efforts to identify instances of unequal treatment in state provision of public services than it had been with similar legislative efforts in prior cases.

As is always true, the scope of the Court's decision in the Lane case remained to be determined by later cases. The doctrine seemed to rest on the "tiered" structure of the Equal Protection Clause (Chapter Four). Congressional legislation would probably be upheld if it involved efforts to address discrimination against women, or if it involved discrimination against older people or those with disabilities in connection with activities that themselves had some constitutional protection. That covers a lot of territory, but not everything. Could Congress require that state prisons make reasonable accommodations to the needs of prisoners with disabilities? Prisoners have fewer constitutional rights than defendants in criminal cases, such as Lane, but they are more under the government's control. Writing before Justice O'Connor announced her retirement, one expert observed that "it is virtually certain that the decision will ultimately be Justice O'Connor's to make," because the Court divided five-to-four in each of the decisions in the area, with Justice O'Connor in the majority in Lane's case. Justice O'Connor's planned departure kept open some paths the Federalism Revolution might yet take by giving its proponents the chance to gain a new vote and limit the Lane decision, perhaps by emphasizing that access to the courts is a more important constitutional value than others.

When William Rehnquist joined the Court, and even when he became Chief Justice, someone suggesting that federal drug and anti-discrimination laws might be unconstitutional would have been regarded as out of touch with constitutional law. It is a measure of the success—and the limitations—of the Federalism Revolution that in 2005 three or four justices, but not five, agreed with those claims.

☙

The Takings Project too ran into a wall in 2005, although the Institute for Justice won the battle to transform its Supreme Court defeat into a public relations victory. The Supreme Court rejected the institute's attempt to dramatically transform takings doctrine by making it impossible for cities to use their power of eminent domain to force people to sell their property—including their homes—so that the cities could transfer it to developers who proposed to use the land for projects like shopping malls that, the developers promised, would make the cities more attractive places to live and work. The doctrinal vehicle for this Institute for Justice proposal was the requirement that the power of eminent domain be exercised only for "public uses." What was most striking about the case was that four justices agreed with the proposed rule that a compensated taking for economic development purposes was not a taking for a public use, in the face of more than a hundred years of cases making it clear that the "public use" requirement was so broad that people had to rely not on the courts but on their own political power to limit the use of eminent domain.

The case the Court considered pitted Susette Kelo against the city of New London, Connecticut. New London was a city in economic decline in 1998, when Pfizer, the pharmaceutical company, announced that it would build a large research facility in the city, near a neighborhood that the city and state had identified as a prime area for economic revitalization. City planners developed a proposal to develop the area near the Pfizer buildings for multiple uses: a hotel where conferences could be held, a "small urban village" with restaurants and shopping areas, a marina, residences, a U.S. Coast Guard Museum, and additional offices. The city believed that the development would ensure that Pfizer carried through on its plans, and that the new buildings and businesses would make the city more attractive—and generate new tax revenue.

The city's problem was that the area to be developed already had many homes on it. Most of the homeowners negotiated sales of their property to the city. Susette Kelo, though, wanted to stay in her house, which she had done a lot to improve. Others who refused to sell included Wilhelmina Dery, who lived in the house she had been born in eighty years earlier. The city offered to pay Kelo and Dery more than they would have received on the open market, but the homeowners did not want to move. Kelo and Dery filed suit in state court trying to block the city's plans. Represented by the Institute for Justice, they argued that all that was going to happen was that the city was going to buy their property and give it to someone else, and that taking one person's property merely to transfer it was not taking it for a "public use." The Connecticut Supreme Court rejected their claim by a four-to-three vote, and Kelo appealed to the Supreme Court.

The Institute for Justice's lawyers believed they had the best case possible for a major challenge to urban redevelopment projects. The facts of the Kelo case placed the homeowners in a very good light, the state supreme court had been closely divided, other state courts had recently started to limit cities' powers to engage in "economic development" takings, such takings had a feel of big companies pushing small homeowners around, and the history of such takings included numerous unattractive episodes in which "urban renewal" meant "Negro removal," as it had been put in the 1960s. All true, but not enough to win at the U.S. Supreme Court. The reason was precedent: Justice Stevens's opinion ran through the cases, beginning with one from 1896, to show that the Court had for generations refused to place serious limits on the eminent domain power. "Legislatures," he wrote, needed "broad latitude" to decide "what public needs justify the use of the takings power."

Four Justices invoked one of the Supreme Court's earliest opinions, in which Justice Samuel Chase said that a "law that takes property from A, and gives it to B" was unconstitutional. Though they were in dissent, the Institute for Justice thought they were right, and was ready with press releases capitalizing on its loss in the Kelo case. It announced a "Hands Off My Home" publicity campaign. The institute and other participants in the Takings Project generated a backlash, but of a sort that vindicated the majority's underlying insight even as the backlash was fueled by hostile comments about the Supreme Court. Members of Congress proposed new legislation to limit the power of state governments to exercise the power of eminent domain. State legislators began to explore limitations on their own power. Yet, of course, that is precisely what the majority thought should happen: Voters upset about government decisions forcing people to sell their houses should exercise political, not judicial, power to stop the government. As the immediate backlash against the Kelo decision died down, city planners and other officials began to make the case that figuring out how, and even whether, to limit the power of eminent domain called for complex policy judgments. In the end, the Court's decision to stay out of the area might be even more strongly vindicated, as legislatures design restrictions more subtle than Justice O'Connor's proposal that there be no takings for economic development.

৩

Having dodged the question of whether the Pledge of Allegiance's reference to a nation "under God" was unconstitutional in 2004, the Court took up two cases involving public displays of religious symbols in 2005. Both involved the Ten Commandments. Before the Court announced its decisions, law professor Jack Balkin joked that Justice O'Connor was going to find five commandments constitutional and five unconstitutional. Not quite. The Court did indeed split the difference, holding that displays posted at courthouses in Kentucky were unconstitutional but that Texas did not have to take down a large stone monument on its statehouse grounds. Justice O'Connor wasn't the key vote, though; Justice Breyer was. He agreed with the majority that the Kentucky displays were unconstitutional because the background made it clear that the reason the counties had for posting them was to promote religion. The Texas monument was different, according to Justice Breyer. It had been erected as part of a program supported by the Fraternal Order of the Eagles during the 1950s, and Justice Breyer thought it important that there had been no real controversy over the display for more than forty years.

The Court's divisions in the Ten Commandments cases indicate how symbolism cases might return to the courts. Justice Breyer's opinion might have meant that long-existing public symbols of religions would be grandparented into the Constitution, while new ones would be struck down. Justice O'Connor's departure reduced the possibility that such a rule would become permanent. Another view of the decisions is that they offer a roadmap to legislatures and city councils that want to endorse religious symbols: They need only obscure the fact that they *want* to support religion by dressing up their decisions in the rhetoric of civic education or acknowledgment of our nation's history. Trial courts will be asked to decide what the city councils' "real" purposes were. Some displays will be allowed, others struck down, perpetuating the conflict over government support for religious symbols.

Justice Scalia, joined by Chief Justice Rehnquist and Justice Thomas, offered a different approach to the problem, more candid but more troubling. They would have allowed governments to endorse monotheism openly, the religious position, Justice Scalia said, held by nearly 98 percent of "all believers" in the United States. Justices Souter and Stevens pointed out that Justice Scalia did not effectively explain why his analysis focused on monotheism rather than Christianity, the religion of more than 90 percent of American believers. And, indeed, Justice Thomas in a separate opinion wrote, "If a cross in the middle of a desert establishes a religion, then no religious observance is safe from challenge," referring to a case involving a memorial cross at a national park. We can expect the Religious Right to take up and extend these hints, defending government support for specifically Christian symbols.

Shortly after the decisions were announced, law professor Noah Feldman published *Divided by God: America's Church-State Problem—and What We Should Do About It*. He proposed to solve the problem by distinguishing between money cases and symbolism cases, giving government wide power to support religious symbolism but limiting its power to provide money to religious institutions. Feldman's proposal, though, did not take into account important features of constitutional law. No one can strike a deal of that sort that has any staying power, and it is not clear that anyone has much interest in doing so anyway. The many demands on tax funds place inherent limits on how much money governments will give to religious institutions, which means that those opposed to government support for religion might get relatively little from the deal that they cannot get from the politics of money. The Religious Right holds out hope that it might squeeze more money out of the political system. More important, its interest in religious symbolism is effectively inexhaustible. At the end of the Rehnquist Court, the Religious Right remained poised to advance its agenda, but, from its point of view, there was still much to do.

◌∕◌

The public reaction to the Kelo decision sometimes took an odd form. Conservatives had become used to criticizing liberal decisions as "activist" without distinguishing between two kinds of activism, one that led courts to overturn decisions by elected legislatures and another that involved departures from some preferred theory of constitutional interpretation. The *Wall Street Journal* demonstrated the confusion of the terms when it denounced the justices for "arrogat[ing] to themselves an almost legislative authority" in the medical marijuana and the takings cases. Yet, in those cases the majority *upheld* what legislatures had done. Any "arrogating" of legislative authority had been done by legislatures themselves. The ambiguities of the conservative condemnation of judicial activism cast some light on the prospects for a Court without Justice O'Connor.

President Bush was committed to naming a modern Republican to the Supreme Court. His models, he said, were Justices Scalia and Thomas. Republican control of the Senate smoothed the president's path. Still, Democrats had signaled their willingness to filibuster a nominee they found "extreme," and President Bush's poll ratings hovered in the low 40s when Justice O'Connor announced her retirement. Under these circumstances, President Bush found it appropriate to nominate a solid conservative, to avoid alienating core Republican activist groups. But doing so risked setting off a political battle that the president might not win. The solution was an updated version of the stealth strategy, but that was predictably a difficult strategy to pursue. Judge Roberts did have a thin public record, so at first Democrats found little to seize on to demonstrate that the president had indeed fulfilled his campaign promises about nominating a judge like Scalia or Thomas. And yet Roberts's solid conservative credentials—his clerkship for Rehnquist; his association with Kenneth Starr; the fact that he was well-established in conservative legal circles; his association with, if not membership in, the Federalist Society—and the very fact that President Bush had to satisfy his base meant that Democrats looked very hard at Roberts's record as its details seeped out. President Bush probably did the best he could by nominating Judge Roberts. The fact that, in the end, Roberts was to replace Rehnquist made confirmation easier, because the most Democrats could fairly claim was that Roberts would be a slightly more conservative and much younger version of Rehnquist, not a nominee who would change the balance on the Court. Roberts's confirmation was reasonably easy, but the process did contain enough storm signals to suggest that the confirmation process for O'Connor's successor would be more contentious, as Senator Arlen Specter warned.

Chief Justice Roberts is undoubtedly a modern Republican. His nomination exposed a line of division that had been obscured when the division that mattered was between traditional and modern Republicans. Early in Roberts's career, modern Republicans were oppositionists, fighting against the constitutional liberalism they saw as the legacy of the Warren Court. They articulated their opposition through vigorous advocacy of judicial restraint, a theme sounded in the fragmentary documentary record from Roberts's early career. As modern Republicans strengthened their position on the Supreme Court, they came to realize that sometimes they wanted to be activists. They defended their activism by insisting that the liberal activism they criticized occurred when judges imposed their own values on the Constitution and that good activism involved striking laws down if they were inconsistent with the Constitution's terms as originally understood. The Federalism Revolution and the Takings Project show how the division between old-style conservative judicial restraint and new-style conservative judicial activism matters. Those initiatives would be doomed if Judge Roberts turns out to be a real devotee of judicial restraint, but they might take on new life otherwise.

Modern Republicans now face the dilemma of the New Deal justices described by Martin Shapiro (Chapter One). Recall that Shapiro argued that those justices had taken over the last battlement of the conservative constitutional order the New Deal replaced. They had to decide whether to dismantle the weapons the conservatives had used by becoming consistent advocates of judicial restraint or to turn those weapons against their adversaries by advancing their new, substantive vision.

The Roosevelt appointees divided among themselves. So might the Roberts Court's modern Republicans, who are going to have to decide how strongly they are committed to the criticisms of judicial activism they deployed quite effectively against their adversaries. Individual justices may well find themselves as ambivalent as the Roosevelt appointees were, although of course on different issues. With nine individuals all pursuing distinctive variations on a single theme, the Roberts Court in its first decade is likely to seem themeless overall. Sometimes it will be activist, sometimes restrained.

The resolution of the Court's ambivalence may come only if things clear up in the national political system. The Roosevelt Court became committed to a liberal vision of constitutional law when, and because, it became clear that the New Deal constitutional vision dominated the national political system. Sustained Republican control of Congress and the presidency might produce a Roberts Court deferring to legislatures dominated by Republicans and mopping up those occasional statutes enacted by the remaining Democratic legislatures.

But unified Republican government might not last. There's some reason to think that Americans actually prefer the kind of divided government we had for most of the time between 1968 and 2002. If divided government comes back, the Roberts Court is likely to be divided too, drifting gradually in a conservative direction but not dramatically or on issues that would excite real resistance from liberals. Most notably, under these conditions the Roberts Court is unlikely to overrule *Roe v. Wade* in its first years.

The Supreme Court did not consider any important cases involving abortion, gay rights, or affirmative action in 2004–5. Nor are important gay rights or affirmative action cases likely to come to the Court soon. Conservatives who thought that the Supreme Court was about to hold that the Constitution required states to allow gay marriages were deluded; even a Court dominated by John Kerry appointees would not have done so anytime soon, much less the Supreme Court we actually have. Justice O'Connor cast the deciding vote in the Michigan affirmative action cases, and at least in theory the Court might revisit the issue. Yet it seems reasonably clear that the proposed twenty-five-year limit for affirmative action represented an implicit statement by the Court that it was going to let the issue simmer for a while, and even the addition of two new justices is unlikely to alter the understanding the other justices came to among themselves.

Abortion issues may come back to the Court soon. One was pending on the docket for decision during the term that began in October 2005, and challenges to the federal partial-birth-abortion ban were working their way to the Court. The Roberts nomination provoked the observation that even without O'Connor there were five votes on the Court to uphold what the *Casey* opinion called the "core holding" of *Roe v. Wade*. Justice Kennedy wrote a strong dissent when the Court invalidated a state partial-birth-abortion statute, and presumably Chief Justice Roberts would agree with that position. But the federal statute would present the Court with an additional question, which perhaps would weigh heavily on Justice Kennedy: How important should adherence to a prior precedent be? Kennedy signed the joint opinion in *Casey*, part of which stressed the importance for the Court's legitimacy of adhering to precedents so that the public would not come to believe that changes in the Court's personnel led to large changes in constitutional law. How Kennedy would reconcile the views he expressed in these two cases will not be known until the federal statute actually gets to the Supreme Court. Senator Specter pressed Judge Roberts to reveal his views about adhering to precedent, but the answers were so opaque that Chief Justice Roberts could follow his expressed views and overrule the partial-birth-abortion decision or, as easily, reaffirm it.

Pro-choice advocates emphasized a different theme. They pointed out that the *Casey* decision developed a new standard, under which regulations of abortion would be invalid only if they imposed an "undue burden" on the right to choose, and argued that the Court might eat away at the right to choose by refusing to find new regulations to be undue burdens. Still, the margin for new regulation was relatively thin: The Court had already approved waiting periods, requirements that abortion providers supply information about the process to their clients, and requirements that parents and spouses be notified unless doing so was not in the woman's best interests, typically because it would endanger her. These requirements might be tightened up a bit, but pro-choice advocates also emphasized—for other purposes—that under *existing* law abortion services were unavailable in 87 percent of the nation's counties. How much more erosion might occur is unclear.

∞

The end of the Rehnquist Court portended no rapid shifts in the fundamentals of constitutional law. If Republicans continue to control the presidency and Congress, eventually a Court dominated by modern Republicans might indeed change constitutional law a great deal—although surely the impact on public policy of such a transformation would be smaller than the transformation wrought by Republican legislative policies.

More interesting, but more speculative, are the possibilities if Republicans foresee Democrats regaining control of the presidency or Congress. The Republican victories in the 2004 elections confirmed that the United States no longer had a divided government. That might not be a permanent condition, though. As law professor Bruce Ackerman suggested years before the Roberts nomination, Democrats might regain the presidency in the 2008 election, and—less likely—get control of the Senate even earlier. Knowing that the opportunities for constitutional transformation might evaporate, the modern Republicans on the Supreme Court might try to consolidate that transformation as quickly as possible, hoping to put in place doctrines that would obstruct whatever political programs a Democrat-controlled government might try to implement. That, though, might provoke a constitutional crisis on the scale that occurred during the New Deal, with Democrats picking up anti-Supreme Court themes that had been the property of Republicans through the Rehnquist years.

In short, the deepest truth about how constitutional law develops is that constitutional law is connected to politics, and what happens in the wider political system will determine the Rehnquist Court's legacy.

NOTES

CHAPTER ONE: *William Rehnquist's Court*

13 "not a woman": Quoted in John W. Dean, *The Rehnquist Choice: The Untold Story of the Nixon Appointment that Redefined the Supreme Court* (New York, 2001), p. 191.

13 "most conservative lawyer": Quoted ibid., p. 129.

15 Martin Shapiro on taking over the fortress: Martin Shapiro, "Fathers and Sons: The Court, the Commentators, and the Search for Values," in *The Burger Court: The Counterrevolution That Wasn't*, ed. Vincent Blasi (New Haven, 1983), p. 220.

16 "most celebrated footnote": Lewis F. Powell, Jr., "*Carolene Products* Revisited," 82 *Columbia Law Review* 1087 (1982), p. 1087.

16 Carolene Products decision: United States v. Carolene Products, 304 U.S. 144 (1938).

17 Jaybird case: Rehnquist's memos are quoted in Mark Tushnet, *Making Civil Rights Law: Thurgood Marshall and the Supreme Court, 1935–1961* (New York, 1994), pp. 110–12.

18 Rehnquist memorandum in *Brown*: My discussion is drawn from ibid., pp. 189–90.

18 Reaction in 1971 to Rehnquist memo: Dean, *Rehnquist Choice*, pp. 274–84, details the controversy.

20 "had lied" and "reconstruct history": Ibid., p. 277.

22 Goldwater's first campaign: Described in Rick Perlstein, *Before the Storm: Barry Goldwater and the Unmaking of the American Consensus* (New York, 2001), pp. 25–26.

22 *U.S. News* article: Quoted in Lucas A. Powe, Jr., *The Warren Court and American Politics* (Cambridge, 2000), p. 140.

23 Polling place challenges: The affidavits are summarized in Dean, *Rehnquist Choice*, pp. 311–13.

23 "I am opposed to all civil rights laws": Quoted in Sue Davis, *Justice Rehnquist and the Constitution* (Princeton, 1989), p. 6, from a 1971 affidavit referring to a conversation held in 1964 after Rehnquist's appearance before the city council.

23 "many . . . would feel": Quoted ibid., p. 6.

24 American Political Science Association speech: Quoted in Perlstein, *Before the Storm*, p. 425.

24 "Bill Rehnquist's mantra": Ibid., p. 461.

24 "Civil Rights and the Common Good": Quoted ibid., pp. 461–62.

27 "Even if he is mediocre": Quoted in Henry J. Abraham, *Justices, Presidents, and Senators: A Political History of the U.S. Supreme Court Appointments from Washington to Clinton*, rev. ed. (Lanham, Md., 1999), p. 11.

27 "someone worse than Poff": Quoted in David Yalof, *Pursuit of Justices: Presidential Politics and the Selection of Supreme Court Nominees* (Chicago, 1999), p. 120.

28 "mediocre" and "obscure," and "some people with stature": Quoted in Abraham, *Justices, Presidents, and Senators*, p. 15.

28 "all those kikes": Quoted in Dean, *Rehnquist Choice*, p. 206.

28 Nixon's first meeting with Rehnquist: Ibid., pp. 85–86.

29 "no racist": Quoted ibid., p. 130.

29 Nixon's lack of enthusiasm: Ibid., p. 139.

29 "arch conservative," "how the hell," and "reevaluate": Quoted ibid., pp. 212, 228, 230–31.

30 "like China": Quoted ibid., p. 243.

30 "among the very best lawyers": Quoted in Abraham, *Justices, Presidents, and Senators*, p. 268.

30 "Democrats jumped on it": Dean, *Rehnquist Choice*, p. 274.

30 Restrictive covenants: Described in Davis, *Justice Rehnquist and the Constitution*, p. 196.

31 "one last bit of advice": Quoted in Dean, *Rehnquist Choice*, p. 285.

31 "counterrevolution that wasn't": Blasi, ed., *Burger Court*, iii.

31 "rootless activism": Vince Blasi, "The Rootless Activism of the Burger Court," ibid., p. 198.

32 "intellectual giant": Quoted from a White House report in Yalof, *Pursuit of Justices, Presidents, and Senators*, p. 153.

32 "most represented": Quoted in David Savage, *Turning Right* (New York, 1992), p. 9.

33 Marshall and Brennan on Rehnquist: Quoted in Keith E. Whittington, "William H. Rehnquist: Nixon's Strict Constructionist, Reagan's Chief Justice," in *Rehnquist Justice: Understanding the Court Dynamic*, ed. Earl Maltz (Lawrence, Kan., 2003), p. 14.

34 Justice Department report on Scalia: Quoted in Yalof, *Pursuit of Justices*, p. 146.

35 "political symbol": Quoted in Abraham, *Justices, Presidents, and Senators*, p. 293.

36 "machinery of death": Callins v. Collins, 510 U.S. 1141 (1994) (Blackmun, J., dissenting from denial of certiorari).

36 Guidelines booklet: *Guidelines on Constitutional Interpretation*, U.S. Department of Justice, Office of Legal Policy (February 19, 1988). Dawn Johnsen of the Indiana University Law School brought the importance of this document to the attention of the scholarly community.

39 Early conservative strategic litigation: The first antiunion campaign is discussed by Daniel Ernst, *Lawyers Against Labor* (Champaign, Ill., 1995). Lee Epstein, *Conservatives in Court* (Knoxville, Tenn., 1985) carries the story forward through the 1970s.

39 NAACP's campaign against *Brown*: I have examined this campaign in Mark Tushnet, *The NAACP's Legal Strategy Against Segregated Education, 1925–1950* (Chapel Hill, 1987).

39 Powell memorandum: Described in Peter Schmidt, "Behind the Fight over Race-Conscious Admissions," *Chronicle of Higher Education* (April 4, 2003), p. A22.

43 Lorson advice: Telephone interview with Frank Lorson, May 2, 2003.

44 Epstein book: Richard A. Epstein, *Takings: Private Property and the Power of Eminent Domain* (Cambridge, 1985).

44 "lunatic fringe": Thomas C. Grey, "The Malthusian Constitution," 14 *University of Miami Law Review* 21 (1986), p. 23.

45 Academic study: John P. Heinz, Anthony Paik, and Ann Southworth, "Lawyers for Conservative Causes: Clients, Ideology, and Social Distance," 37 *Law and Society Review* 5 (2003).

45 "talk about joint efforts" and "keep them informed": Ibid., pp. 36, 37.

45 "epiphany": Quoted in Neil A. Lewis, "Conservative 'Outsiders' Now at Hub of Power," *New York Times*, March 29, 1991, p. B16.

46 "debating group" and "attract bright conservatives": Calabresi quoted in Rex Bossert, "Conservative Forum Is a Quiet Power," *National Law Journal* (September 8, 1997), p. A1.

46 "more than half": Quoted in "The Federalist Society: Judge Scalia's Cheerleaders," *New York Times*, July 23, 1986, p. B6.

46 "we do not run": Quoted ibid.

47 "It is satisfying": Quoted in Heinz, Paik, and Southworth, "Lawyers for Conservative Causes," p. 35.

47 "recommended directly": Neil A. Lewis, "Bush to Reveal First Judicial Choices Soon," *New York Times*, April 24, 2001, p. A17.

47 "cabal": Jerry M. Landay, "The Conservative Cabal that's Transforming American Law," *Washington Monthly* (March 2000), p. 19.

47 "guilt-by-association": Kate O'Bierne, "High Society: Conservative Lawyers and their Wonderful 'Cabal,'" *National Review* (April 30, 2001).

48 "a monstrous infrastructure": Unnamed conservative activist quoted in Heinz, Paik, and Southworth, "Lawyers for Conservative Causes," p. 35.

CHAPTER TWO: *Two Kinds of Republican*

52 "all but clinched her nomination" and "personally opposed to abortion": Deaver and notes from Reagan interview quoted in David Yalof, *Pursuit of Justices: Presidential Politics and the Selection of Supreme Court Nominees* (Chicago, 1999), p. 140.

52 Starr report: Quoted ibid., at 141.

52 "Lighten up, Sandy": Quoted in "Lighten Up, Sandy!," *People* magazine (December 23–30, 1985), p. 147.

52 "no excuses accepted": Sandra Day O'Connor and H. Alan Day, *Lazy B: Growing Up on a Cattle Ranch in the American Southwest* (New York, 2002), p. 243.

53 not "passively plucked": Walter Dellinger, "The Breakfast Table," *Slate* magazine (June 27, 2003).

53 staff briefing: Jeffrey Rosen, "A Majority of One," *New York Times Magazine*, June 3, 2001, p. 37.

53 "a witch": Kim Isaac Eisler, "Majority of Two," *Washingtonian* (December 1996), p. 78.

53 "Maybe in error": Rosen, "Majority of One."

53 "I make my decision": Quoted ibid.

54 Measures of justices' power: The studies are summarized in Paul H. Edelman and Jim Chen, "The Most Dangerous Justice Rides Again: Revisiting the Power Pageant of the Justices," 86 *Minnesota Law Review* 131 (2001).

54 "Writing for an Audience of One": Susan R. Estrich and Kathleen M. Sullivan, "Abortion Politics: Writing for an Audience of One," 138 *University of Pennsylvania Law Review* 119 (1989).

54 "frequently justify exceptions": Nancy Maveety, "Justice Sandra Day O'Connor: Accommodationism and Conservatism," in *Rehnquist Justice: Understanding the Court Dynamic*, ed. Earl Maltz (Lawrence, Kan., 2003).

55 Suzanna Sherry article: Suzanna Sherry, "Civic Virtue and the Feminine Voice in Constitutional Adjudication," 72 *Virginia Law Review* 543 (1986).

55 O'Connor on Sherry: Sandra Day O'Connor, *The Majesty of the Law* (New York, 2003), p. 191.

55 "[A] wise old man": Quoted in ibid., p. 193.

56 "Forward into the 19th century": Ruth Marcus and Joe Pichirallo, "Seeking Out the Essential David Souter," *Washington Post*, September 9, 1990, p. A1.

58 "step aside": Bob Hohler, "Souter's Rise: Ability—and a Few Helping Hands," *Boston Globe*, July 29, 1990, p. 10.

58 "lovefest" and Bush's note: Aric Press, "The Quiet Man," *Newsweek* (August 6, 1990), p. 14.

58 "came from similar backgrounds": Warren B. Rudman, *Combat: Twelve Years in the U.S. Senate* (New York, 1996), p. 169.

59 "in your face": David Lauter and Ronald J. Ostrow, "And Then There Were 2 and Finally 1," *Los Angeles Times*, July 25, 1990, p. A1.

59 "getting quotations from old girlfriends": Ethan Bronner and John Milne, "Souter Calls Himself 'Moderate Conservative,' " *Boston Globe*, October 5, 1990, p. 1.

59 "moving a bookstore": Margaret Carlson, "An 18th Century Man," *Time* (August 6, 1990), p. 19.

59 Proust: Jeffrey Rosen, "Poetic Justice: The Education of David Souter,"

New Republic (March 8, 1993), p. 25.

60 Bar of soap: David Garrow, "Justice Souter Emerges," *New York Times Magazine*, September 25, 1994, p. 36.

60 "no sound bites": David G. Savage, "Supreme Court Ends Term with Souter Leading Way," *Los Angeles Times*, July 3, 1994, p. A1.

60 "thrusts at lions": Board of Education of Kiryas Joel School District v. Grumet, 512 U.S. 687, 708 (1994).

60 "Homer nodded": Lee v. Weisman, 505 U.S. 577 (1992). The words were mistakenly omitted from the official version and were restored in an erratum page published a decade later, in 535 U.S. Reports.

60 "The guy lied": Quoted in Jeremy Rabkin, "The Sorry Tale of David Souter," *Weekly Standard* (November 6, 1995), p. 30.

60 *Greenhouse Effect*: Terry Eastland, "The Tempting of Justice Kennedy," *American Spectator* (February 1993), p. 32. The term *Greenhouse Effect* is sometimes attributed to the federal judge Laurence Silberman. See, for example, Tony Mauro, " 'Kennedy Court' Ponders New Case," *USA Today*, March 19, 1997, p. 3A.

61 "reflecting a racial distribution" and "need for affirmative action": Quoted in "Excerpts from Senate's Hearings on the Souter Nomination," *New York Times*, September 15, 1990, p. 10.

61 "I never had to think about these things": Quoted in Rabkin, "Sorry Tale of David Souter."

61 Souter's aunt: Melvin Levine, quoted in David Margolick, "Bush's Court Choice: Ascetic at Home but Vigorous on Bench," *New York Times*, July 25, 1990, p. A1.

62 Harlan opinion: Griswold v. Connecticut, 381 U.S. 479 (1965).

63 "verbal hand grenades": Alex Kozinski, "My Pizza with Ninó," 12 *Cardozo Law Review* 1583 (1991), p. 1586.

63 "When you work in a small group": ABC News Transcripts, *This Week with George Stephanopoulos*, July 6, 2003.

64 "You live your professional life": Address by Clarence Thomas, Fifteenth Annual Ashbrook Memorial Dinner, February 5, 1999, available at http://www.ashbrook.org/events/memdin/thomas/home_speech.html (visited December 29, 2003).

64 "internally we rarely see each other": Remarks of Justice Thomas on receiving the Oklahoma Citizenship Award on May 8, 2000, available at http://www.ocpathink.org/Pages/Perspective0600.htm (visited December 29, 2003).

66 "not a very polite man": Eisler, "Majority of Two."

67 Merrill argument: Thomas W. Merrill, "The Making of the Second Rehnquist Court: A Preliminary Analysis," 47 *St. Louis University Law Journal* 569 (2003). The article was delivered as a lecture in the fall of 2002.

68 Scalia speech on federalism: Antonin Scalia, "The Two Faces of Federalism," 6 *Harvard Journal of Law and Public Policy* 19 (1982).

CHAPTER THREE: *Clarence Thomas's Constitution*

71 Review of book on Thomas's nomination hearings: Mark Tushnet, "Clarence Thomas: The Constitutional Problems" (reviewing Jane Mayer and Jill Abramson, *Strange Justice*), 63 *George Washington Law Review* 466 (1995). For my response to the reporter's questions, see Tony Mauro, "Should We Just Ignore Thomas?," *Legal Times* (December 4, 1995), p. 11.

72 "Every Clarence Thomas profile": Clarence Thomas, interview by Bill Kauffman, *Reason* magazine, conducted in 1987, available at http://reason.com/cthomasint.shtml (visited December 18, 2003).

72 "strongest man in the world": Quoted in Andrew Peyton Thomas, *Clarence Thomas: A Biography* (San Francisco, 2001), p. 67.

72 "You don't have any control": Quoted in Clarence Thomas, interview by Bill Kauffman, *Reason* magazine.

73 "a small community of blacks": Quoted in Andrew Peyton Thomas, *Clarence Thomas*, p. 59.

73 "not one of these people": Address by Clarence Thomas, Fifteenth Annual Ashbrook Memorial Dinner, February 5, 1999, available at http://www.ashbrook.org/events/memdin/thomas/home_speech.html (visited December 18, 2003)

74 "ABC": Quoted in Juan Williams, "A Question of Fairness," *Atlantic Monthly* (February 1987), p. 70.

74 "Smile, Clarence": Quoted ibid.

74 "acceptance did not come": Ibid.

74 "There is nothing you can do": Quoted ibid.

74 King assassination story: Clarence Thomas, "I am a man, a black man, an American," available at http://www.claremont.org/980821thomas.html (visited December 18, 2003). Thomas told the story in various versions with minor variations among them.

75 "partial to Malcolm X": Quoted in Clarence Thomas, interview with Bill Kauffman, *Reason* magazine.

75 "blatant manifestation": Quoted in Andrew Peyton Thomas, *Clarence Thomas*, p. 125.

75 "captured a lot of the feelings": Quoted in Clarence Thomas, interview with Bill Kauffman, *Reason* magazine.

75 "go back to college": Clarence Thomas, James Madison Day Lecture, James Madison University, March 15, 2001, available at http://www.jmu.edu/jmuweb/general/news/general_200132382450.shtml (visited December 18, 2003).

76 weren't "qualified to be there": Yale law professor, quoted in Andrew Peyton Thomas, *Clarence Thomas*, p. 141.

76 "You had to prove yourself": Quoted ibid, p. 142.

76 "No one can ever know": Quoted in Stephen Henderson, "Clarence Thomas Urges Graduates to Persevere," Knight Ridder Newspapers, May 17, 2003.

76 "dream of going back to Savannah": Quoted in Andrea Jones, "Be Heroes,

Not Victims, Thomas Tells UGA Grads," *Atlanta Journal-Constitution*, May 17, 2003.

76 "plenty of room at the top": Henderson, "Clarence Thomas Urges Graduates to Persevere."

76 "like pouring half a glass of water": Clarence Thomas, interview by Bill Kauffman, *Reason* magazine.

76 "back to an approach": Quoted in Andrew Peyton Thomas, *Clarence Thomas*, p. 164.

77 "She gets mad": Quoted in Williams, "A Question of Fairness," p. 70.

77 "be irreparably ruined": Quoted ibid.

77 "insulted": Clarence Thomas, interview by Bill Kauffman, *Reason* magazine.

77 "playing the group game": Quoted in Williams, "A Question of Fairness," p. 70.

78 "think through what protects individual liberty": Clarence Thomas, James Madison Day Lecture.

78 "the epitome of the right kind of affirmative action": Quoted in Williams, "A Question of Fairness," p. 70.

79 "I want to be on the Supreme Court": Quoted in Andrew Peyton Thomas, *Clarence Thomas*, p. 179.

79 "stepping stone": Ibid., p. 318.

79 "as Jesus prayed": Ibid., p. 320.

79 Announcement statements: Ibid., pp. 345–47.

81 "purely in the context of political theory": Ibid., p. 369.

81 Books have been written: For example, Jane Mayer and Jill Abramson, *Strange Justice: The Selling of Clarence Thomas* (Boston, 1994); David Brock, *The Real Anita Hill: The Untold Story* (New York, 1993), retracted in David Brock, *Blinded by the Right: The Conscience of an Ex-Conservative* (New York, 2002).

83 "I've been called names": Quoted in Kevin Merrida and Michael A. Fletcher, "Supreme Discomfort," *Washington Post*, August 4, 2002, p. W8.

83 "singled out": Clarence Thomas, "I am a man, a black man, an American."

83 "I don't fit in with whites": Quoted in Andrew Peyton Thomas, *Clarence Thomas*, p. 221.

84 "Quotas are for the black middle class": Quoted in Williams, "A Question of Fairness," p. 70.

84 "out of touch with reality": Quoted in Clarence Thomas, interview with Bill Kauffman, *Reason* magazine.

84 "It pains me . . . more deeply than you can imagine": Quoted in Joan Biskupic, "Justice Thomas Takes on His Critics," *Washington Post*, September 23, 1998, p. A1.

84 "time to move on": Quoted ibid.

84 "psycho-silliness": Clarence Thomas, "I am a man, a black man, an American."

84 "habit of listening": Kevin Merrida, responding to an e-mail question in *Washington Post* Live On-Line, August 5, 2002, available at http://dis cuss.washingtonpost.com/wp-srv/zforum/02/magazine_thomas080502 .htm (visited December 18, 2003).

84 "what else could possibly be the explanation . . . ?": Clarence Thomas, "I am a man, a black man, an American."

85 "God is all right": Quoted in Williams, "A Question of Fairness," p. 70.

85 "He's a lonely guy": Quoted in Merrida and Fletcher, "Supreme Discomfort."

85 "condo on wheels": Quoted ibid.

85 Ginni's protectiveness: Ibid.

87 "photographic memory": Tony Mauro, "The Education of Clarence Thomas," *American Lawyer* (August 2, 2001).

87 Railroad case: Norfolk & Western Railway Co. v. Hiles, 516 U.S. 890 (1996).

87 "fun little" opinion: Mauro, "The Education of Clarence Thomas."

87 "proud of an opinion": Ibid.

87 "dry" and "precise": Address by Clarence Thomas, Fifteenth Annual Ashbrook Memorial Dinner.

87 "opportunity to engage in lively prose": Clarence Thomas, "The Virtue of Practical Wisdom."

88 "lifted, almost word for word": Jeffrey Rosen, "Fed Up," *New Republic* (May 22, 1995), p. 13.

90 "whim and fancy": Address by Clarence Thomas, Fifteenth Annual Ashbrook Memorial Dinner, February 5, 1999.

91 Hudson prison case: Hudson v. McMillan, 503 U.S. 1 (1992).

92 "mind-boggling": *Washington Post*, February 26, 1992, p. A16.

92 "cruelest justice": Editorial, "The Youngest, Cruelest Justice," *New York Times*, February 27, 1992, p. A24.

92 Raspberry column: William Raspberry, "Confounding One's Supporters," *Washington Post*, February 28, 1992, p. A23.

92 not a "cure-all": George F. Will, "The Constitution Is Not a Cure-All," *Washington Post*, March 1, 1992, p. C7.

93 "Thomas attempted . . . to distance himself": Scott Douglas Gerber, *First Principles: The Jurisprudence of Clarence Thomas* (New York, 1999), p. 39.

93 "difficult to take seriously": Ibid., p. 41.

94 "splendid example": Quoted in Andrew Peyton Thomas, *Clarence Thomas*, p. 302.

94 Tribe op-ed: Laurence H. Tribe, " 'Natural Law' and the Nominee," *New York Times*, July 15, 1991, p. A15.

95 "a union that, at its root": Clarence Thomas, "The Virtue of Practical Wisdom," speech at the Third Annual Lincoln Day Colloquium & Dinner, Claremont Institute, February 9, 1999, available at http://www.clare mont.org/writings/990209cthomas.html (visited December 8, 2003).

96 Texas sodomy case: Lawrence v. Texas, 123 S. Ct. 2472 (2003).

96 liberal and conservative originalism: Gerber, *First Principles*, p. 47n.

97 Mississippi universities case: United States v. Fordice, 505 U.S. 717 (1992).

98 Kansas City desegregation case: Missouri v. Jenkins, 515 U.S. 70 (1995).

98 School voucher decision: Zelman v. Simmons-Harris, 536 U.S. 639 (2002).

99 "at war with the principle": Adarand Constructors, Inc. v. Pena, 515 U.S. 200 (1995)

99 Michigan affirmative action case: Grutter v. Bollinger, 123 S. Ct. 2325 (2003).

100 "something of a black nationalist": Williams, "A Question of Fairness."

100 rejected the label: Clarence Thomas, interview with Bill Kauffman, *Reason* magazine.

100 "primarily because of their belief in self-help": Ibid.

102 *defensive solidarity*: Clarence Thomas, "I am a man, a black man, an American."

103 "had a relatively undistinguished career": Mark Graber, "Clarence Thomas and the Perils of Amateur History," in *Rehnquist Justice: Understanding the Court Dynamic*, ed. Earl Maltz (Lawrence, Kan., 2003), p. 71.

103 "a jurisprudence based upon a theory": Missouri v. Jenkins, 515 U.S. 70 (1995).

CHAPTER FOUR: *Ruth Bader Ginsburg's Equal Protection Clause*

108 Reed case: Reed v. Reed, 404 U.S. 71 (1971).

109 "showing them the disadvantage": Quoted in Philippa Strum, *Women in the Barracks: The VMI Case and Equal Rights* (Lawrence, Kan., 2002), p. 64.

109 Frontiero case: Frontiero v. Richardson, 411 U.S. 677 (1973).

111 Near beer case: Craig v. Boren, 429 U.S. 190 (1976).

114 VMI details: I have relied on Strum, *Women in the Barracks*, for details about the VMI case.

115 VMI barracks: Witness quoted ibid., p. 44.

115 "break down the 18-year-old": Quoted ibid., p. 45.

115 Self-study committee report: Quoted ibid., p. 32.

116 "political hot potato": Ibid., p. 89.

117 "Girls do it right": Quoted ibid., p. 146.

118 "the strongest assault": Quoted ibid., p. 163.

121 "Thurgood Marshall of gender equality law": Janet Benshoof quoted in Neil Lewis, "Rejected as Clerk, Now Headed for the Bench," *New York Times*, June 15, 1993, p. A1.

121 Ginsburg on *Roe*: Ruth Bader Ginsburg, "Some Thoughts on Autonomy and Equality in Relation to *Roe v. Wade*," 63 *North Carolina Law Review* 375 (1985).

121 "big heart": Quoted in David Yalof, *Pursuit of Justices: Presidential Politics and the Selection of Supreme Court Nominees* (Chicago, 1999), p. 200.

122 "fell in love": Quoted ibid., p. 201.

122 "the strongest and bravest": Quoted in "When Women Could Aspire," *Boston Globe,* June 20, 1993, p. 69.

123 Mississippi University for Women case: Mississippi University for Women v. Hogan, 458 U.S. 718 (1982).

123 Jury exclusion case: J.E.B. v. Alabama ex rel. T.B., 511 U.S. 127 (1994).

123 "very mixed feelings": Conference notes, Harry Blackmun Papers, Library of Congress, box 636, folder 8.

124 VMI case: United States v. Virginia, 518 U.S. 515 (1996).

126 "ending that I loved": Quoted in Strum, *Women in the Barracks,* p. 284.

128 "clarity above elegance": Laura Krugman Ray, "Justice Ginsburg and the Middle Way," 68 *Brooklyn Law Review* 629 (2003), p. 649.

128 "nightmarish images": Board of Education of Pottawatomie County v. Earls, 536 U.S. 822 (2002).

128 "sphinx-like, damage-determining law": Gasperini v. Center for the Humanities, Inc., 518 U.S. 415 (1996).

CHAPTER FIVE: *Antonin Scalia's First Amendment*

134 Brandenburg decision: Brandenburg v. Ohio, 395 U.S. 444 (1969).

135 Chaplinsky case: Chaplinsky v. New Hampshire, 315 U.S. 568 (1942).

136 Draft card–burning case: United States v. O'Brien, 391 U.S. 367 (1968).

138 "often sullen in disposition": Edward J. Cleary, *Beyond the Burning Cross: The First Amendment and the Landmark R.A.V. Case* (New York, 1994), p. 8. Details of the case are drawn from Cleary's account. Cleary says that I participated in a moot court for him just before the oral argument; I'm sure he's right, but I have no recollection of doing so.

139 "pushed the right buttons": Ibid., p. 115.

142 Mitchell case: Wisconsin v. Mitchell, 508 U.S. 476 (1993).

143 Virginia cross burning case: Virginia v. Black, 123 S. Ct. 1536 (2003).

144 "Scalia was putting his finger on": Fried, as quoted in Jon B. Gould, "The Precedent That Wasn't: College Hate Speech Codes and the Two Faces of Legal Compliance," 35 *Law and Society Review* 345 (2001), p. 356.

144 "number . . . clearly rose": Ibid., pp. 359–60.

145 Flag burning case: Texas v. Johnson, 491 U.S. 397 (1989).

147 "Ninomania": http://ninomania.blogspot.com/ (visited December 29, 2003).

147 "Cult of Scalia": http://members.aol.com/schwenkler/scalia/ (visited December 29, 2003).

148 Scalia on affirmative action: Antonin Scalia, "The Disease as the Cure: 'In Order to Get Beyond Racism We Must First Take Account of Race,'" 1979 *Washington University Law Quarterly* 147 (1979).

149 "fancies himself the intellectual": Maureen Dowd, "Nino's Opera Bouffe," *New York Times*, June 29, 2003, Sec. 4, p. 13.

149 "resuscitates the *ne plus ultra*": County of Sacramento v. Lewis, 523 U.S. 833 (1998), p. 861.

150 "marginalized": Kim Isaac Eisler, "Majority of Two," *Washingtonian* (December 1996), p. 78.

150 "Let her answer": Oral argument transcript in Apprendi v. New Jersey, 530 U.S. 466 (2000).

151 "formalistic vision": George Kannar, "The Constitutional Catechism of Antonin Scalia," 99 *Yale Law Journal* 1297 (1990), p. 1300.

151 "growing up Catholic": Ibid., p. 1314.

152 "If the next case": Antonin Scalia, "The Rule of Law as a Law of Rules," 56 *University of Chicago Law Review* 1175 (1989), p. 1179.

152 *Bush v. Gore*: 531 U.S. 98 (2000).

153 "war is really stupid": William H. Freivogel, "Case Involved Clash of Two Determined Women," *St. Louis Post-Dispatch*, October 10, 1993," p. 1B.

154 Information on Ladue: Michael Tackett, "Women's Suit over Yard Sign Pits 1st Amendment, City's Aesthetics," *Chicago Tribune*, January 6, 1991, p. C10.

154 Spink's testimony: William H. Freivogel, "Balancing Property Values and Free Speech: Supreme Court to Review Ladue's Strict Sign Law," *St. Louis Post-Dispatch*, October 10, 1993, p. 1B.

154 Gilleo decision: City of Ladue v. Gilleo, 512 U.S. 43 (1994).

155 five hundred thousand dollars in legal fees: Carolyn Bower, "Ladue's Bill for Fighting Case Could Exceed $467,000," *St. Louis Post-Dispatch*, June 14, 1994, p. 9A.

155 win-loss count: My count is based on a table in Alan J. Howard, "Continuity on the Court: The Rehnquist Court's Free Speech Cases," 47 *St. Louis University Law Review* 835 (2003).

CHAPTER SIX: *Anthony Kennedy and Gay Rights*

156 Georgia sodomy case: Bowers v. Hardwick, 478 U.S. 186 (1986).

158 St. Patrick's Day parade case: Hurley v. Irish-American Gay, Lesbian and Bisexual Group of Boston, 515 U.S. 557 (1995).

159 "except in a formal name": Joyce Murdoch and Deb Price, *Courting Justice: Gay Men and Lesbians v. the Supreme Court* (New York, 2001), p. 436.

161 "pretending to be straight": Ibid., p. 498.

161 Dale case: Boy Scouts of America v. Dale, 530 U.S. 640 (2000).

163 "I'm not a message": Quoted in Andrew Koppelman, "Signs of the Times: Dale v. Boy Scouts of America and the Changing Meaning of Nondiscrimination," 23 *Cardozo Law Review* 1819 (2002), p. 1829.

165 "a large part of many homosexuals' lifestyle": Pamphlet quoted in Murdoch and Price, *Courting Justice*, p. 454.

165 Amendment 2 case: Romer v. Evans, 517 U.S. 620 (1996).

169 "level[ed] the playing field": Quoted in Murdoch and Price, *Courting Justice*, p. 482.

169 Lawrence decision: Lawrence v. Texas, 123 S. Ct.. 2472 (2003).

172 "only visible personal vice": Jeffrey Rosen, "The Agonizer," *New Yorker* (November 11, 1996), p. 85.

173 "preaches that the decadent United States should be destroyed": Quoted in Patricia Williams, "For Which We Stand," *Nation* (May 20, 1992), p. 9.

173 "shy, bookish boy": Joseph R. Tybor, "Judge Kennedy—Rulings with a Knack for Tact," *Chicago Tribune*, November 22, 1987, p. C1.

173 "bashful lobbyist": Cynthia Gorney, "A Cautious Conservatism: Judge Kennedy Lives by the Rules," *Washington Post*, December 14, 1987, p. A1.

173 "you don't see real people": Rosen, "The Agonizer," p. 84.

173 "courteous, stern": Quoted from the *Almanac of the Federal Judiciary* in Robert Reinhold, "Man in the News: Restrained Pragmatist Anthony M. Kennedy," *New York Times*, November 12, 1987, p. A1.

174 Shakespeare freak: Kim Isaac Eisler, "Majority of Two," *Washingtonian* (December 1996), p. 78.

174 "fascinating conversationalists": Terry Carter, "Crossing the Rubicon," *California Lawyer* (October 1992), p. 40.

175 Rehnquist on other constitutional courts: William Rehnquist, "Constitutional Courts—Comparative Remarks," in *Germany and Its Basic Law: Past, Present, and Future—A German-American Symposium*, ed. Paul Kirchhof and Donald P. Kommers (Baden-Baden, 1993).

175 Juvenile death penalty case: Stanford v. Kentucky, 492 U.S. 361 (1989).

175 Mental retardation death penalty case: Atkins v. Virginia, 536 U.S. 304 (2002).

176 "would constantly refer": Rosen, "The Agonizer," p. 86.

177 "Bork was perfect": Michael P. McDonald quoted in Linda Greenhouse, "Hearings to Begin for Court Nominee," *New York Times*, December 14, 1987, p. A1.

177 "raving lunatics": Daniel Popeo quoted in Al Kamen, "Kennedy Moves Court to Right; Justice More Conservative than Expected," *Washington Post*, April 11, 1989, p. A1.

177 "very difficult for any gay person": Quoted in Charles F. Williams, "The Opinions of Anthony Kennedy: No Time for Ideology," *American Bar Association Journal* (March 1, 1988).

177 "moderate Republicanism": Louis Michael Seidman, "Romer's Radicalism," *1996 Supreme Court Review* 67.

178 "this hand-wringing thing": Ibid., p. 82.

178 "destroys a sense of community": Ibid., p. 88.

179 Castro district flag: Meredith May, "Gay Rights Affirmed in Historic Ruling," *San Francisco Chronicle*, June 27, 2003, p. A1.

CHAPTER SEVEN: *The Religious Right's Agenda—Symbols and Money*

180 "missed one" and "Catholics aren't Christians": Quoted in Pamela Colloff, "They Haven't Got a Prayer," *Texas Monthly* (November 2000), p. 118.

181 School prayer decisions: Abington School District v. Schempp, 374 U.S. 203 (1963); Wallace v. Jaffree, 472 U.S. 38 (1985).

184 Lemon test: Lemon v. Kurtzman, 403 U.S. 602 (1971).

184 "a ghoul": Lamb's Chapel v. Center Moriches Union Free School District, 508 U.S. 384 (1993).

184 Crèche case: Lynch v. Donnelly, 465 U.S. 668 (1984).

184 "sleazy": Philip Kurland, "The Religion Clauses and the Burger Court," 34 *Catholic University Law Review* 1 (1984).

186 "absolutely humiliated": Kevin Cullen, "Prayer Challenge: High Court to Hear Church-State Lawsuit," *Boston Globe*, November 6, 1991, p. 29.

186 Graduation prayer case: Lee v. Weisman, 505 U.S. 577 (1992).

187 "looked quite wrong": Quoted in Linda Greenhouse, "Documents Reveal the Evolution of a Justice," *New York Times*, March 4, 2004, p. A1.

187 Football game case: Santa Fe Independent School District v. Doe, 530 U.S. 290 (2000).

187 ACLJ and Sekulow: Steven P. Brown, *Trumping Religion: The New Christian Right, the Free Speech Clause, and the Courts* (Tuscaloosa, 2002), pp. 36–37. I have also drawn on Chapter Two of Hans J. Hacker, "Contesting the Constitution: Conservative Litigating Interests and Their Impact," unpublished Ph.D. dissertation, Ohio State University, 2000.

188 Anthony Griffin: Delida Costin, "Profiles: Anthony Griffin," 4 *Boston University Public Interest Law Journal* 107 (1994).

189 Ray Moore case: for an overview, see Joseph L. Conn, "Down for the Count," *Church & State* (December 1, 2003), p. 4.

192 *Wide Awake* case: Rosenberger v. Rector and Visitors of the University of Virginia, 515 U.S. 819 (1995).

192 "out of steam": Alan Sears, quoted in Brown, *Trumping Religion*, p. 74.

194 Minnesota case: Mueller v. Allen, 463 U.S. 388 (1983).

195 Witters and Zobrest cases: Witters v. Washington Department of Services for the Blind, 474 U.S. 481 (1986); Zobrest v. Catalina Foothills School District, 509 U.S. 1 (1993).

195 Louisiana case: Mitchell v. Helms, 530 U.S. 793 (2000).

197 Mr. Burns: The image comes from Dahlia Lithwick, "Supreme Court Dispatches," *Slate* magazine, January 19, 2000.

197 "imagine you made a hair brush": Oral argument in Wal-Mart Stores, Inc. v. Samara Bros., Inc. 529 U.S. 205 (2000).

197 "second year of law school": Oral argument in Virginia v. Black, 123 S. Ct. 1536 (2003).

197 "pet oyster": Oral argument in Federal Communications Commission v. NextWave Personal Communications Inc., 537 U.S. 293 (2003).

199 Background for Cleveland voucher case: Clint Bolick, *Voucher Wars: Waging the Legal Battle over School Choice* (Washington, D.C., 2003).

200 Voucher case: Zelman v. Simmons-Harris, 536 U.S. 639 (2002).

201 Contemporary *Brown*: Bolick, quoted in "Tax-Funded School Vouchers Upheld," Bloomberg News, June 27, 2002, available in LEXIS/NEXIS, News Group File.

202 "Every proposal to provide for vouchers": James E Ryan and Michael Heise, "The Political Economy of School Choice," 111 *Yale Law Journal* 2043 (2002), p. 2079.

CHAPTER EIGHT: *Holding the Line on Abortion*

205 Missouri case: Webster v. Reproductive Health Services, 492 U.S. 490 (1989).

206 "disagrees with *Roe*": Quoted in David J. Garrow, *Liberty and Sexuality: The Right to Privacy and the Making of* Roe v. Wade (New York, 1994), p. 675.

208 Minnesota two-parent notification case: Hodgson v. Minnesota, 497 U.S. 417 (1990).

209 "high stakes game of chicken": Thomas W. Merrill, "The Making of the Second Rehnquist Court: A Preliminary Analysis," 47 *St. Louis University Law Journal* 569 (2003), p. 631.

209 Pennsylvania abortion/Casey case: Planned Parenthood of Southeastern Pennsylvania v. Casey, 505 U.S. 833 (1992).

215 Holmes on doubt: Abrams v. United States, 250 U.S. 616 (1919).

215 "had to do what he thought was right": Jeffrey Rosen, "The Agonizer," *New Yorker* (November 11, 1996), p. 87.

216 "Caesar about to cross the Rubicon": Terry Carter, "Crossing the Rubicon," *California Lawyer* (October 1992), p. 39.

216 *Flipper* theme song: Richard Lacayo and Julie Johnson, "Inside the Court," *Time* (July 13, 1992), p. 28.

216 Nini, or little Nino: Carter, "Crossing the Rubicon," p. 104.

216 "put off by Scalia's fanged personal attacks": Richard C. Reuben, "Man in the Middle," *California Lawyer* (October 1992), p. 38.

216 "No justice is going to abdicate": Terence Moran, "The Curse of the Third Nominee," *Recorder* (July 6, 1992), p. 1.

220 Nebraska partial birth abortion case: Stenberg v. Carhart, 530 U.S. 914 (2000).

222 "most disappointing loss": Edwin Meese III, "Dialogue: Reagan's Legal Revolutionary," 3 *Green Bag 2nd* 193 (2000), p. 199.

CHAPTER NINE: *Race, Affirmative Action, and Crime*

223 "just schools": Green v. New Kent County School Board, 391 U.S. 430 (1968).

224 Detroit interdistrict remedy case: Milliken v. Bradley, 418 U.S. 717 (1974).

224 Detroit educational remedies case: Milliken v. Bradley, 433 U.S. 267 (1977).

224 Kansas City case: Missouri v. Jenkins, 515 U.S. 70 (1995).

225 Oklahoma City case: Board of Education v. Dowell, 498 U.S. 237 (1991).

225 Atlanta case: Freeman v. Pitts, 503 U.S. 467 (1992).

227 Bakke case: Regents of University of California v. Bakke, 438 U.S. 265 (1978).

228 Richmond case: City of Richmond v. J. A. Croson Co., 488 U.S. 469 (1989).

229 Scalia and Thomas's opposition to affirmative action: Adarand Constructors, Inc. v. Pena, 515 U.S. 200 (1995); Adarand Constructors, Inc. v. Mineta, 534 U.S. 103 (2001).

230 "bagman": Linda Chavez, "Financial Disgrace: The Buying of 'Justice' by Civil-Rights Leaders Will Eventually Backfire," *Chicago Tribune*, November 26, 1997, p. 19.

230 "demonstrates panic": Quoted in Amy Westfeldt, "Rights Groups Pay to Avoid Bias Decision," *Chattanooga Times*, November 22, 1997, p. A5.

230 "She just wants to be a teacher": Quoted in Susan Hayes and Rex Roberts, "A Case of Black and White," *Scholastic Update*, November 3, 1997, p. 2.

231 "put the consideration of race": Michael Greve quoted in Peter Schmidt, "Behind the Fight Over Race-Conscious Admissions," *Chronicle of Higher Education* (April 4, 2003), p. A22.

231 "very choosy" and "tell the story": Terence Pell quoted in Jonathan Groner, "Center Ring," *Legal Times* (December 9, 2002), p. 1.

233 "real handicap": Quoted in Jonathan Groner, "How University Got Support of Military Leaders," *Legal Times*, June 30, 2003, p. 1.

234 "the accumulated wisdom": Quoted in Tony Mauro, "Courtside," *Legal Times* (October 6, 2003), p. 10.

234 Michigan affirmative action cases: Gratz v. Bollinger, 123 S. Ct. 2411 (2003); Grutter v. Bollinger, 123 S. Ct. 2325 (2003).

239 "a complete wipeout" and "pick good targets": Quoted in Marcia Coyle, "The Fallout Begins," *National Law Journal* (July 7, 2003), p. 1.

239 McCleskey case: McCleskey v. Kemp, 481 U.S. 279 (1987).

240 "No study": Quoted in John C. Jeffries, Jr., *Justice Lewis F. Powell, Jr.* (New York,1994), p. 439.

241 Brown and Whren case: Whren v. United States, 517 U.S. 806 (1996).

243 "the perfect case": Quoted in Charles Ornstein, "Seat Belt Case Sparks Fourth Amendment Debate in Supreme Court," *Dallas Morning News*, December 5, 2000.

244 "not exactly a graduate": Quoted in Jan Jarboe Russell, "Small Town Arrest Raises a Big Question," *San Antonio Express-News*, December 7, 2000, p. 5B.

245 "an independent 'free spirit' ": Ibid.

245 "didn't deserve to be arrested": Quoted in Steve Lash, "She Just Wanted an Apology," *Houston Chronicle*, November 24, 2000, p. A1.

245 "the bane of the American legal system": Quoted in Dave Harmon, "Judge Throws Out 2 Suits Against Lago Vista," *Austin American-Statesman*, February 19, 1998, p. A1.

245 Atwater case: Atwater v. Lago Vista, 532 U.S. 318 (2001).

247 "If the city's position is accepted": Quoted in Terrence Stutz, "Buckling In: Woman Drives Seat Belt Case to Supreme Court," *Dallas Morning News*, July 3, 2000, p. 23A.

247 "We know who will be most affected": Quoted in Andrea Ball, "Soccer Mom Gets Her Day in Court," *Austin American-Statesman*, December 3, 2000, p. A1

Chapter Ten: *The Federalism Revolution*

249 Greenhouse on federalism revolution: Linda Greenhouse, "Federalism: States Are Given New Legal Shield by Supreme Court," *New York Times*, June 24, 1999, p. A1.

252 Collapse of judicial resistance to the New Deal: Barry Cushman, *Rethinking the New Deal Court: The Structure of a Constitutional Revolution* (New York, 1998), is the best modern work on this.

252 Farmer Filburn's case: Wickard v. Filburn, 317 U.S. 111 (1942).

253 *Chisholm v. Georgia*: 2 U.S. (2 Dall.) 419 (1793).

254 "states but a truism": United States v. Darby, 312 U.S. 100, 124 (1941).

256 Ohio wage freeze case: Fry v. United States, 421 U.S. 75 (1975).

257 Blackmun, Rehnquist, and O'Connor opinions: Garcia v. San Antonio Metropolitan Transit Authority, 469 U.S. 528 (1985).

258 O'Connor quoting Blackmun: Franchise Tax Board of California v. Hyatt, 123 S. Ct. 1683 (2003).

258 Background of Lopez case: In addition to the reported opinions, see Joseph Calve, "Anatomy of a Landmark," *Texas Lawyer* (July 31, 1995), p. 1.

258 Press conference: Susan R. Klein, "Independent-Norm Federalism in Criminal Law," 90 *Texas Law Review* 1541, 1556 (2002).

261 "not worth the time and money": Ibid., p. 1556. Klein, writing in 2001, says that she was unable to locate *any* post-*Lopez* prosecutions for violations of the old or new Gun-Free School Zones Act.

261 Rehnquist on VAWA: See Judith Resnik, "The Programmatic Judiciary: Lobbying, Judging, and Invalidating the Violence Against Women Act," 74 *Southern California Law Review* 269 (2000), pp. 269–75.

261 Brzonkala case: United States v. Morrison, 529 U.S. 598 (2000).

261 Facts of Brzonkala case: In addition to the reported opinions, my account relies on Ira J. Hadnot, "Supreme Court Weighs Power of States, Interests of Women in Rape Case," *Dallas Morning News*, April 2, 2000, p. 1J; Jan Vertefeuille and Betty Hayden, "Tech Wants Rape Case Dismissed: Accuser Changed Story, School Claims," *Roanoke Times & World News*, January 20, 1996, p. C1; Brooke A. Masters, " 'No Winners' in Rape Lawsuit: Two

Students Forever Changed by Case That Went to Supreme Court," *Washington Post*, May 20, 2000, p. B1; "The Brzonkala Case," *Roanoke Times & World News*, March 6, 1999, p. A2; Michael Hemphill, "Brzonkala, Tech Reach Settlement in Lawsuit; U.S. Supreme Court Case Will Proceed," *Roanoke Times & World News*, February 26, 2000, p. A1; Jan Vertefeuille, "Players Are Not Indicted; Ex-Tech Student to Pursue Rape Claim in Federal Suit," *Roanoke Times & World News*, April 11, 1996, p. A1.

265 Fifty VAWA cases: Resnik, "Programmatic Judiciary," p. 274. Resnik cites the Brief of Law Professors as Amici Curiae in Support of Petitioners in the Brzonkala case for this figure, and I examined the cases cited in that brief.

266 Literacy requirement case: Lassiter v. Northampton Election Board, 360 U.S. 45 (1959).

266 Voting Rights Act decision: Katzenbach v. Morgan, 384 U.S. 641 (1966).

267 Unemployment compensation case: Sherbert v. Verner, 374 U.S. 398 (1963).

267 Peyote case: Employment Division, Department of Human Resources v. Smith, 494 U.S. 872 (1990).

268 Boerne case: My account is drawn from my chapter, "The Story of City of Boerne v. Flores: Federalism, Rights, and Judicial Supremacy," in *Constitutional Law Stories*, ed. Michael Dorf (New York, 2003).

273 Maine probation officers' suit: Alden v. Maine, 527 U.S. 706 (1999).

274 Disabilities discrimination case: Board of Trustees of the University of Alabama v. Garrett, 531 U.S. 356 (2001).

274 Age discrimination case: Kimel v. Florida Board of Regents, 528 U.S. 62 (2000).

275 Family and Medical Leave Act case: Nevada Department of Human Resources v. Hibbs, 538 U.S. 721 (2003).

275 "Some truths are so basic": New York v. United States, 505 U.S. 144 (1992).

276 Term limits case: U.S. Term Limits v. Thornton, 514 U.S. 779 (1995).

276 "case about federalism": Coleman v. Thompson, 501 U.S. 722 (1991).

CHAPTER ELEVEN: *The Takings Project*

279 Suitum case: Information on the background is from Glen Elsasser, "Fighting for Land rights, Woman Finally Gets Case to Supreme Court," *Chicago Tribune*, February 27, 1997, p. N10; Paul Rogers, "Supreme Court Will Hear Private-Property Debate; Tahoe Case Centers on Land," *San Jose Mercury News*, February 6, 1997, p. A1; Alex Barnum, "Top Court to Hear Tahoe Land Case," *San Francisco Chronicle*, February 26, 1997, p. A1; Editorial, "Preserving Tahoe Slow-Growth Idea Up to Supreme Court," *San Francisco Chronicle*, March 16, 1996, p. 8; Kathy Kristoff, "Woman Still Battling for Settlement on Her Land," *Fresno Bee*, June 14, 1998, p. C1; Bettina Boxall, "California and the West," *Los Angeles Times*, June 7, 1999, p. A3. The Supreme Court's decision is Suitum v. Tahoe Regional Planning Agency, 520 U.S. 725 (1997).

281 "green pastel redness": John Hart Ely, *Democracy and Distrust: A Theory of Judicial Review* (Cambridge, 1980), p. 18.

281 Substantive due process: A good short introduction to the idea of substantive due process is John V. Orth, *Due Process of Law: A Brief History* (Lawrence, Kan., 2003).

281 *Lochner v. New York*: 198 U.S. 45 (1905).

282 Coal mining cases: Pennsylvania Coal Co. v. Mahon, 260 U.S. 393 (1922); Keystone Bituminous Coal Association v. DeBenedictis, 480 U.S. 470 (1987).

283 Original meaning of the takings clause: William Treanor, "The Origins and Original Significance of the Just Compensation Clause of the Fifth Amendment," 94 *Yale Law Journal* 694 (1985).

284 Scalia on originalism and the takings clause: Lucas v. South Carolina Coastal Council, 505 U.S. 1003, 1028 n. 15 (1992).

285 "pig in a parlor": Village of Euclid v. Ambler Realty Co., 272 U.S. 365, 388 (1926).

285 Grand Central Terminal case: Penn Central Transportation Co. v. New York, 438 U.S. 104 (1978).

287 Takings Project: Douglas T. Kendall and Charles P. Lord, "The Takings Project: A Critical Analysis and Assessment of the Progress So Far," 25 *Boston College Environmental Affairs Law Review* 509 (1997–98).

288 Lucas case: Lucas v. South Carolina Coastal Council, 505 U.S. 1003 (1992). For background on the Lucas case, I have relied on Vicki Been, "Lucas v. the Green Machine," in *Property Stories*, ed. Gerald Korngold and Andrew P. Morriss (New York, 2004).

289 "no fun regulating": Douglas W. Kmiec, "Clarifying the Supreme Court's Taking Cases: An Irreverent but Otherwise Unassailable Draft Opinion in *Dolan v. City of Tigard*," 71 *Denver University Law Review* 325 (1994), p. 330.

289 Subsequent developments on Lucas's land: Robert V. Percival, *Environmental Regulation: Law, Science, and Policy*, 3rd ed. (Boston, 2000), p. 803.

290 Lucas book: David H. Lucas, *Lucas Versus the Green Machine: Landmark Supreme Court Property Rights Decision by Man Who Won Against All Odds* (Alexander, N.C., 1995).

292 Palazzolo case: Palazzolo v. Rhode Island, 533 U.S. 606 (2001).

292 "everyone was filling": Anthony Flint, "Landlocked on the Coast for 40 Years, Anthony Palazzolo has Battled R.I. Over Property Rights, All the Way to the Supreme Court," *Boston Globe*, November 3, 2002, p. B1.

293 "those guys fighting the Revolutionary War": Ibid.

293 "This land had rights": Carey Goldberg, "A Property Rights Case Tests Wetlands Curbs," *New York Times*, February 17, 2001, p. A14.

293 "Wait a minute": Marcia Coyle, " 'I Will Do No Harm,' " *National Law Journal* (March 26, 2001), p. A17.

295 "largely immune from takings challenges": John D. Echeverria, "A Preliminary Assessment of Palazzolo v. Rhode Island," 31 *ELR News and Analysis* 11112 (September 2001).

296 Nollan case: Nollan v. California Coastal Commission, 483 U.S. 825 (1987).

297 Dolan case: Dolan v. City of Tigard, 512 U.S. 374 (1994).

299 San Jose rent control case: Pennell v. City of San Jose, 485 U.S. 1 (1988).

300 Escondido rent control case: Yee v. Escondido, 503 U.S. 519 (1992).

CHAPTER TWELVE: *Big Business's Constitution*

302 money and sex: Alan J. Howard, "Continuity on the Court: The Rehnquist Court's Free Speech Cases," 47 *St. Louis University Law Review* 835 (2003), p. 846.

303 ideological drift: J. H. Balkin, "Some Realism About Pluralism: Legal Realist Approaches to the First Amendment," 1990 *Duke Law Journal* 375 (1990).

303 Chrestensen case: Valentine v. Chrestensen, 316 U.S. 52 (1942).

304 Pittsburgh ordinance case: Pittsburgh Press Co. v. Pittsburgh Comm. on Human Relations, 413 U.S. 376 (1973).

304 Bigelow case: Bigelow v. Virginia, 421 U.S. 809 (1975).

304 Drug price advertising case: Virginia State Board of Pharmacy v. Virginia Citizens Consumer Council, 425 U.S. 748 (1976).

306 Liquor price advertising case: 44 Liquormart, Inc. v. Rhode Island, 517 U.S. 484 (1996).

307 Massachusetts tobacco case: Lorillard Tobacco Co. v. Reilly, 533 U.S. 525 (2001).

309 Kasky "heartened" by Nike: Quoted in Roger Parloff, "Can We Talk?," *Fortune* (September 2, 2002), p. 102.

310 "the great moral dilemmas": Quoted ibid.

315 Academic research on punitive damages: For a summary, see Marc Galanter, "Shadow Play: The Fabled Menace of Punitive Damages," 1998 *Wisconsin Law Review* 1 (1998).

315 TXO case: TXO Production Corp. v. Alliance Resources Corp., 509 U.S. 443 (1993).

316 BMW case: BMW of North America v. Gore, 517 U.S. 559 (1996).

317 Wrapping things up: State Farm Mutual Auto Insurance Co. v. Campbell, 123 S. Ct. 1513 (2003).

CHAPTER THIRTEEN: *A Supreme Court United?*

320 Delhi Sands flower-loving fly: Matthew Heller, "A Simple Case of Insecticide," *Los Angeles Times Magazine*, February 16, 2003, p. 20; John Copeland Nagle, "The Commerce Clause Meets the Delhi Sands Flower-Loving Fly," 97 *Michigan Law Review* 174 (1998).

323 Vouchers: For a more developed argument on the path voucher law might follow, see Mark Tushnet, "Vouchers after *Zelman*," 2003 *Supreme Court Review* 1.

325 "Neutrality" argument: Frederick Mark Gedicks, "Neutrality in Establishment Clause Interpretation: Its Past and Future," in *Church-State Relations in Crisis: Debating Neutrality*, ed. Stephen V. Monsma (Lanham, Md., 2002), p. 119.

325 Sexual harassment law and the First Amendment: For the most complete collection of First Amendment arguments against sexual harassment law, see Eugene Volokh's Web site, http://www1.law.ucla.edu/~volokh/#HARASSMENT (visited December 15, 2003).

328 Epstein on corporate culture: Richard A. Epstein, "The Constitutional Perils of Moderation: The Case of the Boy Scouts," 74 *Southern California Law Review* 119 (2000), pp. 139–40.

330 "young conservative nominees": David Yalof, *Pursuit of Justices: Presidential Politics and the Selection of Supreme Court Nominees* (Chicago, 1999), p. 100.

331 "turned over the privilege": Neil A. Lewis, "A Republican Senator Forces the Administration to Rethink Strategy on Judicial Appointments," *New York Times*, December 9, 1994, p. B7.

332 Distinction between judicial ideology and judicial philosophy: Thomas L. Jipping, "Winners and Losers Versus How You Play the Game: Should Ideology Drive Judicial Selection," 15 *Regent University Law Review* 1 (2002–03).

333 Kennedy speech: Quoted in Mark Gitenstein, *Matters of Principle: An Insider's Account of America's Rejection of Robert Bork's Nomination to the Supreme Court* (New York, 1992), p. 55.

334 *City Paper* story: The events are described in Michael Pertschuk and Wendy Schaetzel, *The People Rising: The Campaign Against the Bork Nomination* (New York, 1989), p. 6.

335 Anti-Bork coalition's efforts: See ibid.

336 Clarence Thomas strategy meetings: Jane Mayer and Jill Abramson, *Strange Justice: The Selling of Clarence Thomas* (Boston, 1994), pp. 24–25.

337 Bork on *Griswold*: For a discussion of the liberals' strategy, see Pertschuk and Schaetzel, *The People Rising*, pp. 256–58.

338 Meetings on conservative judicial activism: Some of the papers at these meetings are reprinted in "Conservative Judicial Activism," *University of Colorado Law Review*, vol. 73, no. 4 (Fall 2002).

338 Wilkinson's opinion: 169 F.3d 820, 889 (4th Cir. 1999).

339 Graglia: "Order in the Court," *National Review* (November 24, 1997), p. 48.

343 Dahl: Robert Dahl, "Decision-Making in a Democracy: The Supreme Court as a National Policy Maker," 6 *Journal of Public Law* 279 (1957).

343 Klarman: Michael Klarman, *From Jim Crow to Civil Rights: The Supreme Court and the Struggle for Racial Equality* (New York, 2004).

344 "I no longer believe": Paul Weyrich, "The Moral Minority," *Christianity Today* (September 6, 1999), p. 44.

EPILOGUE: *The End of the Rehnquist Court*

349 "to save my life": http://www.angeljustice.org/article.php?list=type&type=27.

349 Medical marijuana case: *Raich v. Gonzales*, 125 S. Ct. 2195 (2005).

350 Roberts opinion on Endangered Species Act: *Rancho Viejo LLD v. Norton*, 334 F.3d 1158 (D.C. Cir. 2003) (opinion dissenting from denial of rehearing en banc).

350 Lane case: *Tennessee v. Lane*, 541 U.S. 509 (2003).

350 Facts of Lane case: Bill Mears, "Court hears wheelchair access case," CNN.com, Jan. 11, 2004.

351 "it is virtually certain": http://www.scotusblog.com/movabletype/archives /2005/05/analysis_grant_1.html .

352 Kelo case: *Kelo v. City of New London*, 125 S. Ct. 2655 (2005).

353 "Negro removal": One source identifies James Baldwin as the source of this phrase. 12 Thompson on Real Property 194, § 98.02(e) (David A. Thomas ed., 1994).

353 "Hands Off My Home": http://www.ij.org/private_property/connecticut/ 7_18_05pr.html.

354 Jack Balkin: http://balkin.blogspot.com/2005/03/my-prediction-on-ten-commandments-case.html .

354 Ten Commandments cases: *McCreary County v. ACLU*, 125 S. Ct. 2722 (2005); *Van Orden v. Perry*, 125 S. Ct. 2854 (2005).

355 Noah Feldman: *Divided by God: America's Church-State Problem—and What We Should Do About It* (New York, 2005).

356 "arrogat[ing] to themselves": "No More Souters," *Wall Street Journal*, July 19, 2005, p. A-14.

360 87 percent of the nation's counties: http://www.guttmacher.org/in-the-know/providers.html .

360 Bruce Ackerman: *"Off Balance," in Bush v. Gore: The Question of Legitimacy* (Bruce Ackerman ed., New Haven: 2002).

INDEX